D0174787

Building Strengths and Skills

Building Strengths and Skills

A COLLABORATIVE APPROACH TO WORKING WITH CLIENTS

JACQUELINE CORCORAN

OXFORD
UNIVERSITY PRESS
2005

OXFORD
UNIVERSITY PRESS

Oxford   New York
Auckland   Bangkok   Buenos Aires   Cape Town   Chennai
Dar es Salaam   Delhi   Hong Kong   Istanbul   Karachi   Kolkata
Kuala Lumpur   Madrid   Melbourne   Mexico City   Mumbai   Nairobi
São Paulo   Shanghai   Taipei   Tokyo   Toronto

Copyright © 2005 by Oxford University Press, Inc.

Published by Oxford University Press, Inc.
198 Madison Avenue, New York, New York 10016

www.oup.com

Oxford is a registered trademark of Oxford University Press

Library of Congress Cataloging-in-Publication Data

Corcoran, Jacqueline.
Building strengths and skills : a collaborative approach to working with clients / Jacqueline
Corcoran.
p. cm.
ISBN 0-19-515430-4
1. Social service. 2. Mental health services. 3. Counselor and client. 4. Solution-focused therapy.
5. Cognitive therapy. I. Title.
HV40.C67 2004
361.3'2—dc22   2004012396

9 8 7 6 5 4 3 2 1

Printed in the United States of America
on acid-free paper

A movement has recently emerged in the helping professions in which the focus is on people's strengths and circumstances rather than their pathology. Prior to this movement, the dominant ideology involved the "expert" practitioner diagnosing and determining what people should do to fix their problems; people were viewed largely in terms of their weaknesses, limitations, and problems. Now, with strengths-based (Saleebey, 2001), resilience (Werner & Smith, 2001), and positive psychology frameworks (Snyder & Lopez, 2002), the emphasis lies instead on people's resilience, strengths, and capacities. Unfortunately, practice models encompassing these frameworks are few. Those that do exist tend to lack balance between a focus on the strengths clients possess and the skills they need to develop. *Building Strengths and Skills: A Collaborative Approach to Working With Clients* takes into account both individual resources and the areas where client skills can be bolstered, offering an eclectic practice approach that interweaves and operationalizes both strengths-based and skills-based practice approaches.

In what has therefore been named the strengths-and-skills-building model, clients are assumed to have the necessary capacities to solve their own problems, and a major focus of treatment is bolstering motivation and resources. When these resources are exhausted or when deficits are identified as a substantial barrier to change, then skill building is introduced.

However, skills are taught in a collaborative fashion and, as much as possible, are made relevant to each client's unique circumstance. *Building Strengths and Skills* offers an assessment and intervention model for practitioners in the helping, social service, and mental health professions.

In addition, the helping process described in *Building Strengths and Skills* can fit any number of roles, including those of case manager, probation officer, caseworker, medical social service worker, counselor, crisis worker, and therapist. Because of this broad potential audience range and setting application, the terms *practitioner, clinician, worker,* and *helper* are used interchangeably in recognition that the skills offered in this book can be therapeutically applied to a wide range of helper relationships and roles with the client. Similarly, the strengths-and-skills-building model can be employed in the different modalities in which clients may be seen, whether individually, in families, or in groups. Regardless of the setting, the role of the helper, or the modality, the principles and techniques of the strengths-and-skills-building model are designed to make contacts with clients maximally therapeutic and productive.

◼ Organization

Chapters 1 through 3 of this book provide an overview of each of the therapeutic approaches—solution-focused therapy, motivational interviewing, and cognitive-behavioral therapy—that together make up the strengths-and-skills-building model. Chapter 4 compares and contrasts the three approaches in terms of their underlying assumptions and discusses the theoretical framework of the strengths-and-skills-building model. Chapter 5 provides an overview of the helping process for the strengths-and-skills-building model, which comprises engagement, problem exploration, solution exploration, goal setting, taking action, and termination. Techniques under each phase of the helping process are delineated.

Chapter 6 has a dual purpose. Its central objective is to familiarize the reader with the strengths-and-skills-building model and to teach the perspective and the skills involved; its secondary purpose is to demonstrate how the model can be applied as crisis intervention in a hospital setting. The reader will see the importance of basic interviewing skills, including the use of open-ended questions and reflection of the client's message and feelings, and learn how these are used to effect in the strengths-and-skills-building model.[1] Chapter 6 further shows that the strengths-and-skills-

---

1. For an overview of foundation skills, the reader is encouraged to consult Cournoyer (2000); Evans, Hearn, Uhlemann, and Ivey (1998); and Hepworth, Rooney, and Larsen (2002). *Building Strengths and Skills: A Collaborative Approach to Working With Clients* assumes reader familiarity with these skills.

building model largely focuses on the strengths clients possess. If there is limited time for contact, such as in crisis intervention settings, practitioner efforts center on strengths and solutions, bolstering client resources for the challenges they face and building their motivation to expend further effort on finding solutions and learning new skills that can help them.

Chapters 7 through 15 focus on applications of the strengths-and-skills-building model to various client problems and populations. These chapters illustrate how the strengths-and-skills-building helping process (engagement, problem exploration, solution exploration, goal setting, taking action, and termination) may be applied in a flexible way to meet the demands of different situations practitioners may encounter. Contributors for these chapters were brought in for their expertise in certain topic areas. After they gained familiarity with the strengths-and-skills-building model, they applied it to their areas in creative and flexible ways. Applications are divided into two categories: diagnosable disorders, as defined by the American Psychiatric Association (APA) *Diagnostic and Statistical Manual of Mental Disorders*,[2] and problems with family violence, to include domestic violence between partners and child maltreatment.

Readers will note that Chapter 8 (on working with juvenile offenders) is the only chapter on youths; however, this does not preclude practitioners from practicing the model with teenagers and children. Chapter 9, the application of the strengths-and-skills-building model in an inpatient substance abuse treatment center, discusses how art therapy techniques can be integrated within the model to reinforce the helping process. Chapter 10 deals with both marital therapy and a situation in which one partner has an anxiety disorder. This chapter is indicative of real-life helping situations, in which a client rarely presents with only one problem; indeed, multi-problem presentations might be the norm in certain helping settings. The book concludes with a chapter covering strengths-based assessments and tracking tools. This chapter is seen as necessary because there are many resources that compile instrument tools measuring deficits, but very few emphasize the assessment of strengths.

The applications are meant to show the range of problems for which the strengths-and-skills-building model can be employed, but this does not mean that the model is limited to these populations and problems. Readers, once familiar with how to interweave the practice components, can feel free to adapt the model to other areas, including work with children, as long as they are knowledgeable about their practice areas and receive supervi-

2. Although the *DSM*'s focus on diagnostic labels and individual psychopathology is seen as at odds with a strengths-based approach, the *DSM* does provide a common nomenclature for problems so that professionals within and between disciplines can converse.

sion for their work. The assumption is that readers already armed with the fundamentals of interviewing can build on these capacities to help clients maximize both strengths and their skills.

References

Cournoyer, B. (2000). *The social work skills workbook.* Pacific Grove, CA: Brooks/ Cole.

Evans, D., Hearn, M., Uhlemann, M., & Ivey, A. (1998). *Essential interviewing: A programmed approach to effective communication.* Pacific Grove, CA: Brooks/Cole.

Hepworth, D. H., Rooney, R., & Larsen, J. (2002). *Direct social work practice: Theory and skills* (6th ed.). Belmont, CA: Brooks/Cole.

Saleebey, D. (2001). *The strengths perspective in social work practice* (3rd ed.). Boston: Allyn & Bacon.

Snyder, C., & Lopez, S. (2002). *Handbook of positive psychology.* New York: Oxford University Press.

Werner, E., & Smith, R. (2001). *Journeys from childhood to midlife: Risk, resilience, and recovery.* Ithaca, NY: Cornell University Press.

ACKNOWLEDGMENTS

To my contributors: for their hard work and valuable applications of strengths-based work, I am truly grateful.

To all those students and colleagues who contributed case examples: Carrie Becker, Kathleen Castello, Kimberly Crawford, LaToya Deese, Roslyn Fenner, Katherine Filipic, Lynn Hafer, Corlis Jones, Liat Katz, Ann Keifer, Lori Kopp, Makita Lewis, Susan Livingston, Holly Matto, Candace Strother, Julie Sherrill, Dossi Toviessi, and Joseph Walsh.

To my father, Patrick Corcoran, for his excellent proofreading skills, and to my mother, Myra Corcoran, for the clinical wisdom she brought to reading drafts of child welfare chapters.

To my editor at Oxford University Press, Joan Bossert, and her assistants, Maura Roessner and, before her, Kimberly Robinson: my appreciation for the professionalism and prompt attention paid to this book and all my projects at Oxford.

CONTENTS

CONTRIBUTORS

CHRISTINE ANKERSTJERNE, M.A., is editor at the Virginia Institute for Social Services Training Activities, Richmond, Virginia.

CARRIE BECKER, M.S.W., is a Presidential Management Fellow in the Division of Policy Evaluation, Office of Research, Evaluation, and Statistics, Washington, DC.

HOLLY BELL, Ph.D., is Research Associate, Center for Social Work Research at the School of Social Work, The University of Texas at Austin, Austin, Texas.

JANICE BERRY-EDWARDS, Ph.D., is Assistant Professor, School of Social Work, Virginia Commonwealth University, Northern Virginia Campus, Alexandria, Virginia.

THERESA J. EARLY, Ph.D., is Associate Professor, College of Social Work, The Ohio State University, Columbus, Ohio.

KRISTIN A. GARELL, M.A., is Admissions and Enrollment Specialist, School of Social Work, Virginia Commonwealth University, Richmond, Virginia.

DIANNA HART, M.S.W., is a therapist at the New Horizons Home-Based Services Program, Prince William Community Services Board, Prince William, Virginia.

MELINDA HOHMAN, Ph.D., is Associate Professor, School of Social Work, San Diego State University, San Diego, California. She is also a trainer in motivational interviewing.

AUDREY JONES, M.S.W., is Foster Care and Adoption Social Worker at Louisa County Department of Social Services, Louisa County, Virginia.

CHRISTINE KLEINPETER, Psy.D., is Associate Professor, Department of Social Work, California State University at Long Beach, Long Beach, California. She is also a trainer in motivational interviewing.

HILDA LOUGHRAN, M.Soc.Sc., is College Lecturer, Department of Social Policy and Social Work, National University of Ireland, Dublin, Ireland. She is a trainer in motivational interviewing and solution-focused therapy throughout Ireland and the United Kingdom.

HOLLY C. MATTO, Ph.D., is Assistant Professor, School of Social Work, Virginia Commonwealth University, Northern Virginia Campus, Alexandria, Virginia.

W. SEAN NEWSOME, Ph.D., is Assistant Professor, Jane Addams College of Social Work, The University of Illinois at Chicago, Chicago, Illinois.

JANE HANVEY PHILLIPS, M.S., M.S.W., is Program Director, Excel Adult Outpatient Services, Millwood Hospital, Arlington, Texas, and Ph.D. candidate at the School of Social Work, The University of Texas at Arlington.

DAVID W. SPRINGER, Ph.D., is Associate Dean for Academic Affairs and Associate Professor, School of Social Work, The University of Texas at Austin, Austin, Texas.

JOSEPH WALSH, Ph.D., is Associate Professor, School of Social Work, Virginia Commonwealth University, Richmond, Virginia.

Building Strengths and Skills

PART I

Introduction of the Strengths-and-Skills-Building Model

1 Solution-Focused Therapy

Developed by de Shazer, Berg, and colleagues (Berg, 1994; Berg & Miller, 1992; Cade & O'Hanlon, 1993; DeJong & Berg, 2001; de Shazer et al., 1986; O'Hanlon & Weiner-Davis, 1989), solution-focused therapy emphasizes the strengths people possess and how these can be applied to the change process. Solution-focused therapy is influenced by the philosophies of constructivism and social constructionism, as well as by strategic family therapy. Constructivism involves the perspective that reality does not exist as an objective phenomenon; instead, it is a mental construction comprised from the assumptions that people hold about themselves and the world (Gergen, 1994; Neimeyer & Mahoney, 1995). Social constructionism takes the position that these mental constructions are formed through social interaction (Berg & DeJong, 1996). In the therapeutic context, worker and client share perceptions through language and engage in dialogue because this is the medium by which reality is shaped (de Shazer, 1994). In solution-focused therapy, language is used to influence the way clients view their problems (as in the past and as surmountable) to help them see the potential for solutions (through past successful attempts and imagining a future without the problem) and to create an expectancy for change (Berg & DeJong, 1996).

Strategic family therapy models from which solution-focused therapy is derived include the Mental Research Institute (MRI) brief therapy model (e.g., Weakland, Fisch, Watzlawick, & Bodin, 1974) and Haley's strategic family therapy (e.g., Haley, 1984). Solution-focused therapy, while maintaining the brief orientation of the MRI model, concerns itself with the development of solutions derived from nonproblem times rather than a problem focus (de Shazer et al., 1986). Haley's model of strategic family therapy was influenced by Milton Erickson, who believed that individuals possess the strengths and resources to resolve their problems and that the practitioner's job is to help clients discover these resources and activate them. Many times, this involves an amplification of symptomatic behavior through the use of paradoxical directives. Solution-focused therapy maintains the strengths-based orientation but relies on paradox as a last resort when more direct attempts to elicit positive behavior have failed.

In this chapter, the assumptions of solution-focused therapy are delineated, and the techniques are briefly summarized. A discussion of solution-focused treatment outcome studies follows.

Assumptions

Solution-focused therapy utilizes a strengths-based perspective in that client strengths, abilities, and resources are emphasized (Durrant, 1995; O'Hanlon & Weiner-Davis, 1989). Clients are assumed to be able to solve their own problems through resources that can be found by eliciting and exploring times when the problem does not exert its negative influence and/or when the client has coped successfully.

Rather than focusing on the past and a history of the problem, attention is oriented to a future without the problem to build vision, hope, and motivation for the client. Extensive historical information is not viewed as necessary because understanding the past will not change the future without action. The past is explored only for exception finding; the focus of conversation between the practitioner and the client becomes how these exceptions—when problems do not occur—can be applied in the future.

The assumption in solution-focused therapy is that change occurs in a systemic way. Small change is all that is necessary as a "spiral effect" takes place: The client takes a step in the right direction; others in the context respond differently; the client feels more empowered and is encouraged toward further change. Both behaving differently and thinking differently are part of the processes of change (de Shazer, 1994). Rapid change is possible; all that is necessary in treatment is for a small change to occur, as this will reverberate into change throughout the system.

Because no one holds the objective truth, individuals are valued for their unique perspectives, with the right to determine their own goals. Clients are encouraged to find the solutions that fit their own worldviews. The practitioner works collaboratively with the client to build the client's awareness of strengths. These strengths are then mobilized and applied to problem situations.

Empirical Basis for Solution-Focused Therapy

The evidence basis for solution-focused therapy is building slowly. Part of the reason for this is the constructivist roots of solution-focused therapy. Assumptions underlying constructivism, such as the importance of subjective meaning and the use of language to form meaning, are antithetical to the positivist, quantitative roots of treatment outcome research. However, a small knowledge base has accumulated. In 2000, Gingerich and Eisengart conducted a review, categorizing 15 studies according to their quality in terms of research design. Five well-controlled studies were identified, all of which showed positive outcomes. More research of solution-focused therapy needs to be conducted, however.

Techniques

Only an overview of techniques is provided here, as specific techniques are integrated into the strengths-and-skills-building model (Chapter 5) and illustrated in subsequent chapters. For a more complete rendering of techniques, along with case examples, see DeJong and Berg (2001).

Solution-Focused Language

Underlying all solution-focused techniques is the use of language to influence perception. One way language is used is to place problems in the past as if they are no longer exerting their negative influence. For example, "So you were losing your temper?" replaces "So you lose your temper?" The implication is that change is already in process.

Another strategic use of language is through what is referred to as definitive rather than possibility phrasing. Definitive phrasing through the employment of words such as *when* and *will* implies that change *will* occur. For example, a practitioner asks, "*When* you are better, what *will* you be doing?" Possibility phrasing with the use of words such as *if* and *could* is used only for the purposes of preparing clients to prevent further problems: "*If* you feel the urge to use drugs, what *could* you do to prevent it from going any further?" The strategic use of language stems from the social constructivist roots of solution-focused therapy in that language is the medium by which reality is shaped.

Joining Strategies for Client Relationships

Solution-focused therapy places a heavy emphasis on joining, which involves building a basis for collaborative work with clients. The attention to language begins with how the practitioner approaches opening contact with the client. See Table 1.1 for sample opening language and its rationale.

A central aspect of the joining process is assessing the relationship the client has with the helping process. Indeed, one of the advantages of solution-focused therapy is that, unlike other approaches that assume a voluntary client is willing to do what is necessary to change, solution-focused therapy acknowledges the different reasons clients may present for treatment and services. Three different client relationships are posed within the model: the customer, the complainant, and the visitor. The customer type of relationship is the client who is motivated and willing to participate in the change process. The complainant type of relationship is motivated chiefly for change in another person rather than for change in the self. The visitor type of relationship is a client who is typically unmotivated and is attending only because he or she has been mandated to do so. Strategies have been designed for each type of client relationship, although they can be used interchangeably. See Table 1.2 for an outline.

Table 1.1		
Language on Opening Contact		
Use	Avoid	Rationale
Words *concern* or *issue*	Word *problem*	*Problem* seen as pathologizing; *concern* seen as conveying the event as a part of life that the client will have to manage, surmount, or solve
"What would you like to see happen as a result of our talking?"	"What brings you here today?" "How can I help you?"	Want to imply internal locus of control (client is capable of resolving problems in collaboration with the worker) rather than external locus of control (something is taking control of the client, someone else can solve the problem)
"What will be happening in your life when our talking has been successful?"	Tentative language: *could, if*	Use definitive language to imply that change will occur and that the work will be successful

Note. From "Client Strengths and Crisis Intervention: A Solution-Focused Approach," by G. J. Greene, M. Y. Lee, R. Trask, and J. Rheinscheld, 1996, *Crisis Intervention, 3*, pp. 43–63.

Table 1.2

Strategies to Engage Clients

Client relationship/ description	Strategies	Description of strategies
Customer: Voluntary; willing to make changes	Orienting toward change	"What will your life look like when your work here is successful?"
Complainant: Motivated for somebody else to change	Coping questions	What resources have been drawn upon to cope with the situation?
	Normalizing	Depathologizing clients' concerns as normal life challenges
	Reframing	Introducing the positive elements of a behavior initially viewed as negative
	Orienting toward goals	"What would you like _____ to be doing instead of [complaint]?"
Visitor: Nonvoluntary; mandated into treatment	Orienting toward meeting the requirements of the mandate	"Whose idea was it that you come here?"
		"What does _____ need to see to know you don't have to come here anymore?"
	Relationship questions	Asking clients to view themselves from the perspective of another
	Siding with the client against an external entity	"What will we need to do to convince _____ you no longer need to come here?"
	Getting client to identify a desired goal	What is something the client is motivated to pursue?
All (Bertolino & O'Hanlon, 2002; Metcalf & Thomas, 1994)	Orienting toward change	"What is concerning you most at this point?"
	Collaborating on client perspective	"What would you like to change or have different in your life?"
	Determining progress toward goals	"What goals do you have for yourself?"
		"What did you [hope/wish/think] would be different as a result of coming to treatment?"
		"How will you know when things are better?"
		"How will you know when the problem is no longer a problem?"

(continued)

Table 1.2 (continued)		
Strategies to Engage Clients		
Client relationship/ description	Strategies	Description of strategies
		"What will indicate to you that coming here has been successful?"
		"How will you know when you no longer need to come here?"
		"What will be happening that will indicate to you that you can manage things on your own?" (Bertolino & O'Hanlon, 2002, pp. 83, 91)
	Encouraging collaboration	"What ideas do you have about how I can help you?"
		"In what ways do you see me helping you reach your goals?"
		"Are there certain things that you want to be sure that we talk about?"
		"How has this conversation been helpful?"
		"In your opinion, do we need to meet again?" (to further empower the client regarding the continuation of therapy based on his/her choice)
		"How will you know when we can stop?" (a collaborative question to define client criteria for termination)
		"What did we do today that you felt make a difference?" (to learn what is instigating change and what is helpful in the process) (Bertolino & O'Hanlon, 2000, p. 82)

The joining techniques discussed here are using idiosyncratic language, relationship questions, and complimenting. Chapter 5 covers other solution-focused joining techniques.

Using Idiosyncratic Language

Practitioners should attune themselves to the idiosyncratic phrasing of the client and adopt this language (Berg, 1994; O'Hanlon & Weiner-Davis,

1989).[1] The assumption is that clients feel understood when the worker uses their language. If a client describes herself as being "down in the dumps," the practitioner should use that term rather than using the term *depression*. If a client describes her "nerves" as acting up, then the practitioner should direct questions about those things that can "soothe her nerves" rather than talking about the client's "anxiety." Professional jargon should be avoided as it emphasizes the practitioner's "expert" role instead of allowing clients to be the experts on their own lives.

Relationship Questions

Relationship questions ask clients to view themselves from the perspective of another (DeJong & Berg, 2001). They are derived from the family systems therapy intervention of circular questioning. Circular questions are often nonthreatening to clients because the questions are posed in such a way that one comments on a situation from the view of an outside observer, typically family members (Fleuridas, Nelson, & Rosenthal, 1986). When people are stuck in a problem, it is often difficult for them to see alternatives. By viewing the problem from another person's point of view ("What would your partner say needs to happen in our work together to know that our time has been successful?"), they can sometimes see other possibilities. Similar to circular questions, relationship questions have the added advantage of allowing people to increase their ability to take on other people's perspectives and see the impact of their behavior on other people.

Compliments

Clients may feel defensive when they first see a practitioner, expecting to be judged and criticized. "Complimenting clients is a way to enhance their cooperation rather than defensiveness and resistance. . . . Clients are usually surprised, relieved, and pleased when they receive a compliment from the clinician. A consequence of therapeutic compliment is that clients are usually more willing to search for, identify, and amplify solution patterns" (Greene, Lee, Trask, & Rheinscheld, 1996, p. 56). The practitioner should be generous with compliments throughout the change process to reinforce the strengths and resources that individuals display. Compliments may be connected to the presenting problem or relate to other aspects of the client's life.

DeJong and Berg (2001) suggest a form of complimenting called "indirect complimenting" in which positive traits and behaviors are implied. Examples of indirect complimenting are "How were you able to do that?"

---

1. Practitioners who work with adolescent clients may want to use caution with this technique, as adolescents may not respect and/or trust a practitioner who adopts teenage slang.

and "How did you figure that out?" These questions push the client to figure out the resources he or she used to achieve success.

Exceptions: Nonproblem Times

A key intervention technique in solution-focused therapy is delving into the details of exceptions, times when the problem does not occur. The purpose is to help people access and expand upon the resources and strengths they use to combat difficulties. Helping individuals find abilities that have served them in the past is easier than teaching them entirely new behaviors (Bertolino & O'Hanlon, 2002). Exception finding also reduces the dichotomous thinking that often afflicts people when they are embroiled in problems. Exceptions help people shrink the all-encompassing nature of problems and see their problems as much more fluid and changeable.

Some guidelines for identifying exceptions include inquiring about incremental rather than radical differences (Murphy, 1997), such as asking "when are things a little better?" rather than when things are "wonderful." A second guideline is to start in the most recent past and then go back in time since recent evidence may exert a more powerful influence (Bertolino & O'Hanlon, 2002). If clients cannot identify any successes, the practitioner can inquire about when a problem is less severe, less frequent, less intense, or shorter in duration (O'Hanlon & Weiner-Davis, 1989). Once an exception is identified, its components are deconstructed. The practitioner asks investigative types of questions, such as those outlined in Table 1.3, to help the client discover the contextual details of the exception. People come to understand, through the process of exception finding, that behaviors are triggered by specific contexts and personal choices rather than ingrained

Table 1.3	
Investigative Questions for Exceptions	
Who	Who is there when the exception occurs? What are they doing differently? What would they say you are doing differently?
What	What is happening before? What is different about the behavior? What happens afterward?
Where	Where is the exception occurring? What are the details of the setting that contribute to the setting?
When	How often is this happening? What time of the day is it?
How	How are you making this happen? What strengths, talents, or qualities are you drawing on?

personality characteristics and hence more under their control than they previously believed.

Externalizing the Problem

Another way to build exceptions is through a technique called externalizing the problem. This technique was originally developed by Michael White from the narrative school (White & Epston, 1990) and has been adopted by solution-focused writers (e.g., Berg, 1994; Bertolino & O'Hanlon, 2002; Dolan, 1991). In externalizing, a linguistic distinction is made between the presenting problem and the person in which the problem behavior is personified as an external entity (the urge to drink, the invitation to argue, the anger). The purpose is to free the person from the belief that the problem is a fixed and inherent quality. It introduces fluidity into the problem, which may have become rigid and seemingly fixed. Externalizing may also introduce a note of humor into the work. Children may select playful names, such as "the crap" (oppositional behaviors; Corcoran, 2002), "the tornado," or "the volcano" (anger). In this way, the oppressive nature of the problem is lifted, and more options for behavior may be revealed. Our experiences of the advantages of "problem talk" led to a compromise between solution-focused therapy and its emphasis on solution talk and the narrative idea of externalization. Dyes and Neville (2000) suggest a further advantage of externalizing, which is to validate people's talk about problems while providing a bridge to discussion of solutions.

After identifying the externalized entity, the next step is to empower people to fight against it by asking relative influence questions. Answering these questions helps clients determine when they have control over the problem and when the problem has control over them. The following questions can be employed (Bertolino & O'Hanlon, 2002, p. 133):

"What's different about the times you're able to control the _____?"
"When can you resist the urge to _____?"
"When are you able to overcome the temptation to _____?"
"What percentage of the time do you have control over _____?"
"How has _____ come between you and your _____?"
"When has _____ recruited you to do something that you later got in trouble for?"
"What intentions do you think _____ has for you?"
"When have you been able to take a stand against _____?"
"Tell me about times when _____ couldn't convince you to _____?"

Individuals can also be invited to extend their awareness of how they combat their problems through a homework task recommended by Murphy

(1997). In this task, clients are asked to pay attention to the times they are able to resist the urge to engage in the problem behavior. "This language highlights people's choices and creates an assumption of accountability, rather than blame or determinism. If the person is not the problem, but has a certain relationship to the problem, then the relationship can change. If the problem invites rather than forces, one can turn down the invitation. If the problem is trying to recruit a client, he or she can refuse to join" (Bertolino & O'Hanlon, 2002, p. 133).

Miracle Question

To help people turn from a problem-focused view to one where change is possible, the miracle question, one of the signature techniques of solution-focused therapy, can be employed. Through the miracle question, people are asked to detail a future when the problem is no longer a problem. The miracle question is phrased as follows: "If a miracle happened in the night while you were sleeping but you didn't know it, what would be the first thing you noticed when you woke up in the morning to let you know that the miracle had occurred and the problem that you came here for was solved?" (de Shazer, 1988).

After posing the scenario, the practitioner works to elicit specific, behavioral details, taking into account the context of the miracle and the different relationships involved: "What will be happening?" "What will happen next?" "What will _____ notice about you?" "What will _____ say?" "Then what will you do?" The miracle question orients clients toward a more hopeful future when the problem does not dominate the picture. By eliciting the concrete details of the actions the client will take, a blueprint is being drawn on how change can occur (Cade & O'Hanlon, 1993).

Scaling Questions

The intervention of scaling questions is primarily designed for goal setting but also acts as a springboard for other techniques, such as relationship questions, exception finding, and task setting. In scaling questions, a rank-order scale of 1 to 10 is created, with 10 representing when the problem is no longer a problem. The practitioner then engages the client in a process of identifying specific and concrete behavioral anchors for 10. Clients are asked for their perception of their current functioning on the scale and then engaged in relationship questions to determine how people influenced by the problem see their behavior. Exception finding can follow ("So you're already a 4? What have you been doing to get yourself to a 4?" "What would _____ say you are doing?"). Incremental change is pursued by asking clients to figure out how they will move one number on the scale toward their goal before the next time they are seen for an appointment. In this way, they are accountable for the tasks they will perform to meet their goals, and progress is measured in a quantifiable fashion over time.

Pessimistic Stance

When individuals have difficulty coming up with exceptions and seem stuck in a problem orientation, as a last-resort intervention the practitioner can take a pessimistic stance. In this technique, the practitioner sides with the client's view of the problem, that it is very serious and difficult. The pessimistic stance involves the following types of questions:

"It sounds like the problem is very serious. How come things are not worse?"

"What are you doing/what steps have you taken/what has helped to keep things from getting worse?" "What else?"

"How has that been helpful? How has that made a difference?" "Would _____ agree?"

"What are you doing to keep going?"

"What is the smallest thing that you could do that might make a difference in your situation?"

"What could others do?"

"How could we get that to happen a little now?"

Asking these questions allows the practitioner to side with the client's position that change will not occur. Consideration of these questions can sometimes produce a shift, with the client beginning to take the opposite view and argue for change.

Homework

Solution-focused writers recommend several formula homework assignments to attune people to their resources and abilities. These include the formula first-session task, keeping track of current successes, the prediction task, and pretending the miracle has happened. Homework assignments are all phrased as suggestions rather than as prescriptions, with the overall purpose of helping people build awareness of their resources and what they are doing well. See Table 1.4 for a delineation of homework assignments.

▬▬▬ Termination

Because change is oriented toward a brief time frame in the solution-focused model, work is oriented toward termination at the beginning of

Table 1.4

Solution-Focused Homework Tasks

Tasks	Description	Uses
Formula first-session task	"Between now and next time, notice all the things that are happening that you want to continue to happen." Murphy's (1997) variation: "Observe when the problem is not occurring or is just a little better, and pay attention to how you are able to make that happen."	The task most often recommended by SFT writers; Greene et al. (1996) suggest it for clients who have difficulty defining specific problems on which they would like to work and those who are challenged to concretely formulate exceptions.
Keeping track of current successes	"Pay attention to and keep track of what you do to overcome the temptation or urge to _____ [perform the symptom or some behavior associated with the problem]."	To help people understand the resources they use to circumvent their problem behaviors
Prediction task	"In the prediction task, the client is asked to predict or rate something, such a 'First thing each morning, rate the possibility of _____ [an exception behavior] happening before noon' (Greene et al., 1996, p. 58)."	When people experience the problems as being outside their control, often clients find that the behavior follows their prediction; as a result, they discover they are much more in control of outcomes than they previously believed.
Pretend the miracle has happened	Select a day to pretend the miracle has occurred and the presenting problem is resolved; keep track of what is different about the day or the individual or how others react	This tasks shows clients that they can enact positive feelings, thoughts, and behaviors that will help them reach a nonproblem state.

treatment. Questions include "What needs to happen so you don't need to come back to see me?" and "What will be different when therapy has been successful?" (Berg, 1994). Once clients have maintained changes on the small concrete goals they have set, the practitioner and client start to discuss plans for termination, as it is assumed that achievement of these small changes will lead to further positive change in the client's life. Termination is geared toward helping clients identify strategies so that change will be maintained and the momentum developed will cause further change to occur. While the practitioner does not want to imply that relapse is inevitable, the client must be prepared with strategies to enact if temptation presents itself or if the client begins to slip into old behaviors. Therefore, it is during termination that possibility rather than definitive phrasing is used. For example, "What *would* be the first thing you'd notice *if* you started to find things slipping back?" "What *could* you do to prevent things from getting any further?" and "*If* you have the urge to do drugs again, what *could* you do to make sure you didn't use?" might be typical inquiries to elicit strategies to use if there is a return to old behavior.

Termination also involves building on the changes that have occurred, with the hope they will continue into the future. Selekman (1993, 1997) has proposed a number of such questions, including "With all the changes you are making, what will I see if I was a fly on your wall 6 months from now?" and "With all the changes you are making, what will you be telling me if I run into you at the convenience store 6 months from now?" (Selekman, 1997). Questions are phrased to set up the expectation that change will continue to happen.

Summary

Solution-focused therapy, a brief treatment model, emphasizes client strengths, resources, and abilities (O'Hanlon & Weiner-Davis, 1989). Because no one holds the objective truth, each person's perspective and way of solving problems is unique and valued. The practitioner's job is to help build client awareness of these strengths and to amplify change toward its application in problematic situations. Rather than being focused on the past and a history of the problem, attention is oriented to a future without the problem to build vision, hope, and motivation for the client. The helper empowers clients to view themselves as capable and resourceful and encourages small, concrete behavioral change, which is assumed to fuel further change in a systemic way.

References

Berg, I. K. (1994). *Family-based services: A solution-focused approach*. New York: W. W. Norton.

Berg, I. K., & DeJong, P. (1996). Solution-building conversations: Co-constructing a sense of competence with clients. *Families in Society, 77,* 376–391.

Berg, I. K., & Miller, S. (1992). *Working with the problem drinker*. New York: W. W. Norton.

Bertolino, B., & O'Hanlon, B. (2002). *Collaborative, competency-based counseling and therapy*. Boston: Allyn & Bacon.

Cade, B., & O'Hanlon, W. H. (1993). *A brief guide to brief therapy*. New York: W. W. Norton.

Corcoran, J. (2002). Developmental adaptations of solution-focused family therapy. *Brief Treatment and Crisis Intervention, 2,* 301–313.

DeJong, P., & Berg, I. K. (2001). *Interviewing for solutions* (2nd ed.). Pacific Grove, CA: Brooks/Cole.

De Shazer, S. (1988). *Clues: Investigating solutions in brief therapy.* New York: W. W. Norton.

De Shazer, S. (1994). *Words were originally magic.* New York: W. W. Norton.

De Shazer, S., Berg, I. K., Lipchick, E., Nunnally, E., Molnar, A., Gingerich, W., et al. (1986). Brief therapy: Focused solution development. *Family Process, 25,* 207–221.

Dolan, Y. (1991). *Resolving sexual abuse.* New York: W. W. Norton.

Durrant, M. (1995). *Creative strategies for school problems: Solutions for psychologists and teachers.* New York: W. W. Norton.

Dyes, M. A., & Neville, K. E. (2000). Taming trouble and other tales: Using externalized characters in solution-focused therapy. *Journal of Systematic Therapies, 19*(1), 74–81.

Fleuridas, C., Nelson, T. S., & Rosenthal, D. M. (1986). The evolution of circular questions: Training family therapists. *Journal of Marital and Family Therapy, 12*(2), 113–127.

Gergen, K. (1994). *Realities and relationships: Soundings in social construction.* Cambridge, MA: Harvard University Press.

Gingerich, W. J., & Eisengart, S. (2000). Solution-focused brief therapy: A review of the outcome research. *Family Process, 39*(4), 477–498.

Greene, G. J., Lee, M. Y., Trask, R., & Rheinscheld, J. (1996). Client strengths and crisis intervention: A solution-focused approach. *Crisis Intervention, 3,* 43–63.

Haley, J. (1984). *Ordeal therapy.* San Francisco, Jossey-Bass.

Metcalf, L., & Thomas, F. (1994). Client and therapist perceptions of solution focused brief therapy: A qualitative analysis. *Journal of Family Psychotherapy, 5*(4), 49–66.

Murphy, J. (1997). *Solution-focused counseling in middle and high schools.* Alexandria, VA: American Counseling Association.

Neimeyer, R., & Mahoney, M. (1995). *Constructivism in psychotherapy.* Washington, DC: American Psychological Association.

O'Hanlon, W. H., & Weiner-Davis, M. (1989). *In search of solutions: A new direction in psychotherapy.* New York: W. W. Norton.

Selekman, M. (1993). *Pathways to change.* New York: Guilford.

Selekman, M. (1997). *Solution-focused therapy with children.* New York: Guilford.

Weakland, J., Fisch, R., Watzlawick, P., & Bodin, A. (1974). Brief therapy: Focused problem resolution. *Family Process, 13,* 141–168.

White, M., & Epston, D. (1990). *Narrative means to therapeutic ends.* New York: W. W. Norton.

2   Motivational Interviewing

Developed over the last 20 years (Dunn, Deroo, & Rivara, 2001), motivational interviewing is "a client-centered, directive method for enhancing intrinsic motivation to change by exploring and resolving ambivalence" (Miller & Rollnick, 2002, p. 25). Developed for the treatment of substance abuse, motivational interviewing is now being applied to other areas of change, such as diet and exercise (Moyers & Rollnick, 2002). It has been employed both as a stand-alone treatment and as a way to engage people in other intervention approaches (Walitzer, Dermen, & Conners, 1999).

Motivational interviewing is enacted within the framework of the stages of change model, with its conceptualization that people need different interventions depending on the level of their motivation to change. Because the stages of change model acts as a backdrop, the model is first described, followed by the guidelines and techniques of motivational interviewing.

Stages of Change Model

In acknowledgment of the reluctance of many substance abusers to change their patterns, Prochaska and colleagues (Connors, Donovan, & Di-

Clemente, 2001; Prochaska & Norcross, 1994) developed the transtheoretical stages of change model. The model offers a novel conceptualization that allows for many different theoretical approaches that are employed at the point where they will be most effective. Six stages of change have been formulated:

1. Precontemplation
2. Contemplation
3. Determination
4. Action
5. Maintenance
6. Relapse

Particular techniques from different theoretical orientations match the relevant stage of change, with a primary focus on building motivation for individuals to take action toward their goals and to maintain changes. Each stage of change is more fully examined in the following sections, with strategies for increasing client's motivation so that movement toward the next change can occur. See Table 2.1 for a summary of the stages and the possible strategies within each one.

Precontemplation

In precontemplation, the individual believes there is no problem behavior and is therefore unwilling to do anything about it. At this stage, the individual sees the problem behavior as possessing more advantages than disadvantages. Individuals in this stage are typically defensive and resistant about their behavior. They lack awareness of the problem, and if in treatment have usually been coerced or pressured to do so by others. In treatment, they are not willing to participate (Connors et al., 2001).

In the precontemplation stage, the practitioner, rather than focusing on behavioral change, focuses on building the client's motivation to change and on increasing awareness of the negative aspects of the problem behavior. Prochaska, DiClemente, and Norcross (1994) advise asking about the impact of the problem both on the individual and on family members and other people who are affected by the problem. For the client to move to the next stage, the advantages of changing have to outweigh the disadvantages.

If a client in precontemplation is initially uninterested in change, the decision can be made to work with family members. For example, reinforcement training (Sisson & Azrin, 1986), also called unilateral therapy (Thomas & Ager, 1993), and the pressures to change model (Barber & Gilbertson, 1997) have effectively induced individuals with substance abuse problems to reduce their intake and seek treatment.

Table 2.1

The Stages of Change and Strategies at Each Stage

Stage of change	Characteristics	Change strategies
Precontemplation	Individual is unwilling to do anything about the problem	Linking the client with social liberation forces
	Individual sees the problem behavior as possessing more advantages than disadvantages	Motivational enhancement interviewing
	Individual is usually coerced or pressured to do so by others	
Contemplation	Individual begins to consider there is a problem and the feasibility and costs of changing the behavior	Providing education on the disorder and the recovery process
	Individual wants to understand own behavior and frequently feel distress over it	Bolstering the advantages of changing and problem-solving about how to ameliorate or lessen the disadvantages
	Individual thinks about making change in the next 6 months	Self-monitoring
		Functional analysis
		Alternative reinforcers for the problem behavior are considered
		Identifying social support systems
Preparation (determination)	Individual is poised to change in the next month	Goal setting
		Developing a change plan
		Developing coping skills
Action	Individual has started to modify the problem behavior and/or the environment in an effort to promote change in the past 6 months	Appraisal of high-risk situations and coping strategies to overcome these are a mainstay of this stage
		Alternative reinforcers to problem behaviors should also be applied
		Assessment of social support systems continues to be essential so that others are a helpful resource for change rather than a hindrance

(continued)

Table 2.1 (continued)

The Stages of Change and Strategies at Each Stage

Stage of change	Characteristics	Change strategies
Maintenance	Sustained change has occurred for at least 6 months	The practitioner should help the individual find alternative sources of satisfaction and enjoyment and continue to support lifestyle changes
		Assisting the individual in practicing and applying coping strategies
		Continued vigilance of cognitive distortions that might be associated with the problem and ways to counteract
		Maintaining environmental control
Relapse	The problem behavior has resumed, another cycle is begun, and the individual reenters at the stage of either precontemplation or contemplation	An opportunity for greater awareness of high-risk situations and the coping strategies needed to address these challenges

Note. Adapted from *Substance Abuse Treatment and Stages of Change: Selecting and Planning Interventions*, by G. Connors, D. Donovan, and C. D. Clemente, 2001, New York: Guilford.

The practitioner can also expose the client in precontemplation to social liberation, which offers people information about the problem and public support for change efforts. Much of this involves harnessing the forces that are already present to help people with problem behaviors. For example, a large self-help network exists for a range of problems, including substance use, overeating, and mental disorders.

Contemplation

In contemplation, individuals begin to consider that there is a problem, and they also begin to consider the feasibility and costs of changing the behavior. They want to understand their behavior and frequently feel distress over it. During this stage, individuals think about making change within the next 6 months. While they may have made attempts to change their behavior in the past, they are not yet prepared to take action at this point; they are engaged in the process of evaluating the advantages and disadvantages of the problem (Connors et al., 2001).

The practitioner's role during this stage is to continue to enhance the client's motivation and to educate him or her on aspects of the disorder and the recovery process. The practitioner works to help bolster the advantages of changing and to brainstorm about how to ameliorate the situation or at least lessen the disadvantages. For instance, if a person identifies, as an advantage of drinking, that he or she handles social situations more smoothly, then perhaps the client's social skills need work so confidence can be inspired without alcohol.

Self-monitoring of problem behavior can help the individual gain awareness of the frequency and intensity of the behavior, the cues that elicit problem behavior, and the consequences that follow. Alternative reinforcers for the problem behavior are considered. Identification of social support systems is critical during this change, so that others can promote change efforts.

Determination

In determination (also called preparation), the individual is poised to change in the next month. Readiness to change is bolstered through goal setting and developing a change plan (Connors et al., 2001). To be prepared to resist problem behaviors, the individual should develop and rehearse coping skills, such as relaxation, visualization of successful outcomes, cognitive restructuring, communication skills, and avoidance of environmental cues, before being placed in high-risk situations.

Action

In action, the individual has started to modify the problem behavior and/or the environment in an effort to promote change in the past 6 months. The individual at this point is willing to follow suggested strategies and activities for change (Connors et al., 2001).

In the action stage, the practitioner works toward maintaining client engagement in treatment and supports a realistic view of change through helping the individual achieve small, successive steps. The practitioner should acknowledge and empathize with the difficulties associated with the early stages of change. Appraisal of high-risk situations and coping strategies to overcome these are a mainstay of this stage. Alternative reinforcers to problem behaviors should also be applied. Assessment of social support systems continues to be essential so that others are a helpful resource for change rather than a hindrance.

Maintenance

In maintenance, sustained change has occurred for at least 6 months. The individual is working to sustain changes achieved to date, and attention is focused on avoiding slips or relapses (Prochaska & Norcross, 1994). The practitioner helps the individual find alternative sources of satisfaction and enjoyment and continues to support lifestyle changes. The practitioner also continues to assist the individual in practicing and applying coping strategies. Clients have to be aware of cognitive distortions that might be associated with the problem. For example, if an individual with an alcohol problem begins to think, "Life is no fun without drinking," recognizing this as a high-risk thought is essential so that the validity of the thought can be questioned: What were the consequences of my drinking? Were they always fun? How else can I experience fun and enjoyment in my life without drinking?

Maintaining environmental control is critical at this stage. For example, an individual with a weight problem has to avoid buying junk food "for the sake of the children." As much as possible, the individual should not put temptation in his or her way. However, he or she must also be armed with the necessary skills to face high-risk situations if they do occur. Continued practice with skills is necessary for this reason.

Relapse

Rather than as failure, DiClemente, Prochaska, and associates (Connors et al., 2001; Prochaska & DiClemente, 1984, 1992) view relapse as an opportunity for greater awareness of high-risk situations and the coping strategies to be developed to address these challenges. The notion that change is a spiral process rather than linear in nature means that relapse is just a normal part of the process of change. In other words, there is one step backward for two steps forward.

Motivational Interviewing

Motivational interviewing is a brief treatment model (one to four sessions) formulated to produce rapid change in which the client's motivation is mobilized. Motivational interviewing avoids prescriptive techniques and training the client in skills; instead, the client's own motivation is galvanized (Miller & Rollnick, 2002). Motivational interviewing is suggested when clients are initially low in motivation for change, specifically, in the precontemplation and contemplation stages of change. Indeed, research supports this finding; the motivational interviewing condition was especially helpful when clients were initially low in motivation (Project MATCH Research Group, 1997).

Empirical Support

Research has been conducted on both the stages of change model and motivational interviewing. Prochaska and DiClemente (1984, 1992) and other originators of the stages of change model claim that it is empirically derived, and it has garnered much research support (e.g., Prochaska, DiClemente, & Norcross, 1994; Velicer, Hughes, Fava, Prochaska, & DiClemente, 1995). According to a recent comprehensive review, however, there is as yet no evidence that people progress systematically through each stage of change (Littell & Girvin, 2002). However, a meta-analysis of 47 studies did reveal that cognitive-affective processes were more indicative of the stages of contemplation or preparation (an effect size of .70), whereas behavioral processes were more common in the action stage (an effect size of .80) (Rosen, 2000). This generally supports the hypothesized movement of change from a cognitive to a more behavioral process as people become ready to take action toward change.

Miller and colleagues have performed extensive research studies on motivational interviewing. Dunn et al. (2001) quantitatively reviewed 29 studies, mainly on substance abuse but also on smoking, HIV risk reduction, and diet and exercise. Moderate to large effects were found for reducing both substance abuse and substance dependence, with maintenance of effects over time. Motivational interviewing was also found to promote engagement in more intensive substance abuse treatment. Although studies have largely been conducted on adults, adolescent substance use also showed significantly positive results from motivational interviewing (Burke, Arkowitz, & Dunn, 2002).

Overall, motivational interviewing was superior to no-treatment control groups and less viable treatments; it was equivalent to more credible alternatives that were often two to three times longer in duration. For example, in the Project MATCH Research Group study (1997, 1998), 952 individuals with alcohol problems from outpatient clinics and 774 from aftercare treatment were provided with either 12-step facilitation (12 sessions), cognitive-behavioral coping skills therapy (12 sessions), or motivational enhancement therapy (4 sessions). Motivational enhancement fared as well as the other two treatments with three times as many sessions, both at posttest (Project MATCH Research Group, 1997) and 3 years later (Project MATCH Research Group, 1998).

In addition to alcohol problems, drug addiction, and dual diagnoses, motivational interviewing has been effective for health-related behaviors related to diabetes, hypertension, and bulimia nervosa. Only mixed findings, however, have been indicated for the use of motivational interviewing for quitting cigarette use and for increasing physical exercise, and no support has been indicated for motivational interviewing for the reduction of HIV risk behaviors in the few studies to date (Burke et al., 2002).

Techniques of Motivational Interviewing

Several guiding principles underlie the techniques of motivational interviewing: expressing empathy, developing discrepancy, rolling with resistance, supporting self-efficacy, and developing a change plan. The general guidelines for motivational interviewing are also expressed in a list of do's and don'ts in Box 2.1. The principles are enacted through listening reflectively and demonstrating empathy, eliciting self-motivational statements, developing strategies to handle resistance, and enacting a decisional balance.

Listening Reflectively and Demonstrating Empathy

The first step for the practitioner is to listen empathically to clients' concerns, reflecting the content of the their messages as well as the underlying feelings. In this way rapport is built, and people feel heard and understood. With the practice of empathy, the practitioner is able to more accurately assess the individual's problems and the person's relationship to the process of change.

Empathic listening and affirming statements are not only practiced initially but also continued throughout the change process. Although these techniques are drawn from nondirective counseling (Rogers, 1951), they differ in several key ways. In nondirective counseling, the client is allowed to decide the content and direction of the discussion, whereas in motivational interviewing, the practitioner systematically directs the process toward building client motivation. Another difference between the approaches is the use of empathy. In contrast to nondirective counseling, in which empathic reflection is used noncontingently, in motivational interviewing empathy reinforces client statements about changing. In nondirective interviewing, the practitioner explores the in-the-moment conflicts and emotions that arise; in motivational interviewing, in order to bolster motivation for change, the practitioner works to create discrepancies between the client's values and goals (such as long-term health) and how the problem stands in the way of these goals (Miller & Rollnick, 1991). Motivational interviewing employs specific techniques to gear the client toward behavior change (Moyers & Rollnick, 2002). The practitioner selectively reflects and affirms change talk and asks the client to elaborate on statements about change.

Box 2.1

Guidelines for Motivational Interviewing

Do's

1. Set a tentative agenda, allowing for flexibility.
2. Begin where the client is.
3. Explore and reflect client's perceptions.
4. Use empathic reflection selectively when clients express reasons to change.
5. Reflect by making paraphrasing and summarizing statements rather than using questions.
6. Use affirmation and positive reframing of the client's statements to bolster self-efficacy.
7. Present a brief summary at end of each contact.
8. Use phrases like "I wonder if…" and "some people find…" to probe about problem behaviors gently.

Don'ts

1. Argue, lecture, confront, or persuade.
2. Moralize, criticize, preach, or judge.
3. Give expert advice at the beginning.
4. Order, direct, warn, or threaten.
5. Do most of the talking.
6. Debate about diagnostic labeling.
7. Ask closed-ended questions.
8. Ask a lot of questions (more than three in a row) without reflecting.
9. Offer advice and feedback until later stages, when sufficient motivation has been built.

Note. Adapted from "Shifting the Balance: Motivational Interviewing to Help Behaviour Change in People with Bulimia Nervosa," by S. Killick and C. Allen, 1997, *European Eating Disorders Review* 5(1), pp. 35–41; *Motivational Interviewing: Preparing People to Change Addictive Behavior* (2nd ed.), by W. Miller and S. Rollnick, 2002, New York: Guilford; and "A Practical Guide to the Use of Motivational Interviewing in Anorexia Nervosa," by J. Treasure and W. Ward, 1997, *European Eating Disorders Review, 5*, pp. 102–114.

Eliciting Self-Motivational Statements

The next step in the change process is to elicit from clients arguments in favor of change. The practitioner avoids advice giving at this point and simply poses a series of questions that the client might answer in a way that favors change. Conversation leads to exploring the disadvantages of the status quo and the advantages of changing. The exploration helps the individual examine the discrepancy between goals and values in terms of health, future well-being, success, and family relationships, on the one hand, and current behaviors, on the other. The practitioner inquires about how the problem affects the individual and those close to him or her and the extent of the client's concerns about the problem. The practitioner also asks "questions about extremes": what the future may be like if a change is not made and what will be different if the individual does take steps to eradicate the problem. Table 2.2 details the types of questions that can be asked.

These open-ended questions are a starting point for a conversation about the client's relationship to change. Reflective statements are made to client responses, following the general guideline that the practitioner should strive to make three statements following a question. The array of questions, therefore, is not delivered in a rapid-fire way but is used selectively to invoke possibilities for change in the client.

Developing Strategies to Handle Resistance

Miller and Rollnick (1991) define resistance as a sign that the practitioner's tactics do not match the client's stage of change and discuss their adaptation of Chamberlain and colleagues' categorization system for client signs of resistance. The four main categories are arguing, interrupting, denying, and ignoring. For descriptions of these behaviors, see Table 2.3.

Confrontation is avoided in response to these behaviors because it may lead to escalation of resistance. Instead, variations of reflective responses are used that have a directive aspect to move potential power struggles toward change instead (Moyers & Rollnick, 2002). Strategies to handle client resistance include simple reflection, amplified reflection, double-sided reflection, shifting focus, agreement with a twist, reframing, clarifying free choice, and using paradox. These are briefly summarized here.

Simple reflection acknowledges a client's feeling, thought, or opinion so that the client continues to explore his or her problem rather than becoming defensive ("You're not sure you're ready to spend a lot of time changing right now") (Carroll, 1998). Simple reflection allows further exploration rather than evoking defensiveness.

Amplified reflection goes beyond simple reflection in that the client's statement is acknowledged—but in an extreme fashion. The purpose of such a statement is to bring out the side of the client that wants to change. An amplified reflection, such as the statement "You really like drinking, and you don't think you'll ever want to change," typically has the effect of getting the client to back down from an entrenched position, allowing for the possibility of negotiation about change (Moyers & Rollnick, 2002).

Double-sided reflection reflects both aspects of the client's ambivalence. When people are exploring the possibility of change, they are divided between wanting to change and wanting to keep the behavior that has become problematic ("You're not sure cocaine is that big a problem, and at the same time a lot of people who care about you think it is, and getting arrested for drug possession is causing some problems for you")

Table 2.2

Questions to Elicit Self-Motivational Statements

Disadvantages of the status quo

Problem recognition	What things make you think that this is a problem?
	What difficulties have you had in relation to _____ [problem]?
	In what ways do you think you or other people have been harmed by _____ [problem]?
	In what ways has this been a problem for you?
	How has _____ [problem] stopped you from doing what you want to do?
Concern	What is there about _____ [problem] that you or other people might see as reasons for concern?
	What worries you about _____ [problem]?
	What can you imagine happening to you?
	How do you feel about _____ [problem]?
	How much does that concern you?
	In what ways does this concern you?
	What do you think will happen if you don't make a change?
Querying extremes	What concerns you the most about this in the long run?
	Suppose you continue on as you have been, without changing. What do you imagine are the worst things that might happen to you?
	How much do you know about what can happen if you [continue with the problem behavior], even if you don't see this happening to you?

Advantages of changing

Intention to change	The fact that you're here indicates that at least a part of you thinks it's time to do something. What are the reasons you see for making a change?
	When you are 100% successful and things work out exactly as you would like, what would be different?
	What things make you think that you should keep on the way you have? And what about the other side? What makes you think it's time for a change?
	What are you thinking about _____ [problem] at this point?
	I can see that you're feeling stuck at the moment. What's going to have to change? How would you like for things to be different?
	What would be the good things about _____ [changing]?
	What would you like your life to be like 5 years from now?
Optimism about change (self-efficacy)	What makes you think that if you did decide to make a change, you could do it? What encourages you that you can change if you want to?
	What do you think would work for you, if you decided to change?
	When else in your life have you made a significant change like this? How did you do it?
	How confident are you that you can make this change?
	What personal strengths do you have that will help you succeed?
	Who could offer you helpful support in making this change?
Querying extremes	What might be the best results you could imagine if you make a change?
	If you were completely successful in making the changes you want, how would things be different?

Note. Adapted from *Motivational Interviewing: Preparing People to Change Addictive Behavior* (2nd ed.), by W. Miller and S. Rollnick, 2002, New York: Guilford.

Table 2.3

Signs From the Client That the Practitioner Needs to Change Strategies

Signs	Description
Arguing	Questioning or disagreeing with the practitioner's stance or credentials
Interrupting	Cutting off or talking over the practitioner in an inappropriate or defensive manner
Denial	Client fails to recognize issues, participate, or take responsibility
	Blaming, disagreeing, finding excuses, minimizing
	Presents with hopelessness about changing or is not willing to change
Ignoring	Client fails to track the practitioner's speech, doesn't answer, or derails the line of discussion

Note. Adapted from *Motivational Interviewing: Preparing People to Change Addictive Behavior* (2nd ed.), by W. Miller and S. Rollnick, 2002, New York: Guilford.

(Carroll, 1998). Double-sided reflection can also pull the client's attention to the inconsistency between the person's problem behavior and his or her goals and values (Moyers & Rollnick, 2002), as in "Your relationship is very important to you, and your drug use is causing problems in the relationship."

Shifting focus moves the client's attention from a potential impasse to avoid polarization. When the client begins to argue against what the practitioner might feel is the best course, the practitioner should immediately shift his or her position and redirect the focus ("I think you're jumping ahead here. We're not talking at this point about you quitting drinking for the rest of your life; let's talk some more about what the best goal is for you and how to go about making it happen"). The general guideline for shifting focus "is to first defuse the initial concern and then direct attention to a more readily workable issue" (Miller & Rollnick, 2002, p. 102).

Agreement with a twist involves agreement with some of the client's message but in a way that then orients the client in the direction toward change ("I can see why you'd be troubled about you and your wife's arguments about your use. I wonder what needs to happen so you don't need to keep talking about this"). Reframing takes arguments clients use against change and alters the meaning of the information to promote change instead. A common example involves the tendency of drinkers to consume large quantities without experiencing ill effects and loss of control. This tendency is sometimes used as an excuse for why the drinking is not a problem. This excuse is reframed as tolerance of alcohol, which is actually symptomatic of problem drinking.

Clarifying free choice involves communicating that it is up to the client whether he or she wants to change, rather than getting embroiled in a debate or an argument about what the client must do ("You can decide to take this on now or wait until another time"). "When people perceive that their freedom of choice is being threatened, they tend to react by asserting their liberty. Probably the best antidote for this reaction is to assure the person of what is surely the truth: in the end, it is the client who determines what happens" (Miller & Rollnick, 2002, p. 106).

Paradox involves siding with the client's resistance, which then causes the client to take the other side of the argument for change ("You've convinced me that you're not ready to do anything about this right now. It's not the right time for you"). Sometimes clients who have been entrenched in a negative position vis-à-vis change start to argue from the other side of their ambivalence for change when the practitioner joins with their position.

Enacting a Decisional Balance

A decisional balance is a motivational technique that weighs the costs and benefits of change. The advantages and disadvantages of change have been a continual focus of motivational interviewing, but in this intervention, they are gathered together more formally through a chart (Table 2.4). The client has the main responsibility for coming up with the pros and cons, but the practitioner should elaborate on what has been stated, with the following types of prompts when a reason for change has been given (Miller & Rollnick, 2002, p. 80).

Table 2.4

Decisional Balance

Advantages of changing	Disadvantages of changing	Advantages of problem behavior	Disadvantages of problem behavior
What will the client get out of changing in terms of emotions, thoughts about the self, physical health, relationships, and/or other social networks?	What is the effort involved in changing? What will have to be lost in the different domains (emotions, thoughts, physical health, relationships, other social networks, the environment)?	What does the client get in terms of the different domains?	What is lost in terms of the different domains?

- Asking for clarification: In what ways? How much? When?
- Asking for a specific example
- Asking for a description of the last time this occurred

The advantages of changing should also be elaborated upon by asking the client to detail the difference it would make to have a particular advantage present in his or her life.

From compiling and synthesizing various studies of different problem behaviors involving 3,858 subjects, Prochaska, Velicer, et al. (1994) confirmed that in precontemplation the disadvantages of changing outweigh the advantages. In contemplation, the advantages of changing have increased, and when clients are ready to take action, the disadvantages have decreased, meaning that the pros outweigh the cons. The practice implication, therefore, is to first increase the advantages of changing and then help the client work on decreasing the disadvantages.

People usually understand the benefits of changing, and the list is weighted toward this end. However, the disadvantages of changing often sustain the problem—in other words, there are many important reasons why people keep problem behaviors in their lives. Constructing a decisional balance offers a way to discover these reasons. The practitioner can then assist the client in deciding which of these factors needs to be addressed first. These factors may be, as primary examples, lack of resources (e.g., lack of financial means as a reason to stay in a violent relationship; lack of child care as a barrier to substance abuse treatment), lack of social skills (e.g., unable to relate to others except through drug-taking activities; unable to solve problems other than through aggression), or belief systems that keep the problem in place, such as personal beliefs about being powerless to change and distorted beliefs about the power of alcohol and drugs in substance abuse. Finding out the disadvantages of changing will help determine the nature of the goals that will be constructed.

Supporting Self-Efficacy and Developing a Change Plan

A critical component of motivational interviewing involves building client self-efficacy, which is defined by Miller and Rollnick (2002) as a person's confidence that he or she can succeed at change efforts. Therefore, the practitioner should assess not only clients' willingness to change but also their confidence that they could make changes if they desired to. The practitioner's confidence in the client's abilities also acts as an influence on the client's belief about change. Ways to elicit and strengthen confidence talk include scaling the level of confidence from 1 to 10, reviewing past successes, discussing personal strengths and supports, brainstorming, giving information and advice, reframing, and asking questions about hypothetical change. See Table 2.5 for more detail on these interventions, which also

Table 2.5

Building Confidence and Readiness to Change

Evocative questions	"How might you go about making this change?"
	"What would be a good first step?"
	"What obstacles do you foresee, and how might you deal with them?"
	"What gives you some confidence that you can do this?"
Ruler assessment	"How confident are you that you could _____? On a scale from 1 to 10, where 1 is not at all confident and 10 is extremely confident, where would you say you are?"
	"Why are you at a _____ and not 1?"
	"What would it take for you to go from _____ to [a higher number]?"
Reviewing past successes	"When in your life have you made up your mind to do something, and did it? It might be something new you learned, or a habit that you quit, or some other significant change that you made in your life. When have you done something like that?"
	"What did you do that worked?"
	"Was there specific preparation for change?"
	"What did you do to initiate and maintain change?"
	"What obstacles were there, and how did you surmount them?"
	"To what did you attribute your success?"
	"What did this mean about your resources, skills, and strengths?"
Personal strengths and supports	"What is there about you, what strong points do you have that could help you succeed in making this change?" (Elaborate on personal strengths named.)
	"What sources of social support do you have?"
	"Are there others you could call for support? In what ways? Who else could help with change?"
Brainstorming	Freely generating as many ideas as possible for how a change might be accomplished
Reframing failure	Reframing unsuccessful attempts as learning
	Reframing explanations of failure thought to be due to internal, stable factors (i.e., inability) to external, unstable factors (i.e., effort)
Hypothetical change	"Suppose that you did succeed and are looking back on it now: What most likely is it that worked? How did it happen?"
	"Suppose that this one big obstacle weren't there. If that obstacle were removed, then how might you go about making this change?"
	"Clearly you are feeling very discouraged, even demoralized about this. So use your imagination: If you were to try again, what might be the best way to try?"

have considerable overlap with solution-focused therapy techniques (Chapter 1). These interventions may result in a person's readiness to negotiate a change plan in which goals are set, options for change are considered, a plan is formulated, and commitment is made to the plan.

Summary

The stages of change model and motivational interviewing take into account the level of motivation for change and are designed for those who have not yet committed to action to change problem behavior. The techniques and intervention questions elicit from clients in a nondefensive way the reasons why they should change. The practitioner does not advise or tell clients what to do but rather, using a collaborative process, bolsters motivation so that clients are willing to take action toward solving their problems.

References

Barber, J. G., & Gilbertson, R. (1997). Unilateral interventions for women living with heavy drinkers. *Social Work, 42,* 69–78.

Burke, B., Arkowitz, H., & Dunn, C. (2002). The efficacy of motivational interviewing and its adaptations: What we know so far. In W. R. Miller & S. Rollnick (Eds.), *Motivational interviewing* (2nd ed., pp. 217–250). New York: Guilford.

Carroll, K. (1998). *A cognitive-behavioral approach: Treating cocaine addiction.* Retrieved August 28, 2001, from http://www.drugabuse.gov/TXManuals/CBT/CBT1.html.

Connors, G., Donovan, D., & DiClemente, C. (2001). *Substance abuse treatment and stages of change: Selecting and planning interventions.* New York: Guilford.

Dunn, C., Deroo, L., & Rivara, F. (2001). The use of brief interventions adapted from motivational interviewing across behavioral domains: A systematic review. *Addiction, 96,* 1725–1742.

Killick, S., & Allen, C. (1997). Shifting the balance: Motivational interviewing to help behaviour change in people with bulimia nervosa. *European Eating Disorders Review, 5*(1), 35–41.

Littell, J., & Girvin, H. (2002). Stages of change: A critique. *Behavior Modification, 26,* 223–273.

Miller, W., & Rollnick, S. (1991). *Motivational interviewing* (1st ed.). New York: Guilford.

Miller, W., & Rollnick, S. (2002). *Motivational interviewing: Preparing people to change addictive behavior* (2nd ed.). New York: Guilford.

Moyers, T., & Rollnick, S. (2002). A motivational interviewing perspective on resistance in psychotherapy. *JCLP/In Session: Psychotherapy in Practice 58,* 185–193.

Prochaska, J., & DiClemente, C. (1984). *The transtheoretical approach: Crossing traditional boundaries of therapy*. Malabar, FL: Krieger.

Prochaska, J., & DiClemente, C. (1992). Stages of change in the modification of problem behaviors. In M. Hersen, R. Eisleer, & P. M. Miller (Eds.), *Progress in behavior modification* (Vol. 28). New York: Academic Press.

Prochaska, J., DiClemente, C., & Norcross, J. (1994). *Changing for good*. New York: Avon.

Prochaska, J., & Norcross, J. (1994). *Systems of psychotherapy: A transtheoretical analysis* (3rd ed.). Pacific Grove, CA: Brooks/Cole.

Prochaska, J., Velicer, W., Rossi, J., Goldstein, M., Marcus, B., Rakoeski, W., et al. (1994). Stages of change and decisional balance for 12 problem behaviors. *Health Psychology, 13,* 39–46.

Project MATCH Research Group. (1997). Matching alcoholism treatments to client heterogeneity: Project MATCH posttreatment drinking outcomes. *Journal of Studies on Alcohol, 58,* 7–29.

Project MATCH Research Group. (1998). Matching alcoholism treatments to client heterogeneity: Project MATCH three-year drinking outcomes. *Alcoholism: Clinical & Experimental Research, 22,* 1300–1311.

Rogers, C. (1951). *Client-centered therapy*. Boston: Houghton Mifflin.

Rosen, C. (2000). Is the sequencing of change processes by stage consistent across health problems: A meta-analysis. *Health Psychology, 19,* 593–604.

Sisson, R. W., & Azrin, N. H. (1986). Family-member involvement to initiate and promote treatment of problem drinkers. *Journal of Behavioral Therapy and Experiential Psychiatry, 17,* 15–21.

Thomas, E. J., & Ager, R. D. (1993). Unilateral family therapy with spouses of uncooperative alcohol abusers. In T. J. O'Farrell (Ed.), *Treating alcohol problems: Marital and family interventions* (pp. 3–33). New York: Guilford.

Treasure, J., & Ward, W. (1997). A practical guide to the use of motivational interviewing in anorexia nervosa. *European Eating Disorders Review, 5,* 102–114.

Velicer, W., Hughes, S., Fava, J., Prochaska, J., & DiClemente, C. (1995). An empirical typology of subjects within stage of change. *Addictive Behaviors, 20,* 299–320.

Walitzer, K., Dermen, K., & Conners, G. (1999). Strategies for preparing clients for treatment: A review. *Behavior Modification, 23,* 129–151.

3   Cognitive-Behavioral Theory and Intervention

JACQUELINE CORCORAN AND
JOSEPH WALSH

This chapter provides a brief overview of cognitive-behavioral therapy, a broad class of present-focused interventions with a shared focus on changing cognition (thoughts, beliefs, and assumptions about the world), changing behavior, and building clients' coping skills. The cognitive and behavior theories represent different perspectives on human behavior, but they can be integrated into a holistic approach to working with clients. Cognitive theory focuses on the rationality of one's thinking patterns and the connections between thoughts, feelings, and behaviors. Behavior theory is not concerned with internal mental processes but rather with how human behavior, whether adaptive or problematic, is developed, sustained, or eliminated through its external reinforcement. Both theories deny the significance of unconscious mental processes in human behavior. This chapter first traces behavior theory and then adds the cognitive realm, with a focus on applications of the theory for change.

Behavior Theory

Behaviorism has been prominent in the social sciences since the first half of the 20th century, and it became a popular theory among clinical practitioners in the 1960s. Among its pioneers were Pavlov (1932, 1934), Watson (1930), and Skinner (1953). The rise of behaviorism reflected the new emphasis in the social sciences on empiricism (observable evidence) in evaluating the outcomes of clinical intervention. Because it does not rely on the client's mental capabilities, it is a popular theory for use with children and other noncognitively oriented populations, such as persons with mental retardation and other cognitive disabilities. Today's service delivery environment, with its focus on concrete outcome indicators, owes a great debt to the behaviorists, who remain the most diligent group of practitioners in measuring intervention outcomes (Granvold, 1994).

Basic Assumptions and the Nature of Problems and Change

The basic principles and assumptions of behavior theory are as follows (Granvold, 1994; Wilson, 2000):

- Behavior is what a person does, thinks, or feels that can be observed. Inferences about a person's mental activity should be minimized because it cannot be directly observed. Clinical assessment should focus on observable events with a minimum of interpretation.
- People are inherently motivated to seek pleasure and avoid pain. They are likely to behave in ways that produce encouraging responses or positive reinforcement.
- People behave based on their learning—by direct environmental feedback and also by watching others behave and interact.
- Behavior is amenable to change. A prerequisite for clinical change is that the behavior of concern must be defined in terms of measurable indicators.
- Intervention should focus on influencing reinforcements or punishments for client behaviors. Consistent and immediate reinforcement produces change most rapidly.
- Thoughts and feelings are also considered behaviors subject to reinforcement principles.

All behavior is influenced by the same principles of learning, which include classical conditioning, operant conditioning, and modeling. In short, behaviors change when the reinforcements in the person's environment change. Reinforcement can be understood as any environmental feedback that encourages the continuation of a behavior, and punishment is feedback that discourages the continuation of a behavior. Clinical intervention always involves the rearrangement of a client's reinforcement contingencies so that more desirable or functional behaviors will result.

Classical Conditioning

Conditioning is a process of developing patterns of behavior through responses to environmental stimuli or specific behavioral consequences (Wilson, 2000). The earliest behavioral research involved classical conditioning, in which an initially neutral stimulus comes to produce a conditioned response after being paired repeatedly with a conditioned stimulus (Pavlov, 1932, 1934). In Pavlov's famous research, food (the conditioned stimulus) naturally produced salivation (an involuntary response) in dogs. A bell (the unconditioned stimulus) initially failed to evoke salivation. However, over time, after the bell was paired with the food, the dogs started to salivate when presented with the bell alone. The bell at this point attained the status of a conditioned stimulus because it was capable of producing a response.

Classical conditioning plays a role in the understanding of many behavioral problems that clients experience (Gambrill, 1994). For example, previously neutral cues, such as certain places (e.g., restaurants or bars), people, or feeling states (e.g., boredom) may become associated with problem behaviors such as overeating or substance abuse. Many anxiety-related disorders are also classically conditioned. For instance, a dog bite might generalize to a fear of all dogs. A series of stressful classroom presentations in grade school might generalize to a person's long-standing fear of public speaking or social interaction.

During clinical intervention, the principles of classical conditioning are reversed. For example, if a client experiences an urge to use drugs when experiencing a particular emotion, such as boredom, the conditional pairing between boredom and drug use could eventually lose its association if the person abstained from using drugs to counteract boredom over a period of time. The urge to use drugs is thus extinguished.

Classical conditioning is also involved in the treatment of anxiety. Fear-laden situations, such as public speaking, are rank-ordered by the client and practitioner according to the level of fear they invoke. Clients learn to face each event or item on the list, starting with the least anxiety provoking, by learning to pair relaxation exercises rather than anxiety with the event. Relaxation processes might include deep breathing, deep muscle relaxation, and visualization. In this process of systematic desensitization (Wolpe, 1958), people work their way through the rank ordering of fears until they are no longer plagued by the anxiety.

Operant Conditioning

The main premise of operant conditioning is that future behavior is determined by the consequences of present behavior (Skinner, 1953). Attention is also paid to the *antecedent*, or prior, conditions that may trigger the behavior. Two types of reinforcement—positive and negative—are postulated in this model. Both positive and negative reinforcement encourage the continuation of a behavior. *Positive* reinforcement encourages the continuation of a behavior preceding it. For instance, alcohol use is positively reinforced by the resultant feelings of well-being and pleasant social interaction with others. *Negative* reinforcement is the process by which an aversive event is terminated by the individual's behavior and, therefore, the behavior is reinforced. Alcohol use, for example, is negatively reinforcing if it leads to escape from negative feelings (Carroll, 1998). Compulsive behaviors, such as overeating or substance abuse, are reinforced positively by the feelings of well-being that are created and the social interaction with others involving the food or substance. In practice, clients are helped to seek out behaviors that can offer alternative reinforcements—that is, other activities such as relationships, work, or hobbies—so they will not be as prone to indulging in the problem behavior.

Operant conditioning principles can also be enacted when people assume environmental control over the behavior of others. For example, operant behaviorism for parents of children with behavior problems is called *parent training* (Patterson, 1971). In this intervention, parents are taught to reinforce their children's pro-social behaviors and extinguish negative behaviors through ignoring them or using punishments (providing adverse consequences for the negative target behavior).

Modeling

People also learn behaviors by watching others engage in them and be reinforced for them (Bandura, 1977). Modeling is a pervasive means of learning for children and adolescents. For instance, children may learn to act appropriately in school by seeing classmates praised for listening to the teacher and criticized for talking while the teacher is lecturing. People may begin using alcohol or acting aggressively because they have seen their parents and other relatives acting this way. Along with didactic instruction and discussion, modeling is one of the chief methods of behavioral change. By modeling, the practitioner shows the client how to enact a new behavior. The client then practices the new behavior (called behavioral rehearsal) and receives supportive feedback and suggestions for its refinement.

Covert modeling can also be used for intervention purposes. In covert rehearsal, the practitioner guides the client through a process of imagining the completion of steps toward a successful outcome related to a goal. For example, an anxious client who must give a formal presentation may imagine herself approaching the public speaking situation with ease and with the expectation that she will do well. She visualizes and feels herself speaking in a confident and calm manner and then receiving a warm reception from the audience. The practitioner "walks" the client through this process, and then the client rehearses it herself prior to and during the actual event.

In summary, all situations in which people find themselves (except for truly novel ones) "cue" or prompt behaviors based on principles of classical conditioning (paired associations with certain aspects of the setting), operant conditioning (prior experiences in similar situations), or modeling (watching others behave and receive feedback). During the first day of class during a new academic year at a new school, for example, a student may be inclined to socialize with others based in part on conditioned positive associations of the classroom setting with other peer situations. He may respond eagerly to the instructor's questions because he anticipates positive reinforcement. Finally, he will watch how students behave in this new school to learn what other classroom behaviors are reinforced by other students and the instructor.

Goals of Intervention

The goals of behavioral intervention are to help the client achieve new, desirable behaviors by manipulating the environment to change reinforcement contingencies. For example, returning to the last scenario, if a child behaves in school in ways that are disruptive to the classroom process, the practitioner can devise a plan in which those negative behaviors are extinguished and new, more acceptable classroom behaviors are reinforced. One of the challenges in behavior therapy, however, is to identify the specific responses that are reinforcing to the client among the many responses that he or she receives. A teacher's displeasure with acting-out behaviors might serve as punishment to some students but as reinforcement to others.

Behavioral Assessment

The clinical practitioner can perform a comprehensive behavioral assessment through *functional analysis,* a process in which the client's problem behavior is broken down into its specific manifestations, the environmental conditions (cues) that produce it, and the consequences that follow. The practitioner asks questions of the client about environmental cues in each of five areas that may be related to the problem situation, as noted in Figure 3.1 (Carroll, 1998).

Listed below are examples of assessment questions for the problem behavior (Bertolino & O'Hanlon, 2002).

When do you experience the behavior?
Where do you experience the behavior?

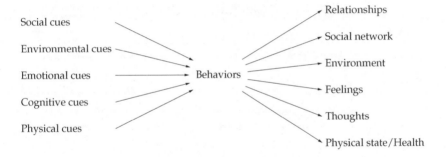

Figure 3.1. Environmental Cues in Each of Five Areas That May Be Related to the Problem Situation

How long does the problem typically last?
What happens immediately after the behavior occurs? That is, what do you do?
What bodily reactions do you experience?
How long do these reactions last?
How often does the problem typically happen (once an hour, once a day, once a week)?
What is the typical timing (time of day, week, month, year) of the problem?
What do the people around you usually do when the problem is happening?

The practitioner also works to discover the specific reinforcers and consequences of the problem behavior. See Table 3.1.

From this functional analysis, the reinforcers and triggers that are keeping the problem in operation are determined. The assessment leads into a process in which the practitioner and client construct concrete target behaviors that include attention to the antecedent conditions and contingencies required to bring about the desired new behaviors. Homework assignments for the client in which these conditions are applied are crucially important for the success of the model. Learning and putting behavioral principles into operation are the only way they will work.

Goal Setting and Intervention Principles

The process of goal setting and intervention in behavior theory is quite systematic.

Table 3.1

Five Areas of Functional Analysis

Domain	Antecedents (triggers, cues)	Consequences (reinforcers)
Social	With whom does the client spend most of his time? Does he have relationships with people who do not have the problem? Does he live with someone who is involved in the problem?	How has his social network changed since the problem began or escalated? How have his relationships been affected?
Environmental	What are the particular environmental cues for the problem? What is the level of her day-to-day exposure to these cues? Can some of these cues be easily avoided?	What people, places, and things have been affected by the problem? Has her environment changed as a result of the problem?
Emotional	What feeling states precede the occurrence of the problem?	How does he feel afterward? How does he feel about himself?
Cognitive	What thoughts run through her mind, or what beliefs does she have about the problem?	What is she thinking afterward? What does she say to herself?
Physical	What uncomfortable physical states precede the problem occurrence?	How does he feel physically afterward? What is his physical health like as a result?

1. The client's problems are stated in behavioral terms. Measurable objectives related to problem reduction are developed.
2. The practitioner and client gather baseline data (its current occurrence) on the problem behavior.
3. The steps required to reach problem resolution, moving from easier to more difficult, are specified.
4. The client's personal and environmental resources for making changes are specified. Any other people who will participate in the intervention plan are identified and sought out for consultation.
5. Possible obstacles to goal achievement are identified in advance, and plans are made to minimize them.

6. An appropriate intervention strategy is chosen with the participation of the client and with an emphasis on positive consequences of behaviors.
7. The client's behavior changes are documented on a regular basis, and the intervention process is evaluated regularly.
8. The intervention ends after the client achieves his or her goals with the likelihood of goal maintenance.

Ending intervention in behavior theory is a process of *fading*. That is, after an intervention has been under way for some length of time and the client has acquired the desired new behaviors, any artificial supports (including the practitioner and the reinforcement schedule) are gradually eliminated (or faded). This fading includes reducing the frequency of meetings between client and practitioner.

▨ Cognitive-Behavioral Theory

Behavioral theory is focused on *overt* behaviors that can be observed and measured. By the early 1960s, however, the importance of a person's *covert* operations, or cognition, was identified as significant to clinical intervention and added to the theory. This broader focus became known as cognitive-behavioral theory. From the perspective of cognitive theory, it is conscious thoughts that are the primary determinants of feelings and behavior (Beck, 1995; Granvold, 1994; Greenberger & Padesky, 1995; Lantz, 1996). Cognitions, or thoughts, include self-statements, beliefs, attitudes, appraisals, assumptions, expectations, attributions, attitudes, ideas, perceptions, expectations, schemas, and scripts (Azar, Barnes, & Twentyman, 1988; Dobson & Dozois, 2001).

Many mental, emotional, and behavioral problems are the result of cognitive misperceptions. Thinking patterns can feature acquired distortions in thought processing or cognitive biases that dismiss certain relevant environmental information from one's judgment. These may lead in turn to maladaptive emotional responses. "Rational" thinking can be thus understood as thinking that is based on external evidence, is life preserving, keeps one directed toward personal goals, and decreases internal conflicts.

Nature of Problems and Change

Many problems in living result from misconceptions—conclusions that are based too much on habits of thought rather than external evidence—that people have about themselves, other people, and their life situations. These misconceptions may develop for any of three reasons. The first is the simplest: The person has not acquired the information necessary to manage a novel situation. This is often evident in the lives of children and adolescents. They face many situations at school, at play, and with their families that they have not experienced before, and they are understandably not sure how to respond. This lack of information is known as a cognitive *deficit* and can be remedied with education.

The other two sources of misperception are more complex and rooted in personal *schemas*, or systematic patterns of thinking, acting, and solving problems, that are too rigid to manage new situations. The first of these involves the concept of *causal attribution*, which refers to three sets of systematic assumptions, or core beliefs, that people carry about the sources of power in their lives. First, a person might think from an underlying premise that his or her life situation is *more* or *less* changeable. Second, a person may perceive the source of power to make changes as existing *within* or *outside* the self. Third, a person might assume that his or her experiences are limited in their implications to the *specific situation* or that they have *global implications*. For example, a woman who is unable to provide for her family during a period of temporary unemployment might assume that she is a thoroughly incapable parent.

The final sources of misperceptions rooted in schemas are specific *cognitive distortions* of reality. Because of their tendency to develop thinking habits, people often interpret new situations in biased ways. These patterns are generally functional—all people utilize cognitive distortions at times—and they create difficulty only when they become too rigid to allow for the input of new information. Table 3.2 includes some widely held cognitive distortions, also known as "irrational beliefs," as identified by Beck (1976).

The nature of change in cognitive-behavioral theory is apparent in its hyphenated term. That is, clients can be helped to change in three ways (Young, Weinberger, & Beck, 2001):

1. Cognitively, by teaching them how to identify and change distorted thinking
2. Behaviorally, by offering skills training to improve coping capability
3. Experientially, by helping clients set up natural experiments so they can test the extent to which their beliefs about an event are rational

In the latter two ways, new skills and experience lend themselves to more adaptive thinking.

In clinical assessment, the practitioner evaluates the client's schemas, identifies any faulty thinking patterns or cognitive deficits, and considers the evidence supporting the client's conclusions about his or her life situation. When those conclusions seem valid, the practitioner initiates a process of problem solving or teaches coping skills. When the conclusions are distorted, the practitioner utilizes techniques to help clients adjust their

Table 3.2

Common Irrational Beliefs

Irrational beliefs	Examples
Absolute thinking: viewing events in all or nothing way	"I must always do well and have the approval of others."
	"If I don't do it perfectly, then I might as well not do it at all."
Catastrophizing: seeing minor situations as disastrous	A low grade: "This is the end of my graduate career."
Low frustration tolerance: inability to put up with minor inconveniences or uncomfortable feelings	A 10-minute wait: "This is ridiculous—spending all day in a line."
Overgeneralization: drawing the conclusion that all instances of some kind of situation or event will turn out a particular way because one or two did.	A bad batch of brownies leads to "I can't bake."
Personal worthlessness: a specific form of overgeneralization associated with failure	An individual is worthless if a paper isn't written perfectly.

Note. From *Cognitive Therapy and the Emotional Disorders*, by A. T. Beck, 1976, New York: International Universities Press.

cognitive processes in ways that better facilitate goal attainment. The practitioner guides the client through the process, but the client is responsible for implementing these strategies. As thinking changes, so do emotions and behaviors.

Intervention Principles

Cognitive interventions focus on present rather than past behavior (Leahy, 1996). The past is important for discovering the origins of a client's thinking patterns, but it is present thinking that motivates behavior. The nature of the practitioner–client relationship is important, as it must catalyze the client's difficult process of questioning basic assumptions and considering alternatives (Mattaini, 1997). The practitioner must demonstrate positive regard for the client while alternately functioning as a model, coach, collaborator, and trusted representative of "objective" thinking. The practitioner is active, participating in discussions and in the mutual development of change strategies.

There are many particular strategies for cognitive intervention, but they fit into two general categories (Spiegler, 1993). The first of these is *cognitive restructuring* (Emery, 1985). The practitioner assesses the client's patterns of thinking, determines with the client that some of them are not effective for managing important life challenges, and through a series of discussions and exercises, helps the client experiment with alternative ways of approaching challenges that will promote goal attainment. Some strategies toward this end include the following:

- Didactic teaching—filling information gaps for the client (Bandura, 1977)
- Attribution training—helping the client understand that emotions, behavior, and potential for goal attainment are more related to arbitrary thought patterns than the client might initially believe (Berlin, 2002)
- The ABC review—a reflective or paper-and-pencil technique in which the client learns to differentiate appraisals of situations from their emotional and behavioral consequences and then considers alternative ways of appraising those situations (Beck & Freeman, 1990)
- Double standard technique—helping clients see that they hold themselves more accountable for problems than they would hold other persons in the same situation (Leahy, 1996)
- Point-counterpoint technique—reviewing with the client the relative arguments for and against a certain belief on the basis of external evidence, as well as the costs and benefits to the client for maintaining certain attitudes (Young, 1990)

The second category of cognitive interventions is *cognitive coping* (Spiegler, 1993). The practitioner helps the client learn and practice new or more effective ways of dealing with stress and personal affects. All of these involve step-by-step procedures for the client to master new skills. Space precludes covering all techniques, but some are discussed here.

- Self-instruction training
- Problem solving
- Communication skills training
- Relaxation training, including deep breathing and visualization
- Self-reinforcement

As with behavioral interventions, cognitive interventions require the client to be active in resolving problems, including practicing solution strategies with the clinician and in natural settings.

Cognitive Restructuring

Cognitive restructuring is a core technique to use in helping people identify and change nonadaptive thinking patterns. Cognitive restructuring was formulated from two different schools of cognitive therapy: rational-emotive therapy by Ellis (Ellis & McLaren, 1998) and cognitive therapy by Beck (Beck, 1976; Beck & Freeman, 1990). Both schools share the assumption that problematic reactions result from interpretations of situations that are often negative or illogical (as described in Table 3.2).

In rational-emotive therapy, the ABC model of cognitive restructuring is used (Figure 3.2). ABC represents a process of cognitive processing in which A is an activating effect, B is a person's belief about the event, and C is the consequence of A and B for the person (emotion and then actions).

For instance, if A is an event that occurs (a rainy day) and C, the consequence, is the person's emotion of depression, then the B (the belief) might be "Everything's gray and ugly. Nothing can go well on a day like this." If the same activating event (rain) occurs and the resultant emotion (consequences or C) is contentment, the belief might be "Today I can stay home and read. It'll be really cozy." Clients often make the assumption that A directly causes C, but except in certain reflexive actions (such as placing a finger on a hot stove and then abruptly pulling it back) there is always a cognitive event, B, that intervenes between the two.

To change a client's belief systems, three processes are necessary. The first is to help the person identify the thoughts preceding and accompanying the distressing emotions and nonproductive action ("What was going through your mind?"). Some clients may require more tangible ways to grasp their thinking patterns (Cournoyer, 2000). They may be asked to engage in imagery work ("Close your eyes, take a deep breath, and see yourself in that situation. What are you doing? What are you feeling? What are you thinking?"). The practitioner may invite other clients to participate in a role-play. By reenacting a problematic situation, some clients can more easily retrieve the thought patterns that maintain the problem.

The second process is to help clients determine the validity of their thoughts by questioning them in the following categories (McKay, Davis, & Fanning, 1997):

- What is the evidence for the belief?
- What are alternative ways of thinking about the event?
- If what the client believes is true, what is the worst that could happen? (This type of question confronts the cognitive distortion of catastrophizing. It is based on the idea that the feared negative consequences about a situation are often not as dire as the client assumes.)

A (activating event) ⟶ B (belief, thought) ⟶ C (emotion, action)

Figure 3.2. The ABC Model of Cognitive Restructuring

Table 3.3 delineates examples of questions that practitioners can ask in each of these categories.

The third process is to challenge the client's irrational beliefs by designing natural experiments—tasks that can be carried out in daily life to test the validity of the beliefs. For instance, if a college student believes that if she speaks out in class everyone will laugh at her, she might be asked to volunteer an answer in class to find out what the reactions of others would be. By changing clients' actions, cognitions and emotions are also indirectly modified. The actions clients perform provide data to refute their illogical beliefs about themselves and the world.

Cognitive Coping

In contrast to cognitive restructuring, which helps clients alter their negative and irrational thoughts and beliefs that maintain problems, cognitive coping involves skills training that targets both covert and overt cognitive operations with the goal of helping clients more effectively manage their challenges. People can modify their cognitive distortions by successfully enacting coping skills because their improved capabilities can change some of their assumptions about the world. If people have good coping skills, they more successfully elicit reinforcement from the environment. Several of these skills are described in detail below.

Self-Instructional Training

Self-instructional training is a means of giving clients an internal cognitive framework for instructing themselves in how to cope effectively with problem situations (Meichenbaum, 1999). It is based in part on the premise that many people as a matter of course engage in internal speech, giving themselves pep talks to prepare for certain challenges. Further, when people find themselves in difficult situations that evoke tension or other negative emotions, their thinking may become confused, and their ability to cope diminishes.

To help them cope, clients are trained in self-talk skills in the following areas (Meichenbaum & Deffenbacher, 1988; Spiegler, 1993).

- Focusing on the stressful situation: "I'll be okay; this is just a problem to be solved." "It's okay to feel discouraged, but you can deal with this."
- Making coping statements: "I can do this." "I'm doing just fine." "I'm nervous, but I can handle this." "It'll be over soon."
- Making self-reinforcing statements: "You did a good job." "That was tough, but you stuck to it." "Next time it'll be even easier."

Preparing an internal or written script for stressful situations can help a client recall and systematically implement the coping strategy previously selected.

Table 3.3

Questions to Examine the Validity of Thoughts

Types of questioning	Definition	Questions
"What is the evidence?"	To what extent is this thought an overgeneralization? Involves analyzing faulty logic and providing information to dispel unrealistic fears; asks the fundamental question,	Are there exceptions to the generalizations? What are the likely consequences and outcomes of the situation? Are there experiences from the past that could lead to another conclusion? What are the real odds that what is feared will actually occur? What in the past leads you to expect a better outcome than you fear? Out of all the times you've done or felt this in the past, how many times did the catastrophe occur? What has usually happened during similar circumstances in the past?
Looking at alternative scenarios	Provide an alternative interpretation of the situation	How could you use your social skills or problem-solving skills to handle the situation? Could you create a plan to change the situation? Is there someone you know who might deal with this differently? What would that person do? How long is this experience likely to last? How can you cope with it for that period?
Worst-case scenario	To examine how the client can cope if the worst fear comes true Can be taken even further to exaggerate the situation to point of absurdity	"So what if it happens?"

Note. From *Thoughts and Feelings: Taking Control of Your Moods and Your Life*, by M. McKay, M. Davis, and P. Fanning, 1997, Oakland, CA: New Harbinger.

Self-instruction training has mainly been studied in relation to children and school task completion, but it can also be taught to adults (Spence, 1994).

When using this technique, a client and practitioner develop a step-by-step self-instruction script following their completion of a plan for confronting a problem. Such a script may be written down or memorized by the client. The practitioner and client then visualize and walk through the problem situation together so the client can rehearse its implementation. The client then uses the script in his or her natural environment, either before or during an assigned task.

Problem-Solving Training

The problem-solving process helps clients learn how to produce a variety of potentially effective responses when faced with problem situations (D'Zurilla & Nezu, 2001). The practitioner and client (a) define the problem, (b) brainstorm, (c) evaluate the alternatives, (d) choose and implement an alternative, and (e) evaluate the implemented option. See Table 3.4 for delineation of each of the problem-solving steps.

Communication Skills Training

The wide spectrum of communication skills interventions includes attention to clients' social skills, assertiveness, and negotiation skills. Positive communication builds relationships and closeness with others, which in turn improves mood (Clarke, Lewinsohn, & Hops, 1990). Social support provides not only a source of positive reinforcement but also buffers individuals from stressful life events. In addition, processing the effects of problems with other people may change one's perspective on problem-generating events. When a person can openly state feelings and reactions to interpersonal situations, other people understand clearly how they might continue their positive behaviors or change their negative behaviors.

The components of communication skills training include using "I" messages, reflective and empathic listening, and making clear behavior change requests. In "I" messages, a person talks about his or her own position and feelings in a situation, rather than making accusatory comments about another person. The basic format for giving "I" messages is "I feel (the reaction) to what happened (a specific activating event)." For example, a person says, "I feel worried when you stay out past curfew on Saturday night" rather than "How dare you stay out so late!" which may make the other person feel defensive.

Listening skills include both reflective listening and validation of the other person's intent. The purpose of reflective listening is to ensure that one understands the speaker's perspective. It decreases the tendency of people to draw premature conclusions about the intentions and meaning of another's statement (Cordova & Jacobson, 1993).

Table 3.4

Problem-Solving Process

Defining the problem	1. Find the real problem (What is behind the problem or what caused it? Why should the problem be solved?) 2. Break down complex problems into their subcomponents 3. Take on one problem at a time 4. Describe in behavioral terms
Brainstorming	1. Generate and write down all possible solutions, even those that seem impossible or silly 2. Encourage spontaneity and creativity by avoiding critical comments
Evaluating the alternatives	1. Mark out patently irrelevant or impossible items 2. Discuss each viable alternative as to its advantages and disadvantages 3. List information that may need to be gathered to pursue viable options
Choosing and implementing an alternative	1. Select one or more strategies that seem to maximize benefits over costs 2. Work on skills (e.g., assertiveness, coping) that might be necessary to successfully implement solution
Evaluating the implemented option	1. Explore "failures" for the elements that went well, in addition to those still needing work 2. Perhaps select another option from the list

Note. Adapted from *Depression in Marriage: A Model for Etiology and Treatment*, by S. Beach, E. Sandeen, and K. O'Leary, 1990, New York: Guilford; "Problem-Solving Therapies," by T. D'Zurilla and A. Nezu, 2001, in K. Dobson and S. Keith (Eds.), *Handbook of Cognitive-Behavioral Therapies* (2nd ed., pp. 211–245), New York: Guilford; and "Couple Distress," by J. G. Wheeler, A. Christensen, and N. Jacobson, 2001, in D. Barlow (Ed.), *Clinical Handbook of Psychological Disorders: A Step-by-Step Treatment Manual* (3rd ed., pp. 609–630), New York: Guilford.

Reflective listening involves paraphrasing back the feelings and content of the speaker's message with the format: "What I hear you saying is . . ." or "You seem to feel . . . [feeling word] when [or because]. . . ." Beyond reflection, validation is an advanced skill conveying a message that, given the other person's perspectives and assumptions, his or her experiences are legitimate and understandable ("I can see that if you were thinking I had done that, you would feel that way") (Beach, Sandeen, & O'Leary, 1990).

A third component of communication skills training teaches people to make clear behavior requests of others. Such requests should always be:

- Specific ("pick up your toys") versus global ("clean up around here")
- Measurable ("I would like you to call once per day")

• Stated as the presence of positive behaviors rather than the absence of negative behaviors ("Give me a chance to change and look over the mail when I come home" rather than "Stop bothering me with your questions")

Praising or complimenting is also considered an essential communication skill because it reinforces desired behaviors in others so that they will continue to occur. Another purpose is to create a positive atmosphere in

Table 3.5		
Communication Skills		
Skill	Description	Format
"I" messages	A person talks about his or her own position and feelings in a situation, rather than making accusatory comments about another person	"I feel [the reaction] to what happened [a specific activating event]."
Reflective listening	Paraphrasing back the feelings and content of the speaker's message with the format to ensure that one understands the speaker's perspective	"What I hear you saying is…" or "You seem to feel…[feeling word]" when [because]…"
Validation	Conveying a message that, given the other person's perspectives and assumptions, his or her experiences are legitimate and understandable	"I can see that if you were thinking I had done that, you would feel that way."
Making behavior requests of others	Asking people to change their behavior	Requests should be behaviorally specific, measurable, and stated as the presence of positive behaviors.
Giving praise and compliments	To reinforce the positive behaviors of others	1. Be specific about what is being praised. 2. Couple verbal praise with eye contact, a smile, and/or physical affection. 3. Praise effort and progress rather than achievement 4. Praise soon after the behavior is performed.

the relationship so that other interventions will be more effective when they are applied. See Table 3.5 for a listing of these techniques. For clients to develop communication and other skills in the cognitive-behavioral model, the practitioner, in addition to using didactic instruction, also encourages role-play so that learning can generalize to the challenging situations the client faces. The steps for role-plays are delineated in Table 3.6.

Table 3.6	
Steps in Role Playing	
Step	Rationale
1. Practitioner models skills.	The practitioner demonstrates the skill so that the client can experience what it looks like. Pressure is reduced on the client as he or she is not expected to perform a new behavior before it is modeled. The practitioner gains a fuller appreciation of the challenges the client faces; the client's taking on the perspective of the other person (family member, boss, friend) allows the client to more easily understand this other person's position. Taking on other roles introduces a note of playfulness and humor to a situation that may have been previously viewed with grim seriousness.
2. Modeling is processed.	The practitioner can share the difficulties he or she experienced in the process so that the client receives validation for the problem and the client can learn that a "coping model" as opposed to a "mastery model" is adequate to get new interaction patterns going. Client can verbalize what was different as a result of the new interaction pattern; practitioner can clarify any elements of the skill that were still unclear and bolster confidence in the client.
3. The client behaviorally rehearses the new skill.	The client practices the new behavior. This process allows for misunderstandings about the material to come to light for clarification. When the client experiences a difference, it enhances his or her confidence that the skill can be generalized to a real-life situation.
4. The client and practitioner process the behavioral rehearsal.	The client expresses what it was like to try on the new behavior, discusses what was different. Practitioner offers compliments on areas that went well and feedback for improvement, if necessary. Client and practitioner discuss potential barriers and challenges and how to circumvent. Client may be offered another opportunity to behaviorally rehearse.

Note. From *Direct Social Work Practice: Theory & Skills* (6th ed.), by D. H. Hepworth, R. Rooney, and J. Larsen, 2002, Belmont, CA: Brooks/Cole.

Empirical Evidence

Cognitive-behavioral therapy was developed out of experimental research, and the structured interventions lend themselves to manualized treatments and outcome research. Cognitive-behavioral therapy has been validated for many mental health disorders, such as depression (Dobson, 1989; Gaffan, Tsaousis, & Kemp-Wheeler, 1995; Gerson, Belin, Kaufman, Mintz, & Jarvik, 1999), anxiety (Bakker, van Balkom, Spinhoven, & Blaauw, 1998; Feske & Chambless, 1995; Gould, Otto, & Pollack, 1995), substance abuse and dependence (DeRubeis & Crits-Christoph, 1998; Irvin, Bowers, Dunn, & Wang, 1999), bulimia nervosa (Whittal, Agras, & Gould, 1999), and schizophrenia (Pilling et al., 2002). Cognitive-behavioral therapy also has been found to helpful with marital (Dunn & Schwebel, 1995) and family problems (Corcoran, 2000).

Summary

Cognitive-behavioral therapy is a structured approach with a primary emphasis on thoughts and behaviors. The assumption is that individuals can learn skills and manage reinforcement principles, which will help them manage painful feelings and problematic behaviors more effectively. Cognitive-behavioral therapy is used in the strengths-and-skills-building model when people are ready to take action toward their problems and when a lack of knowledge or skills appears to represent a barrier to more effective functioning.

References

Azar, S. T., Barnes, K. T., & Twentyman, C. T. (1988). Developmental outcomes in physically abused children: Consequences of parental abuse or the effects of a more general breakdown in caregiving behaviors? *The Behavior Therapist, 11,* 27–32.

Bakker, A., van Balkom, A., Spinhoven, P., & Blaauw, B. (1998). Follow-up on the treatment of panic disorder with or without agoraphobia: A quantitative review. *Journal of Nervous and Mental Disease, 186,* 414–419.

Bandura, A. (1977). *Social learning theory.* Englewood Cliffs, NJ: Prentice-Hall.

Beach, S., Sandeen, E., & O'Leary, K. (1990). *Depression in marriage: A model for etiology and treatment.* New York: Guilford.

Beck, A. T. (1976). *Cognitive therapy and the emotional disorders.* New York: International Universities Press.

Beck, A. T., & Freeman, A. (1990). *Cognitive therapy and depression.* New York: Guilford.

Beck, J. S. (1995). *Cognitive therapy: Basics and beyond.* New York: Guilford.

Berlin, S. B. (2002). *Clinical social work practice: A cognitive-integrative perspective.* New York: Oxford University Press.

Bertolino, B., & O'Hanlon, B. (2002). *Collaborative, competency-based counseling and therapy.* Boston: Allyn & Bacon.

Carroll, K. (1998). *A cognitive-behavioral approach: Treating cocaine addiction.* Retrieved August 28, 2001, from http://www.drugabuse.gov/TXManuals/CBT/CBT1.html.

Clarke, G., Lewinsohn, P., & Hops, H. (1990). The adolescent coping with depression course. Retrieved December 19, 2003, from http://www.kpchr.org/public/acwd/acwd.html.

Corcoran, J. (2000). *Evidence-based social work practice with families: A lifespan approach.* New York: Springer.

Cordova, J., & Jacobson, N. (1993). Couple distress. In D. H. Barlow (Ed.), *Clinical handbook of psychological disorders: A step-by-step treatment manual* (2nd ed., pp. 481–512). New York: Guilford.

Cournoyer, B. (2000). *The social work skills workbook.* Pacific Grove, CA: Brooks/Cole.

DeRubeis, R., & Crits-Christoph, P. (1998). Empirically supported individual and group psychological treatments for adult mental disorders. *Journal of Consulting and Clinical Psychology, 66,* 37–52.

Dobson, K., & Dozois, D. (2001). Historical and philosophical bases of the cognitive-behavioral therapies. In K. Dobson (Ed.), *Handbook of cognitive-behavioral therapies* (2nd ed., pp. 3–39). New York: Guilford.

Dobson, K. S. (1989). A meta-analysis of the efficacy of cognitive therapy for depression. *Journal of Consulting and Clinical Psychology, 57,* 414–419.

Dunn, R., & Schwebel, A. (1995). Meta-analytic review of marital therapy outcome research. *Journal of Family Psychology, 9,* 58–68.

D'Zurilla, T., & Nezu, A. (2001). Problem-solving therapies. In K. Dobson & S. Keith (Eds.), *Handbook of cognitive-behavioral therapies* (2nd ed., pp. 211–245). New York: Guilford.

Ellis, A., & McLaren, C. (1998). *Rational emotive behavior therapy: A therapist's guide* (Vol. 2). Atascadero, CA: Impact Publishers.

Emery, G. (1985). Cognitive therapy: Techniques and applications. In A. T. Beck & G. Emery (Eds.). *Anxiety disorders and phobias: A cognitive perspective* (pp. 167–313). New York: Basic Books.

Feske, U., & Chambless, D. (1995). Cognitive behavioral versus exposure only treatment for social phobia: A meta-analysis. *Behavior Therapy, 26,* 695–720.

Gaffan, E., Tsaousis, I., & Kemp-Wheeler, S. (1995). Researcher allegiance and meta-analysis: The case of cognitive therapy for depression. *Journal of Consulting and Clinical Psychology, 63,* 966–980.

Gambrill, E. D. (1994). Concept and methods of behavioral treatment. In D. K. Granvold (Ed.), *Cognitive and behavioral treatment: Methods and applications* (pp. 32–62). Pacific Grove, CA: Brooks/Cole.

Gerson, S., Belin, T., Kaufman, A., Mintz, J., & Jarvik, L. (1999). Pharmacological and psychological treatments for depressed older patients: A meta-analysis and overview of recent findings. *Harvard Review of Psychiatry, 7,* 1–28.

Gould, R., Otto, M., & Pollack, M. (1995). A meta-analysis of treatment outcome for panic disorder. *Clinical Psychology Review, 15,* 819–844.

Granvold, D. K. (1994). Concepts and methods of cognitive treatment. In D. K. Granvold (Ed.), *Cognitive and behavioral treatment: Methods and applications* (pp. 3–31). Pacific Grove, CA: Brooks/Cole.

Greenberger, D., & Padesky, C. A. (1995). *Mind over mood: A cognitive therapy treatment manual for clients.* New York: Guilford.

Irvin, J., Bowers, C., Dunn, M., & Wang, M. (1999). Efficacy of relapse prevention: A meta-analytic review. *Journal of Consulting & Clinical Psychology, 67,* 563–570.

Lantz, J. (1996). Cognitive theory and social work treatment. In F. J. Turner (Ed.), *Social work treatment* (4th ed., pp. 94–115). New York: Free Press.

Leahy, R. L. (1996). *Cognitive therapy: Basic principles and applications.* Northvale, NJ: Aronson.

Mattaini, M. A. (1997). *Clinical practice with individuals.* Washington, DC: NASW Press.

McKay, M., Davis, M., & Fanning, P. (1997). *Thoughts and feelings: Taking control of your moods and your life.* Oakland, CA: New Harbinger.

Meichenbaum, D. (1999). *Cognitive-behavior modification: An integrative approach.* Cambridge, MA: Perseus.

Meichenbaum, D., & Deffenbacher, J. (1988). Stress inoculation training. *Counseling Psychologist, 16,* 69–90.

Patterson, G. R. (1971). *Families: Application of social learning theory to family life.* Champaign, IL: Research Press.

Pavlov, I. P. (1932). Neuroses in man and animals. *Journal of the American Medical Association, 9,* 1012–1013.

Pavlov, I. P. (1934). An attempt at a physiological interpretation of obsessional neurosis and paranoia. *Journal of Mental Science, 80,* 187–197.

Pilling, S., Bebbington, P., Kuipers, E., Garety, P., Geddes, J., Orbach, G., et al. (2002). Psychological treatments in schizophrenia: I. Meta-analysis of family intervention and cognitive behaviour therapy. *Psychological Medicine, 32,* 763–782.

Skinner, B. F. (1953). *Science and human behavior.* New York: Macmillan.

Spence, S. (1994). Practitioner review: Cognitive therapy with children and adolescents. *Journal of Child Psychology and Psychiatry, 35,* 1191–1228.

Spiegler, M. (1993). *Contemporary behavior therapy* (2nd ed.). Belmont, CA: Brooks/Cole.

Watson, J. B. (1930). *Behaviorism.* Chicago: University of Chicago Press.

Wheeler, J. G., Christensen, A., & Jacobson, N. (2001). Couple distress. In D. Barlow (Ed.), *Clinical handbook of psychological disorders: A step-by-step treatment manual* (3rd ed., pp. 609–630). New York: Guilford.

Whittal, M., Agras, W., & Gould, R. (1999). Bulimia nervosa: A meta-analysis of psychosocial and pharmacological treatments. *Behavior Therapy, 30,* 117–135.

Wilson, G. T. (2000). Behavior therapy. In R. J. Corsini & D. Wedding (Eds.), *Current psychotherapies* (6th ed., pp. 205–240). Itasca, IL: F. E. Peacock.

Wolpe, J. (1958). *Psychotherapy by reciprocal inhibition.* Stanford, CA: Stanford University Press.

Young, J., Weinberger, A., & Beck, A. (2001). Depression. In D. Barlow (Ed.), *Clinical handbook of psychological disorders: A step-by-step treatment manual* (2nd ed.). New York: Guilford.

Young, J. E. (1990). *Cognitive therapy for personality disorders: A schema-focused approach.* Sarasota, FL: Professional Resource Exchange.

4   Integration of Models

Now that solution-focused therapy, motivational interviewing, and cognitive-behavioral therapy have been discussed separately, this chapter highlights some of the similarities and differences between models. The integration of the models is discussed so that both strengths and skill building are emphasized. An outline of how the integration is achieved within the helping process follows. Subsequent chapters demonstrate how the integrative strengths-and-skills-building model can be applied to various problems individuals may experience.

Comparison of Models

Similarities and differences between practice models are explored here along certain dimensions, including the stance toward strengths and behavioral change, the client's relationship to the change process, the time needed to enact change, the degree of structure and direction required, and the system level at which change is targeted. These dimensions are listed in Table 4.1. Solution-focused therapy and motivational interviewing are compared in Table 4.2.

Table 4.1

Comparisons Between Models

Dimensions	Solution-focused therapy	Motivational interviewing	Cognitive-behavioral therapy	Strengths-and-skills-building model
Strengths versus deficits	Clients are assumed to have the necessary resources to solve their own problems.	Once they are sufficiently motivated, clients can employ available resources to change their behavior.	Problems arise out of misapplying reinforcement principles, coping skills deficits, and distorted belief patterns.	Client strengths, abilities, and resources are emphasized, but when these are exhausted or when deficits are identified as a barrier to change, then skill building may be necessary.
Stance toward behavioral change	Targets cognitive and behavioral change toward specific and concrete measurable goals; interconnection between perceptions and behaviors	Works with perceptions of the problem initially, then to define goals when client is motivated to work on the problem.	Targets cognitive and behavioral change toward specific and concrete measurable goals; interconnection between thoughts, feelings, and behaviors.	When a client is ready to take action, specific and concrete measurable goals are targeted.
Method of change	Perceptions are changed through a focus on success and resources and by the strategic use of language to imply that change will occur. Small changes in behavior are made, which will affect client perception in a transactional process.	Perceptions are explored for advantages of the problem; seeks to create dissonance between a person's values/ goals and the problem behavior, so that the desire to change is seen as more advantageous.	People are trained on how to apply reinforcement principles and how to improve their skills. They are taught to recognize irrational thoughts and replace them with more realistic appraisals.	Uses all of the preceding methods.

(continued)

Table 4.1 (continued)

Comparisons Between Models

Dimensions	Solution-focused therapy	Motivational interviewing	Cognitive-behavioral therapy	Strengths-and-skills-building model
Type of client who benefits	Strategies are designed for clients who are in different relationships to the change process.	Clients who are in precontemplation (not considering there is a problem) or contemplation (are contemplating change).	Motivated for change and is organized and conscientious about following change tactics.	Strategies are designed for clients who are in different relationships to the change process.
Compliance and resistance	Resistance is not a useful concept; need to collaborate to find out what the client wants.	Resistance is the problem of the practitioner, signifying a need to adjust change strategies to match the client's position.	Importance of completing homework assignments for success. Problem solving around barriers to compliance.	Takes into account all the preceding
Length of change	Brief: as little as one session	Brief: as little as one session	Brief: 12–16 sessions commonly reported	Brief: as little as one session
System level of change	Context of behavior more important than individual characteristics	Focus on work with an individual's motivation; the interpersonal transactions between client and practitioner are a significant part of change process.	Behavioral: considers the reinforcement contingencies involved in dyadic relationships. Cognitive: centers on cognitions of the individual	A systemic orientation, including the importance of individual cognitions. Behavioral principles of learning are also understood to play a role in both the problem and its solution.

Table 4.2

Comparison Between Strengths-Based Models (Solution-Focused and Motivational Interviewing)

Similarities

Language is used strategically

Brief in nature

Focus on strengths and resources

Collaboration

Respect for the individual's relationship to the change process

Use of scaling questions

Focus on self-efficacy (motivational interviewing) and building hope and vision (solution focused) as these factors are considered necessary for change

Focus on hypothetical future without the problem

Draw on past successes to build change in the present

Motivation is a strength

Client motivation is encouraged by an emphasis on strengths

Differences

Solution-focused therapy doesn't work on developing discrepancy

Solution-focused therapy doesn't work with ambivalence as actively, although motivation can be scaled

Motivation is only one strength

Motivational interviewing involves more exploration of the problem

Solution-focused therapy works more actively to elicit and amplify strengths

Primary intervention for solution-focused therapy is the use of questions rather than statements, whereas motivational interviewing relies more on statements

Strengths Versus Deficits

Solution-focused therapy takes a strengths-based approach in that client strengths, abilities, and resources are emphasized. Clients are assumed to have the necessary resources to solve their own problems. Evidence of these resources is found by eliciting and exploring times when the problem the client brings does not exert its negative influence. During sessions, clients are empowered through questioning, rather than asked to follow through with structured interventions. When homework is assigned, a common first-session task is to ask clients to notice all that is happening in their lives that they want to continue experiencing. This assignment is phrased as a suggestion to help people become attuned to the positive aspects and successes of their lives.

In contrast, cognitive-behavioral therapy targets deficits in people's skills, such as their ability to solve problems, to think rationally, and to communicate. Details of the problem are elicited through a functional analysis. People's problems are assumed to arise as the result of misapplying reinforcement principles, and clients are trained to employ them more effectively. They are prescribed skills to help them gain more positive reinforcement from the environment, and coping behaviors are taught through instruction, modeling, and behavioral rehearsal. A further assumption of cognitive-behavioral therapy is that people in distress demonstrate distorted belief patterns and that they need help in altering these patterns to make them more realistic. A possible drawback of this approach is highlighted by Greene, Lee, Trask, and Rheinscheld (1996): "The use of cognitive restructuring to replace negative, irrational thinking with positive rational thinking and tasks to implement alternative courses of action reflect a perspective that sees clients as having deficits that need fixing, rather than strengths and solution behavior that can provide a foundation for change and growth; such a view can reinforce the client's negative, self-fulfilling prophecy" (p. 46).

Cognitive-behavioral therapy assumes that working with the principles of reinforcement, building skills, and identifying and changing thought patterns will lead the client to make necessary changes. The way of change in cognitive-behavioral therapy, therefore, is clearly delineated. Clients may, however, find this prescriptive approach artificial and irrelevant to the problem. Moreover, the focus on their deficits may have the unfortunate consequence of making clients feel worse about themselves and more hopeless about change. Finally, the requirements of homework assignments, such as identifying negative thinking and challenging belief patterns, may place too much of a burden on certain types of clients. Experiencing additional failure through the inability to complete homework may lead to more negative spirals: "I can't even do this." "I'm lazy and worthless." "I'll never get better."

Similarly, motivational interviewing explores perceptions without having to label them and replace them with "rational" thoughts (Miller & Rollnick, 1991). Ambivalence toward change is viewed as a natural process, and the client can decide whether a change is needed (Killick & Allen, 1997). In motivational enhancement interviewing, the responsibility for how individuals change their behaviors is left to clients; the assumption is that clients can employ available resources to change behavior and that training is not required. Another similarity between solution-focused therapy and motivational interviewing is the importance of developing client hope and vision about the possibility of change. Motivational interviewing discusses self-efficacy, "which refers to a person's belief in his or her ability to carry out and succeed with a specific task" (Miller & Rollnick, 2002, p. 40). Solution-focused therapy builds hope and vision by focusing on client strengths and successes and by helping the client detail a future without the problem.

One difference between solution-focused therapy and motivational interviewing is that solution-focused therapy avoids discussion of the problem, whereas motivational interviewing focuses on the extent of the problem's impact to bolster individuals' motivation to change. However, recent writers on solution-focused therapy (Bertolino & O'Hanlon, 2002; DeJong & Berg, 2001; Murphy, 1997) show more willingness to explore the role of the problem with the rationale that people need to feel heard and validated for their concerns. In addition, problems that are clearly delineated are considered to lead to better solutions (Greene et al., 1996; Murphy, 1997).

Stance Toward Behavioral Change

All three models target cognitive and behavioral processes. In motivational interviewing, the initial goal is to build clients' motivation when they are initially not willing to change, rather than focusing on behavioral change. People's perceptions of their problems are the focus of the early part of the helper's contact. As the work moves into the action stage, actual behavior becomes more the focus (Treasure & Ward, 1997).

Both cognitive-behavioral therapy and solution-focused therapy target cognitive and behavioral change toward specific, concrete, measurable goals (Corcoran, 2000). Solution-focused therapy and cognitive-behavioral therapy share the value of perspective changing as a necessary aspect of mastering problems. Both models suggest that if a new view is formulated, feelings of well-being and productive action will follow. Another shared assumption is that a change in behavior can result in a different perspective.

The difference is that in solution-focused therapy, perceptions are changed through a focus on success and resources and by the strategic use of language. "When our time here is successful, what will be different?" rather than "If our time here is successful, what could be different?" implies that change will occur (e.g., DeJong & Berg, 2001; de Shazer et al., 1986). A focus on strengths, therefore, is the way to influence perspective changing. In contrast, cognitive-behavioral interventions focus on irrational beliefs and skills deficits. Thoughts that are deficient in terms of their rationality are systematically examined for flaws in logic and then subject to replacement with a more productive line of reasoning. Skills—such as problem-solving training, social skills training, assertiveness training, and communication skills training—are also taught (e.g., Barlow, 2001; Meichenbaum, 1999).

Cognitive-behavioral therapy and motivational enhancement interviewing differ mainly in their stance toward skills training. In motivational enhancement interviewing, the responsibility for how individuals are to change their behaviors is left to clients; the assumption is that clients can employ available resources to change behaviors and that training is not required. In contrast, cognitive-behavioral therapy maintains that learning and practice of specific coping skills is necessary. At the same time, Moyers and Rollnick (2002) make the point that motivational interviewing draws from behavioral principles in that a client's speech is reinforced in the direction of change.

Type of Client

Cognitive-behavioral therapy was developed with White, middle- to upper-class clients who were voluntarily seeking treatment for their complaints. Young, Weinberger, and Beck (2001) list the characteristics of clients who benefit from their cognitive-behavioral protocol: (a) introspective, (b) able to reason abstractly, (c) well organized, (d) conscientious about carrying out responsibilities, (e) employed, (f) not excessively angry, and (g) less dogmatic and rigid in thinking. To a great degree, the client in a cognitive-behavioral model needs to be motivated and willing to implement skills.

The type of client described by Young et al. (2001) in solution-focused terms is the "customer," the voluntary client who comes to treatment motivated to make changes. In addition to the customer, solution-focused therapists describe a second type of client relationship, the "complainant," who is interested not in change for the self, but in change for someone or something else. The third type of client relationship, the "visitor," is involuntary and mandated to treatment by an outside person or entity. The visitor type of relationship is similar to the client who is in precontemplation according to motivational interviewing and the stages of change model. Therefore, both solution-focused therapy and motivational interviewing take into account the relationship of the person to the change process and adjust strategies accordingly, whereas cognitive-behavioral therapy assumes that the person is already motivated and will be organized and conscientious about following change tactics. In solution-focused therapy and motivational enhancement, the client does not necessarily have to be motivated; the role of the practitioner is to engage clients where they are in the stages of change, build their motivation, and enlarge on the concerns and strengths that they show.

The assumption is that people are rational beings and that rational thought will serve them well. The solution-focused practitioner instead views individuals as constructing their reality in ways that make sense for them based on their experiences, dialogue with others, and unique perspective of the world. The solution-focused practitioner does not know how the individual should solve a particular problem because each person is seen as the expert on his or her own life. In contrast, the cognitive-behavioral therapist is convinced that the problem can be solved in a methodical, fairly prescribed pattern.

Compliance and Resistance

Because cognitive-behavioral therapy is designed for clients who are motivated and willing to comply with treatment, the client is advised from the start about the importance of completing homework and that treatment success is predicated on compliance (e.g., Barlow, 2001; Garland & Scott, 2002). The cognitive-behavioral approach to lack of cooperation with implementation of techniques or missed sessions is to problem-solve around barriers to compliance (Carroll, 1998).

Motivational interviewing and solution-focused therapy take a different stance toward compliance and resistance. Both models share an aversion to the concept of "resistance." In motivational interviewing, specific principles and strategies are engaged for building motivation; it is assumed that otherwise change will not occur (Miller & Rollnick, 2002). In motivational enhancement interviewing, "resistance" is the problem of the practitioner rather than the problem of the client, signifying that the practitioner needs to adjust his or her change strategies to match the client's position toward change. In solution-focused therapy, resistance is not considered a useful concept (Berg, 1994; Bertolino & O'Hanlon, 2002; O'Hanlon & Weiner-Davis, 1989). The client determines the goals and the strategies to be taken, based on the client's own unique worldview and problem-solving skills; therefore, the concept of resistance becomes moot.

Length of Change

Cognitive-behavioral therapy, solution-focused therapy, and motivational enhancement interviewing share a brief orientation toward change. Cognitive-behavioral therapy protocols for various problems are often discussed in terms of approximately 12 to 16 sessions (Barlow, 2001). In solution-focused therapy, rapid change is possible, even as quickly as one session. In motivational interviewing, a four-session protocol has been set up for the treatment of those with substance abuse problems and found effective through Project MATCH (1998), but change has been reported in only one session in a number of studies (see Burke, Arkowitz, & Dunn, 2002).

Theoretical Bases

All three of the models stem from differing theoretical bases. One of the theoretical influences of solution-focused therapy is constructivism, the view that knowledge about reality is constructed from social interactions (Berg & DeJong, 1996). Therefore, the concept of the "expert" practitioner— who categorizes, diagnoses, and solves client problems objectively—is viewed with skepticism. Sharing perceptions with others through language and conversational dialogues is the medium by which reality is shaped (de Shazer, 1994). Thus, the solution-focused practitioner uses language and questioning to influence the way clients view their problems, the potential for solutions, and the expectancy for change (Berg & DeJong, 1996). The constructivist roots and the philosophy of subjective reality are incompatible with the empirical tradition, which explains why solution-focused therapy has been slow to gather quantitative outcome studies, and those that have been conducted have often been of poor methodological quality.

Behaviorism arose out of laboratory research; therefore, cognitive-behavioral therapy has a long-standing empirical tradition. Cognitive-behavioral therapy has been studied more than any other psychotherapy and has amassed much empirical support (see Chapter 3). The underlying theoretical basis involves classical conditioning, operant conditioning, and modeling.

The System Level of Change

Solution-focused therapy has a systemic orientation, and the context of a behavior matters more so than individual characteristics, whereas cognitive-behavioral therapy centers on the individual and, specifically, the cognitions of the individual. Behavioral theory tends to consider the reinforcement contingencies involved in dyadic relationships—for instance, the parent–child dyad and marital couples—rather than the entire system. Motivational interviewing works with the ambivalence of the individual client, considering the advantages and disadvantages of the problem behavior, as well as how goals and values are dissonant with the problem. However, in motivational interviewing, motivation, rather than a stable internal quality of the individual, is seen as being affected by the interaction between practitioner and client (Killick & Allen, 1997). The context of the helping relationship, therefore, is emphasized.

Assumptions of the Strengths-and-Skills-Building Model

Strengths Versus Deficits

The integrative model takes a strengths-based perspective in that client strengths, abilities, and resources are emphasized. Clients are assumed to have the necessary strengths (including cognitive resources) to solve their own problems, and a major focus of treatment is bolstering motivation and resources. When these resources are exhausted or when deficits are identified as a substantial barrier to change, then cognitive-behavioral skill building is introduced. However, skills are taught in a collaborative fashion and, as much as possible, are made relevant to the client's unique circumstance. This integration is designed so that the practitioner can maximize both strength finding and skill building.

Stance Toward Behavioral Change

In the strengths-and-skills-building model, the client's level of motivation is considered in determining goals. If a client is initially unmotivated for change, the advantages of changing have to be increased, and the disadvantages of changing have to be decreased. Some of the disadvantages may involve belief systems that need to be addressed, and resources to help circumvent the problem behavior may have to be accessed. When a client is ready to take action, specific and concrete measurable goals are targeted (Corcoran, 2000).

Type of Client

In the strengths-and-skills-building model, the practitioner approaches clients based on their worldview and their motivation toward change. Solution-focused therapy takes into account the different client relationships, including those who are mandated to attend treatment. Motivational interviewing techniques are used to bolster the motivation of clients who are in the precontemplation and contemplation stages of change. Motivational interviewing, as well as solution-focused therapy, focuses on *why* clients may go about changing their problem, whereas cognitive-behavioral and solution-focused therapy focuses on *how* clients might do so. Therefore, motivational interviewing and cognitive-behavioral therapy may be viewed as complementary (Baer, Kivlahan, & Donovan, 1999; Carroll, 1998), with motivational interviewing beginning the process before the practitioner turns to cognitive-behavioral skill building. As Baer et al. (1999) have also discussed, in integrating motivational and skills-based treatment, high-risk situations (in addition to temptations and slips) can be interpreted as indicators of skills deficits and/or motivational needs. The strengths-and-skills-building model takes into account the level of motivation, as well as the client's attitude toward the change process.

Compliance and Resistance

The therapeutic work involves a collaborative process. The practitioner needs to assess where the client is in the change process and use appropriate strategies accordingly. When the practitioner encounters resistance, it is a signal to change tactics. The strengths-and-skills-building model also focuses on building skills and their implementation. When barriers present themselves, the focus shifts to problem solving, behavioral rehearsal, and other strategies to help the client cope with challenges that may arise.

Length of Change

The strengths-and-skills-building model can be employed in crisis situations in only one session. Overall, it is a brief model, with the idea that change can be enacted in a short time frame.

Level of Structure

As much as possible, clients' resources and problem-solving abilities, including their belief systems and ways of thinking (cognitions), are tapped for solutions. Only then are these capacities supplemented with information about how to apply effective reinforcement and coping skills that might help people more successfully manage life difficulties. In the strengths-and-skills-building model, task formulation and tracking progress on assigned tasks are an important part of the helping process, but first it must be determined that the client is ready to take action steps toward change. Initially, it may be necessary to bolster motivation for change by eliciting client arguments for change, and by increasing the advantages of changing and decreasing the disadvantages.

The System Level of Change

Like solution-focused therapy, the strengths-and-skills-building model poses a systemic orientation, with the context of a behavior playing a crucial role. However, individual cognitions are also considered to influence and be influenced by the context. In addition, behavioral principles of learning are understood to play a role in both the problem and its solution.

■ Summary

This chapter has summarized the similarities and differences between the three therapies—solution-focused therapy, motivational interviewing, and cognitive-behavioral therapy—that comprise the strengths-and-skills-building model. Solution-focused therapy and motivational interviewing are found more similar in their approach, if not their underlying assumptions. Cognitive-behavioral therapy is more deficit-based than the other two approaches discussed; however, the precept of motivational interviewing is that more action-oriented techniques, such as those found in cognitive-behavioral therapy, are useful when people are ready to change their behavior. This precept is adopted for the integrative strengths-and-skills-building model. As much as possible, client strengths, resources, and motivation are identified, reinforced, and amplified. Cognitive-behavioral skill building is used to bolster areas where clients have knowledge or skill gaps that seem to interfere with the attainment of their goals. The aim throughout is a collaborative process in which the individual, not the practitioner, is seen as the ultimate expert on his or her life.

References

Baer, J., Kivlahan, D., & Donovan, D. (1999). Integrating skills training and motivational therapies: Implication for the treatment of substance dependence. *Journal of Substance Abuse Treatment, 17*(1–2), 15–23.

Barlow, D. H. (Ed.). (2001). *Clinical handbook of psychological disorders* (3rd ed.). New York: Guilford.

Berg, I. K. (1994). *Family-based services: A solution-focused approach*. New York: W. W. Norton.

Berg, I. K., & DeJong, P. (1996). Solution-building conversations: Co-constructing a sense of competence with clients. *Families in Society, 77*, 376–391.

Bertolino, B., & O'Hanlon, B. (2002). *Collaborative, competency-based counseling and therapy*. Boston: Allyn & Bacon.

Burke, B., Arkowitz, H., & Dunn, C. (2002). The efficacy of motivational interviewing and its adaptations: What we know so far. In W. R. Miller & S. Rollnick (Eds.), *Motivational interviewing* (2nd ed., pp. 217–250). New York: Guilford.

Carroll, K. (1998). *A cognitive-behavioral approach: Treating cocaine addiction*. Retrieved January 16, 2004, from nida.nih.gov/TXManuals/CBT/CBT1.html.

Corcoran, J. (2000). Brief solution-focused theory. In N. Coady & P. Lehman (Eds.), *Theoretical perspectives in direct social work practice: An eclectic-generalist approach*. New York: Springer.

DeJong, P., & Berg, I. K. (2001). *Interviewing for solutions* (2nd ed.). Pacific Grove, CA. Brooks/Cole.

De Shazer, S. (1994). *Words were originally magic*. New York: W. W. Norton.

De Shazer, S., Berg, I. K., Lipchick, E., Nunnally, E., Molnar, A., Gingerich, W., et al. (1986). Brief therapy: Focused solution development. *Family Process, 25*, 207–221.

Garland, A., & Scott, J. (2002). Using homework in therapy for depression. *JCLP/In Session: Psychotherapy in Practice, 58*(5), 489–498.

Greene, G. J., Lee, M. Y., Trask, R., & Rheinscheld, J. (1996). Client strengths and crisis intervention: A solution-focused approach. *Crisis Intervention, 3*, 43–63.

Killick, S., & Allen, C. (1997). Shifting the balance: Motivational interviewing to help behaviour change in people with bulimia nervosa. *European Eating Disorders Review, 5*(1), 35–41.

Meichenbaum, D. (1999). *Cognitive-behavior modification: An integrative approach.* Cambridge, MA: Perseus.

Miller, W., & Rollnick, S. (1991). *Motivational interviewing.* New York: Guilford.

Miller, W., & Rollnick, S. (2002). *Motivational interviewing: Preparing people to change addictive behavior* (2nd ed.). New York: Guilford.

Moyers, T., & Rollnick, S. (2002). A motivational interviewing perspective on resistance in psychotherapy. *JCLP/In Session: Psychotherapy in Practice, 58*(2), 185–193.

Murphy, J. (1997). *Solution-focused counseling in middle and high schools.* Alexandria, VA: American Counseling Association.

O'Hanlon, W. H., & Weiner-Davis, M. (1989). *In search of solutions: A new direction in psychotherapy.* New York: W. W. Norton.

Project MATCH. (1998). Matching alcoholism treatments to client heterogeneity: Project MATCH three-year drinking outcomes. *Alcoholism: Clinical and Experimental Research, 23,* 1300–1311.

Treasure, J., & Ward, W. (1997). A practical guide to the use of motivational interviewing in anorexia nervosa. *European Eating Disorders Review, 5,* 102–114.

Young, J., Weinberger, A., & Beck, A. (2001). Depression. In D. Barlow (Ed.), *Clinical handbook of psychological disorders: A step-by-step treatment manual* (2nd ed.). New York: Guilford.

5   Phases of the Strengths-and-Skills-Building Model

Now that the theoretical basis for the model has been discussed, this chapter describes a template of the helping process for the strengths-and-skills-building model. Specific techniques, procedures, and principles are drawn from each of the three theories: solution-focused therapy, motivational interviewing, and cognitive-behavioral therapy. Subsequent chapters illustrate how the integrative model can be adapted to different problem areas and populations. Although guiding principles are offered for how techniques can be applied, clinical judgment and the needs of the particular client dictate the choice of techniques and the order in which they are used.

The outline for the helping process follows the phases of engagement, exploring the problem, exploring the solution, goal setting, taking action, and evaluation and termination. See Table 5.1 for how techniques from each theoretical approach are integrated at each of these different phases of the helping process.

Engagement

Initial engagement involves joining, the practitioner's task of establishing a positive, mutually cooperative relationship (Berg, 1994), which is pivotal

Table 5.1

Integration of the Model

Stage of the helping process	Model	Techniques
Engagement	SFT	See Table 5.2
Exploration of the problem	MI	Questions to elicit self-motivational statements; decisional balance
	SFT	Problem-solving attempts; experience with previous helpers
	CBT	Functional analysis
Exploration of the solution	SFT	Exception finding
Goal setting	SFT	Miracle question; scaling questions
Taking action: implementation of plan	SFT CBT	Application of exceptions; teaching strategies and skills
Termination	SFT	Termination questions

to the rest of the work. From the opening words of contact, the practitioner should attend to language, which conveys certain meanings about the problem and its solvability. See Table 1.1 for sample opening phrases and their justification. As was described in Chapter 3, essential to the joining process is the practice of empathy, a skill that is continued throughout the interview process. The practitioner must listen empathically to clients' concerns, reflecting the content of their messages, as well as their feelings. In this way, rapport is built, and the individual feels heard and understood (Hepworth, Rooney, & Larsen, 2002). With the practice of empathy, the practitioner is also able to more accurately assess the individual's problems and relationship to the process of change.

Another essential aspect of engagement is assessing and engaging clients in the change process. As explained in Chapter 1, solution-focused therapy poses three different client relationships: the "customer," the "complainant," and the "visitor." The customer type of relationship is the client who is motivated and willing to participate in the change process. The person in the complainant type of relationship seems initially motivated but actually is not as interested in changing himself or herself as for another person to change. The visitor type of relationship involves a client who is typically unmotivated and attends services only because he or she has been mandated to do so. The visitor is similar to the person who is in the precontemplation phase of the Stages of Change model. In precontemplation, the individual believes there is no problem behavior and therefore is unwilling to do anything about it. At this stage, the individual sees the problem behavior as possessing more advantages than disadvantages. Typically, individuals in this stage are defensive and resistant about their behavior. They lack awareness of the problem and, if in treatment, have usually been coerced or pressured to do so by others. In treatment, they are not willing to participate (Connors, Donovan, & DiClemente, 2001).

Solution-focused therapy offers many engagement techniques for the different client relationships (Table 5.2). The techniques highlighted in the next section are those that are shared across at least two of the practice models, including reframing, normalizing, coping questions, and aligning with the client's position.

Reframing

One of the central tenets of solution-focused therapy is that the practitioner should recognize that every problem behavior contains within it an inherent strength (O'Hanlon & Weiner-Davis, 1989). One technique that can be used throughout the helping process that can also be employed as early as joining is reframing—a technique by which the practitioner introduces people to a new way of viewing the problem. In other words, clients are given credit for positive aspects of their behavior (Berg, 1994), or their motives are cast in a benevolent light. Through reframing, individuals are introduced to a novel way of viewing some aspect of themselves, others, their problem, or their situation. A new perspective on the problem can generate new actions in accordance with this frame of reference (Bertolino & O'Hanlon, 2002). Table 5.3 lists problem behaviors and their corresponding possible reframes.

Reframing is also used as a technique in cognitive-behavioral therapy and motivational interviewing. In cognitive-behavioral therapy, reframing is offered when people provide attributions that are problematic. Reframing is used to reflect a more functional attribution-making pattern (i.e., one that represents internal versus external control and one that represents temporary versus enduring circumstances) (Gotlib & Abramson, 1999; Weiner, 1985).

Motivational interviewing employs reframing as a technique to deal with "resistance." People's arguments for why they should continue their problem behavior are turned upside down to argue for change. Miller and Rollnick (2002) give the example of people who argue that they do not need to change their drinking habits because alcohol does not affect them like it does other people; for instance, they can drive and carry out other tasks. The practitioner instead points out that a higher tolerance for alcohol

Table 5.2

Strategies to Assess and Engage Different Client Relationships

Client relationship description	Strategies	Description of strategies
Customer: Voluntary; willing to make changes	Orient toward change	"What will your life look like when your work here is successful?"
Complainant: Motivated for somebody else to change	Coping questions	What resources have been drawn upon to cope with the situation?
	Normalizing	Depathologizing clients' concerns as normal life challenges
	Reframing	Introducing the positive elements of a behavior initially viewed as negative
	Orienting toward goals	"What would you like _____ to be doing instead of [complaint]?"
Visitor: Nonvoluntary; mandated into treatment	Orienting toward meeting the requirements of the mandate	"Whose idea was it that you come here?" "What does _____ need to see to know you don't have to come here anymore?"
	Relationship questions	Asking clients to view themselves from perspective of another
	Siding with the client against an external entity	"What will we need to do to convince _____ you no longer need to come here?"
	Get client to identify a desired goal	What is something the client is motivated to pursue?
	Elicit self-motivational statements: Get clients to argue for their own change	"In what ways do you think you or other people have been harmed [by your problem]?" "How has your (problem) stopped you from doing what you want to do?" "What do you think will happen if you don't make a change?" "The fact that you're here indicates that at least a part of you think it's time to do something?" "What are the reasons you see for making a change?"

all table

Table 5.3

Reframes of Common "Problem" Behaviors

Nags	Concerned about bringing out the best in someone
Lazy	Laid back, mellow, relaxed, taking it easy
Pushy	Assertive, in a hurry, action oriented
Impatient	Action oriented, has high standards
Uncaring	Detached, allows room for others
Depressed	Overwhelmed, introspective, quiet, slowing down
Hyperactive	Energetic
Anger problems	Emotional
Shy	Takes a little time to know people
Controlling	Providing structure and direction, conscientious, wants to make sure that things get done
Defiant	Independent, assertive, committed
Argumentative	Caring enough to disagree
Immature	Fun hearted, playful
Impulsive	Spontaneous, energetic
Withdrawn	Introspective, contemplative, observant
Passive	Ability to accept things as they are, laid back
Rigid	Steadfast and committed to a plan of action
Boring	Dependable, steady, consistent, reliable; follows through
Codependent	Cares about people, nurturing, kind

Note. Adapted from _Family-Based Services: A Solution-Focused Approach_, by I. K. Berg, 1994, New York: W. W. Norton; _Collaborative, Competency-Based Counseling and Therapy_, by B. Bertolino and B. O'Hanlon, 2002, Boston: Allyn & Bacon; _Direct Social Work Practice: Theory & Skills_ (6th ed.), by D. H. Hepworth, R. Rooney, and J. Larsen, 2002, Belmont, CA: Brooks/Cole; and _Solution-Focused Counseling in Middle and High Schools_, by J. Murphy, 1997, Alexandria, VA: American Counseling Association.

often is one of the signs of a problem and something for the client to consider.

Normalizing

Normalizing is also compatible with cognitive-behavioral therapy in that sometimes education (information taken in cognitively) is necessary to allay people's concerns and fears. For instance, if people are grieving the loss of a loved one and feel that they are "going crazy" because they haven't "snapped out of it," information about the length of the grieving process and the phases that are common might help them depathologize their reactions.

Normalizing works with the negative spiral that sometimes occurs with problems. Some people become so concerned with the problem that they escalate it to greater proportions. A common example involving adolescents is when parents center on a teen's style of dress as a source of contention, and frequent arguments about this topic ensue, causing the relationship to deteriorate. Experimentation with style and other aspects of identity can be normalized as typical adolescent-stage behavior. By depathologizing the concerns, the original problem is kept in proportion to its nature.

Normalizing may also involve the reactions and concerns people often experience when they encounter a specific problem or problems. For example, crime victims, cancer patients, caregivers of the elderly, and sexual abuse victims and their families need information about the problem and its particular dynamics and phases in order to prepare them for what to expect. However, rather than being delivered in a lecture format, information should be conveyed in a collaborative manner (as described in a later section).

Coping Questions

Extreme negativity from clients about their circumstances should act "as a sign of great desperation and a signal for empathetic help. In such a situation, the client could perceive the clinician's focus on the positive as being artificial and imposing" (Greene, Lee, Trask, & Rheinscheld, 1996, p. 54). In these circumstances, the solution-focused intervention of coping questions can be asked; these questions not only validate the extent to which people have struggled but also ask clients to reflect on the resources they have used to manage their struggles. Clark (1997) further adds, "Coping questions can help victims look at their resourcefulness and strengths, not the painful event. People who have been victimized don't need to relive or recount the pain; they've been living with it. It is far better to foster a sense that they have survived in the face of such adversity" (pp. 98–102).

Examples of coping questions include the following (Bertolino & O'Hanlon, 2002):

"How have you coped with the problem?"
"How do you manage? How do you have the strength to go on?"
"This has been a very difficult problem for you. How have you managed to keep things from getting even worse?"
"How have you managed to keep your sanity and hope in the midst of these problems?"

"What qualities do you possess that you seem to be able to tap into in times of trouble?"

"What is it about you that allows you to keep going?"

"What would others say are the qualities that you have that keep you going?"

"In the midst of what has happened, how have you managed to keep going?"

"What percentage of the time are you dealing with this? How do you cope during this time? What makes it a little better the other percentage of the time?"

In a cognitive-behavioral orientation, additional questions can be asked: "What do you tell yourself to keep going?" "What do you say to yourself to keep your sanity and hope when things are really hard?"

By asking specifically about cognitions that are used to help the individual cope, a strengths-rather than deficit-based way of targeting cognitive resources is employed (i.e., coping thoughts are targeted rather than "irrational" thoughts).

Coping questions allow "clients to shift their views and attribute change or control to their personal qualities, internal abilities and resources, and actions" (Bertolino & O'Hanlon, 2002, p. 137). They also help the practitioner know which resources may be amplified, as well as what areas may need developing for skill building. Finally, those who struggle with adversity are usually doing something to prevent the problem from getting even worse. "These questions imply that the client is competent and resilient in dealing with the problem, if only to stop it from getting worse. Regardless of whether or not clients answer these questions, the implication of competence conveys the counselor's respect for their ideas and resources" (Murphy, 1997, pp. 80–81).

A great deal of material has also been amassed in the cognitive coping literature on how people cope with unexpected, stressful life events (Folkman, 1984; Lazarus & Folkman, 1984). *Coping* has been defined as "cognitive and behavioral efforts to master, reduce, or tolerate the internal and/or external demands that are created by the stressful transaction" (Folkman, 1984, p. 843). Folkman (1984) classified coping strategies into two main types: problem-focused and emotion-focused. Problem-focused strategies focus on the use of problem solving and action plans, whereas emotion-focused strategies involve the control of negative or distressing emotions.

When people are asked specifically about their coping strategies, they may report a wide variety of responses. For example, qualitative research with caregivers of the elderly found that caregivers drew on an array of positive coping strategies with the reframe that caregiving was an opportunity rather than a burden (Berg-Weger, Rubio, & Tebb, 2001; Schulz et al.,

1997). Caregivers derived a sense of competence and satisfaction from managing the caregiving challenge, learning new skills, and negotiating informal and formal supports and resources. They coped with caregiving because of family loyalty or obligation and the chance to grow closer and spend more time with a family member. Care recipient appreciation for their efforts helped caregivers cope, as did the knowledge that the elderly family member was receiving optimal care. Spirituality, faith, or religious support was also named as a major coping mechanism.

These studies illustrate the many possible resources people use when coping with difficult life circumstances. The practitioner should routinely inquire about a person's means of coping to reinforce positive strategies. Such a discussion also aids people in viewing themselves as more self-efficacious. Moreover, the practitioner may gain valuable information about coping mechanisms that are unhealthy (e.g., drinking alcohol); at this point, the practitioner may choose to shift toward motivational interviewing techniques.

Aligning With the Client's Position and Perspective

The practitioner is advised to convey acceptance of the client's positions and perspectives rather than becoming invested in who is "right" and who is "wrong." This stance is particularly necessary toward clients who are mandated to attend treatment. If the practitioner becomes polarized from a client's position, the client is likely to become defensive and even more entrenched in a position against change (Berg, 1994). Indeed, whenever possible, the practitioner should strive to align with the client against external entities that are desirous of the client's change: "I wonder what we need to do here to convince _____ [the judge, your husband, your probation officer] that you don't need to come here anymore?"

Another part of aligning with the client is rolling with resistance. Strategies for rolling with resistance include simple reflection, double-sided reflection, shifting focus, agreement with a twist, and paradox (Chapter 2; Miller & Rollnick, 2002).

Summary of Engagement

The techniques employed show that from the point of joining, the practitioner is oriented toward strengths ("What are you doing to cope?") and to change ("What will _____ need to see to know you don't need to come here anymore?"). Indeed, the integrative model adapts from solution-focused therapy that intervention is integral to assessment. That is, while the client's problems and strengths are being assessed, techniques are also used to create momentum for change.

■■■■ Problem Exploration

After engagement, the next stage is to help the client explore the problem and build motivation to change. Exploration of the problem and its effects on the individual's life include continuing to ask questions that will elicit the client's motivation (motivational interviewing), discovering past problem-solving attempts (solution-focused therapy), and a functional analysis to explore details of the problem, its triggers, and its consequences, both negative and positive (cognitive-behavioral). The relative importance of these techniques depends on the client's relationship to the change process. For instance, if a client is involuntary, more time will be spent on motivational interviewing; if a client is already motivated to change, the practitioner can choose techniques that work more proactively toward change. Finally, problem exploration might also include having clients complete measurement tools that assess the problem behaviors under question. (For a resource of such measures, see Corcoran, 2000.)

Eliciting Self-Motivational Statements

The next step in the change process is to elicit arguments from clients in favor of change. The practitioner poses a series of questions that the client might answer in a way that favors change. Conversation will lead into exploring the disadvantages of the status quo and the advantages of changing. The exploration involves helping the individual examine the discrepancy between current behavior and goals and values related to health, future well-being, success, and family relationships. The practitioner inquires about how the problem affects the individual and those close to him or her and the extent of the client's concerns about the problem. The practitioner also asks "questions about extremes": questions about what the future may be like if a change is not made and what will be different if the individual does take steps to eradicate the problem. Table 2.2 shows the types of questions that can be asked.

Problem-Solving Attempts

Another part of the problem exploration process is finding out how individuals have handled their problems and how these efforts have worked. This gives the practitioner important information for intervention purposes. First, it is helpful for service providers to learn in a detailed way what has been tried and in what ways: "When you say you used time-out, tell me, what did you do? What happened?" The practitioner may find in many instances that the efforts were applied inconsistently or in a manner that sabotaged the client's success. In line with cognitive-behavioral assumptions, sometimes people may have to be educated about a more effective way to apply possible solutions. Second, information about unsuccessful problem-solving attempts also assists the practitioner in avoiding the same tactics (Murphy, 1997). At the same time, it is useful for practitioners to ask in a detailed way about what has been attempted. Third, fruitless problem-solving efforts may escalate the problem. Sometimes people's attempts to solve the problem actually add another layer to the problem rather than alleviating it. For instance, a woman who senses her partner has pulled away her and nags the partner to spend more time with her may cause the partner to pull further away.

Another reason to inquire about previous problem-solving attempts is that people who are caught up in stressful circumstances may become so immersed in the problem that they lose sight of what has been effective for them in the past (Murphy, 1997). In addition, asking people how they have tried to solve their problems gives them credit for their efforts and the sense they have competence and the capacity for effectiveness. For these various reasons, the following types of questions can be asked:

What have you tried?
What has been helpful?
What have you done about this problem so far?
How did it work?
What have others done?
What have other people suggested doing about it?
What strategies have you used to deal with your problem and how successful have they been?

Another avenue of exploration for previous problem-solving attempts may be people's experiences with helpers in the past. What has been the client's experience with other helpers? What was helpful and what was not helpful?

Answers to these questions may give the practitioner and the client ideas about where future interventions may need to be applied. These questions give clients credit for knowing what is best for them and put them in charge of their own treatment. A collaborative relationship is thus built between the practitioner and the client about the best course of action to follow. Practitioners, however, can fall into certain traps when inquiring about previous problem-solving attempts. Table 5.4 lists some of these common pitfalls and solutions for how to address these.

Functional Analysis

A functional analysis is derived from cognitive-behavioral therapy and focuses on the specific, concrete behaviors and interactional patterns of prob-

Table 5.4

Helping Clients With Their Problem-Solving Attempts: Pitfalls and Solutions

Pitfalls	Solutions
Concentrating on all the professional services that have been provided (e.g., anger management course at school for a 16-year-old girl, family therapy with mother, punitive attempts to control problem behavior by school)	Focus instead on what the clients have done (the 16-year-old daughter and her mother)
Failing to give credit for the efforts clients have made in being active problem solvers in their own lives	Highlighting and complimenting efforts individuals have made on their behalf
Failing to note when clients' problem-solving attempts have actually exacerbated the problem	Compliment clients on the efforts they have made; focus on the original problem and ask for exceptions to that problem
Not asking enough detail to find out what people have specifically done; missing opportunities to fill in gaps in clients' implementation of techniques (e.g., parent reports using time-out by sending child to her room for 2 hours)	Compliment clients on the efforts they have made; ask about the specifics of what they have tried ("When you say you used time-out, tell me what you did and how that worked out"); ask permission to provide information on gaps in knowledge or implementation (guidelines for time-out: a minute for each year of the child's age in a place where there is no reinforcement)

lems. Attention is given to the antecedents of the behavior and its consequences, as these, according to behavioral principles, influence the occurrence of the problem. Similarly, solution-focused writers discuss "video talk" ("If I were to videotape you, what would I see you doing?"), that is, encouraging people to talk about behaviors in concrete and sensory-based ways rather than in global and general terms (Bertolino & O'Hanlon, 2002; Hudson & O'Hanlon, 1993). In order to do this, the practitioner can choose among the following array of questions (Bertolino & O'Hanlon, 2002; Spiegler, 1993):

- When you experience the behavior, what do you do?
- How do you feel?
- What are you thinking?
- What bodily reactions do you experience?
- How do you react?

- What do you say and do?
- How long do these reactions last?
- How often does the problem typically happen (once an hour, once a day, once a week)?
- What is the typical timing (time of day, week, month, year) of the problem?
- Where does the problem typically happen?
- What does the client, and others who are around, usually do when the problem is happening?

A functional analysis further works to discover the antecedents of the problem. Carroll (1998) discusses the following domains that may trigger or influence the problem behavior and also the areas that may be influenced: social, environmental, emotional, cognitive, and physical. (See Table 3.1 for questions to ask in these various domains.) Related to consequences is exploring the pros and cons of committing the problem behavior (a decisional balance from motivational interviewing). See Chapter 2's discussion of the decisional balance technique and Table 5.5. Table 5.6 lists some of the ways functional analyses can be maximized.

Exploring the Solution

Exploration of the solution involves discussion of the strengths that people display and exception finding. The practitioner can also utilize strengths-based measurement tools to assess and track strengths (see Chapter 15). Practitioner judgment dictates whether this stage precedes problem exploration, depending, for example, on the time constraints and the type of problem (see Chapter 8 on depression).

Exception Finding

One main way to explore solutions is exception finding, in which the practitioner explores with clients their pasts to discover times when the problem did not exert its negative influence. The focus is on successes people have enjoyed, starting in the present and working backward, as recent exceptions are more powerful for counteracting negative stories (Bertolino & O'Hanlon, 2002). Rather than teaching new skills, exception finding emphasizes the capacities clients already possess.

Once an exception is elicited, the practitioner asks about the resources the client drew upon, including the cognitive resources, and the details of the context.

Table 5.5

Steps in Using the Decisional Analysis

Asking questions	What do you get out of the problem behavior?
	What do you lose?
	What will you get out of changing?
	What will you lose by changing?
Selectively reinforce change statements	"You would really like to be in shape again."
Develop discrepancy between goals/values and current problem behavior	"On one hand, your relationship with your son is more important to you than anything else, and you're finding that your alcohol use is making the relationship worse."
Discover what needs the problem behavior meets	"You find that to deal with your stress, you drink to relax."
How else have these needs been met in a functional way?	Solution-focused exception finding
How else could these needs be met in a functional way?	Cognitive-behavioral skill building
Goal setting	What disadvantages of changing need to be addressed first?
	How can the advantages of change be bolstered?

- How: "How did you get that to happen?" "How are you managing to do this?"
- What: "What did you do differently?" "What's different about those times?"
- Who: "Who was there?" "What did _____ do?" "How was that helpful?"
- "What would be more helpful?" "What would _____ say you did differently?"
- When: "When is the problem a little bit better?" "At what times of the day and what days?" "Before or after?"

To tap cognitive resources, clients can further be asked, "What were they thinking to make this happen?" "What were they telling themselves?" "What did they think and feel as a result of doing that?"

At times, when people talk about exceptions, they attribute credit to externals ("I didn't do anything different. He was nice that day/the sun was shining/she didn't give me a hard time"). Similarly, cognitive-

Table 5.6

Functional Analysis: Pitfalls and Solutions

Pitfalls	Solutions
Failing to pick up on an opportunity to track a behavior/allowing the client to speak in generalities (Christensen et al., 1999)	When clients speak in generalities around a recurrent or a critical problem, ask them questions to elicit behavioral details: "To help me get a better sense of what happens when you 'just lose it' with the kids, tell me what happened the last time this occurred. Where were you? What was going on?"
Not choosing a specific circumstance (e.g., 16-year-old girl acts out when she is with her natural mother)	Select a typical incident, the most recent, or the most severe (e.g., look at last Saturday night when conflict came to a head between mother and daughter)
Using general language (e.g., 16-year-old girl showing oppositional behaviors)	Use behavioral, concrete descriptors (e.g., 16-year-old on a visit with her natural mother yelled at her mother when her mother didn't want to let her go out with her old friends from the neighborhood)
Failing to examine both triggers and consequences	Explore triggers and consequences from possible domains of functioning (see Table 3.1) to help individual understand the situations and states that make a behavior likely to happen and the costs and benefits of committing a particular behavior
Tracking sequences too quickly (Christensen et al., 1999)	Record the information in writing; get information about behavioral sequences, thoughts, feelings, body sensations, and so on
Failing to exploit the information gained in the functional analysis	Prioritizing antecedents, using problem-solving process on priorities, and developing a plan for how to manage triggers; explaining principles of reinforcement that encourage behaviors; bolstering the advantages of changing and working on decreasing the disadvantages of changing

behavioral theorists have discussed the problematic nature of attributing positive events to entities or people outside the self ("My supervisor was just nice to me") and attributing negative events to internal factors that are global and stable in nature ("I'm just stupid") (Weiner, 1985).

In solution-focused therapy, careful questioning is used to elicit the role the client played in the exception: How did you make that happen? What part did you have in creating that? For example, a 14-year-old boy claimed that he did not skip school when the teacher saw him before class. He elaborated that if she saw him and then he did not turn up for class, he would definitely get in trouble. He was credited with this idea—making sure the teacher noticed him earlier in the day—which would then force him to attend class. The teen was able to follow through with this strategy to prevent himself from skipping. Solution-focused therapy aims to empower clients to see the role they take in events.

Exception finding seems to some people to be overly simplistic; however, practitioners at times do not thoroughly exploit exception finding. Table 5.7 addresses some of the pitfalls practitioners fall prey to and how they can be addressed.

After the exception has been identified, its contextual details elicited,

Table 5.7	
Exception Finding: Pitfalls and Solutions	
Pitfalls	Solutions
Finding exceptions too early before a person feels understood for the problem (Christensen et al., 1999)	Track problem sequences first (see functional analysis) to understand the problem behavior; use coping questions; use externalizing as a bridge between problem and solution exploration (Dyes & Neville, 2000)
Process is abandoned too quickly when client is unable to come up with an exception	Inquire about when a problem is less intense, frequent, or severe; identify an exception that happens during the session; ask a relationship question about what others would see as an exception; ask about the percentage of time the problem is experienced, and then what is better the other percentage of the time; if all else fails, ask the client coping questions or what he or she is doing to prevent the problem from becoming even worse
Failing to elicit details of the exception	Use the investigative questions (who, what, where, when, how) to elicit contextual details of the exception; write the details down to emphasize their importance
Not applying solutions to problem situations	Spend sufficient time on the exception so that clients begin to feel more successful and able to invoke further change; ask clients how they can use their strengths to help them with their problems; role play to try out skills in different situations; identify where there are gaps in knowledge and skills and work with the client to correct these
Clients attribute exceptions to events ("the sun was shining") and people ("she was just acting nice") rather than to their own efforts (Berg, 1994)	Ask questions about what they were doing differently when "the sun was shining" or "she was just acting nice"

and the client's role in the exception explicitly defined, the next phase of exception finding is to help the client enlarge upon exceptions in order to resolve the problems that still plague him or her. For purposes of structuring the helping process, this step is discussed under Task Setting later in this chapter.

Finding Strengths

The practitioner must also be alert to the strengths individuals bring to other contexts, such as work settings (e.g., organizational skills, assertiveness, problem-solving abilities), their hobbies (e.g., gardening, crafts, handiwork, sports), and pastimes (attending church, socializing with friends). One study worked purposefully to elicit the strengths and resilience family members demonstrated in taking care of an individual with mental illness (Marsh et al., 1996). In this study, family members were asked open-ended questions about resilience in the following areas: personal or family qualities or strengths that had developed as a result of dealing with the illness, the contributions either the person with the illness or other family members had made, the gratifications individuals had experienced in their role as family members, whether the family member with mental illness had experienced adaptation or recovery, and resources that had promoted positive change. This study indicates that many facets of difficult circumstances can be explored to find the strengths that have been employed or developed. Murphy (1997) suggests the following phrasing to elicit strengths: "Think of a specific difficulty or challenge that you have successfully overcome or coped with in your own life. How did you manage to do this? What type of attitudes, beliefs, and actions contributed to your success in this situation? How could these attitudes, beliefs, and actions be adapted and applied to your current difficulty?" (p. 118).

Many agencies require either clients or practitioners to complete detailed assessment forms of a client's educational and employment history, network of social support, health status, and so forth. Although a great deal of history taking is not seen as necessary from a strengths-based perspective, such assessments can identify exceptions and strengths. Bertolino and O'Hanlon (2002) suggest an excellent series of questions for this purpose (Box 5.1). In the same way, potential risk behaviors and situations, such as suicidal or homicidal thoughts or history, substance abuse, health problems, or medication use, can be explored in a way that both protects client safety and elicits client strengths (Box 5.2).

Strengths-Based Assessment Questions

Employment

- How did you come to work at your current place of employment?
- How did you get yourself into position to get the job?
- What do you think your employer saw in you that might have contributed to your being hired?
- What have you found to be most challenging or difficult about your job?
- How have you met or worked toward meeting those challenges and difficulties?
- What keeps you there?
- What skills or qualities do you think your employer sees in you?
- What qualities do you think you possess that are assets on the job?
- (If self-employed) How did you have the means to start your own business?
- (If unemployed) What kind of employment would you like to see yourself involved with in the future?

School

- How did you manage to make it through _____ (ninth grade, high school, trade school, junior college, a 4-year university, 2 years of college, graduate school, etc.)?
- What qualities do you possess that made that happen?
- What did you find most challenging about school?
- How did you manage any difficulties that you may have encountered while in school? (e.g., completing homework assignments, tests, getting to school on time, moving from one grade to another, teacher/classmates relationships, sports)
- In what ways did school prepare you for future challenges?

Family and Social Relationships

- Who are you closest to in your _____ (life, family, etc.)?
- What do you appreciate most about your relationship with _____?
- What would (he, she, they) say are your best qualities as a _____ (friend, spouse, parent, child, grandparent, colleague, etc.)?
- How is that helpful for you to know that?
- What does it feel like to know that?
- Which relationships have been more challenging for you?
- How have you dealt with those challenges?
- Whom can you go to for help?
- Who has made a positive difference in your life?
- How so?
- What difference has that made for you?
- When are others more helpful to you?

Hobbies and Interests

- What do you do for fun?
- What hobbies or interests do you have or have you had in the past?

(continued)

Strengths-Based Assessment Questions

Hobbies and Interests

- What kinds of activities are you drawn to?
- What kinds of activities would you rather not be involved with?
- What would you rather do instead?

Previous Treatment Experiences

- What did you find helpful about previous therapy _____ (individual, couples, family, group, etc.)?
- What did the therapist do that was helpful?
- How did that make a difference for you?
- What wasn't so helpful?
- (If currently or previously on psychotropic medication) How was the medication helpful to you?
- What, if anything, did the medication allow you to do that you wouldn't have otherwise been able to do?
- What qualities do you possess such that you were able to work with the medication to improve things for yourself?

Note. From *Collaborative, Competency-Based Counseling and Therapy*, by B. Bertolino and B. O'Hanlon, 2002, Boston: Allyn & Bacon, pp. 76–77.

Goal Setting

Both solution-focused and cognitive-behavioral therapies work toward specific and measurable goals. With solution-focused therapy, negotiation for goals begins at the start of the session with questions such as "What needs to happen so you know coming here is a success?" Goals are to provide focus to the work so that both the worker and the client agree on what will be done. Measurable goals also help the client and practitioner monitor the progress of the intervention and how well it is meeting the achievement of goals (Hepworth et al., 2002). However, the integration of motivational interviewing means that goals are formulated at the client's particular stage of change.

When people are mired in their problems, sometimes they have difficulty seeing beyond their unhappy circumstances. As a result, they might need help in constructing a vision of a nonproblem future. The miracle question (or its adaptation, the dream question) from solution-focused therapy and hypothetical change questions from motivational interviewing may allow clients to project themselves into a nonproblem future that fuels their sense of hope. The intervention may also act as a blueprint for the changes that need to be made and how these will be achieved. Table 5.8

Box 5.2

Risk Assessment in a Strengths-Based Way	
Area of risk	Sample questions
Suicide risk	Have you had thoughts about hurting yourself now or in the past? What did you do to get past that point?
	Things sounded really hard then. How did you manage?
	How did you stop things from getting even worse?
	What needs to happen now so that you feel a bit better?
	What will that look like?
Medications	Have you been on medications? How were they helpful? How were they not helpful?
	"What percentage of the change you've experienced is a result of the medication and what percentage do you think is your own doing?"
	"What are you able to do as a result of feeling better from taking medication?" (Bertolino & O'Hanlon, 2002)
Abuse	Has there been abuse (physical, sexual, family violence)? How did you cope?
	How were you able to survive that time?
	What needs to happen so that you are safe?
	What will that look like?
Health	How is your health? What do you do to take care of yourself?
	How have you been able to cope with the (health problem)?
	When are you able to get the best of it, compared with when it is able to get the best of you?

reviews these interventions and some reasons why the practitioner might choose one over another. Table 5.9 discusses some of the pitfalls in using miracle questions and how the practitioner can maximize their use.

Several guidelines are helpful to consider in formulating goals. First, a rationale for goals should be explained to the client: to provide focus to the work, to get helper and client agreement about what should be done, to monitor progress of the intervention, and to know when the work is complete. Second, the type of goals pursued will depend on where the client is in the process of change. If clients are unmotivated, goals may be oriented toward meeting the requirements of the mandate: "Whose idea was it that you come here? What does _____ need to see to know that you don't have to come here anymore?"

Table 5.8

Future-Oriented Change Questions

Miracle question	"If a miracle happened in the night while you were sleeping but you didn't know this miracle had occurred, what would be the first thing you noticed when you woke up in the morning to let you know a miracle had occurred?"	Practitioner delivery makes it sound contrived; client might feel the intervention is artificial, feels patronized.
Dream question	"Suppose that tonight while you are sleeping you have a dream. In this dream you discover the answers and resources you need to solve the problem that you are concerned about right now. When you wake up tomorrow, you may or may not remember your dream, but you do notice you are different. As you go about starting your day, how will you know that you discovered or developed the skills and resources necessary to solve your problem? What will be the first small bit of evidence that you did this? ... Who will be the first person to notice that you have and are using some of the resources you discovered in your dream? What will they be noticing about you that will be evidence to them that you have and are using some of these resources?" (Greene et al., 1998, p. 397)	This question was formulated by Greene et al. (1998) because they believed the miracle question implied an external locus of control, and they wanted a question that was more reflective of the client's internal sense of control.
Hypothetical change	"Suppose that you did succeed and are looking back on it now: What most likely is it that worked? How did it happen?" "Suppose that this one big obstacle weren't there. If that obstacle were removed, then how might you go about making this change?" "Clearly you are feeling very discouraged, even demoralized about this. So use your imagination: If you were to try again, what might be the best way to try?"	Might be more palatable for some clients as just questions, not discussion about dreams and miracles
Variations of future-oriented, hypothetical questions	"Imagine yourself in the future when the problem is no longer a problem. Tell me where you are, what you are doing and saying, and what others around you are doing and saying."	Practitioner can find phrasing that suits the client's level of understanding and personality.

Table 5.9

Miracle Question: Pitfalls and Solutions

Pitfalls	Solutions
Failing to help the client develop a detailed picture (25-year-old female with relationship problems said her family would be speaking to her, her relationship with her boyfriend would not be strained, her boyfriend would notice she was more laid back and open to communication, she would have control over her emotions, and her stress headaches and upset stomach would not be present)	Push for details and specifics of the miracle, ask for the presence of positive behaviors rather than the absence of negatives (client said her family would be speaking to her [which family member would be speaking to her, what would they be saying, what would she be doing and saying?], her relationship with her boyfriend would not be strained [what would it be like instead, what would they be doing together, what would they be saying together?], her boyfriend would notice she was more laid back and open to communication [what would he specifically notice about her behavior, what would she be saying, how would she say it?], she would have control over her emotions [what would she be doing?], her stress headaches and upset stomach would not be present [how would she be feeling instead?]
The client turns the answer into outlandish fantasies (winning the lottery, having someone die, recovering from an incurable illness).	Phrase the miracle question in terms of "when the problem you came here for is solved"; validate ("wouldn't that be nice") and move on to a more realistic picture
Practitioner feels it's fake and contrived.	Use one of the variations, such as the dream question or the hypothetical change question, or just ask a question about the future without the problem ("When this problem you have with temper disappeared one day, how would similar situations be handled? What exactly would you do?").

For those who are starting to consider change, goal setting may involve working on enhancing the advantages of changing and reducing the disadvantages. This might mean building coping skills so that clients have alternatives to the problem behavior. It might also mean making referrals so that clients are linked to resources that may help. For instance, a woman who is in a violent relationship may need to learn how to obtain a protective order from the county attorney's office. Goal setting to build motivation may further involve working with belief systems that present barriers to change. For example, if a woman believes she should stay married even if there is violence in the relationship, then this belief system may be targeted.

Third, the goal should be one which the client is motivated and interested in achieving. At the same time, a goal may have to be reframed so that it is within the client's control and works with the system that is most amenable to change. For instance, in the complainant relationship, the client may be most motivated for a child, a partner, or a workmate to be different rather than changing his or her own behavior. The practitioner emphasizes in these situations that the client (or the practitioner) cannot make a person outside the helping relationship become different. However, clients can influence others' behavior by changing their own actions. Systemic notions underlie this idea; if there is change in one part of a system, then change can ricochet to other parts of the system.

A fourth important guideline for goal construction is that a minimum number of goals should be formulated. When clients enter into the helping process, many times they are overwhelmed by many simultaneous stressors, such as divorce, death of a family member, a family move, financial problems, health problems, and behavior problems in children. Goals must be prioritized with the client's input: "Which of these goals is most important for you to center on? Which one would make the most difference to you right now?" Of course, the practitioner may offer input into which of the goals might make the most difference. For instance, goals having to do with safety (getting a protective order, severing contact with an abusive partner) would be of foremost priority and might assist the progress of other goals, such as bolstering mood and improving behavior of children in the household.

The practitioner who notices behaviors that cross-cut domains of the client's life in which difficulty is experienced may also offer input. For example, a client may report anger problems at work, with children, and with a partner. A possible goal in this situation may be to improve communication skills and anger management.

A minimum number of goals is critical because the client needs to achieve success and experience some confidence as a result of efforts. If efforts are scattered around many diverse goals, the client is unlikely to achieve success in any one area. Along with the guideline of prioritizing goals, some goals may also have to be partialized (broken down into smaller subgoals or tasks). An example is drawn from Chapter 11, in which a typical goal in a family violence situation may be for a woman to leave her abusive partner. This overall goal might contain within it some substantial subgoals. For example, a woman might have to obtain job training and find employment to become financially independent; she might have to locate transportation so that she is able to attend training and employment; she might have to find reliable and safe child care for her children. Each of these subgoals is a major goal in its own right.

A fifth guideline is that goals should be feasible in light of baseline behaviors, and that they can be attained in a brief time frame. The assumption is that small changes can lead to a more empowered view of the self, as well as different reactions from other people in the system; these changes can then spiral into further change. For example, if a teenager is currently flunking all classes, then a goal of achieving honor roll grades is unrealistic; a more feasible aim might be to pass certain classes.

A sixth guideline is that goals should be stated in terms of the presence of positive behaviors rather than the absence of negative behaviors. For instance, rather than "stop talking back at school," the goal should be phrased as "comply with directions" or "work quietly in the classroom." To get the client thinking within this frame, the question can be asked: "What will you be doing instead of [the problem behavior]?" The practitioner must continue to persist because clients often continue to talk about the absence of negatives. This tendency, however, keeps the focus on negative behavior rather than on what is desired. To retain the emphasis on the presence of positive behaviors, the goal can also be phrased in the format of "how" or "what" questions (Christensen, Todahl, & Barrett, 1999): "How can I find some new friends that don't use drugs and alcohol?" "How can I get enough income so that I can support myself and the children without my husband's income?"

A seventh guideline is that goals should be considered in terms of final outcome rather than in terms of formal services in which clients will participate (Christensen et al., 1999). For instance, rather than "attending a parenting skills group," the goal should focus on what the parent is expected to achieve as a result of attending the group. This helps both practitioner and client develop a mind-set toward outcome rather than simply "going through the motions" of attending different services.

Eighth, the client's level of commitment to the goal should be determined: "How important is this for you to achieve?" Commitment or motivation to a certain goal can be determined quickly through the use of a scale: "From 1 to 10, with 1 being not at all important and 10 being very important, where would you place yourself?" Hepworth et al. (2002) recommend that clients should at least be at a 7 in relation to wanting to achieve the goal; otherwise, they may not be sufficiently motivated. More discussion of scaling questions follows.

Scaling Questions

No matter what goal is targeted for work, scaling questions (adopted from solution-focused therapy and integrated with cognitive interventions to maximize their effectiveness) are useful for quantifying goals and measuring progress. "Almost any aspect of a client's life can be scaled, including progress toward finding a solution, confidence about finding a solution, motivation to work on a solution, severity of a problem, the likelihood of hurting self or another person, self-esteem, and so on" (DeJong & Miller, 1995, p. 732). The following steps are used with scaling questions: constructing the scale, rank ordering on the scale, asking relationship questions, task setting, and measurement.

Constructing the Scale

First, the client must decide on a goal for which he or she has the motivation to expend effort. Questions to orient clients toward goals include the following (Bertolino & O'Hanlon, 2002, pp. 82–83, 91):

"What is most concerning you at this point?"
"What would you like to change/have different in your life?"
"What goals do you have for yourself?"
"What did you (hope/wish/think) would be different as a result of coming to treatment?"
"How will you know when things are better?"
"How will you know when the problem is no longer a problem?"
"What will indicate to you that coming here has been successful?"
"How will you know when you longer need to come here?"
"What will be happening that will indicate to you that you can manage things on your own?"

A scale is constructed around goals the client is motivated to achieve, whether the goal is "getting the judge off my back," "feeling better," or "figuring out whether I should leave my husband." A scale from 1 to 10 is built, and the two sides are anchored, with 1 at a low point (a client overdosing, for instance, or when a parent lost control and hit a child) or, more typically, when the client made the call to get help. Detailing the negative behaviors at 1 is avoided because attention should focus on the positive behaviors the client wants rather than the negative behaviors that must be eliminated. "When the problem is no longer a problem" is 10, which is anchored with concrete behavioral indicators and, with a cognitive-behavioral integration, the positive thoughts accompanying these behavioral changes. A focus on 10 allows clients who previously viewed their problems as "hopeless" and "overwhelming" to see the possibility of change and gives them hope for the future.

Note that 10 should be realistic and achievable within a brief time frame, rather than "when everything is perfect." The solution-focused approach assumes that small changes occurring within a short time frame create a more empowered view of the self in clients and have a positive impact on other people in the system, which then leads to further change. Feasibility of goals might be determined by asking about obstacles that may impede progress. In this way, the client is slated to meet with success.

An advantage of the scales is that even vague and abstract goals, such as "feeling better," can be quantified. Indeed, writers of the motivational interviewing approach also recommend the use of scales for clients to rate the importance of doing something about the problem and their confidence that they can do something about it (Miller & Rollnick, 2002). Another abstract entity that can be used for scaling questions involves negative belief systems that get in the way of life functioning. The way to work with such belief systems through scales is to anchor the negative belief at 1 and the opposite, more functional belief at 10. For instance, a client with a problem in managing anger identifies the functional belief as "People will do what they're going to do. The only person I have control over is myself." This belief system is made concrete by asking the client to name the behaviors that accompany such a belief. The gradations of the scale and the concrete rendition of a continuum help people loosen their hold on the dichotomized thinking that underlies cognitive distortions and leads to problem behaviors. As the reader goes through the different techniques associated with the scaling intervention, he or she should be cognizant of the pitfalls involved to ensure that the intervention is maximized (Table 5.10).

Rank Ordering

The next part of the scaling intervention asks clients to rank-order themselves in relation to 10. Clients often place themselves at a number implying that change has already occurred, which allows them to see that their problems are not as all-encompassing as they previously believed. Occasionally, clients place themselves at a 1; in these cases, the practitioner can inquire about times when the problem is "less severe, frequent, intense or shorter in duration" (O'Hanlon & Weiner-Davis, 1989, p. 86) or what the client is doing to prevent problems from getting even worse.

Asking Relationship Questions

Relationship questions, questions about where others may perceive the client, are also asked: "Where would your supervisor place you on the scale?" Very often clients who suffer from cognitive distortions view themselves differently from how others experience them. Getting clients to perceive themselves from someone else's perspective may help them see themselves more realistically. With certain problems such as depression, clients tend to see others as ranking them higher on their competence and hope for the future than they themselves do (see Chapter 8). With other problems such as juvenile offending, clients tend to view themselves as doing better than what others may perceive (see Chapter 7). In either type of case, clients can be challenged to appraise themselves more appropriately through the viewpoints of other people.

Table 5.10

Scaling Questions: Pitfalls and Solutions

Deciding which goal is a priority for the client (working on the client's anger management)	Allow the client to determine the priority goal (working on managing the children's behavior)
Phrasing the goal in terms of absence of negatives ("when the client is not feeling depressed")	Phrase the goal in terms of presence of positives ("feeling better")
Not fleshing out a detailed picture of 10 (when the problem the client came for is solved)	Find at least three behavioral indicators of what will be happening when the problem is solved; use videotape analogy so that clients can visualize positives ("if I was looking through a videoplayer, what would I see you doing?"); push for behavioral specifics (rather than "husband and wife would be getting along," they would be "spending 30 minutes talking about their day together," "doing a fun activity once a week," and "eating dinner together five out of seven nights."
Talking about when everything is "perfect"	Concentrate on "when the problem the client came for is solved."
Anchoring each point in the 10-point continuum	Simply spend time anchoring 10 to get clients focused on where they are heading.
Wanting to convince the client of a different rank ordering that is perceived as unrealistic (either too high or low)	Take client's rank ordering at face value; use relationship questions to get a disparities (for example, a child might rank self at 7, but rank a parent's perception at 3); then focus on what is needed to move one number up on the scale.
Not using the full range of techniques within the scaling question	Use anchoring, rank ordering, relationship questions, exception finding, complimenting, and task setting.
Failing to track the scale over time	Measure client's progress by tracking numbers on the scale over time.
Not taking advantage of the many uses to which scaling questions can be put	Scale goals, confidence, and motivation.

Task Setting

Task setting can also be formulated from the solution-focused scale. Clients are called on to determine how they will move up one rank order during the time between sessions. Asking clients to come up with their own answers is seen as more empowering than relying solely on the training model of cognitive-behavioral therapy, in which the practitioner prescribes information or a task. Tasks may also derive from the exceptions that people have already identified. The client is asked to summarize the plan of how to apply identified resources to the problem, including strategies for coping with obstacles that may be encountered.

When tasks are difficult to formulate or when barriers present themselves, the solution-finding process (a variation of the cognitive-behavioral technique of problem solving) can be used. The steps are (a) defining the problem, (b) defining the solution hypothetically through visualization of a nonproblem future, (c) brainstorming, (d) evaluating the alternatives, (e) choosing and implementing an alternative, and (f) evaluating the alternative. Table 5.11 has more details on the solution-finding process, and Table 5.12 shows common pitfalls with their commensurate solutions.

For generalization of suggested solutions to occur in problem situations, it may be necessary at this point to teach effective reinforcement and coping skills and to use cognitive-behavioral methods of change, such as role playing and behavioral rehearsal, so that clients can practice and improve their skills (see Chapter 3).

Conveying Information in a Collaborative Way

In the strengths-and-skills-building approach described in this book, people's existing resources and unique problem-solving capacities are plumbed before any information or education is provided for skills deficits. However, this approach recognizes that people sometimes do not have the skills to enact change. Any deficits, such as communication and assertiveness skills, that might impede progress are identified and corrected. However, when people are taught skills or provided education, information should be imparted in a collaborative way so that the client is engaged in the process.

Miller and Rollnick (2002) recommend circumstances under which advice is offered: first, if a person explicitly requests such information; second, if the client gives permission to do so; or third, if the information is important to the client's safety. This guideline also follows the solution-focused therapy guideline that people's resources should be tapped for solutions. Then, when providing advice, the practitioner should use tentative language, such as the following: " 'Would it be all right if I told you

Table 5.11

Solution-Finding Process

Defining the problem	1. Breaking down complex problems into their subcomponents 2. Taking on one problem at a time 3. Describing in behavioral terms
Defining the solution	Dream question: If at night you dreamed that you used your internal resources to solve your problem, what would be the first thing you would notice in the morning when you woke up? What else? What would _____ notice about you?
Brainstorming	1. Generate and write down all possible solutions, even those that seem impossible or silly. 2. Encourage spontaneity and creativity by avoiding critical comments. 3. Ask relationship questions: What would other people say about how to solve the problem? 4. What has worked in the past?
Evaluating the alternatives	1. Mark out patently irrelevant or impossible items. 2. Discuss each viable alternative as to its advantages and disadvantages. 3. More information may be needed about certain possible solutions.
Choosing and implementing an alternative	1. Select one or more strategies that seem to maximize benefits over costs. 2. Work on skills (e.g., assertiveness, coping) that might be necessary to successfully implement a solution.
Evaluate alternatives	Asking: "What did you learn?" "How can you do more of the same?" (if successful) "What needs to happen differently next time?"

a concern that I have about what you're proposing to do?' 'I have an idea here that may or may not be relevant. Do you want to hear it?' 'There are a few things that may or may not be important to you here, and I want to make sure that you know them before we go on. You probably already know some of these, but I want to make sure. Would that be all right with you?' " (Miller & Rollnick, 2002, p. 132). Table 5.13 shows other ways to give advice to clients in a collaborative way.

When information is provided, clients should be asked to make it relevant to their own circumstances. Carroll (1998) provides suggestions on how this may be achieved:

• Ask clients to provide concrete examples from their own experiences on how material can be applied: "Can you think of a time last week when that happened to you?"

Table 5.12

Problem Solving: Pitfalls and Solutions

Pitfalls	Solutions
Taking on a superficial problem	Try to find the real problem. (If being late to work is caused by children not being ready in the morning or having conflict with spouse in the morning, then the latter problems should be addressed.)
Making the problem too vague and general (my teen daughter is impossible)	Take on one specific problem at a time, phrased in the positive (to get my teen daughter to do her chores); break complex problems into separate components.
During brainstorming, not coming up with enough solutions	Allow the client to come up with as many solutions as possible; mention that they can be silly, creative, outlandish, etc.; ask the client relationship questions (what would other people he or she knows say is a possible solution); make an off-the-wall solution to spur the creative process; if more than one person is taking part in the process, make sure to get feedback from everyone.
During brainstorming, people start criticizing ideas	Remind clients that this is the brainstorming phrase, and later they can evaluate their ideas; when people criticize, ask them to come up with an alternative solution instead.
An idea is selected, but not implemented	Flesh out the details of the plan in writing, practice any skills necessary, determine barriers, and gain a commitment from the client

Note. Some ideas adapted from "Parent-adolescent conflict and relationship discord," by S. Foster and A. Robin, 1998, in *Treatment of Childhood Disorders* (2nd ed., pp. 601–646), New York: Guilford.

- Elicit clients' views on how they might use particular skills: "Now that we've talked about this, what do you think would work best for you? Which of these techniques have you used in the past? Is there any other way you've tried to manage this?"
- Elicit clients' reactions to the material: "Does this seem like it's an important issue for us to be working on right now, or do you have something else in mind?"
- Ask clients to describe the skill in their own words: "Just to make sure you're confident about what you want to do, can you tell me what you you're going to do when you tackle this?"
- Pay attention to clients' verbal and nonverbal cues (e.g., lack of eye

Table 5.13

Ways to Qualify Advice Giving

Practitioners should first ask themselves:	"Have I elicited the client's own ideas and knowledge on this subject?"
	"Is what I am going to convey important to the client's safety or likely to enhance the client's motivation for change?"
Obtain client's permission:	"Would it be all right if I told you a concern that I have about what you're proposing to do?"
	"I have an idea here that may or may not be relevant. Do you want to hear it?"
	"I think I understand your perspective on this. I wonder if it would be okay for me to tell you a few things that occur to me as I listen to you, which you might want to consider."
	"I don't know if this will matter to you, or even make sense, but I am a little worried about your plan. Would you mind if I explained why?"
	"There are a few things that may or may not be important to you here, and I want to make sure that you know them before we go on. You probably already know some of these, but I want to make sure. Would that be all right with you?"
Qualify advice:	"I don't know if this would work for you or not, but I can give you an idea of what some other people have done in your situation."
	"This may or may not make sense to you, but it's one possibility. You'll have to judge whether it applies to you."
	"I can give you an idea, but I think you'd have to try it out to see if it would work for you."
	"All I can give you, of course, is my own opinion. You're really the one who has to find out what works for you."
If a person directly asks for advice, show reluctance initially:	"I'll be happy to give you some ideas, but I don't want to get in the way of your own creative thinking, and you're the expert on you. I'm not sure if you really want or need my advice. Maybe you have some ideas of your own about what to do."
	"Of course I can tell you what I think, if you really want to know. But I don't want you to feel like I'm telling you what you have to do."
Offer a cluster of options:	"Well, there really isn't any way that works for everybody. I can tell you about some approaches that other people have used successfully, and you can see which of those might fit you best."
	"Let me describe a number of possibilities, and you tell me which of these makes the most sense for you."

contact, one-word responses, yawning): "I notice that you keep looking out the window, and I was wondering what your thoughts are on what we're talking about today."

Tracking Tasks

When clients have their next contact with the helper, the practitioner is advised to check in about completion of the task, spending at least 5 minutes discussing the assignment to illustrate its importance (Carroll, 1998). If the practitioner does not attend to tasks, clients will conclude that they are not very important and will not take them seriously. When people say that they were unable to complete or did not get around to the agreed-upon task, the practitioner should reinforce homework behavior rather than noncompliance. When practitioners say, "Oh, that's okay" or "No problem," clients again get the message that tasks are not important. Instead, time should be spent discussing what got in the way and negotiating the task for the following week. It could be, for instance, that the task was too ambitious for the client, and it needs to be broken down into smaller, more manageable pieces. Webster-Stratton and Herbert (1993) have a series of recommended questions to ask when the client has difficulty following through with tasks.

What makes it hard for you to do the assignment?
How have you overcome this problem in past?
What advice would you give to someone else who has this problem? ✓
What can you do to make it easier for you to complete the assignment this week?
What assignment might be more useful for you?
What thoughts come to mind when you think about this assignment?
What makes it hard to do?
Does this seem relevant to your life?
How could we make this more helpful?

If the task did not work out as planned, the practitioner should convey that there is no such thing as a failure. Instead, the focus can be: "What did you learn? What needs to be done differently next time?" This approach encourages the client to continue testing out new skills and activities.

Progress continues to be monitored on the solution-focused scale, which makes movement toward goals quantifiable and measurable. The practitioner may find that the client has progressed on the scale without even having completed the agreed-upon task. It might be that the client has a new perspective on the problem or that he or she has done something else differently that week that accounts for change. The solution-focused scale can be used in subsequent sessions to track progress over time and to determine when goals have been met.

Evaluation and Termination

Because change is oriented toward a brief time frame in the strengths-and-skills-building model, work is oriented toward termination at the beginning of intervention. Questions include "What needs to happen so you don't need to come back to see me?" and "What will be different when therapy has been successful?" (Berg, 1994). Goal achievement is evaluated through discussion of progress, scores on strength-or problem-based measurement tools, or incremental changes on client-devised scales. Once clients have maintained changes on the small, concrete goals they have set, the practitioner and client start to discuss plans for termination, as it is assumed that achievement of these goals will lead to further positive changes in the client's life.

Termination, guided by the accomplishment of goals (Murphy, 1997), is geared toward helping clients identify strategies so that progress will be maintained and momentum developed for further change. Although the practitioner does not want to imply that relapse is inevitable, the client must be prepared with strategies to enact if temptation presents itself or if the client begins to slip into old behaviors. Therefore, it is during termination that *possibility* rather than *definitive* phrasing is used. For example, "What *would* be the first thing you'd notice *if* you started to find things slipping back?" "What *could* you do to prevent things from getting any further?" and "*If* you have the urge to do drugs again, what *could* you do to make sure you didn't use?" might be typical inquiries to elicit strategies to use if there is a return to old behavior (O'Hanlon & Weiner-Davis, 1989). Bringing up the possibility of temptation to return to old patterns is a way to normalize people's fears about what may happen with their hard-earned changes (Bertolino & O'Hanlon, 2002). Once potential obstacles are identified, the practitioner can explore with the client how they may be handled. Cognitive-behavioral methods, such as rehearsal, may also be necessary to prepare the client for difficult situations.

Termination further involves building on the changes that have occurred, with the hope they will continue into the future. Selekman (1993, 1997) has proposed a number of such questions, including "With all the changes you are making, what will I see if I was a fly on your wall six months from now?" and "With all the changes you are making, what will you be telling me if I run into you at the convenience store six months from now?" (Selekman, 1997). Questions are phrased to set up the expectation that change will continue to happen.

Another way to handle termination, especially when a client withdraws from services before the agreed-upon time period, is to write the person a letter. White and Epston (1990) have discussed the importance of narrative methods, particularly letter writing, to emphasize client strengths.

Many agencies send out form letters to clients who terminate prematurely. Practitioners may consider adding a strengths-based portion to such letters, affirming clients' resources and successes, delineating the exceptions that have been identified, and highlighting the goals clients have for their lives and the progress they have made thus far. If a client is involuntary, the practitioner may want to compliment the person for the courage to approach services and to explore and consider change. In summary fashion, the practitioner may also cover the advantages and disadvantages for continuing a certain problem behavior, empathizing with the struggle involved. The practitioner should strive to end on a positive note, emphasizing the positive goals clients have for themselves and the wisdom they have for making choices that are in their best interest. (See Chapters 7 and 8 for examples of this technique.)

▆▆▆▆ Cultural Diversity

Much attention now focuses on helpers and clinicians gaining "cross-cultural competence." However, as DeJong and Berg (2001) state, "Each individual is a composite of several dimensions of diversity (class, ethnicity, gender, physical ability/disability, sexual orientation, race, religion, and so forth)" (p. 257). Therefore, practitioners may have knowledge of and experience with a particular population, but they do not know a particular individual with a unique history, traits, strengths, and limitations. To make assumptions about that person because of cultural membership is tantamount to stereotyping. Instead, the client is considered the expert; practitioners should respectfully inquire about clients' worldview and distinctive ways of solving problems (DeJong & Berg, 2001).

Although ferreting out personal biases toward cultural groups and gaining knowledge about a particular group's history, customs, strengths, and struggles are encouraged, there is no formulaic way to understand culture. Further, most available evidence is in the form of case reports, with a lack of empirical knowledge guiding professionals on how to proceed (Goldberg, 2000). Therefore, Dean (2001) proposes "that we distrust the experience of [cultural] competence and replace it with a state of mind in which we are interested, and open but always tentative about what we understand."

Summary

This chapter outlined and detailed the phases of the helping process of the strengths-and-skills-building model. The helping process comprises engagement, exploration of the problem, exploration of the solution, taking action, and evaluation and termination. The reader can see in the case applications that follow in the chapters ahead that not all techniques from each phase are employed in work with each client. Rather, techniques should be selected that fit the client situation and the particular time frame of the helping relationship. For instance, if a practitioner sees a client in a one-time crisis intervention contact, the emphasis may be on techniques that emphasize identifying and bolstering strengths. If a client is already motivated to do something about the problem, then motivational interviewing techniques may not be seen as necessary and instead other problem exploration techniques, such as a functional analysis, may be highlighted.

In addition, the phases of the helping process serve as constructive parameters to define helping activities and direct focus but are not rigidly sequenced as separate or distinct intervention units. As Matto states in Chapter 9, "Assessment is not relegated to intake but is ongoing, treatment goals may change or be revisited and modified, and client motivation can naturally be expected to wax and wane across the trajectory of the intervention. Problem-exploration and solution-finding opportunities are not necessarily linear; rather, strengths are identified and solution pathways constructed at all points in the process."

The crux of the skills-and-strengths-building model is that while people have strengths and resources, they also may need help in learning specific strategies and skills. The practitioner works in a collaborative way, with respect for the client's perspective and unique strengths, to help build on existing resources, as well as to identify areas of limitation on which the client is motivated to work. Collaboration and respect for the client's resources are paramount throughout the phases of the helping process.

References

Berg, I. K. (1994). *Family-based services: A solution-focused approach.* New York: W. W. Norton.

Berg-Weger, M., Rubio D. M., & Tebb, S. S. (2001). Strengths-based practice with family caregivers of the chronically ill: Qualitative insights. *Families in Society, 82*(3), 263–272.

Bertolino, B., & O'Hanlon, B. (2002). *Collaborative, competency-based counseling and therapy.* Boston: Allyn & Bacon.

Carroll, K. (1998). *A cognitive-behavioral approach: Treating cocaine addiction.* Retrieved August 28, 2001, from http://www.drugabuse.gov/TXManuals/CBT/CBT1.html

Christensen, D., Todahl, J., & Barrett, W. (1999). *Solution-based casework: An introduction to clinical and case management skills in casework practice.* New York: Aldine de Gruyter.

Clark, M. (1997). Interviewing for solutions. *Corrections Today, 59*(3), 98–102.

Connors, G., Donovan, D., & DiClemente, C. (2001). Substance abuse treatment and the stages of change: Selecting and planning interventions. New York: Guilford.

Corcoran, J. (2000). *Evidence-based social work practice with families: A lifespan approach.* New York: Springer.

Dean, R. (2001). The myth of cross-cultural competence. *Families in Society, 82,* 623–631.

De Jong, P., & Berg, I. K. (2001). *Interviewing for solutions* (2nd ed.). Pacific Grove, CA: Brooks/Cole.

De Jong, P., & Miller, S. D. (1995). How to interview clients for strengths. *Social Work, 40*(6), 729–736.

Dyes, M. A., & Neville, K. E. (2000). Taming trouble and other tales: Using externalized characters in solution-focused therapy. *Journal of Systemic Therapies, 19,* 74–81.

Folkman, S. (1984). Personal control and stress and coping processes: A theoretical analysis. *Journal of Personality and Social Psychology, 46,* 839-852.

Foster, S., & Robin, A. (1998). Parent-adolescent conflict and relationship discord. In E. Mash & R. Barkley (Eds.), *Treatment of childhood disorders,* (2nd ed., pp. 601–646). New York: Guilford.

Goldberg, M. (2000). Conflicting principles in multicultural social work. *Families in Society, 81,* 12.

Gotlib, I., & Abramson, L. (1999). Attributional theories of emotion. In T. Dalgleish & M. Power (Eds.), *Handbook of cognition and emotion* (pp. 613–636). New York: Wiley.

Greene, G., Lee, M. Y., Mentzer, R., Pinnell, S., & Niles, D. (1998). Miracles, dreams, and empowerment: A brief therapy practice note. *Families in Society, 79,* 395–399.

Greene, G. J., Lee, M. Y., Trask, R., & Rheinscheld, J. (1996). Client strengths and crisis intervention: A solution-focused approach. *Crisis Intervention, 3,* 43–63.

Hepworth, D. H., Rooney, R., & Larsen, J. (2002). *Direct social work practice: Theory & skills* (6th ed.). Belmont, CA: Brooks/Cole.

Hudson, P. O., & O'Hanlon, W. H. (1993). *Rewriting love stories: Brief marital therapy.* New York: W. W. Norton.

Lazarus, R., & Folkman, S. (1984). *Stress, appraisal, and coping.* New York: Springer.

Marsh, D., Lefley, H., Evans-Rhodes, D., Ansell, V., Doerzbacher, B., La-Barbera, L., et al. (1996). The family experience of mental illness: Evidence for resilience. *Psychiatric Rehabilitation Journal, 20*, 3–12.

Miller, W., & Rollnick, S. (2002). *Motivational interviewing: Preparing people to change addictive behavior* (2nd ed.). New York: Guilford.

Murphy, J. (1997). *Solution-focused counseling in middle and high schools.* Alexandria, VA: American Counseling Association.

O'Hanlon, W. H., & Weiner-Davis, M. (1989). *In search of solutions: A new direction in psychotherapy.* New York: W. W. Norton.

Schulz, R., Newsom, J., Mittelmark, M., Burton, L., Hirsch, C., & Jackson, S. (1997). Health effects of care giving: The caregiver health effects study: An ancillary study of the cardiovascular study. *Annal of Behavioral Medicine, 19*, 110–116.

Selekman, M. D. (1993). *Pathways to change: Brief therapy solutions with difficult adolescents.* New York: Guilford.

Selekman, M. D. (1997). *Solution-focused therapy with children: Harnessing family strengths for systemic change.* New York: Guilford.

Spiegler, M. (1993). *Contemporary behavior therapy* (2nd ed.). Belmont, CA: Brooks/Cole.

Webster-Stratton, C., & Herbert, M. (1993). What really happens in parent training? *Behavior Modification, 17*, 407–457.

Weiner, B. (1985). *Human motivation.* New York: Springer-Verlag.

White, M., & Epston, D. (1990). *Narrative means to therapeutic ends.* New York: W. W. Norton.

6 Learning the Model
Applications to a Hospital Setting

The purpose of this chapter is to demonstrate the strengths-and-skills-building model—its principles and practice techniques. It shows how the model builds on basic helping skills, such as effective listening, for strategic effect. All examples in this chapter were drawn from social service work in a hospital setting, which leads to the secondary purpose of the chapter—to illustrate how the strengths-and-skills-building model can be applied in medical placements.

Often in social service medical practice, there is only a single contact focused on assessing needs, planning discharge, and providing referrals for ongoing services. The following cases show how a social services practitioner, untrained in the strengths-and-skills-building model, approached contacts with clients. After each case scenario is presented, commentary explains how the model could have been applied. Finally, a case study demonstrates how the strengths-and-skills-building model can be put into practice.

Case I

"Filip" is a 50-year-old man recently admitted to the hospital for liver failure due to a history of alcohol and drug abuse. Filip was hospitalized after discharging himself from a medical shelter before he was ready to be released. He was born in Argentina but has lived in the United States for 30 years and is a U.S. citizen; he currently lives in Virginia, and his family of origin lives in New York. Filip's wife is deceased, and his two children, who live in Tennessee, won't talk to him. He has attended some college. Filip no longer has a place to live because he lost his apartment 6 months ago.

The medical shelter will not allow Filip to return. The practitioner's role is to help him find a place to stay where staff will also take care of his medical needs. After the practitioner has gathered some initial background information, the following interview takes place:

PRACTITIONER: What did you have surgery for?

FILIP: I think I had fluid in my lungs.

PRACTITIONER: Do you know why you had fluid in your lungs?

FILIP: It has to do with my illness. [He reveals a large scar on his stomach.]

PRACTITIONER: I see.

FILIP: It's a nasty one.

PRACTITIONER: Do you know what is going on with you medically?

FILIP: I have lung problems and liver problems.

PRACTITIONER: Do you still use alcohol?

FILIP: No, I don't drink or use any drugs. I know I can't.

PRACTITIONER: Have you received any treatment for your drug and alcohol problems?

FILIP: Yes, and I don't hang around my friends anymore who do drink because it's not good for me.

PRACTITIONER: I am happy to hear that. You need to take care of yourself.

FILIP: I just can't believe I let my life get like this, and I have no one, and I have nothing.

PRACTITIONER: I hear what you're saying. It must be difficult, but you can take care of yourself now.

FILIP: Yes.

PRACTITIONER: Do you have anyone to stay with now?

FILIP: No, my family is in New York. They want me to get better here first.

PRACTITIONER: If you could go back to the medical shelter, would you?

Commentary

The practitioner is focused on her agenda of ensuring the client has a place to stay after discharge and of making sure he understands that he can no longer use alcohol because of his medical condition. However, Miller and Rollnick (2002) suggest that a worker provide an agenda but express it in tentative terms—that is, invite the client to share his or her concerns. For example, after introducing herself, the practitioner could have stated, "My job is to talk with you about how you're doing right now and to help you figure out where you can go after you are discharged, so that you can continue to recover. You've been through surgery, and that takes some time and rest to get over. But that might not be what's on your mind right now, so we can also talk about what is most concerning you at the moment." This opening statement begins a collaborative process in which the client has an equal say in what is being discussed.

In this case, the priority for the client may be his physical pain. Filip does allude to the fact that he has a "nasty" scar and even shows it to the worker. Although we don't know from the scenario what motivates him to reveal the scar, it could have been to impress on the practitioner that he is feeling physically debilitated. Filip also volunteers details about his emotional state ("I just can't believe I let my life get like this, and I have no one, and I have nothing") even though the practitioner does not ask him questions about his feelings or state of mind—questions that typically start an interview. The practitioner attempts to show empathy ("I hear what you're saying. It must be difficult . . .") but quickly follows with premature reassurance ("but you can take care of yourself now"). This seems to have the effect of shutting down any further exploration of Filip's feelings, as he merely responds, "Yes." Filip's feelings could have been reflected with this statement: "You're feeling lonely and sad because of all you have lost from alcohol." A reflecting statement might have encouraged Filip to explore the losses he sustained from alcohol use.

Another opportunity for a reflecting statement occurs when Filip says he has no one to stay with, and his family wants him "to get better here first." The worker could have said, "You seem to understand why they're taking this position." This again might have provided an entrée into the losses caused by alcohol abuse, specifically Filip's impaired relationships (for instance, his children in Tennessee won't speak to him). This might have led to a discussion of the values he has held in his life, followed by an exploration of the discrepancy between these values and his alcohol use.

This interview consisted mainly of closed-ended questions that were designed to lead the client to the responses that the practitioner wants: "What did you have surgery for?" "Do you know why you had fluid in your lungs?" "Do you still use alcohol?" "Have you received any treatment for your drug and alcohol problems?" "Do you have anyone to stay with now?" "If you could go back to the medical shelter, would you?" Instead, open-ended questions should have been used ("How are you feeling?" "Where are you on your drinking now?" "What is your understanding of your medical condition?") to allow Filip to state and explore his concerns.

Another line of inquiry the practitioner could have pursued is the reasons Filip left the medical shelter and what he sees as the advantages and disadvantages of staying there. This is important to explore because it might indicate how much control Filip has over his drinking problem (for instance, he might have left the shelter in order to drink or use drugs). This information might result in a better assessment of the type of facility Filip needs and could circumvent some potential problems at the next placement.

The practitioner could have inquired further about the support systems available to Filip. This information is critical in determining where he should be placed. Proximity to his support system would help him recover from his illness and maintain sobriety. The worker does discover in her interview that Filip no longer associates with substance-abusing peers. This information deserves more attention and perhaps an indirect compliment: "A lot of people find that very difficult, to stop hanging around a group of people that use. How were you able to do that?" Acknowledging Filip's hard work would have encouraged him to discuss the strengths that he used. Filip also mentions having been in treatment previously. The practitioner could have gathered more information about the treatment, such as when it occurred and in what ways it was helpful and not helpful for him. These questions position Filip in the expert role in determining what is best for him.

Case 2

"Pete" is a 56-year-old White man. He lives with his wife, whom he says is a supportive partner. Pete has a 30-year history of alcohol abuse but has recently decreased the amount of alcohol he drinks to four to five beers per week. He was admitted to the hospital after a recent doctor's appointment; tests have determined that his liver has ceased functioning, and he will need a transplant. For Pete to be placed on the transplant list, he must completely quit drinking. The practitioner's agenda is to discuss Pete's current drinking and to provide him with information on alcohol rehabilitation.

PETE: I don't really have time to talk. I'm going for a procedure.
PRACTITIONER: Why don't we talk until you have to leave?
PETE: Well, if you think that would work.
PRACTITIONER: I have some information for you. I wondered how you are feeling.
PETE: You're from social work? The doctor insists my liver is ruined because I'm drinking. I used to drink a lot, but other things impact my liver.

PRACTITIONER: What do you mean by that?

PETE: I used to drink hard liquor, beer—everything.

PRACTITIONER: When did you start drinking?

PETE: When I was 20.

PRACTITIONER: Do you still drink?

PETE: A little, but not like I used to.

PRACTITIONER: How much do you drink?

PETE: Four to five beers a week.

PRACTITIONER: Do you understand why it's important for you to quit totally?

PETE: I do.

PRACTITIONER: Do you think you can quit?

PETE: Not on my own. I think I would need help.

PRACTITIONER: That's good that you recognize you need help. There are a lot of programs and resources available.

PETE: I know.

PRACTITIONER: Have you had treatment in the past?

PETE: Yes, I went to AA.

PRACTITIONER: How long ago was that?

PETE: In 1997—I went for about a year.

PRACTITIONER: Why did you stop going?

PETE: I didn't like the religious part.

Commentary

This interview gets off to a poor start. When the client says he has another appointment, the practitioner probably should ask if the client would prefer to talk at a more convenient time. This would convey to Pete that he has some control over the process. Instead, Pete seems to become immediately defensive about his drinking. He may feel forced into a discussion and therefore adopt a resistant or hostile attitude. Furthermore, the "procedure" Pete is about to undergo certainly will distract him from an open discussion.

When Pete says that things other than drinking impact his liver, the practitioner asks an appropriate clarifying question: "What do you mean by that?" However, her subsequent questions are all closed-ended: "When did you start drinking?" "Do you still drink?" "Do you understand why it's important for you to quit totally?" "Do you think you can quit?" "Have you had treatment in the past?" "How long ago was that?" Another closed-ended question, "Why did you stop going?" is also problematic because "why" questions imply a judgmental attitude, which may arouse further defensiveness. Had the practitioner asked open-ended questions, she might have elicited Pete's understanding of his medical position and the consequences of continued drinking. The worker might have asked the following open-ended questions: "What is your understanding of your medical condition?" "What needs to happen from here?" "What is your plan for future treatment?"

Miller and Rollnick's (2002) general principle is that an interview should not be solely questions, and that for every question three statements by the worker should follow. Some examples of statements the practitioner might make take the form of reflecting comments. For example:

PETE: I used to drink hard liquor, beer—everything.
PRACTITIONER: So you used to drink more than you do now.

PETE: The doctor insists my liver is ruined because I'm drinking. I used to drink a lot, but other things impact my liver.
PRACTITIONER: It's not just alcohol that has ruined your liver.

PETE: I don't think I could quit on my own. I think I would need help.
PRACTITIONER: So you recognize that you might need help to quit.

PETE: I went to AA for about a year, but I stopped because I didn't like the religious part.
PRACTITIONER: AA worked for you, and you struggled with the religious part.

This last statement is an example of a double-sided reflection in which two sides of a client's ambivalence are reflected in the same comment. The statement captures both sides of the client's experience about attending AA, encouraging the client to acknowledge the positive side of the experience without contradicting or arguing with the client.

Furthermore, the practitioner could have evoked some of Pete's potential strengths when he mentioned that he was able to stop drinking hard liquor and reduce his overall drinking: "How were you able to do this?" "What resources did you use to get this to happen?" Taking time to reinforce and attend to Pete's strengths will encourage his further efforts in this direction.

If Pete had revealed that he has simply substituted beer for hard liquor, then the technique of reframing might be used. In reframing, the client's argument that there is not a problem ("I now drink beer rather than hard liquor") is turned around so that it becomes an argument for change ("Actually, a serving of each type of drink has the same alcohol content, so you may be consuming as much alcohol now as you were before").

It is not the practitioner's job to instruct the client that he must not drink anymore; it is to get him to consider if he is willing to stop drinking.

If the client is hesitant to commit to quitting drinking, a decisional balance might be constructed: "I know this is a lot to give up right now. Let's look a little more closely at where you stand on this. What do you get out of drinking? What are some of the not so good things about drinking?" The practitioner and client then spend time together detailing some of these pros and cons, which the practitioner should write down for the client's further edification. This helps the client clarify in his own mind how his drinking will affect his medical condition, as well as how it will affect other areas of his life.

The client reveals that he did avail himself of Alcoholics Anonymous (AA) for a year, which is a significant amount of time. Rather than focusing on why he stopped, the practitioner should have concentrated on how he was able to attend for so long, even though he struggled with some of the philosophy. What did he get out of going? What parts of it were helpful for him? The practitioner also could have validated his experience—that many people struggle with the religious aspects of AA: "What did you hear people say about this in meetings?" "How did people resolve their struggle?" "What did your sponsor say about this part of it?" It is also important to get the client's input on what would work better for him when he tries to make a change.

As the interview draws to a close, the worker should summarize their conversation, expressing the pros and cons Pete has identified about alcohol use and the value of taking care of his health and continuing to be around for his wife. At that point, the client might be more amenable to hearing about the different available treatment options.

Case 3

"LaTrice" is a 35-year-old African American woman who was released from prison and put on parole 4 weeks previously. LaTrice came to the emergency room when she experienced numbness in her leg. Tests have revealed that LaTrice has a blood clot in her lung and will need to receive injections for treatment.

LaTrice served 3 years in prison for dealing drugs. She is currently homeless and without an income, and she has previously been diagnosed with bipolar disorder and HIV. Although LaTrice lives in Virginia, her mother and sister live in Georgia. She has an uncle who lives 2 hours away, but she doesn't want to contact him.

The practitioner will help LaTrice address her multiple needs: shelter, medication to treat her blood clot, substance abuse treatment, and HIV services.

LaTRICE: I don't understand what's going on.

PRACTITIONER: I'm trying to get medication for you as well as find you a shelter or a place for you to go.

LaTRICE: Well, I don't understand why there was stuff in my urine.

PRACTITIONER: What do you mean?

LaTRICE: The nurse said my urine was positive for drugs, and that's why I'm still here.

PRACTITIONER: Well, that's not necessarily why you are still here.

LaTRICE: My parole officer said I could go to an aftercare program.

PRACTITIONER: Well, that was if you had a clear drug screen. Your drug screen did show a positive result for barbiturates.

LaTRICE: I don't know why. I haven't used except once.

PRACTITIONER: So, you are saying you used drugs only once recently?

LaTRICE: Yes, and I was honest about that.

PRACTITIONER: Well, the urine showed a positive screen for barbiturates.

LaTRICE: Well, I am just going to leave. I don't need you. I don't need to be here. You can't arrest me.

PRACTITIONER: No, I'm not trying to arrest you. I am trying to help you find a place to stay and get your medication. You can leave if you want to leave. That is your choice. But you really should consider the consequences of leaving without your meds and with no place to go and no way to get there.

LaTRICE: Does my parole officer know there was a drug test?

PRACTITIONER: Yes, and she knows it was positive.

LaTRICE: Well, I'm just leaving—I don't need this.

PRACTITIONER: Please think about your actions before you go. If you can wait just a little while longer, I will have your meds, and I will give you a voucher to get to a shelter.

LaTRICE: Okay, okay, okay.

Commentary

This scenario is another example of how important it is to set a flexible agenda. In this case, the practitioner is most concerned about obtaining the client's medication to treat her blood clot and getting the client to a shelter. These are important tasks but seem to blind the practitioner, at least for a time, to the fact that LaTrice is most worried about getting arrested and being sent back to prison.

It is important to side with the client rather than working at cross-purposes with her. First, to avoid a confrontational situation, the practitioner could have complimented LaTrice for knowing she needed medical attention and seeking help. Also, it's probable that the rules of confidentiality would dictate that if LaTrice came in for medical treatment on her own, her parole officer wouldn't necessarily need to be informed of a positive drug screen. That her parole officer has been informed makes LaTrice feel that she is being punished for seeking help for her medical needs. Rather than getting into an argument about the specifics of the drug use, the practitioner could have sided with the client ("What can we do to show your parole officer that this is working out?").

The client also reveals an implicit strength when she says she has used drugs only once in the 4 weeks since her release. The practitioner could have explored with her how she was able to overcome temptation for the majority of this period. This focus would have emphasized what the client has been doing well, rather than underscoring LaTrice's dirty drug screen and her numerous problems. This strategy might have also garnered more cooperation and less defensiveness from the client.

Another avenue for intervention could have involved coping questions. The client has many overwhelming stressors affecting her simultaneously. How has she been able to manage? How has she been able to face all this at once? These questions would have also revealed some of the strengths of which the client has availed herself. If LaTrice does not volunteer information about her support system, the practitioner should inquire about her relatives, her non-substance-abusing peers, or other supportive persons in her life.

Case 4

"Rena" is a 29-year-old Pakistani woman who recently moved to the United States after an arranged marriage. Rena, who lives in Virginia, has no job, no income, and only one relative other than her husband in the United States—who lives in Vermont. Rena resides with her husband in an efficiency apartment. Her husband attends a state university located in the area.

The practitioner received a referral from the outpatient clinic of the hospital regarding concerns that Rena is being abused by her husband. The practitioner phones Rena to discuss the violence and to provide information about available resources.

RENA: He is hitting me all the time, and he pulls the phone out of the wall when I try to get help.
PRACTITIONER: Can you get out of the apartment when you are arguing? Can you stand near the door so you can walk out?
RENA: I could. I did go to the neighbors' once, but then my husband was pounding on their door.
PRACTITIONER: Do you know what to do to keep yourself safe?

RENA: I am not sure.

PRACTITIONER: You should stay out of the kitchen and bathroom and stay near the door when you argue.

RENA: Okay.

PRACTITIONER: Do you feel safe now?

RENA: Yes, because he isn't here. But he hits me all the time.

PRACTITIONER: You know, nobody has a right to hit you.

RENA: I learned it is against the law in the U.S. when I went to the counselor at the university.

PRACTITIONER: So you have talked to someone about this?

RENA: Yes, I don't want it to be like this.

PRACTITIONER: Have you thought of a safety plan?

RENA: I don't know.

PRACTITIONER: Well, we can talk about it.

Commentary

After introductions, the practitioner could have started the interview with an initial assessment of the client's immediate safety. What is her current level of concern? Is she safe at the moment to talk? The practitioner doesn't inquire about this until later in the interview ("Do you feel safe now?"). However, if the client's safety is not immediately assessed, the phone conversation might place a family violence victim at even greater risk.

In this scenario, the practitioner is quick to give advice ("Can you get out of the apartment when you are arguing? Can you stand near the door so you could walk out?" "You should stay out of the kitchen and bathroom and stay near the door when you argue"). This is important information to convey, but the practitioner should listen and assess the level of risk in terms of frequency, duration, and severity, as well as display empathy. Open-ended questions may be useful to uncover this information, rather than the closed-ended questions the practitioner typically uses in this scenario.

Rena talks about different ways she has tried to deal with the violence. Had the practitioner made a more concerted effort to examine these previous problem-solving attempts, she would be acknowledging Rena as an active participant in making efforts to improve her situation. Also, gathering information about previous attempts to solve the problem would allow the practitioner to focus information and education on avenues the client has not pursued. The advice the practitioner does offer will be more useful, which may help to establish trust and credibility.

The practitioner could have also explored with the client what she viewed as her options. What kind of social support does Rena have available to her? She has a relative in Vermont. Is this a possible resource? Rena also mentions going to the neighbors' to keep safe and seeking counseling at the university her husband attends. The practitioner and the client can discuss the reasons she went to counseling, what she learned from that encounter, and whether she plans to continue. She could be complimented for acting so resourcefully when she is a stranger to the country and this is all so unfamiliar to her.

If the client talks about leaving the relationship, the reasons for leaving should be discussed, as well as the other side—the reasons she has for staying in the relationship. This decisional balance may reveal what needs to be addressed so that the client feels she has more options available to her. For instance, the client may talk about her lack of money as a possible barrier to leaving the relationship. The practitioner might then ask the client's permission to have another conversation about exploring these options, which might include the problem-solving process. Or she might refer her to resources for battered women that will help address these concerns.

In this scenario, the practitioner brings up the safety plan on two occasions, but it seems apparent from the client's responses ("I am not sure"; "I don't know") that Rena doesn't understand what a safety plan is. The practitioner should have explained that, while Rena has obviously taken some steps to protect herself, together they can develop these ideas further into a plan to ensure that she is kept as safe as possible from violence.

The practitioner can also explore with the client how family violence is handled in her native land and in the United States, as well as the differing cultural values and beliefs the couple might have. Despite cultural differences, Rena seems open to accessing the available resources to deal with the violent situation in which she has found herself, and she deserves a lot of credit for her efforts. (For more on intervention with victims of domestic violence, see Chapter 11.)

Case 5

"Linda" is a 40-year-old White woman who is in the hospital after she overdosed on prescription drugs when faced with eviction from her apartment, her home for 11 years. Linda then contracted an infection and remains in the hospital. She will be sent to the psychiatric floor when she is medically cleared.

Linda has not worked in 15 years because of a chronic illness (rheumatoid arthritis), but she is working on her second master's degree. Her mother lives in the area, and her father is deceased. She has contact with one of her two sisters but reports limited contact with the other sister and her mother. Linda reports that none of her family members will allow her to live with them. Other members of her support system include one friend and her therapist.

This is a second contact between the practitioner and the client. Its purpose is securing Linda enough income so that she can support herself.

PRACTITIONER: I wanted to follow up with you regarding your father's pension plan. You and I had discussed this as a possible source of income for you.

LINDA: Did you get in touch with my ex-husband?

PRACTITIONER: Yes, he gave me the information, and I have found out what we need to do to proceed.

LINDA: Well, good. I can't talk to him, you know.

PRACTITIONER: Yes, you have mentioned that. How do you feel about that, Linda?

LINDA: It makes me very sad. He was my best friend for years.

PRACTITIONER: I can understand how that must be hard. He did give me the information, and we can move forward with the process as soon as possible.

LINDA: Okay, let's see. We need my doctor to give you some information.

PRACTITIONER: Yes, we do.

LINDA: You know, I wasn't planning to be in here. I mean, I have two master's degrees, and I spent the last 2 years vacationing in Cambridge.

PRACTITIONER: So your ex-husband was nice?

LINDA: He supported me all these years. After he stopped, I lost my apartment.

PRACTITIONER: How do you feel about him not supporting you anymore?

LINDA: It makes me sad, but he had no choice. His new wife said she would divorce him if he kept talking to me and helping me.

PRACTITIONER: Well, it's important that we work to get you some resources that help you with taking care of yourself.

Commentary

While following up on the plan for finding options for the client's income, the practitioner successfully elicited the client's feelings about the circumstances she finds herself in. However, there could have been more reflection of the client's statements and feelings. As Hudson and O'Hanlon (1993) point out, if people are not validated, then they will not move on; however, if all they are is validated, they will not move on. Some examples of productive reflection follow.

LINDA: I just got kicked out of my apartment. I don't have a job. I'm in pain all the time. My family doesn't like me. I can't believe I'm here.

PRACTITIONER: You sound really overwhelmed by all that's happening.

LINDA: My ex-husband has been paying for my apartment since I've been in school. But now his wife won't let him.

PRACTITIONER: So now you're in a situation where you have to support yourself, and you feel ill prepared.

LINDA: You know, I wasn't planning to be in here. I mean, I have two master's degrees, and I spent the last 2 years vacationing in Cambridge.

PRACTITIONER: You're feeling shocked that with everything you have going on, you find yourself in here.

LINDA: I've never had to support myself. We were married for 15 years. I don't know how I'm going to do this.

PRACTITIONER: It's scary to think about supporting yourself.

PRACTITIONER: How do you feel about him not supporting you anymore?

LINDA: It makes me sad, but he had no choice. His new wife said she would divorce him if he kept talking to me and helping me.

PRACTITIONER: There's a real sense of loss since he not only supported you; you said he was your best friend. You're sad, but you do understand his position.

Despite the client's recent circumstances and her long-term unemployment, the client has a number of apparent strengths. For example, she has one master's degree and is working on another. From these accomplishments, we can assume that she is intelligent and has high motivation, a strong work ethic, and problem-solving skills if she is able to meet the demands of graduate school. These possible strengths can be elicited, reinforced, and then applied to the problem areas she is facing now, such as her loss of income and her present homelessness.

More discussion of social support is warranted. Is the friend she mentions an option for temporary housing? How can Linda later reciprocate if the friend is available for this? What about her graduate program and her classmates? Are there resources available at the university, such as a listing of people looking for roommates? Are there people in her classes who might be available for support? What needs to happen with her family to improve relations?

The "miracle question" or one of its variations might help Linda because she finds herself so overwhelmed by her present circumstances. The miracle question could help Linda envision a future without these problems. It also might point the way to the steps necessary to make the "miracle" more of a reality.

▇ Case 6

"V.J." is a 15-year-old male from India. He came to the United States for a youth leadership conference for 2 weeks and was suddenly hospitalized due to cellulitis. Everyone from the conference returned home. V.J.'s family lives in India, except for a brother who lives in Delaware. V.J. attends college in India. He's anxious to leave the hospital and return home, although he isn't medically ready for discharge.

PRACTITIONER: I understand you have some concerns about being here.

V.J.: Yes, I do. My insurance expires today, and I need to go home now.

PRACTITIONER: So you're worried that insurance won't cover your stay after today? Well, I contacted your insurance company, and they will continue your coverage since you were admitted prior to expiration.

V.J.: Okay, but I'm missing school.

PRACTITIONER: I'll provide you with a letter for your school letting them know you're hospitalized.

V.J.: Okay, I need to go home, though.

PRACTITIONER: I understand it must be difficult for you to be here away from your family. It may even be scary.

V.J.: A little. I just don't want to be billed.

PRACTITIONER: Your insurance will cover your visit. I understand your anxiety, but you need to get well and healthy before you leave the country. It has to be a long flight back to India.

V.J.: Seventeen hours!

PRACTITIONER: Well, you don't want to be sick and flying on a plane for 17 hours, you know.

V.J.: You're right.

PRACTITIONER: I know it's hard being here alone, but it's really the best thing for you. You also need to be honest with your parents.

V.J.: What do you mean?

PRACTITIONER: Well, I heard that you told your father that you're okay to go home.

V.J.: Who told you that?

PRACTITIONER: Your father. But you're not medically cleared according to the doctor.

Commentary

The practitioner in this scenario did an excellent job in arranging resources for the client to allay some of his very legitimate concerns. For example, she ensured that his travel insurance would keep covering his medical care, and she offered to write V.J. a note that would excuse his absence from school. The practitioner tried to convey empathy on a number of occasions, although she typically followed empathic statements with advice giving or reassurance. The client might have needed to express his concerns further before he could be reassured by her efforts, as the following examples demonstrate:

V.J.: My insurance expires today, and I need to go home now.
PRACTITIONER: So you're worried that insurance won't cover your stay after today?

V.J. could then be allowed to elaborate on this worry. After venting, he might be more able to take in the practitioner's information that she had made sure that his hospital stay would be covered.

V.J.: I just don't want to be billed.
PRACTITIONER: You're worrying that your parents will have to pay for this, and that it will be too much.

V.J.: I'm missing school.
PRACTITIONER: So another thing you're worried about is that you're getting behind in school while you're here.

V.J. might then have proceeded to talk about the cost of schooling to his parents and his fear of wasting their money, the competitive nature of his program, or worries about having to withdraw from school and getting behind. Rather than assuming that her medical note to the school would solve his problems, the practitioner could have been a bit more tentative when offering to write the note because she isn't familiar with how schools in India might handle this circumstance. Eliciting from the client the effect the note might have on his plight might have been helpful.

Coping questions might also be a line of intervention to pursue, as this young man is facing some very difficult circumstances alone and seems to be getting some pressure, rather than support, from his family about the cost of medical care. Coping questions could be asked about what resources he is using to manage the situation: "I don't know that many young men your age could handle this. You came to this country as part of a group and now you're here alone, after having gone through a medical procedure. How are you managing? How did you deal with all this?" Answers to these questions will indicate that, despite his anxieties about being alone, spending his parents' money, and missing school, he has shown a lot of strengths in the face of difficult circumstances.

Although suggestions have been provided, overall this interview seems to proceed well, until the practitioner confronts the client on being honest with his parents about his discharge. This has the effect of making him defensive. If this point needs to be addressed, one method would be to inquire about the amount of contact V.J. has had with his relatives since he was hospitalized. This would have also served the purpose of assessing the parental support he has received while in the hospital. This conversation might have led into the concerns his parents have that he will run up a bill that they can't afford to pay. The practitioner could also have asked more directly how V.J.'s parents feel about him staying. As she has since given V.J. information that might alter his perception of the situation (the travel insurance will pay for the medical stay), she might then ask about the impact this information will have on his parents. This would set up a more collaborative position with the client so that she is helping him with the pressure his parents have placed on him, instead of adding to the amount of stress he feels.

Now that we've explored some ways the contacts a practitioner has in a medical setting can be made more strengths-oriented, we discuss a case example of the strengths-and-skills-building model in a medical setting in detail.

Case Study I

"George" is a 47-year-old White man admitted to the hospital for cirrhosis of the liver and complications from diabetes, both secondary to chronic alcohol use. George is separated and has an 8-year-old son who lives with his wife. Last year, George buried his 42-year-old brother, who died of complications of alcohol use.

George currently lives alone and is unemployed. He supports himself through Social Security disability insurance due to a diagnosis of clinical depression. Prior to being on disability, George was a long-distance truck driver for 20 years. By his report, he has been in and out of substance abuse treatment programs over the last several years. The purpose of the interview is to provide the client with referrals for substance abuse treatment and information on how to take better care of himself.

After the practitioner has introduced herself:

GEORGE: I don't know why I need a practitioner. They were supposed to call my doctor to see when I can get out of here. I *need* a doctor. I don't *need* no practitioner.

PRACTITIONER: George, it sounds like you really want to get out. It says that you've been here a week and a half. It must be really frustrating being here all that time.

The practitioner begins with the client's concerns and manages his anger by reflective listening and expressing empathy.

GEORGE [a little calmer]: Yeah, and this is the third time this year! How would you like it having to lie here forever and eat this nasty food?

PRACTITIONER: I think I would really dislike it. How do you think you could avoid coming here again?

GEORGE: If I could be in better health and not be sick all the time, I wouldn't have to be in this godforsaken place. Then I could actually walk around and eat good food instead of this lousy crap! [points at food]

PRACTITIONER: Now, let me ask you a somewhat strange question. Suppose that while you are sleeping tonight a miracle happens. The miracle is that the problem that brought you here today is solved. But because you are asleep, you don't know that the miracle has happened. When you wake up, what would be the first sign to you that things are *different*, that a miracle has happened?

GEORGE [after a long pause, his face relaxes and he smiles]: Now that is a strange question! I don't know. I guess I'd be healthy and not tired. I'd get up early and feel like I wanted to get up and do things. I'd get out of my house. I'd go see my son and maybe play a game of catch with him. He's a really good kid. He deserves to have a dad who can play ball with him.

PRACTITIONER: So you'd have more energy, you'd get up, and do things and spend more time with your son. That sounds really nice. He must be a pretty special kid. So when the miracle happens, what will your son notice about you?

GEORGE: My son would notice that I'd be fun to be with—you know, a good dad. Just tossing the ball around like a couple of guys. I'd be patient and smile with him. I wouldn't scare him. [pause] I'd, um, be sober.

PRACTITIONER: So what will you be doing to feel better, stay sober, and play with your son? What will your day look like after the miracle?

GEORGE: I'd get up—let's say it was a Saturday—and instead of grabbing a beer, I'd call my son. I'd shower in the morning. I usually don't shower in the morning or sometimes I just don't—you know, 'cause I don't feel like it. But with this dream thing, I'd shower and get up, at 8 A.M., you know, 'cause my son, he's an early riser. And I'd call my son. I'd get my best bat—I got the professional kind, you know, like Mickey Mantle used [smiles, sits up in hospital bed]—and mitt and grab a couple of balls. I'd have to practice a bit before seeing my son, so he doesn't think his ole man can't hit or nothin'. I'd feel good enough to practice for a while. Then I'd go over to my wife's house and hit a couple of balls with him. [swinging an imaginary bat in the air] I'd show him how to hit some, then I'd let him try it. He'd get the hang of it. He's a quick learner, that kid.

At the beginning of the interview, the client is ill-tempered and complaining about being in the hospital and feeling sick all the time, without acknowledging how his drinking plays a role in his circumstances. Rather than confronting the client on the part he plays, the practitioner sides with him on what an awful experience it is to spend so much time at the hospital. Then, in nonblaming language, she empowers him to look at what he can do to make sure he doesn't end up in the hospital again. The client says he wouldn't be in the hospital "if I could be in better health and not be sick all the time." At this point, the practitioner could have asked what better health looks like, using language that implies that change will occur: "When you have better health, what will that look like?" More than likely, this line of questioning would get George to focus on what he will have to do differently in terms of either cutting down or abstaining from alcohol and otherwise taking care of his health. However, if these types of responses do not spontaneously emerge, the practitioner could further inquire about what George "will be doing when he has better health" or when he is on the first step he needs to take to bring himself closer to the picture of "better health" he has fleshed out.

By using the intervention of the miracle question, this practitioner takes an equally viable course of action. The miracle question gives the client permission to think of all the possibilities that could occur. This circumvents the current problems in which he finds himself mired and begins the process of motivating him to change his behavior so that it will be more congruent with a future without the problem.

The miracle question reveals the importance of the client's relationship with his son. George recognizes the incongruence of drinking with his value of spending time with his son. As George says, "Instead of grabbing a beer, I will call him to play ball." He doesn't want to "scare" his son, which seems to imply that his son might find him scary when he is drinking. When clients mention, in describing their miracle, negative behaviors they no longer want, practitioners can focus on the presence of positive behaviors instead (e.g., "What will you be doing to make sure he isn't scared?").

In this case, the miracle question has led George to his most important goal: to forge a better relationship with his son and to spend time with him. In order to meet this goal, George already recognizes that he will have to at least curtail his drinking. Like many clients, George can be engaged in a goal that is most important to him, which might not be the goal professionals would have chosen for him (becoming and staying sober). However, part of the way for George to reach his goal will be for him to address his drinking problem, at least during the times he plans to spend time with his son.

PRACTITIONER: That sounds like a lot of fun [referring to the miracle of playing baseball with son]. I bet you'd be really good with your son. So, let me ask you this. You will probably get discharged from the hospital this week. Let's say you were to do one part of the miracle the Saturday after you got discharged. Which part will you be doing?

GEORGE: Nothing. It's a nice dream, but I can't do none of that. My wife won't let me see my son, and I haven't seen him in forever. She says she doesn't want me drunk around him.

PRACTITIONER: What would it take for your wife to let you play baseball with your son?

GEORGE: If I quit drinkin' and I could prove to her that I'd quit.

At this point, the practitioner tries to move the client toward taking action. However, this seems premature as the client quickly plummets from "the miracle" and becomes stuck once again in his present circumstances. The practitioner persists by siding with the client against an external entity (his wife), and then George makes his most direct statement about the need not only to achieve but also to maintain sobriety. The client has made a clear connection between his relationship with his son and his alcohol use. He recognizes that he cannot build a relationship with his son while he uses alcohol.

PRACTITIONER: So, it sounds like that in order to see your son like you'd like to, you would need to work on your drinking. And, in order to do that, we might need to get a handle on when you drink.

GEORGE: Well, I started to drink real bad when me and my wife were fighting a lot. My brother was sick around that time, and I lost my job, and my wife got real angry because I wasn't working. I got depressed and started drinking, and I guess it just became a habit. Now I drink just 'cause the beer's there, I mean there's really nothin' to do but drink. Like I said, I'm not workin' and I can't see my son.

PRACTITIONER: So, it sounds like you really had a lot going on, and you got overwhelmed and now you drink because you're in the habit of it. There is beer in the house, and you have nothing else to do during the day.

Because the client is not yet ready to take action, the practitioner starts to examine the patterns of his drinking and more specifically the antecedents of the client's drinking behavior. These seem to include environmental antecedents, such as having beer stocked in the house, and emotional antecedents, such as feeling that there are no other activities to do. She offers simple reflection, which conveys empathy about his previously "overwhelming" circumstances, and then offers her understanding of the present circumstances that seem to maintain his drinking.

Because it seems that George has gotten past a lot of the circumstances that led to his feeling depressed, and that his current situation is less overwhelming than it once was, the practitioner could have explored how he was able to cope during that time, focusing at least initially on the strategies other than drinking he had used to manage these circumstances. For example, the client says he lost his job. Somehow, he had summoned the resources to explore the possibility of disability insurance for his depression and had managed to forge through the rather lengthy procedures to get the disability insurance granted.

The practitioner knows that the client's brother had become sick and eventually died at the age of 42 of health problems due to chronic alcohol use. This information could be used to help motivate the client to pursue a different course than his brother's. One strategy for motivation would be to ask relationship questions, such as "What do you think your brother would want for you now?" "How would he want your life to be different from his?" and "What would he want you to learn from what he went through?"

The practitioner here continues the interaction with the problem-solving process:

PRACTITIONER: You mentioned before that you would like to quit drinking to be able to spend more time with your son. You also listed some factors that have contributed to your drinking: namely, boredom, feeling overwhelmed, and having beer in the house. What's the one thing that really seems to contribute the most?

GEORGE: Ain't nothing to do, I guess.

PRACTITIONER: Is it okay if we spend some time now, coming up with some options for having activities to do during the day? Let's just get silly and creative right now rather than having you commit to any one thing. Then we could just look at some options, okay?

Because the client has named several issues that contribute to his drinking, it is important to focus on only one problem at a time, so as not to overwhelm the client further. The practitioner changes the focus from the negative ("Ain't nothing to do") to the positive (having activities to do during the day) to focus the client on what he wants rather than on what he doesn't want. She asks the client's permission to proceed rather than moving ahead with her agenda, reassuring him that there is no need to take action at this point.

Though the client agrees to take this step with the practitioner, initially he is still stonewalled:

GEORGE: I really can't think of anything except watching TV, and I already do that.

To get beyond the impasse, the practitioner asks an exception-finding question:

PRACTITIONER: Tell me about a time in the last month when you did not drink.
GEORGE [considers for a moment, shaking his head; suddenly he brightens]: The 30th. It was my son's birthday, and I didn't drink a drop all day.
PRACTITIONER: So what was different about that day?
GEORGE: Well, I knew I was gonna see my son, and it was important to him that I was okay, that I didn't embarrass him at his party, so I didn't drink. And you know what? [smiles] I was kind of actually looking forward to it, so I didn't even think of grabbing a beer. I made a real soapbox car to give him.
PRACTITIONER: You were really creative with the gift for your son! You seem like a pretty smart and innovative guy. I bet you can name 12 things that you can do to keep yourself occupied.

The practitioner builds on the client's previous success with exception-finding questions. Different aspects of the exceptions are uncovered. Clearly, George's son is a motivating force for him. Could he use his handiwork skills to make other things? Could he spend his time during the day getting healthy so that he could see his son again? For instance, could he attend a treatment program or an AA meeting? Is socializing with others a critical factor? Perhaps he could arrange to spend time with nondrinking friends or attending AA meetings.

After the practitioner suggests these things, George starts to interrupt: "I've tried all that. It don't work for me. I've been in and out of those things." The practitioner then reminds him of one of the rules of brainstorming, which is to simply produce ideas rather than criticizing them in any way. (Later, the practitioner will return to George's previous treatment experiences, giving him credit for the experience and positioning him as the expert on his own life: "What was most helpful for you?" "What was least helpful?" "What would be most helpful for you the next time?")

The practitioner then asks George about his future plans for employment, prompting him to brainstorm further. George says his health is too poor to think about working full-time, and anyway all he knows how to do is drive trucks. The practitioner then asks him to think about how he can prepare himself for at least part-time work. She suggests visiting a job training center, so he can start to build some skills for the future. At the end of their time together, George is tired but seems more hopeful that he can make some changes in his life.

Summary

This chapter has covered some of the pitfalls practitioners commonly encounter when trying to implement the strengths-and-skills-building model. It further illustrated the way different strengths-and-skills-based techniques can be applied in a way that emphasizes collaboration, building client motivation, and enhancing client strengths. Additionally, the chapter has shown that this model is sufficiently flexible to include medical settings and demonstrated that it can be implemented in a one-contact, crisis-oriented situation.

References

Hudson, P. O., & O'Hanlon, W. H. (1993). *Rewriting love stories: Brief marital therapy.* New York: W. W. Norton.

Miller, W., & Rollnick, S. (2002). *Motivational interviewing: Preparing people to change addictive behavior* (2nd ed.). New York: Guilford.

PART II

Disorders

7 Treatment of Adolescents With Disruptive Behavior Disorders

JACQUELINE CORCORAN AND
DAVID W. SPRINGER

The disruptive behavior disorders—namely, attention-deficit/hyperactivity disorder (ADHD), conduct disorder (CD), and oppositional defiant disorder (ODD)—are some of the most common encountered by practitioners working with at-risk adolescents and juvenile delinquents (Kronenberger & Meyer, 2001). Approximately half of all adolescents receiving mental health treatment also have coexisting substance abuse problems (McBride, VanderWaal, Terry, & VanBuren, 1999). Both conduct disorder and hyperactivity have been associated with substance abuse problems and delinquent behavior (Hawkins, Catalano, & Miller, 1992). Adolescents with disruptive behavior disorders are often referred to treatment (not necessarily willingly) by their parents, a judge, a school counselor, or another helping professional. The case of Richard, which is used throughout this chapter, explores the strengths-and-skills-building model as applied to adolescent disruptive behaviors. Additional case examples are interspersed throughout the chapter to demonstrate the phases of the helping process and selected techniques.

Case Study

Richard is a 16-year-old African American male who is currently in foster care. Richard has not had contact with his biological mother in a couple of years and is unaware of and has no contact with his biological father. Richard is transitioning from his foster family to live with his Aunt Mavis, with whom he lived before entering foster care. Aunt Mavis is an aunt by marriage who is no longer married to Richard's maternal uncle. According to Aunt Mavis, she was forced to place Richard into foster care because Richard would not respect the rules of her home, such as abiding by curfews and completing chores. Richard often loses his temper and takes little responsibility for his behavior. Finding it difficult to sustain attention, being easily distracted, talking excessively and interrupting others in class, and fidgeting in his seat, he has had problems in school since he was a young child. Richard was recently picked up by a police officer for fighting at school and taken to the local juvenile assessment center. Rather than being expelled, he is now attending the alternative learning center (ALC). Richard has voiced that he is unhappy in his current foster home and wants to return to Aunt Mavis's home; however, he does not want it to be as restrictive as it was the first time. Aunt Mavis views the return as workable if Richard agrees to follow her rules and enter treatment. While Richard wants to return to live with Aunt Mavis, he is reluctant to meet with the therapist or to enter treatment.

Application of Strengths-and-Skills-Building Model

We begin with a brief discussion of the interventions that encompass the strengths-and-skills-building model—solution-focused therapy, motivational interviewing, and cognitive-behavioral therapy—before turning to the application. Solution-focused therapy (SFT) has been conceptually applied to the population of juvenile offenders (Clark, 1997; Corcoran, 1997) and has been evaluated in one study (Seagram, 1997) that examined the efficacy of SFT in improving attitudes and behaviors and reducing antisocial thinking and behavior among adolescent offenders in a secure facility. In a matching design, 40 youths were rank-ordered according to sentence and then alternately assigned to the treatment ($N = 21$) or control ($N = 19$) group. The majority of the sample (85%) had a history of violent behavior. Augmenting traditional services, the SFT treatment consisted of a group orientation session and three individual assessment sessions, followed by 10 weekly SFT sessions, each lasting 45 to 60 minutes. Among the key findings was that the treatment group had significantly fewer reported antisocial tendencies and substance abuse.

Gingerich and Eisengart (2000) caution that SFT is still in the process of moving from an "open trial" phase of investigation to an "efficacy" phase. More research needs to be conducted on the effectiveness of SFT before it can truly be held up as an evidence-based approach. Nevertheless, SFT techniques, either on their own or integrated with motivational interviewing and cognitive-behavioral therapy, may be useful to practitioners in their work with juvenile offenders.

The effectiveness of motivational interviewing or its adaptations has been critically examined in three published reviews to date (Burke, Arkowitz, & Dunn, 2002; Dunn, DeRoo, & Rivara, 2001; Noonan & Moyers, 1997), generally revealing positive results. In addition, research over the past decade suggests that the authoritarian approach to prompt behavior change is less effective than interventions like motivational interviewing that target internal motivation (Ginsburg, Mann, Rotgers, & Weekes, 2002). Although the use of motivational interviewing with adolescents and their parents appears promising, only a few well-controlled studies with at-risk adolescents have been conducted (Baer & Peterson, 2002).

Cognitive-behavioral therapy has been used successfully to treat youths with antisocial problems and ADHD. Robinson, Smith, Miller, and Brownell (1999) studied cognitive-behavioral interventions delivered in the school system. Twenty-three studies comprised the meta-analysis, which included 1,132 participants. On ADHD symptoms, the mean effect size of treatment was .79, and for aggression, the mean effect was .64. In addition, treatment effects were maintained over time.

Another meta-analysis focused on cognitive-behavioral treatment (including self-statement modification, reinforcement, problem solving, and other cognitive-behavioral treatment combinations) for impulsive symptoms in youths (Baer & Nietzel, 1991). Despite a mean of only 7 hours of treatment, results were impressively strong when direct observation of behaviors was the outcome measure (a mean effect size of .83). Results were moderate when teacher ratings were used (a mean effect of .35). However, relying on parent ratings, a negative effect was shown (a mean effect of −.10). It appears that the less biased the observer, the more children were viewed as benefiting from treatment.

An additional meta-analysis has been conducted on cognitive-behavioral treatments, mainly delivered in group settings, for antisocial youth (Bennett & Gibbons, 2000). Studies were included if they used "anger management, assertiveness training, cognitive restructuring, relaxation, social problem solving or social skills training as interventions" (p. 3) and employed cognitive-behavioral methods, such as rehearsal, modeling, and coaching, to deliver content. Results of 30 treatment outcome studies concluded that cognitive-behavioral therapy is at least slightly, if not moderately, effective with antisocial children and teenagers. There is reason to believe that the older the child, the more benefit experienced from cognitive-behavioral treatment, given the increased cognitive capacity of adolescents (Bennett & Gibbons, 2000; Durlak, Fuhrman, & Lampman, 1991).

A behavioral approach to the treatment of conduct problems involves parent management training (PMT), a summary term for therapeutic strategies in which parents are trained in skills for managing their child's problem behavior (Kazdin, 1997). These skills involve effective command giving, setting up reinforcement systems, and using punishment, including taking away privileges and assigning extra chores. Although PMT programs may differ in focus and therapeutic strategies used, they all share the common goal of enhancing parental control over children's behavior (Barkley, 1987; Eyberg, 1988; Forehand & McMahon, 1981; Patterson, Reid, Jones, & Conger, 1975; Webster-Stratton, 2001). The PMT approaches are typically used for parents with younger children (Serketich & Dumas, 1996), but they have been successfully adapted for parents with adolescents (Bank, Marlowe, Reid, Patterson, & Weinrott, 1991; Barkley, Edwards, Laneri, Fletcher, & Metevia, 2001; Barkley, Guevremont, Anastopoulos, & Fletcher, 1992). To date, parent management training is the best treatment for youth with oppositional defiant disorder (Brestan & Eyberg, 1998; Hanish, Tolan, & Guerra, 1996).

Engagement

Engagement, as applied to work with adolescents, uses techniques for assessing and engaging clients who are "visitors" to the intervention process. By the time they have been mandated to attend services, teens have typically experienced countless lectures and advice-giving sessions. Such tactics tend to be counterproductive, as they contribute to client defensiveness and an even more entrenched pattern (Cade & O'Hanlon, 1993). Rather than telling the individual what to do, the practitioner asks questions that invite the teen to take responsibility for change: "What do you think you need to do so you don't have to come here anymore?" "What will convince your probation officer [your mother, the judge] that you don't need to come anymore?" (Berg & Miller, 1992). These orienting questions help workers join with clients whose main goal involves avoiding services. The questions indicate that the therapist is not invested in their continued presence in treatment and is willing to work with them to that end.

Very often, youths who present for behavior problems have experienced life stressors, such as poverty, overcrowded living conditions, large family size, parental divorce, incarceration of parents, parental substance abuse, and community violence. Often, an agenda for helpers is to process clients' feelings about all the losses and difficulties they have experienced. However, youths often resist such tactics and avoid the discussion by remaining uncooperative or uncommunicative. Rather than getting into a struggle with clients about what they "should be dealing with" and pushing them in a direction that they may find intrusive and irrelevant, the strengths-and-skills-based approach targets the goals that clients need to achieve so that they are no longer getting into trouble for their behavior. This is often the main goal of the youths (to have people leave them alone) and of the referrers. Of course, if an adolescent is willing to discuss painful feelings about the past, then the worker focuses on that, but usually it is the case that clients do not choose to pursue this avenue. In other words, it is the solution-focused belief that it is easier to build on strengths and past successes than to try to correct past failures and mistakes. The strength-based perspective focuses on positives and solutions rather than negative histories, problems, and deviance.

One way that the worker can address some of the difficulties youths have experienced is through asking coping questions. Coping questions are a way to engage clients who may not be interested in processing feelings and the past but whose strengths need to be validated and encouraged. These are illustrated with the example of Richard.

THERAPIST [to Richard]: You have been through a lot in the past year, with no longer living with your aunt, being placed in a foster home, and now going to the alternative learning center, which you say you don't like. How are you managing to cope with all that? How do you deal with all the stress?

RICHARD: I don't know. I didn't have much choice.

THERAPIST: Well, you always have a choice.

RICHARD: It really wasn't that bad.

THERAPIST: I think you have survived a lot. How can you use that strength to make changes now?

RICHARD [considers for a moment, obviously taken aback]: I know I can do anything when I want to do it.

THERAPIST: So, on a scale of 1 to 10, with 10 being you really want to change as far as listening to your teachers and aunt, where are you on this scale?

RICHARD: I'd say a 5. Sometimes I do, sometimes I don't. [The practitioner may want to switch to motivational questions here, such as "What would need to happen so you got up to a 6?"]

Coping questions can also be directed toward how teens stick with difficult circumstances. For example, the therapist says to Richard: "A lot of students who have gone through what you have would have dropped out of school by now. What keeps you coming to the ALC instead of dropping out?" His answers help him see that he has used certain resources to persevere and that he can use these strengths to succeed in the alternative school setting.

Finally, part of the engagement process involves handling the adolescent's "uncooperative behaviors," including (but certainly not limited to) lack of response and blaming others. Certain tools enable the practitioner to respond to such stances in a calm manner so that responsibility for change is placed on the adolescent and work proceeds in a productive way.

First, consider the following options for dealing with the "I don't know" stance that some adolescents take.

1. Allow silence (about 20 to 30 seconds).
2. Rephrase the question.
3. Ask a relationship question (adolescents sometimes feel put on the spot by having to answer questions about themselves but can take the perspective of others to view their behavior).
4. Say, "I know you don't know, so just make it up," which bypasses teens' resistance or fear that they don't know or don't have the right answer. Or, using presuppositional language, say, "Suppose you did know . . ."
5. Speak hypothetically about others: "What would [pro-social peers that teens respect] say they do to keep out of trouble [get passing grades or get along with their parents]?"

There are also options for responding when adolescent clients blame others and fail to take responsibility for their actions.

1. Bertolino and O'Hanlon (2002) suggest that practitioners reflect the clients' statements back, leaving out the part they perceive as making them unaccountable for their actions, as was done with Richard when discussing his anger management issues at school and at home.

RICHARD: He called me a name, so I hit him.
THERAPIST: You hit him.

RICHARD: Aunt Mavis yelled at me, so I yelled back.
THERAPIST: You yelled at your aunt.

2. Explore the details of the context: "What are you doing when your aunt is talking to you in a normal tone?" "What are you doing when your teacher treats you with respect?" "What are you doing when the other boys at school are leaving you alone?" These tools can certainly be used throughout the change process, not just during the stage of engagement, but it is important to set them up from the start.

Problem Exploration

Problem exploration begins with discussion of the problem behaviors vis-à-vis the client's motivation to change them. Once the client has demonstrated sufficient motivation to change, a functional analysis may help uncover the details and context of the behavior that are holding it in place.

Motivational Interviewing

One objective of motivational interviewing is to amplify the discrepancy between current behavior and a person's goals and values (Miller & Rollnick, 2002). When clients talk about what they hold important, the practitioner can reflect the ambivalence that is involved with change: "On one hand, freedom and being able to do what you want to do is very important to you, and if you sneak out of the house to hang around with your friends and cause trouble, then you will go back to juvenile and that will stop you from having the freedom you would like."

When using motivational interviewing, practitioners are attempting to assist clients in talking themselves into changing, rather than using direct persuasion. Resistance is sidestepped—it is not confronted directly—because direct confrontation is likely to escalate resistance rather than reduce it. Two categories of responses are most common: reflective and strategic. We focus next on reflective responses.

The reflective responses are variations of reflective listening but with a directive component to move the interaction away from a power struggle and toward change. The practitioner might choose to make an amplified reflection, in which the client's resistance is slightly overstated. This takes advantage of the natural tendency of a person to speak against either side of a decision about which he or she is ambivalent. It is likely to produce verbal backpedaling, away from the strong position of refusing to proceed and toward a less entrenched opinion where negotiation is possible. The value of an amplified reflection is that it is the adolescent, rather than the practitioner, who makes the argument toward the desired change.

Consider the case of Richard. The therapist is conducting a family therapy session with Aunt Mavis and Richard to prepare for Richard's return home. You may recall that they often argue over chores. Richard has been basically nonresponsive through much of the session while Aunt Mavis does all the talking. Richard says, for the second time, "I wouldn't yell at her if she didn't yell at me first."

THERAPIST: So you're saying that you react to your aunt? [simple reflection]
RICHARD: Isn't that what I just said? If she's going to yell at me, why shouldn't I yell back?

THERAPIST: So, after your aunt yells at you, the *only* way you can communicate with your aunt is to yell at her. [amplified reflection]

RICHARD: Yes, she never listens anyway whether I yell or not. Why should I change?

THERAPIST: You're right. It's up to you whether or not you want to change. [clarifying free choice]

RICHARD: Whatever.

THERAPIST: Okay, so you want to talk about how it's difficult to communicate without yelling at home. What else is there at home that you want to change? [shift focus]

This exchange between Richard and the therapist accomplishes at least two objectives. The first is to begin to engage Richard in the treatment process by validating where he is coming from, which is extremely important when working with juvenile offenders. Second, the therapist is sending the message early on that Richard is responsible for whether change takes place or not.

Next, the therapist continues by questioning Richard about previous attempts at therapy and inquiring about how long he attended, what he learned, what has been helpful, and so on.

RICHARD: All I have to say about therapy is that it's stupid. That counselor thought he had me figured out, but he didn't know what he was talking about.

THERAPIST: You think there is no way that a counselor can really help you. There's just no point. [amplified reflection]

RICHARD: Well, I haven't talked to anyone yet who has done me any good. I really think it's the guys who talk all that stuff who need therapy. [Being teased is what led up to Richard's fight at school.]

THERAPIST: So, there's really no need for you to be here. We shouldn't be concerned about you, since it's the boys at school that need help.

RICHARD: No, I just don't think I should be here. I mean, I'm not a psycho.

THERAPIST: So, you think if you can't handle a problem on your own, you're a crazy person. [amplified reflection]

RICHARD: I'm not crazy. But nobody can fix this.

THERAPIST: The way you see it, the situation can't be changed at all. [amplified reflection]

RICHARD: No, I'm not saying that. Just—I can do it on my own.

Rather than try to persuade Richard how helpful counseling would be for him, which would probably lead him to resist this idea, the practitioner asked him about past experiences. This helps Richard feel validated, using his own experiences to realize what has been useful. Because Richard is denying that any piece of it has been helpful (not an unusual tactic by juveniles), the practitioner adjusts her strategies in response to his "resistance" on this matter.

The therapist may also want to ask evocative questions to help the juvenile increase readiness for change. The first line of questioning encourages the adolescent to explore the disadvantages of the status quo.

1. "What worries you about your current situation?"
2. "What makes you think that you need to do something about_____?"
3. "What difficulties or hassles have you had in relation to_____?"
4. "What is there about _____ that you or other people might see as reasons for concern?"
5. "In what ways does this concern you?"
6. "How has this stopped you from doing what you want to do in life?"
7. "What do you think will happen if you don't change anything?"

The following exchange between Richard and the therapist illustrates how this line of questioning might unfold.

THERAPIST: Richard, let's talk about what landed you at the alternative learning center.

RICHARD: Okay, sure, what about it?

THERAPIST: Well, I'm just wondering, what worries you the most about being there?

RICHARD: It sucks.

THERAPIST: Yeah, I know that you don't like it, but what about it sucks the most?

RICHARD: I want to hang with my friends at my regular school. I mean, I know a couple of guys at ALC, but it's not the same.

Next, encourage the adolescent to examine advantages of change.

1. "How would you like for things to be different?"
2. "What would be the good things about [changing]?"
3. "What would you like your life to be like 5 years from now?"
4. "If you could make this change immediately, by magic, how might things be better for you?"
5. "The fact that you're here indicates that at least part of you thinks it's time to do something. What are the main reasons you see for making a change?"
6. "What would be the advantages of making this change?"

Let's continue with the interaction between Richard and his therapist to highlight how some of these questions might be applied.

THERAPIST: So, one good thing about being allowed to go from the ALC back to your regular school is that you get to see your friends every day?

RICHARD: Yeah.

THERAPIST: Let's say for a minute that you could magically make this happen, and that you were back at your regular school tomorrow. How would things be better?

RICHARD: I already told you. I'd see my friends.

THERAPIST: So, you'd have the freedom to see your friends?

RICHARD: Yeah, right now I can't see them because Aunt Mavis picks me up from ALC, and I have to go straight home. It's like I can't do anything.

THERAPIST: Sounds like you miss your freedom.

RICHARD: Big time.

THERAPIST: So being able to see your friends is one advantage of doing what you need to do to leave the ALC. What's another?

RICHARD: People might get off my back a little, and I'll be able to do somethings.

As part of this exploration process, the worker should instill in the juvenile optimism about change through posing some of these questions.

1. "What makes you think that if you did decide to make a change, you could do it?"
2. "What encourages you that you can change if you want to?"
3. "What do you think would work for you, if you decided to change?"
4. "When else in your life have you made a significant change like this? How did you do it?"
5. "How confident are you that you can make this change?"
6. "What personal strengths do you have that will help you succeed?"
7. "Who could offer you helpful support in making this change?"

THERAPIST: Richard, you're saying that you want your freedom, want people off of your back, and want to be able to hang out with your friends at your regular school. What's the first thing that you have to do for some of these things to happen?

RICHARD: I need to follow the rules at the ALC so they'll let me go back to school in 30 days like they said.

THERAPIST: What makes you think you can do what you need to do, like follow the rules at the ALC and at home, to get back to your school?

RICHARD: I don't know. I just need to think twice before I do something stupid.

THERAPIST: Think about times in the past that you've been able to catch yourself like this. How were you were able to do that?

RICHARD: I thought ahead to what kind of trouble I would get in if I got caught.

THERAPIST: Okay, good. Is there someone at the ALC that can help you with this?

RICHARD: What do you mean, like a teacher?

THERAPIST: Yeah, either a teacher or someone else in class.

RICHARD: You know, there's this girl, Yolanda, who doesn't really belong there, and we get along pretty well. But I'm not sure how she can stop me before I do something.

Once the adolescent has started voicing an interest in changing, the worker may have to guide the client past perceived obstacles and fears associated with change. The focus here is on the adolescent's intention to change.

1. "What are you thinking about _____ at this point?"
2. "I can see that you're feeling stuck at the moment. What's going to have to change?"
3. "What do you think you might do?"
4. "How important is this to you? How much do you want to do this?"
5. "What would you be willing to try?"
6. "Of the options we've mentioned, which one sounds like it fits you best?"
7. "Never mind the 'how' for right now. What do you want to have happen?"
8. "So what do you intend to do next?"

Note in question 4 that the worker asks the client how important this change is to him or her. Here, it may be helpful to use the importance ruler to get the client's rating of importance for doing something about the problem.

1. "Why are you at a _____ and not zero?"
2. "What would it take for you to go from _____ to [a higher number]?"

Continuing with the exchange between Richard and the therapist:

THERAPIST: So, you think Yolanda might be able to help, but you're not sure how exactly. What do you think you might do to let her know that you're about to do something that could get you in trouble?

RICHARD: I could just tell her, you know, so that she can talk me out of it. Or we could have a signal if we're not supposed to be talking. I know that I'm not supposed to do certain things, but I don't always stop myself. She's really smart, and a better student than the rest of us, so I trust her.

THERAPIST: I'm glad that you trust her. Suppose Yolanda isn't around for a day. Who else at the ALC can you talk to or signal when you feel like you might do something that you're not supposed to?

RICHARD: Mr. Arrich is pretty cool.

As the worker explores this with the adolescent, have the client elaborate on a topic before moving on quickly to another reason because it can have the effect of eliciting further change talk. In other words, explore the decisional balance with the client. This can be done by:

- Asking for clarification: In what ways? How much? When?
- Asking for a specific example
- Asking for a description of the last time this occurred
- Asking "What else?" within the change topic

When there seems to be little desire for change, another way to elicit change talk is to ask the client to describe the extremes of his or her (or others') concerns. In this sense, querying extremes might help the adolescent imagine the extremes of consequences that might ensue.

1. "What concerns you the most about _____ in the long run?"
2. "Suppose you continue on as you have been, without changing. What do you imagine are the worst things that might happen to you?"
3. "How much do you know about what can happen if you [continue with the problem behavior] even if you don't see this happening to you?"

At the other extreme, it can be useful to imagine the best consequences that could follow from pursuing a change.

1. "What might be the best results you could imagine if you make a change?"
2. "If you were completely successful in making the changes you want, how would things be different?"

THERAPIST: Richard, when this plan works, and you're able to get help from Yolanda or Mr. Arrich when you're headed for some trouble, how would things be different?

RICHARD: I'd quit getting in trouble, and I could go back to my regular school.

Motivational questions were also used in a family session with Richard and his Aunt Mavis to talk about his difficulties with managing his anger:

THERAPIST: Richard, in what way do you think you or other people have been harmed by your anger? [problem recognition]

RICHARD: I had to leave Aunt Mavis's home, and the teacher puts me in time-out at school. I'm at the ALC because I got in a fight.

THERAPIST: In what ways does this bother you? [problem recognition]

RICHARD: I don't like being at the ALC 'cause I miss my friends at school.

THERAPIST: The fact that you are here indicates that at least part of you thinks it's time to do something. What are the reasons you see for making a change? [eliciting intention to change]

RICHARD: I want to stay out of trouble so that I get back to my regular school and live with Aunt Mavis again.

THERAPIST: When you think about living with your aunt, what are you worried or concerned about? [eliciting concern about possible changes]

RICHARD: If I go back to Aunt Mavis's and nothing changes, this placement may not work. If it doesn't work, then I'll be separated from my family again, and I'll have to go back to foster care.

THERAPIST: It sounds like you have really thought about what might happen if something doesn't change. How much does that concern you? [eliciting intention to change]

RICHARD: A lot! I'm tired of moving around and I want to be with my family. I need to make this work.

THERAPIST: So you see a need for a change, and that you are a part of that change. [Richard nods.] The fact that both of you are here indicates that you think it's worth working on.

THERAPIST TO AUNT MAVIS: In what ways do Richard's anger and his possible return home concern you? [elicitation of concern]

AUNT MAVIS TO RICHARD: I want this to work. That is why I agreed to come here in the first place.

By the end of this conversation, Aunt Mavis and Richard are joined on their motivation to work on his return home. At this point, the therapist may turn toward examining in more detail the specific problem behaviors and the context that is holding them in place.

Functional Analysis

The strengths-and-skills-building model considers change more likely when specific, concrete behaviors are targeted rather than diagnostic or other labels (Cade & O'Hanlon, 1993). This is in contrast to some long-term therapies that often focus on relatively fixed and stable characteristics of people, such as their personalities (O'Hanlon & Weiner-Davis, 1989). As an example, a youth who has destroyed someone's property or harmed others is easier to impact than a "conduct disorder," a youth who talks back to teachers is easier to manage than an "oppositional defiant disorder," and a youth who fails to finish school assignments is easier to deal with than an "attention-deficit/hyperactivity disorder." Cade and O'Hanlon (1993) advise that any diagnostic category can be broken down "into a pattern of discrete personal and interpersonal behaviors that repeats under a particular set of circumstances such that elements in the pattern might more easily be acted upon" (p. 63).

Therefore, with Richard, we might have posed the following types of questions.

1. When you have an argument with your aunt [get into trouble at school], what do you do? How do you feel? What are you thinking? What bodily reactions do you experience?
2. What seems to trigger your anger? What is going on? Where does this occur? What time of day, and on what days of the week? What feelings and thoughts do you have right before a fit or an outburst of anger?
3. Murphy (1997) suggests paying particular attention to the other people involved with the problem. Richard, therefore, could be asked the following: Who is usually around when the problem occurs? Which teachers report more or less of a problem? Does the problem occur more often with one particular teacher? What are the students and others saying and doing right before the problem happens? What happens afterward? How do you react? What do you say and do? How long do these reactions last? What do you do after your fits? How do you feel? What thoughts run through your mind? How do teachers usually respond to the problem? What do they say? What do they do? How do the other students respond to the problem?
4. What strategies have you used to deal with your problem, and how successful have they been? [previous problem-solving attempts]
5. If I recorded the problem on a videotape, what would I be seeing?

When the problem is clearly defined and understood, the therapist can focus on collaborating with the client to build on strengths to shift the patterns of problem behaviors.

Solution Exploration

Exploration of strengths entails exception finding, externalizing, helping adolescent clients internalize their successes, and, if nothing else works, assuming a paradoxical stance.

Exception Finding
One of the main principles of the solution-focused approach is the identification of "exceptions," periods of time when the problem is either not present or is less of a problem (Berg, 1994; Berg & Miller, 1992; Cade &

O'Hanlon, 1993; O'Hanlon & Weiner-Davis, 1989). Exceptions are the means by which solutions to problems are mapped out, using the client's own unique resources and ways of solving problems. The practitioner's task is to help clients identify and access these exceptions, amplifying and enhancing clients' capacities. In Richard's case, strategies included counting to 10 to keep anger in check, staying home and going to sleep instead of driving around with gang members, and entering school unpersuaded by peers who have decided to skip. When these "exceptions" to misbehavior were identified, the therapist congratulated Richard and asked further questions to reinforce positive change: "How did you get that to happen?" "How are you managing to do this?" "What's different about those times?" "What would you need to do to get that to happen again?"

In the following interchange during one of the family sessions with the therapist, Richard and his aunt were asked to identify times when their relationship was being repaired.

THERAPIST [to Richard]: What would be the first thing you noticed that showed your aunt was beginning to trust you again?

RICHARD: She would start letting me go to the mall to hang out with my friends.

THERAPIST: What will you do differently to make this happen?

RICHARD: I don't know, I guess I would not have a bad attitude at home, and been more helpful. Maybe I would have asked to go to the mall for a little while, agreeing to call her once I got there and when I left. That way she would know I got there safe, and know when to expect me back home. She always worries that something bad is going to happen to me, or that I will get back with the same bad crowd, but I have told her those days are over.

AUNT MAVIS: I like to know where he is. I want him to go where he says he is going and come home when he says he will be home. I am an old woman, and I can't afford to be worried all the time about this child.

THERAPIST: Have there been times in the past where you felt like your aunt trusted you?

RICHARD: Yeah, before I got in trouble and got sent away. This one time I helped her clean out the storage room and earned $30. She let me take the bus to the mall and hang out with my friends the whole afternoon.

THERAPIST: How did you get that to happen?

RICHARD: Well, we set a time for me to come home. I called her when I got there at around 3:00 P.M. Then I checked back in at about 5:30 P.M., and I called her when I left the mall and was home by my 9:00 P.M. curfew.

AUNT MAVIS: That is all I want him to do. When I know what friends he is hanging out with, when he checks in, and when he comes home like he's supposed to, I have no problems with letting him go places.

When clients are unable to come up with exceptions to the problem, the therapist can inquire about times when the problem is "less severe, frequent, intense or shorter in duration" (O'Hanlon & Weiner-Davis, 1989, p. 86). An example of this intervention can be demonstrated with a frequent source of problems for offenders involving physical assaults (Corcoran, 1997). Even the most hardened gang member can usually talk about a time when a fight was avoided, by either "walking away," telling the person "he ain't worth it," or "not listening when someone was messing with me." For the occasional adolescent who claims to always fight when challenged, the question can be asked, "When were you able to avoid going past the shoving stage?" Even if clients state that another person outside themselves was responsible for the exception ("A teacher broke us up"), credit can still be given to the client for doing something to contribute to the solution: "So you picked a place for the fight where you knew someone could stop you." As can be seen from these examples, there is always the potential to place a positive, strength-based emphasis even on serious circumstances.

The therapist, in our example, invited Richard to find times in the past when his aunt did allow him to have freedom. At this point, the client moved out of the mind-set of "she never lets me do anything" to a willingness to compromise with his aunt. At the end of the session, his aunt stated she was glad to see that her nephew not only remembered the times when he was allowed to go places but also remembered what he had done to earn the freedom.

Another way to use exception finding is in discussing feeling identification and management. Teens usually tolerate a discussion of feelings if it is posed in a solution-focused way and in the service of the immediate goal—to get themselves out of trouble. Teens are asked to identify emotions that lead to risky and illegal behaviors and then to identify the pro-social ways they have used in the past to cope with these feelings. Responses from teens have included calling a friend or girlfriend or boyfriend when bored, telling themselves that a person who caused them to feel humiliation didn't matter and couldn't affect how they felt about themselves (positive self-talk), and telling the teacher they needed to take a break when feelings of frustration over schoolwork loomed large. These sample responses emphasize the strengths and capacities teens already possess that they can continue to use in the future.

A further use of exception finding is in combination with one of the main principles of motivational interviewing, which is to develop discrepancy between the values a person holds and the current problem behavior.

To gain more awareness of their values, teens can be given a list of emotional states and then asked to rank-order them by the value they place on them. These emotional states include love, success, freedom, intimacy, security, adventure, power, passion, comfort, and health (Robbins, 1992). In a focus on solutions, teens are then asked to create a picture of how they could experience their priority emotional state in a pro-social way. Some teens discuss strategies they need to take to avoid "getting locked up," which results in a loss of freedom. Spending time with members of the opposite sex has been identified not only as a way to get more "love" but also as a way to stay away from negative peers. Teens also say playing sports and talking to members of the opposite sex are ways they could get excitement without committing illegal acts.

Externalizing the Problem

Exceptions can also be identified through a narrative intervention formulated by Michael White, called externalizing the problem (White, 1995; White & Epston, 1990), which has been adopted by some solution-focused therapists (Berg, 1994; Dolan, 1991; Selekman, 1997). Externalizing the problem involves making a linguistic distinction between the presenting problem and the person. Instead of the problem being one of personal dynamics and an inherent quality, it is seen as an external entity. Externalization enables clients to take a less serious approach to their problems, frees them to come up with options, and thus empowers them to "fight against" their external oppressors[1] (White & Epston, 1990). "Externalizing the problem is a two-step process:

1. Map the influence the problem has over the identified client, family members, and significant others (peers, relatives, and involved helping professionals).
2. Map the influence the identified client, family members, and significant others have over the problem" (Selekman, 1997, p. 84).

The therapist used this technique to explore Richard's ADHD symptoms with Richard and Aunt Mavis during a family therapy session.

THERAPIST [to Richard]: How long has ADHD been giving you a hard time?
RICHARD: For as long as I can remember. Since I was a kid.

1. Another variation of externalizing the problem is to ask clients to draw their problems personified as an external entity (examples: a monster, a ball of fire, a volcano) and tell about the times they exerted control over these externalized qualities (what's different about the times they can control "the monster"?). Chapter 9 presents methods of integrating art into techniques.

THERAPIST: When ADHD gets the best of you, what sort of things does it make you do?

RICHARD: You know, I can't sit still, I just can't focus. I get in a lot of trouble with my teachers because I just say sh–, I'm sorry [laughs], crap. It's like I can't even help it.

AUNT MAVIS: He won't listen either. He's like a toy train that's wound too tight. He just goes and goes without thinking.

RICHARD [laughs]: I'm not no toy train.

THERAPIST: So, both of you are frustrated by what ADHD is doing to Richard at school and to your relationship with each other.

AUNT MAVIS: You know, I never thought of it that way, but yeah. It really does get the best of us sometimes.

THERAPIST: Richard, when you say that ADHD controls how you act, how do you feel at those times?

RICHARD: Pissed off, because everyone's trying to tell me what to do, and they need to mind their own business.

[Now that the influence has been mapped out, the therapist switches gears to focus on times that Richard and his aunt have been able to influence ADHD. This "restorying" process allows them the opportunity to feel a sense of control and to align themselves against ADHD.]

THERAPIST: Richard, what percentage of the time do you have control over ADHD?

RICHARD: I don't know.

THERAPIST: Suppose you did know, what do you think it would be?

RICHARD: I guess, like 50% of the time.

THERAPIST: Fifty percent, okay, that's good. What's different about the times that you're able to keep ADHD from getting the best of you? What do you do that's different?

RICHARD: I feel calmer.

THERAPIST: What do you do that makes you feel calmer?

RICHARD: I'm not fighting with Aunt Mavis. I take my medication. I don't sit by Tyrone in class.

AUNT MAVIS: It's true, ever since he was little, when he sits up front in class he gets less distracted. The medication does seem to help, but he hasn't been taking it lately.

THERAPIST: What about your teacher? How does she help letting ADHD get the best of you?

RICHARD: She's not nagging at me and stuff.

THERAPIST: What she's doing instead?

RICHARD: She's leaving me alone.

THERAPIST: What are you doing when she's leaving you alone?

RICHARD: Doing what I'm supposed to, I guess.

By identifying the ways in which Richard and his aunt are able to fight back against ADHD, they both felt an increased sense of hope that they could build on past successes to combat this problem.

Maria, 16, was in trouble with the juvenile court for her marijuana use. She started the following externalizing interchange by saying that it was difficult to quit smoking because it is "everywhere she goes."

PROBATION OFFICER: You said it's everywhere you go. I'm sure there are instances when you are resisting the urge to smoke. Could you tell me about some of these times? [Here, the "urge to smoke" is externalized. The question presupposes that there are occasions when Maria is able to resist.]

MARIA: When I am home with my mom or when I'm exercising.

PROBATION OFFICER: How are you managing to resist the urge at home?

MARIA: I don't have time to smoke because I sleep a lot at home. When I am at home, I usually stay in my room because none of my friends are around.

PROBATION OFFICER: That's great how you're able to do that. So staying at home is one thing that helps you. You also mentioned that you exercise. What is it about exercising that helps you resist the urge to smoke?

MARIA: When I exercise, I'm thinking about other things, like getting fit, feeling energized, and seeing if I could beat my running record.

This example demonstrates how the probation officer was able to elicit from Maria ways that she could "resist the urge to smoke" when she initially expressed hopelessness about the possibility, given that it was *always* around. The solution-focused line of questioning revealed that there were exceptions. Maria not only presented some effective ways to avoid substance abuse (staying at home, exercising) that could be built on but also presented some other possibilities to explore, which included keeping away from friends with whom she smoked and focusing on positive goals.

Getting Clients to Internalize Success

Often people see the exceptions to their problem behavior as outside their control: "I didn't do anything different. She was just not in a bad mood for once." This is a particular risk when adolescents are taking medication. As Richard identified, when clients benefit from medication management and experience change in the direction of their desired goals, we want to help them recognize their contributions to that change. For example, the therapist might have asked Richard some of the following questions:

"You mentioned that you think the medication you're taking is helping. How are you working with the medication to make things better?"

"In your mind, what does the medication you're taking allow you to do that you might not otherwise be able to do?"

"What percentage of the change you've experienced is a result of the medication, and what percentage do you think is your own doing?"

"What are you able to do as a result of feeling better from taking medication?"

Assuming a Pessimistic (Paradoxical) Stance

For those cases in which clients absolutely resist all of the helper's attempts to be positive and strength-based, the clinician sometimes has to switch to a "pessimistic" frame. The adolescent is then forced to assume a more positive frame in order to convince the therapist that "things really aren't so bad" (O'Hanlon & Weiner-Davis, 1989).

For instance, 15-year-old Sonia was detained for solicitation and was now on probation. Sonia was living with her father, the father's girlfriend, and the girlfriend's 13-year-old daughter because living with her mother had become problematic. One night, the community-monitoring officer reported that Sonia and the 13-year-old were siding together against the parents. The father was very angry with Sonia for her "smart mouth," as was the girlfriend, who said that Sonia was a negative influence on her daughter. "They both ganged up on us out there." The father said he didn't want to see Sonia's face because he was afraid he would just "kick her ass across the room." Sonia, in turn, said she didn't want to speak to her father—he was unreasonable to the point where he may be violent with her.

The community-monitoring worker, whose job was to make sure that teens were in their homes and following their sanctions from the courts, had come into this situation. He had attempted to understand each side's position and to set up negotiations between the two factions that had developed. Both parties remained adamant that the situation was impossible and that it would never work out. The family resisted all of the community-monitoring worker's efforts to instill calm while reaching a compromise.

Upon her arrival, the therapist was briefed by the community-monitoring worker on what had already been tried. After brief conversations with both sides, in which they both essentially maintained the same stance that things could not be worked out, the therapist decided against "doing more of the same" and took a paradoxical stance instead. To both parties, the therapist said that they had all tried to give the living arrangement a good chance. They had done their best, but obviously it was not going to work out.

Because it was nighttime and Sonia's probation officer was not available, the therapist recommended that the community-monitoring worker contact the probation officer in the morning to discuss other options for placement of Sonia. In the meantime, the family would have to make alternative arrangements for Sonia to stay somewhere safe for that evening, given the concerns about Sonia's father becoming violent. The family members concurred that Sonia's mother was not a long-term option but that it would be okay to have Sonia stay with her that night as a temporary solution. In the therapist's presence, Sonia then paged her mother, and it was agreed between them that she would arrive shortly to pick up Sonia. Sonia stated that she felt safe enough for now and was fine with the therapist leaving while she waited for her mother.

The next day, the therapist learned from the community-monitoring worker that he had stopped back later that night to check on the situation to find that the entire family (Sonia included) was amicably watching TV. The family dismissed the community monitor's concerns, saying that everything was fine and that Sonia had canceled the page to her mother. The family had decided to give this living arrangement another shot.

This example illustrates how clients are forced to shift their position when the clinician either accepts or exaggerates the position that the client insists on. Paradoxical interventions, when used appropriately, empower clients by validating their fears about change. They allow clients to operate out of their own ambiguity and arguments as to why they should attempt to do so. If the clinician argues for client change, the side of the client that does not want to do so may be galvanized into a defensive stance. If the worker shifts to a case against change, the client may then demonstrate a desire and a capacity for change (Cade & O'Hanlon, 1993).

When the client shows readiness for change and the problem and solutions have been explored, the practitioner can turn efforts toward assisting the client in goal formulation.

Goal Setting

The strengths-and-skills-building model focuses on well-formulated and concrete goals that can be achieved within a brief time frame. Miracle questions and scaling questions are interventions that can be used in the service of goal setting.

Miracle Questions

Miracle questions (de Shazer, 1988; Selekman, 1993) may prove useful with adolescents who are not yet engaged in the treatment process, as they invite clients to examine and evaluate their situation. The miracle question bypasses the present problem and projects the client into a nonproblem future. In this way, teens and their parents can begin to see possibilities they hadn't before considered. The miracle question intervention is illustrated here with Maria, the Hispanic 16-year-old mentioned earlier, who was mandated to attend therapy by the juvenile courts for her marijuana use and physical fighting. The focus of this contact with her probation officer and her mother was on Maria's tendency to have smoked marijuana on a daily basis. Maria was still reporting cravings from this level of use.

PROBATION OFFICER: Pretend a miracle happened during the night, and you no longer had the urge to smoke when you woke up in the morning. What would be different?

MARIA: I would wake up with energy. I would think clearly, and I wouldn't be hungry all the time.

PROBATION OFFICER: That's good, Maria. Mom, what differences would you notice about Melissa's behavior?

MARIA'S MOTHER: I wouldn't have to wake her up in the morning, and she would be more talkative. She would go to school without hassles and not run around with the wrong group of friends.

PROBATION OFFICER: Maria, how would your friends at school know that something is different?

MARIA: I probably wouldn't hang out with them as much when they're smoking.

PROBATION OFFICER: Melissa, tell me about times this is already happening.

The miracle question gets Maria to flesh out the details of a future without the problem. This intervention can then lend itself to exception finding ("tell me about times this is already happening").

Scaling Questions

Once the problem has been identified and mutually agreed upon, the scaling question can assist in goal formulation and evaluation. In this intervention, clients are asked to construct an actual scale on paper. They then anchor 10, listing three behavioral indicators stated in concrete, specific, and positive terms of what they will be doing. In other words, rather than stating "not hanging out with gang members all night," the alternative positive phrasing would be "being home at curfew." Youth are then told to rank their progress.

The scaling technique serves a number of purposes. First, teens provide their own goals and progress rather than being told what to do. This is significant in itself, considering the amount of advice giving and lectures to which the juvenile offender has typically been subjected. Second, scaling questions allow juveniles to recognize the progress they have made toward pro-social behavior. When asked, "What will it take for you to move up one number?" Richard navigated the direction of change: "look for a job," "walk away from fights," and "ignore people who mess with you."

Scaling questions can also be used to assess the context of the behavior. "Relationship questions" are explored with clients to help them understand the influence of their behavior on others (Berg, 1994). Relationship questions assist juvenile offenders in viewing themselves from another's perspective. Teens are asked how the people who are affected by their behavior would view their progress. They are instructed to not only rank themselves but also say how their parents or probation officers might position them on a scale and what they would need to do differently to move up on that scale. "What would your probation officer say is the first step you need to take to enroll in a GED program?" "What would your older brother say is the first step you need to take to resist the influence of gangs in your life?" "What would your caseworker say needs to happen for you to continue to stay clean?" "What would your mother have to see to know you were moving up one number on the scale for school attendance?" In this way clients, viewing themselves from another's perspective, provide themselves with behavioral prescriptors for change.

Other intervention questions explore the influence of the clients' behavior on others. For instance, when individuals complain about their parents always being onto them, they are asked, "What are you doing differently when your parents are not onto you?" Often, these types of questions have to be repeated until adolescents grasp the language, which presupposes that each person's behavior influences the other's. Then teens realize by their answers that they are in part responsible for the interaction: "I guess I'm doing the chores I'm supposed to," "I'm just in my room, listening to music," or "I'm telling her what happened at school that day." Answers elicited by these kinds of questions empower juveniles to change the sequence of interactions.

Taking Action

Although the intervention approaches (e.g., motivational interviewing, solution-focused techniques) reviewed earlier in this chapter are recommended for use when juveniles are "resistant" to the change process, we recommend that practitioners reserve cognitive-behavioral interventions for when adolescents are engaged in the treatment process. Attribution retraining, behavior management, and parent training are discussed as possible techniques in this section.

Attribution Retraining

Youths with poor impulse control are often characterized by a style of cognitive processing that impedes their ability to effectively problem-solve in social situations (Dodge, Price, Bachorowski, & Newman, 1990). Given the tendency to make hostile attributions regarding neutral events, they may be quick to react with aggression (Dodge et al., 1990; Bienert & Schneider, 1995), particularly when impulse control is low.

Richard's physical fights with classmates started, he claims, because they stare at him in a threatening way and make comments that challenge him to fight. He is convinced they are making derogatory remarks about him. In one instance, Richard said, "What are you looking at?" The other boy responded in kind, and the argument escalated into a physical altercation. In order to stop responding aggressively to cues in the environment, a goal will therefore to be to train Richard to interpret events in his environment in a more neutral fashion through attribution retraining.

Attribution retraining was used to address the threat and hostile intention Richard attributed to his classmates. In attribution retraining, the practitioner asks the youth a series of perspective-taking questions.

THERAPIST: Richard, what do you think might be going on with the guys at school who egg you on?

RICHARD: Man, I don't know what their problem is.

THERAPIST: Yeah, I know you don't know for sure. But pretend for a minute like you did know. What's your best guess?

RICHARD: Maybe they're just jealous of my girlfriend, because she's so good looking. All the guys want to go out with her.

Rather than using this as a rationale for fighting, the possible motivation of his classmates was reframed as a compliment for Richard. When people looked at him or talked about him with others, he could see this as an indication that they admired him and his girlfriend's attractiveness.

Perspective-taking questions also helped Richard see the role he takes in interactions.

THERAPIST: Hey, Richard, if you held up a mirror to your face when this stuff is going on, how would you describe your facial expression?

RICHARD: Mean looking I guess. You know, angry. But I can't help it.

THERAPIST: Now, compare that mean look to the expression on your face when you're hanging out with your girlfriend or your friends.

RICHARD: Well, I look happy.

THERAPIST: So, you can control your facial expression from one situation to the next. What else do you have control over?

When Richard was led through the steps of what occurred during his physical fights, he could also see how he escalated arguments by making statements such as "What are you looking at?" "What's your problem?" and "You want some?" He was then asked how people would tend to respond to these comments, and he could see that they were reciprocating some of his own hostility. The therapist continued to deconstruct each incident in which Richard felt that classmates were "trying to get on his nerves," so that he could understand and then change his role in the situation.

Parent Management Training

Parent management training (PMT) is a critical component of treatment with adolescents. Parents and other caregivers can be taught ways to structure the home environment so that desirable, pro-social behavior is encouraged in the adolescent and antisocial or oppositional behavior is extinguished or punished. Consider the following illustration of PMT with Richard and his Aunt Mavis.

THERAPIST: Mavis, you've said that you're not sure how to deal with Richard when he doesn't follow your rules or when he talks back. You've tried yelling, and that doesn't seem to work. How have you rewarded him when he does follow the rules, and how have you imposed consequences when he doesn't? [This validates Aunt Mavis's past attempts, while amplifying the need to acknowledge Richard's pro-social behaviors and impose consequences for negative behaviors.]

AUNT MAVIS: I'm not sure what you mean—like giving him money when he's good? I don't like that.

THERAPIST: No, not money. When Richard is home on time, for example, how could he be rewarded? What's important to him?

AUNT MAVIS: Those computer games!

RICHARD: Yeah!

THERAPIST: So, Richard, you'd like more time playing computer games. Aunt Mavis, what's a reasonable amount of extra Nintendo time each time Richard makes it home on time?

AUNT MAVIS: You can have 30 extra minutes on Nintendo if you get home when you're supposed to.

RICHARD: Man, only 30 minutes!

AUNT MAVIS [raising voice]: Don't give me lip, you're lucky you're getting anything at all!

THERAPIST [coaching Aunt Mavis on how to respond to Richard]: Mavis, I imagine that you're feeling frustrated with Richard, because you're trying to reward him for good behavior, and he doesn't seem to appreciate it. Rather than getting into a shouting match right now, which we've all agreed doesn't work, tell Richard what you'd like to see from him instead. [If needed, the therapist could model for Aunt Mavis how this might sound.]

AUNT MAVIS: Richard, I want to be able to give you things, reward you, when you're good. But, when you talk back like that, it makes me not want to give you any wiggle room. I just feel like pulling the reins even tighter.

THERAPIST: Good, Mavis. Richard, what was it like for you to hear what your Aunt Mavis is saying now, rather than yelling at you?

RICHARD: It's okay. I don't feel like yelling back.

The therapist would continue coaching and modeling Aunt Mavis on using effective parenting skills (e.g., time-out, rewarding pro-social behavior, imposing consequences for undesirable behavior) and encouraging parental self-care. For a more detailed exposition on parent management training, see Cavell's (2000) excellent book on the topic.

Problem-Solving Training

Problem-solving skills training is a cognitively based intervention that has been used to treat aggressive and antisocial youth (Kazdin, 1994). The problem-solving process helps clients learn how to produce a variety of potentially effective responses when faced with problem situations (D'Zurilla & Nezu, 2001). Regardless of the specific problem-solving model used, the primary focus is on addressing the thought process to help adolescents address deficiencies and distortions in their approach to interpersonal situations (Kazdin, 1994). Techniques that are used include didactic teaching, practice, modeling, role playing, feedback, social reinforcement, and therapeutic games (Kronenberger & Meyer, 2001). The problem-solving approach has five steps for the practitioner and client to address (see Table 3.4).

Problem-solving training was utilized in an adolescent girls' group at Ridgedale High School, located in a lower-class section of a large city. Ridgedale High served neighborhoods that experienced much criminal activity. Drug dealing, prostitution, grand and petty theft, and burglaries occurred at a high rate. As one preventive measure, the school offered a number of coping groups for students who were considered at risk for developing delinquent behaviors. One such group was offered to female adolescents who demonstrated chronic school truancy. This 8-week time-limited group, like others at the school, was led by a local mental health professional. This "academic and personal success" group used the problem-solving model as a basis for intervention.

The practitioner devoted the first meeting to acquainting the girls with each other and generating topics for discussion. Subsequent meetings included structured discussions among the girls about ways to problem-solve with regard to the topic for that day. During one group meeting, the issue of safe sex was selected as a topic. The girls agreed that they did not want to become pregnant, and some were opposed to the idea of having sex, but all of them had faced difficulty with boys who were sexually aggressive.

The practitioner's responsibilities each week included teaching and encouraging the problem-solving model as an effective way to address a variety of problems in living. She said that engaging in this practice, while productive in isolation, was often more effective when done in the group setting, with the benefit of immediate input from others. In the first part of this meeting, the girls were asked to specify a problem related to the general topic of safe sex. They quickly agreed that they wanted to learn how to reject the advances of boys who tried to talk them into sex. The practitioner asked the girls to role-play several scenarios during the meeting to get a clearer idea of the situations they had in mind. This was helpful and also provided the girls with some amusement as they acted out the parts.

The girls next brainstormed possible solutions to the challenge. Because all ideas are welcomed and none censored, this task was also fun for the girls. They could laugh and be outrageous with each other while sharing suggestions about physically protecting themselves, making specific and assertive verbal responses, limiting their dates to certain kinds of settings, avoiding related topics of conversation, addressing their preferences before a date began, and many others. It is important in this step for the practitioner to encourage additional responses after the group members decide they are finished. Members often stop participating when a list contains as few as five alternatives, believing that such a list is sufficient, but when pressed they can usually suggest many more.

In the group setting, it is not necessary that each member agree on one item from the list for implementation. Each girl can select her own solution, and it is supported so long as the member can articulate reasons for the choice that represent a logical cost-benefit thought process. The practitioner, whose goal is to teach a generalizable problem-solving process, asked the girls to make a commitment to implement their solution if and when the problem situation arises. In this particular instance, the girls agreed that greater assertiveness would help them maintain control of situations when alone with a boy. The girls could not all implement their strategy in the context of a date situation during the next week, but they could practice assertiveness skills in a variety of other contexts with boys.

The following week the girls shared their experiences with exercising assertive behavior with boys at school and over the weekend and noted whether they considered these episodes to be successes or failures. Several of the girls had in fact been on dates. One had specifically experienced the problem of aggressive behavior with a boy and described how she had responded. The girls helped each other evaluate their task implementation and again were constructive in their comments. As a final stage in this process, they helped each other refine their approaches to assertiveness and consider new strategies for the coming weeks.

Evaluation and Termination

Termination is the time to review progress and strategies for handling triggers, such as boredom and anger, that may lead to oppositional or antisocial behaviors. Selekman (1993, 1997) has a number of solution-focused questions to use with adolescents (see also Chapter 5) for the maintenance and amplification of changes made. Another way to handle the termination process is through letter writing. Here is an example of such a letter to a client who was in a drug treatment program as part of his probation.

Dear DeWayne:
I'm writing to let you know that I enjoyed working with you over the past several weeks. You did an excellent job setting a goal of completing your GED. I know that it was sometimes difficult for you to attend class regularly, but you made significant change on this over the last 2 weeks. I also appreciate the way you have been able to provide helpful, empathetic feedback to other people during group therapy.

You were able to identify times when you overcame your temper. You said that when you stopped to think about the consequences of your actions, you avoided reacting so quickly. We also discussed your ability to walk away from a situation when you felt you were going to lose your temper.

You have demonstrated a great deal of courage over the past several weeks. I understand that coming to a drug treatment program and discussing the challenges you've had in the past was difficult. I appreciate the honesty you demonstrated and your willingness to discuss the possibility of making changes in your life.

We discussed the pros and cons of your drug use during several of our sessions. You acknowledged that your use caused problems with your school and family and that you also had problems with the police. On the other hand, you stated you felt more confident when you were using drugs. That took a lot of insight and honesty to realize and state this. We started to talk about some other ways to feel confident without the use of drugs.

I know it's difficult for you to decide what course to take in your life right now. I just want you to remember that you met your initial goal of staying clean and sober for 7 days. That was quite an accomplishment!

Please remember that additional resources are available to you if you choose to seek it. Feel free to call this agency at any time if you would like to return or receive services. Also, AA and NA groups are available to you at any time.

Sincerely,
Claire

This letter demonstrates a number of strengths-based principles. Borrowed from solution-focused therapy, it uses language to put problems in the past ("You acknowledged that your use caused problems with your school and family and that you also had problems with the police"), implying that the issues that plagued DeWayne were no longer exerting their negative influence. Exceptions were highlighted—times when he was able to control his temper—as well as his strengths and progress toward the goals he had set. The letter summarized the advantages of DeWayne's drug use and its costs. Raising his confidence had become a target for work since that has been identified as a main reason for keeping his use in place. Serving as a concrete reminder, the letter can be referred to when DeWayne needs to bolster his motivation and his confidence that he can change.

Summary

This chapter has demonstrated that solution-focused therapy and motivational interviewing can be used together to build strengths and motivation and to get teens to take responsibility for the change process. Cognitive-behavioral interventions can be employed when teens show readiness to take action. Overall, we encourage practitioners to *start where the client is*, matching treatment interventions to the client's diagnosis and corresponding treatment goal(s) while taking into consideration the type of relationship the client has with the change process. Adolescents with disruptive behavior disorders are complex and challenging clients who demand sophisticated treatment using promising practices such as those presented in this chapter.

References

Baer, J. S., & Peterson, P. L. (2002). Motivational interviewing with adolescents and young adults. In W. R. Miller & S. Rollnick (Eds.), *Motivational interviewing* (pp. 320–332). New York: Guilford.

Baer, R. A., & Nietzel, M. T. (1991). Cognitive and behavioral treatment of impulsivity in children: A meta-analytic review of the outcome literature. *Journal of Clinical Child Psychology, 20,* 400–412.

Bank, L., Marlowe, J. H., Reid, J. B., Patterson, G. R., & Weinrott, M. R. (1991). A comparative evaluation of parent training interventions for families of chronic delinquents. *Journal of Abnormal Child Psychology, 19,* 15–33.

Barkley, R., Edwards, G., Laneri, M., Fletcher, K., & Metevia, L. (2001). The efficacy of problem-solving communication training alone, behavior management training alone, and their combination for parent–adolescent conflict in teenagers with ADHD and ODD. *Journal of Consulting and Clinical Psychology, 69*, 926–941.

Barkley, R. A. (1987). *Defiant children: A clinician's manual for parent training.* New York: Guilford.

Barkley, R. A., Guevremont, D. C., Anastopoulos, A. D., & Fletcher, K. E. (1992). A comparison of three family therapy programs for treating family conflicts in adolescents with attention-deficit hyperactivity disorder. *Journal of Consulting and Clinical Psychology, 60*, 450–462.

Bennett, D., & Gibbons, T. (2000). Efficacy of child cognitive-behavioral interventions for antisocial behavior: A meta-analysis. *Child and Family Behavior Therapy, 22*, 1–15.

Berg, I. L. (1994). *Family-based services: A solution-focused approach.* New York: W. W. Norton.

Berg, I. L., & Miller, S. (1992). *Working with the problem drinker.* New York: W. W. Norton.

Bertolino, B., & O'Hanlon, B. (2002). *Collaborative, competency-based counseling and therapy.* Boston: Allyn & Bacon.

Bienert, H., & Schneider, B. H. (1995). Deficit-specific social skills training with peer-nominated aggressive-disruptive and sensitive-isolated preadolescents. *Journal of Clinical Child Psychology, 24*, 287–299.

Brestan, E. V., & Eyberg, S. M. (1998). Effective psychosocial treatments of conduct-disordered children and adolescents: 29 years, 82 studies, and 5,272 kids. *Journal of Clinical Child Psychology, 27*(2), 180–189.

Burke, B. L., Arkowitz, H., & Dunn, C. (2002). The efficacy of motivational interviewing and its adaptations: What we know so far. In W. R. Miller & S. Rollnick (Eds.), *Motivational interviewing: Preparing people for change* (2nd ed., pp. 217–250). New York: Guilford.

Cade, B., & O'Hanlon, W. H. (1993). *A brief guide to brief therapy.* New York: W. W. Norton.

Cavell, T. A. (2000). *Working with parents of aggressive children: A practitioner's guide.* Washington, DC: American Psychological Association.

Clark, M. D. (1997). Interviewing for solutions. *Corrections Today, 59*(3), 98–102.

Corcoran, J. (1997). A solution-oriented approach to working with juvenile offenders. *Child and Adolescent Social Work Journal, 14*, 277–288.

De Shazer, S. (1988). *Clues: Investigating solutions in brief therapy.* New York: W. W. Norton.

Dodge, K. A., Price, J. M., Bachorowski, J., & Newman, J. P. (1990). Hostile attributional biases in severely aggressive adolescents. *Journal of Abnormal Psychology, 99*, 385–392.

Dolan, Y. (1991). *Resolving sexual abuse.* New York: W. W. Norton.

Dunn, C., DeRoo, L., & Rivara, F. P. (2001). The use of brief interventions adapted from motivational interviewing across behavioral domains: A systematic review. *Addiction, 96*(12), 1725–1742.

Durlak, J., Fuhrman, T., & Lampman, C. (1991). Effectiveness of cognitive-behavior therapy for maladapting children: A meta-analysis. *Psychological Bulletin, 110,* 204–214.

D'Zurilla, T., & Nezu, A. (2001). Problem-solving therapies. In K. Dobson & S. Keith (Eds.), *Handbook of cognitive-behavioral therapies* (2nd ed., pp. 211–245). New York: Guilford.

Eyberg, S. (1988). Parent-child interaction therapy: Integration of traditional and behavioral concerns. *Child and Family Behavior Therapy, 10,* 33–45.

Forehand, R. L., & McMahon, R. J. (1981). *Helping the noncompliant child: A clinician's guide to present training.* New York: Guilford.

Gingerich, W. J., & Eisengart, S. (2000). Solution-focused brief therapy: A review of the outcome research. *Family Process, 39*(4), 477–498.

Ginsburg, J.I.D., Mann, R. E., Rotgers, F., & Weekes, J. R. (2002). Motivational interviewing with criminal justice populations. In W. R. Miller & S. Rollnick (Eds.), *Motivational interviewing: Preparing people for change* (2nd ed., pp. 333–346). New York: Guilford.

Hanish, L. D., Tolan, P. H., & Guerra, N. G. (1996). Treatment of oppositional defiant disorder. In M. A. Reinecke, F. M. Dattilio, & A. Freeman (Eds.), *Cognitive therapy with children and adolescents* (pp. 62–78). New York: Guilford.

Hawkins, J. D., Catalano, R. F., & Miller, J. Y. (1992). Risk and protective factors for alcohol and other drug problems in adolescence and early adulthood: Implications for substance abuse prevention. *Psychological Bulletin, 112*(1), 64–105.

Kazdin, A. E. (1994). Psychotherapy for children and adolescents. In A. E. Bergin & S. L. Garfield (Eds.), *Handbook of psychotherapy and behavior change* (4th ed., pp. 543–594). New York: Wiley.

Kazdin, A. E. (1997). Practitioner review: Psychosocial treatments for conduct disorder in children. *Journal of Child Psychology and Psychiatry and Allied Disciplines, 38,* 161–178.

Kronenberger, W. S., & Meyer, R. G. (2001). *The child clinician's handbook* (2nd ed.). Needham Heights, MA: Allyn & Bacon.

McBride, D. C., VanderWaal, C. J., Terry, Y. M., & VanBuren, H. (1999). *Breaking the cycle of drug use among juvenile offenders.* Retrieved October 24, 2002, from http://www.ncjrs.org/pdffiles1/nij/179273.pdf.

Miller, W. R., & Rollnick, S. (2002). *Motivational interviewing* (2nd ed.). New York: Guilford.

Murphy, J. (1997). *Solution-focused counseling in middle and high schools.* Alexandria, VA: American Counseling Association.

Noonan, W. C., & Moyers, T. B. (1997). Motivational interviewing: A review. *Journal of Substance Misuse, 2,* 8–16.

O'Hanlon, W. H., & Weiner-Davis, M. (1989). *In search of solutions: A new direction in psychotherapy.* New York: W. W. Norton.

Patterson, G. R., Reid, J. B., Jones, R. R., & Conger, R. E. (1975). *A social learning approach to family intervention: Vol. 1. Families with aggressive children.* Eugene, OR: Castalia.

Robbins, A. (1992). *Awakening the giant within*. New York: Simon & Schuster.

Robinson, T. R., Smith, S. W., Miller, M. D., & Brownell, M. T. (1999). Cognitive behavior modification of hyperactivity-impulsivity and aggression: A meta-analysis of school-based studies. *Journal of Educational Psychology, 91*, 195–203.

Seagram, B. C. (1997). *The efficacy of solution-focused therapy with young offenders*. Unpublished doctoral dissertation, York University, Ontario.

Selekman, M. D. (1993). *Pathways to change: Brief therapy solutions with difficult adolescents*. New York: Guilford.

Selekman, M. D. (1997). *Solution-focused therapy with children: Harnessing family strengths for systemic change*. New York: Guilford.

Serketich, W. J., & Dumas, J. E. (1996). The effectiveness of behavioral parent training to modify antisocial behavior in children: A meta-analysis. *Behavior Therapy, 27*, 493–518.

Webster-Stratton, C. (1981; revised 2001). *Incredible years parents and children training series*. Seattle, WA: Incredible Years.

White, M. (1995). *Re-authorizing lives: Interviews & essays*. Adelaide, South Australia: Dulwich Centre Publications.

White, M., & Epston, D. (1990). *Narrative means to therapeutic ends*. New York: W. W. Norton.

8 Depression

JACQUELINE CORCORAN AND
JANE HANVEY PHILLIPS

According to estimates from the two major mental health epidemiologic surveys of the United States, the Epidemiologic Catchment Area study and the National Comorbidity Survey, 6.5% of adults have had a major depressive episode, 5.3% experienced major depressive disorder, and 1.6% were diagnosed with dysthymia (Surgeon General, 2002). The Mental Health Report from the Surgeon General cites major depression as the leading cause of disability worldwide. Depression has a negative impact on the economy in terms of reduced productivity and in greater use of health care resources. Further, this report cites that major depressive disorders cause more than a quarter of deaths by suicide (Surgeon General, 2002). For these reasons, people with depression must be identified and treated.

This chapter discusses how to apply the strengths-and-skills-building model to the problem of depression. The emphasis is on solution-focused and cognitive-behavioral therapies. The purpose is to empower the client with a focus on what is going well and to take concrete steps toward a depression-free future. Motivational interviewing does not play as large a role in the treatment of depression. Motivational interviewing was designed for those who believe their problem is not a problem, and people who seek help for depression usually are motivated to feel relief from their pain. However, its use may be prescribed when people's motivation for task implementation needs to be bolstered (see Rollnick, Mason, & Butler, 1999, for an example) or when they are indulging in problematic coping efforts (e.g., substance abuse) to handle their depression.

In this chapter, cognitive-behavioral therapy and solution-focused therapy are discussed separately, followed by their integration.

Cognitive-Behavioral Therapy

Cognitive-behavioral therapy has had a long history of use with depression (e.g., Young, Beck, & Weinberger, 2001). The cognitive-behavioral view of depression assumes that people so afflicted have a negative view of self (worthless, inadequate, unlovable, and deficient), the environment (overwhelming, insurmountable obstacles, involves failure or loss), and the future (hopeless, their efforts will be insufficient to change, may involve suicidal ideation or attempts). Events are distorted to fit these negative views. Interventions center on identifying and replacing these negative distortions with ones that are more realistic and lead to feelings of well-being. Interventions include logical discourse, examination of evidence, tracking dysfunctional thoughts, behavioral experiments to test assumptions and negative beliefs, problem solving, role playing, imagery restructuring, diversion or relaxation techniques, and rating activities for pleasure and mastery.

Studies have indicated the superiority of cognitive-behavioral therapy for depression over wait-list controls, and its comparable performance to pharmacotherapy even for those who are severely depressed (DeRubeis, Gelfand, Tang, & Simons, 1999). However, certain characteristics in clients may lead to more beneficial outcomes. In a discussion of the type of client who benefits from cognitive-behavioral therapy for depression, Young et al. (2001) list that they are (a) introspective, (b) able to reason abstractly, (c) well organized, (d) conscientious about carrying out responsibilities, (e) employed, (f) not excessively angry, and (g) less dogmatic and rigid in thinking. However, many clients do not possess these characteristics, and other approaches may need to be integrated within the model to help them.

Solution-Focused Therapy

A couple of conceptual articles and case studies (Andrews & Clark, 1996; O'Hanlon, 1993) have applied solution-focused therapy to the problem of depression. Softas-Nall and Francis (1998) describe a solution-focused approach to dealing with adolescent suicidality. Assessment focuses on identifying the times when the adolescent feels safe from suicidal thoughts and what was different during those times. Scaling questions can be used to determine lethality, with 10 anchored as "feeling very safe."

Johnson and Miller (1994) build a case that solution-focused therapy addresses the depressogenic attribution style posited by Seligman (1990), in which people with a tendency toward depression explain negative events as permanent (vs. temporary), pervasive (vs. proximal), and personally caused (vs. externally caused). Exception-finding questions emphasize that events are proximal and contextually driven. Outcome questions, those that ask clients to create a vision of a future without the problem, stress that negative events are temporary and will not persist into the future. Externalizing questions cast the negative event as an external entity rather than a characterological problem. Only one study to date has examined the effect of solution-focused therapy on 10 clients (Lee, Greene, Mentzer, Pinnell, & Niles, 2001). Decreased depression was found at posttest, as well as at 6 months follow-up.

While not directly addressing depression, Kok and Leskela (1996) build a rationale for the use of solution-focused therapy for inpatient psychiatric hospital settings, where many of the cases involve depression and suicide, given the increasing demand from insurance companies and health management organizations for accountability and cost-effective treatment. The authors argue that brief hospital visits do not allow for in-depth examination of clients' past life events; instead, a solution-focused approach emphasizes a future-oriented perspective working toward the client's discharge. Although diagnoses are antithetical to a solution-focused approach, the authors accept the use of diagnoses for pragmatic reasons, such as insurance reimbursement, accreditation purposes, and a common language to enable hospital staff to more clearly define problems and their solutions. Because mental illness includes a biological component, medication can be helpful in improving mood and is seen as a potential solution. In addition, medication compliance may help clients become more adept at formulating and realizing solutions (Kok & Leskela, 1996).

Trautman (2000) also discussed combining medication with solution-focused therapy. On the negative side, he argues that medications emphasize the idea of help stemming from an external rather than an internal source. On the positive side, if an individual accepts that there is a biological disorder for which they are not to blame, they may be empowered to take action on their behalf. Trautman (2000) likens this to the Alcoholics Anonymous view of alcoholism in which people see themselves as afflicted with a disease that is out of their control. This empowers people to take action since guilt is therefore reduced.

Strengths-and-Skills-Building Model

The phases of treatment outlined for the strengths-and-skills-building model—engagement, solution exploration, problem exploration, goal setting, taking action, and termination—are described here, along with the techniques that accompany them.

Engagement

Techniques to engage the client in a collaborative process include listening and validation, using the client's idiosyncratic language, normalizing, and asking coping questions.

Listening and Validation

Often people need to feel heard, validated, and understood for their suffering before they are able to move on to other interventions. If depressive concerns are not attended to and understood, individuals may view the worker's efforts to shift the focus as irrelevant and premature (Beach, Sandeen, & O'Leary, 1990). During this stage, the practitioner may gain information about how long the depressive symptoms have been in existence and their severity, as well as any stressors identified that contribute to depression; however, from a solution-focused perspective, it is not advised to spend a great deal of time on history taking and gathering information about the problem, as a focus on the problem might further enhance a depressed viewpoint. At the same time, it is understood that such information may be necessary for the formulation of a diagnosis for insurance reimbursement purposes or agency requirements. In addition, it is necessary to assess suicidality (see Sommers-Flanagan & Sommers-Flanagan, 1995), and in cases of suicidality, a safety plan will have to be developed. See Box 8.1 for a listing of symptoms of depression and Box 8.2 for a sample safety plan.

Using Idiosyncratic Language

During this period of discussing depressive concerns, the practitioner should reflect clients' descriptions of their experiences, rather than professional jargon. If, for example, a client describes herself as "down in the dumps," the practitioner should use that term rather than "depressed." One rationale for the use of idiosyncratic language is to depathologize clients' concerns; the other is that clients feel understood when the worker uses their language. At the same time, some clients gain enormous relief from having a diagnosis applied to their symptoms because it helps them understand and name their experience (Miller & Rollnick, 2002) and know

Symptoms of Major Depression

- Persistent sad, anxious, or "empty" mood
- Feelings of hopelessness, pessimism
- Feelings of guilt, worthlessness, helplessness
- Loss of interest or pleasure in hobbies and activities that were once enjoyed
- Decreased energy, fatigue, being "slowed down"
- Difficulty concentrating, remembering, making decisions
- Insomnia, early-morning awakening, or oversleeping
- Appetite and/or weight loss or overeating and weight gain
- Thoughts of death or suicide; suicide attempts
- Restlessness, irritability
- Persistent physical symptoms that do not respond to treatment, such as headaches, digestive disorders, and chronic pain

Note. From *Depression*, by National Institute of Mental Health (NIMH), 2001, retrieved January 16, 2002, from http://www.nimh.nih.gov/publicat/depression.cfm

that there are resources and treatment at their disposal. The practitioner, therefore, should follow the client's lead on what is most helpful.

Normalizing

To further the nonpathologizing stance, the technique of normalizing may be used, in which clients' problems are validated as struggles that anyone in their position would face. For example, a mother of three boys described recently undergoing the loss of a beloved grandmother and a romantic break-up, which required a move to another residence and resulted in financial problems. The practitioner normalized that anyone going through these stressors would experience difficulty. Many times people who see a

Sample Safety Plan

I agree that I will not hurt myself. If I have thoughts of harming myself, I will call
_____ (friend or family member) at phone number _____,
_____ (friend or family member) at phone number _____,
_____ (crisis hotline) at phone number _____.

Signature _____

helper have experienced multiple challenges, and understandably their resources have been strained.

Annette Montgomery, a 28-year-old White woman, was distressed because her father had died 4 months ago, and she was still looking at his pictures and crying daily. Her roommates told her that she needed to stop looking at her father's pictures, as it was making her feel worse, but Annette said she kept returning to them. "It's sick, isn't it?" she asked. She didn't want to spend time with her family or with friends and was spending most of her free time lying in bed. She felt she must be going crazy to be acting this way. This woman experienced immense relief when she learned that the grief process was often experienced intensely and that, although it was deeply painful, her experience was quite normal.

Solution Exploration

A focus on strengths should occur early in the treatment process. Although the clinician must assess the readiness of the client for particular techniques, coping questions may serve as a bridge between validation and strengths-based work. Other techniques to garner strengths include orienting the client toward the future, exception finding, externalizing, and assessing and amplifying strengths.

Coping Questions

Coping questions not only validate the extent to which individuals have struggled but also ask clients to reflect on their resources, in terms of the attitudes, beliefs, abilities, qualities, and behaviors that they have used to manage their struggles. They also are helpful to assess people's coping mechanisms and where their skills need bolstering.

The following questions can be asked: "These sound like very difficult circumstances. How are you able to manage?" "Not everyone could do this. How are you able to cope?" In response to these questions, a 42-year-old African American woman said, "What choice do I have? I need to work and keep the house clean and feed the kids. No one else is going to do it for me."

The practitioner, a community mental health worker, said, "There's always a choice. How have you been able to follow through with the choice to put your children first?" This question led to a response by the woman that, despite how she felt, she often acted in an opposite way. "My mother was a drug addict and us kids never knew where we'd sleep or if we'd get any food some days. I don't ever want my kids to have those worries. When I feel like just sitting on the sofa, I remind myself that my kids are depending on me. I don't ever want to be like my mother, so I get up, and go to work, and take care of my kids."

When people feel particularly hopeless, they can also be asked, "How have you kept things from getting worse?" Answers to this question help people realize that they are employing their resources rather than being mired in helplessness. A 45-year-old White woman, who had experienced chronic depression, said that attending "Tough Love" groups helped her from becoming overwhelmed by the conflict she was experiencing with her teenage children. She discussed the support she received from the group and how useful it was to understand she wasn't alone in having such problems.

Another avenue of coping questions involves inquiry about the percentage of time the individual feels depressed. This helps people understand that despite the cognitive distortion that the depression is all-pervasive and all-encompassing, it is rarely experienced 100% of the time. Further questions can be asked about how individuals are able to cope during this time and what makes them feel a bit better the rest of the time.

A 56-year-old White man, recently forced into retirement, initially stated he is "always depressed." The clinician asked if there is a percentage of time that he does not feel depressed. After some thought, he replied that about 10% of the time, he doesn't feel depressed. The clinician asked him to identify times when this happened, and he said it was during his evening walk with his wife. The clinician then asked him what it was about the evening walk that relieved his depression. He replied that he enjoyed the physical activity and being with his wife because she had a good sense of humor and could make him laugh. The clinician encouraged the client to identify other times of the day that he could add physical activity or time with his wife as ways to increase the percentage of time he felt better. He noted that he could join a health club or walk with his neighbor in the morning. He also said he could meet his wife for lunch several times a week and that they used to do this often when he was working. By helping him identify the activities associated with a more positive mood, it was possible to improve the percentage of time he was feeling good.

Some people will name, in response to coping questions, the pleasurable activities they pursue to help themselves feel better, such as exercise, journaling, having hot baths or showers, talking on the phone, reading, craft making, and other creative activities. Clarke, Lewinsohn, and Hops's (1990) cognitive-behavioral conceptualization of depression notes the importance of positive reinforcement. One of the main interventions, therefore, is helping people increase the number of pleasurable activities they engage in, particularly those that involve others' support. The practitioner is advised to help clients with depression develop a list of activities that they can pursue on a daily basis. Some clients need permission to pursue activities they enjoy; others have to identify activities that make them feel slightly better or experiment with activities that are pleasurable for others so they can discover what is helpful for them.

An additional list can also be drawn up of pleasant activities the client can initiate when faced with a particularly debilitating, depressed mood (Bass, 1994). Louden (1992) further advises that the list should include the different sense modalities by which people experience the world. The client is advised to start with one item on the list and keep pursuing each item until the mood shifts and they experience some relief, and then to start over if the depression has still not lifted. See Box 8.3 for a sample list of items that may be chosen.

In a discussion of coping, some clients name coping mechanisms that may be dysfunctional for them in terms of their physical or mental health or their interpersonal relationships. Common dysfunctional coping mechanisms are alcohol or drug use, excessive television watching, and sleeping. The decisional balance technique is a way of addressing some of these mechanisms so that the client can come up with reasons to abandon the

---

Box 8.3

Sample List of Comfort Activities

Put on relaxation tape.
Put on motivational tape.
Play loud music.
Play soft music.
Have a warm bath.
Call _____ with phone number _____ .
Call _____ with phone number _____ .
Call _____ with phone number _____ . If not home, call _____ (phone) or _____ (phone).
Journal feelings.
Journal how you would like things to be.
Take a walk.
Drink a cool beverage.
Drink a hot beverage.
Write a positive affirmation 100 times.
Pray.
Yell into pillow and punch pillows.
Read.
Rent a movie.
Go to a movie.
Give yourself a head or foot massage.
Repeat list if necessary.

Note. See also *The Courage to Heal: A Guide for Women Survivors of Child Sexual Abuse*, by E. Bass, 1944, New York: HarperCollins; and *The Woman's Comfort Book: A Self-Nurturing Guide for Restoring Balance in Your Life*, by J. Louden, 1992, San Francisco: Harper.

behavior rather than the practitioner getting into a position of lecturing or advising the client about what he or she must do.

For example, Dionna, a 17-year-old African American, said that when she felt down, she sought out sexual relations with a man. When the practitioner asked her to consider the pros and cons of this behavior, Dionna admitted that while she felt good about herself when someone showed an interest in her, afterward, when they had gotten "what they wanted," sometimes she felt even worse. The practitioner worked further with Dionna, who came up with the following advantages to having sexual intercourse to cope with her depression: caused her mood to shift temporarily and she felt better about herself during the seduction process and the act itself. The disadvantages were the following: The mood shift didn't last long and she felt worse about herself afterward, she worried about whether the person would call her again, she had gotten a sexually transmitted disease, and other people called her a "slut."

After the decisional balance, clients are asked to come up with their own conclusions about how well the behavior works for them. Many clients, having gone through this process, readily admit that the behavior is hurting rather than helping. This exercise may open the door to the possibility of exploring other coping techniques that have fewer negative consequences for themselves. For example, Dionna was willing to consider some other ways to handle her depressed mood.

Enhancing Social Support

As a specific type of coping resource, research has repeatedly shown the importance of a support network to help people manage their depression (e.g., Kalil, Born, Kunz, & Caudill, 2001; Skaersaeter, Agren, & Dencker, 2002; Wildes, Harkness, & Simons, 2002). One symptom of the disorder, however, is a tendency to isolate. Some questions to assess social support include the following (Murphy, 1997):

- What people are available in the social support network?
- Of all the people in your life, who helps you the most?
- What does that person do or say that really helps you?
- Who are your heroes?
- What is it about_____that you like?
- What do you think_____would do if faced with this problem?
- Would you be willing to try something like that?

James Davis, a White 17-year-old high school student, reported feeling very lonely, with no friends. He went to see the school practitioner because he had started to have thoughts of suicide. He told the worker that he didn't really have a plan; he was just tired of feeling so alone. Through questioning, he was able to acknowledge that he had access to social support through school activities. When asked who had helped him the most in his life or whom he would consider his heroes, he thought for a while before responding that his basketball coach was one of his heroes because he had encouraged him to participate in the sport. The worker asked James what the coach had said or done that had really helped him. James replied that several times Coach Jones had said, "I trust you to do your best." The worker asked James if there was something special he particularly liked about Coach Jones, to which James replied, "Coach is friendly to all the kids, even nonplayers." At this point, the worker was able to ask James what he thought the coach would do if he wanted more friends. James replied that he didn't think the coach would have this problem because he was so friendly. The worker pointed out that James was assuming it was easy for Coach Jones to make friends because of the coach's behaviors, but James didn't really know whether this was the case or not. The worker encouraged James to identify specific behaviors the coach exhibited that made him seem friendly. James stated that the coach went to most of the extracurricular school functions. When asked if he would be willing to go to some of the school's extracurricular activities in order to begin increasing his social contacts, James agreed and said he would make arrangements to meet Coach Jones at an upcoming track meet.

The following steps are involved in social skills training (Clarke et al., 1990):

1. How to approach others, what to say to get a conversation going, how to join a group, how to be a good listener
2. Appropriate self-disclosure
3. Sharing and cooperation skills
4. Problem-solving and conflict-resolution skills

In James's situation, it was not enough to attend more extracurricular school functions. He needed appropriate social skills to nurture the contacts he made. The practitioner helped James identify ways to approach other students and join a conversation. The first step was to identify some areas of interest for him so he would be able to carry on a conversation with people who had similar interests. He acknowledged having a concern for abandoned animals and noted that there was a club for students who volunteered every Saturday at the local animal shelter and then went out for lunch after their work there. The practitioner helped James identify topics for discussion that would provide an appropriate amount of self-disclosure and explained the importance of limiting self-disclosure at first. She also encouraged him to offer assistance to his peers, without being pushy, and provided an opportunity for James to role-play hypothetical scenarios. Finally, James was given information about problem-solving and conflict-resolution skills and, again, was given an opportunity for role play.

Orienting Toward the Future

When people seek help for depression, they are often in a state of hopelessness and helplessness and are experiencing a great deal of emotional pain. Solution-focused interventions, therefore, are very helpful for the beginning stage of the work because they orient people to strengths and to a vision of a more hopeful future: "What will indicate to you that coming here has been successful?" "How will you know when you longer need to come here?" "What will be happening that will indicate to you that you can manage things on your own?" (Bertolino & O'Hanlon, 2002). Clients usually react with surprise to these questions; they may have some difficulty initially producing answers because of the characteristic negative thinking of depression, in which the future is seen as only an extension of a painful present. However, being pushed to answer these questions helps the client begin to view possibilities for the future.

Exception Finding

The main intervention for solution-focused therapy is exception finding, in which the practitioner explores their pasts with clients to discover times when the problem was not exerting its negative influence and then applies these exceptions to the problem areas. (For details on the exception-finding process, see Chapter 1.) People with depression may talk about exceptions in a way that gives credit to externals: "I didn't do anything different. My supervisor was just nice that day." Similarly, cognitive-behavioral theorists have discussed the problematic nature of attributing positive events to entities or people outside the self ("My supervisor was just nice to me") and attributing negative events to internal factors that are global and stable in nature ("I'm stupid") (Weiner, 1995). In solution-focused therapy, careful questioning is used to elicit the role the client has played in the exception.

Clara Martinez, a 24-year-old single Hispanic woman, reported feeling lonely and depressed. She complained that nobody ever wanted to spend time with her. The worker asked if there was ever a time when Clara participated in activities with other people. "Well, last weekend, some of my coworkers from the new job asked me to go to a movie with them," she responded. Then she added, "They must have done it just to be polite." The practitioner responded to this statement by asking, "Well, how did you arrange the situation so that you'd be present when your coworkers were discussing their weekend plans?"

"I didn't really 'arrange' it," Clara said. "I just walked over to get a soda out of the machine and they were standing around the soda machine talking."

The worker pointed out that she could have chosen to avoid the group but didn't: "What were you thinking as you approached the group?"

"I thought, 'I really want a soda and they're usually friendly to me, so it's probably safe to go to the machine. If anyone looks at me, I'll just say "hi" and head back to my office.' " She went on to explain that people looked friendly enough, so she joined the group. The worker questioned her more closely about how she handled the movie conversation, and they discovered from the ensuing conversation that Clara had taken a more active role than she had at first given herself credit for. Clara stated that she heard her coworkers talking about the movie and she asked one of them if he had seen it. He said he hadn't and asked if she had. When she responded that she hadn't seen it either, he asked if she would like to go with the group to see it. Through these questions, Clara was empowered to see the role she took in events.

The next phase of exception finding is to help clients enlarge upon identified exceptions in order to resolve the problems that still plague them. How could these attitudes, beliefs, and actions be adapted and applied to the current difficulty? For generalization to occur, it may be necessary to engage in cognitive-behavioral methods of change, such as role-play, so that clients can practice their skills. Let's continue with our example of Clara, the woman at the soda machine. She successfully engaged her coworkers in conversation that time but continued to avoid social situations. The practitioner encouraged Clara to identify the aspects of the previous situation that worked well for her in order to adapt them to new situations. Clara responded that even though her heart was pounding as she approached the group, she felt good that she had made the effort and asked someone a question. The practitioner validated Clara's anxiety and provided positive feedback about her efforts. "Now let's role-play another situation using the same techniques that worked for you at the soda machine. You've mentioned that you would like to get to know your neighbors better. I'll play the role of your next-door neighbor and assume I'm out watering my plants." Clara joined the role-play by walking up to the worker and saying, "I've never seen flowers like that. What are they?" The worker kept the role-play going and allowed Clara several opportunities to continue the conversation, which she did with occasional coaching. By the end of the session, Clara was feeling quite comfortable about her ability to engage others, at least briefly, in conversation. The practitioner was able to point out that this is a skill that is useful in many situations.

Externalizing

Another way that exceptions can be mined is through the intervention of externalizing. Externalizing interventions can be used when the client defines or describes the depression in symbolic ways (e.g., the cloud, the fog, the blackness, the tunnel, the pit, heaviness). The practitioner asks questions that help the client gain a perspective of depression so that it is seen not as internal to the client but as an external entity. The depression is cast outside the individual, and through questioning, the client is asked how he or she can overcome, gain control over, or stand up to the depression. In this way, clients are freed up to consider "depression" not as an intrinsic part of their beings or personalities but as something that can be fought against and overcome. It also lightens up the often serious ways that depression is considered so that more options are revealed.

Drawings are one way that symbolic images of depression can be externalized. When clients are asked to draw their images, they are also asked about how the depression in their pictures can be shifted or transformed so that it is no longer a problem. In Clara's picture, she described swirling black lines as her depression, but she said that there were now small pieces of yellow light shining through the darkness, which meant that the black was not all-encompassing. When asked to account for the yellow spaces, Clara said that it was due to the progress she had made in treatment. This gave her a sense of hope that change was possible.

Another way depression can be externalized is to have clients write dialogues with their depression in which depression speaks to them and they speak back to it. A similar technique is to write letters to the externalized entity (Dear Depression/Blackness/Cloud/Tunnel, etc.). The following formula adapted from Dolan (1991) can be used in the letter writing:

- Thank the depression for the purpose depression has served, whether it is surviving brutal childhood circumstances or some other kind of protective function.
- Address the depression for the ways it has hindered positive feelings and experiences.
- Say good-bye to the depression, conveying the attributes and coping skills that will enable the person to manage without it.

The following letter was written by a 23-year-old White woman, Alisa, who saw a counselor for depression and anxiety. Initially, she was having trouble with a romantic breakdown, her relationship with her mother, and the type of career to pursue. She wrote the following letter:

Dear Depression,
I am writing a letter to you to say good-bye, that I don't need you anymore. You helped protect me from feelings that were too strong and that I didn't know how to handle. When I was a child, no one was around to help me with my feelings. But the bad thing was I didn't really feel anything but you. You shut me down. You made me feel bad about myself, and that I wasn't worth anything. But I am worth something. I have learned that now from being in therapy.

I have learned about my feelings, and that they aren't too much for me to handle. I would rather feel them than just feel your blackness. My feelings are pure, like water flowing out of a spigot, instead of you, jamming up the pipes. I know how to manage my feelings, like writing down what happens to me, and calling friends, and going to therapy. I don't need you now. Thank you, but good-bye.

Sincerely,
Alisa

This step allowed Alisa to have a new perspective of depression as existing not within but outside herself, where she could be empowered to stand up to it. She was able not only to list her strengths but also to convincingly argue that they were strong enough to circumvent depression's influence.

Assessing Strengths

A major part of the work in focusing on solutions and strengths is to discover what the client brings in terms of personal and contextual resources that can be applied to the current problems. Murphy (1997) suggests being attuned to the resources people might inadvertently reveal in conversation. For example, people might show certain strengths in their work setting, such as the ability to manage time, people skills, organizational skills, or creativity, that they can bring to bear on their problems. Murphy (1997) also advises asking people directly about their job skills, hobbies, talents, interests, and other resources with the following types of questions:

- What kinds of things do you enjoy doing?
- What would your friends/relatives/coworkers/colleagues say that you are good at if I asked them?
- How can these talents and skills be utilized in your work?

Linda Hawthorne was a 51-year-old divorced White woman whose youngest child had moved 1,200 miles away from home to go to college 2 months ago. Linda sought the help of the practitioner on the advice of her employer, who had noticed a decline in Linda's productivity at work. During Linda's initial contact with the worker, she reported that she began feeling depressed as she helped her son prepare for college, and the depression worsened after he left. The practitioner asked Linda what a typical day was like for her. Linda replied that she woke up just in time to quickly get dressed and go to work. After work, she said, she didn't feel like doing anything and would usually just watch TV and go to bed; she felt useless now that her children had all left home. When the practitioner asked Linda what she enjoyed, Linda replied that the only activities she liked doing were those she used to do with her children. The practitioner took another approach and asked what Linda what types of things Linda was able to do well. When Linda didn't reply, the worker asked, "What would people at work say you're good at?" Linda replied that several coworkers had told her how much they admired the way Linda had decorated her office, and two of her coworkers had even asked her to help them decorate their offices. The worker asked if she enjoyed decorating, and Linda said she guessed she did. Further questioning and prompting by the worker helped Linda make plans to redecorate her home in the upcoming weeks, tying this into symbolically changing her environment in a positive way to introduce a new phase of her life.

Problem Exploration

Problem exploration for working with depression involves the difficulties individuals often have with managing and expressing their feelings and working with their problematic belief systems. (For an extensive list of maladaptive schemas, see Young et al., 2001.) A strengths orientation is taken to address these problem areas.

Feeling Identification and Management

People with depression may lack awareness of their feelings beyond the blanket of depression, so it is often necessary to teach clients how to identify their feelings and then manage them. Although exhaustive lists of feeling words can be consulted (for instance, Hepworth, Rooney, and Larsen [2002] have an excellent delineation), sometimes it's easier to teach clients the four basic feelings: anger, sadness, fear, and happiness. Once the client can identify these feelings, an exercise is for the client, as homework, to write down 5 to 10 feelings per day with a brief explanation of the trigger. (This exercise and other journaling ideas are provided in Box 8.4.) This

---

Box 8.4

Journaling Ideas

1. Write a list of feelings with brief explanations ("I feel mad because my boyfriend flirted with someone else"; "I feel scared because I have to make a presentation"; "I feel sad because my wife won't give me affection").
   Rationale: People with depression often do not know what specific feelings have triggered a depressive episode. Knowing trigger feelings helps to identify the needed coping mechanisms.
2. Write in present tense about how the individual wants things to be rather than the way they presently are.
3. Write a list of things daily that happened that the individual would like to have continue to happen.

---

information helps the client gain awareness of feelings, those that seem to act as a cue for depression and those that are unexpressed. The information also assists the practitioner in targeting interventions that help clients manage feelings that are difficult for them. Skills, such as coping, communication, or assertiveness, may need to be taught.

For example, a 15-year-old White girl explained that she "cut on" her wrists with a razor blade. Discussion of specific situations when this had occurred determined that certain triggers were associated with her urge to cut, particularly incidents when people had made statements that were hurtful, such as when her boyfriend called her "stupid" or when her parents criticized her. She was taught ways to express her feelings that earned people's respect and were more likely to get her what she wanted (the use of "I" messages, asking for specific behaviors from others).

Mary Hernandez, 28, found from recording her feelings each day that she seemed to regularly experience sadness and fear but not anger. The practitioner then asked her to come up with "I feel angry" statements, but Mary was unable to do so. The practitioner encouraged her by saying, "I know you don't feel it right now, but if you were to feel angry, what would you feel angry about?" Mary was then quickly able to name anger toward her husband for allowing their children to do things she had already told them they couldn't do—even after she had requested that he not override her decisions. She also named anger at her supervisor for asking Mary to work late when her supervisor knew Mary had to collect her children from day care by a certain time in the evening; otherwise, she was charged extra. From this point, the practitioner could work with Mary on exception finding, times when she was successful in acting as a united front with her husband for the discipline of their children or when she was able to stand up to her supervisor's unreasonable demands. Gaps in skills could be identified from these exceptions, and then training on specific skills, such as assertiveness, could then be a focus of the work.

Sung-Yu Kim, a 20-year-old Asian American community college student and waitress, said that her depression begins with boredom and spirals from there. First, the practitioner asked how Sung-Yu has been successful in coping with that feeling in the past: "Tell me about a time when you were bored but you were able to get out of it without letting it go any further." Sung-Yu responded that what worked for her in the past was to call up a friend and meet for a walk, a meal, or shopping. She said that sometimes, though, "no one was around," and then she succumbed to depression. The practitioner then took one of the steps from the problem-solving process and asked Sung-Yu to brainstorm options for how to manage this difficult emotion. She encouraged Sung-Yu to come up with as many ideas as possible, however silly or absurd. Sung-Yu came up with the following list: (a) call up and see if she was needed at work so she could make some money, (b) do schoolwork, (c) take a walk, (d) work out at the gym, (e) write in her journal, (f) go to a bookstore, (g) go have a latte, (h) clean her apartment, (i) get her hair cut, (j) put on makeup, (k) rent a video, (l) go to a movie, (m) flirt with a guy, and (n) dance along with a music video.

Feeling identification is important so that individuals can be aware of their emotional triggers for depression and can more effectively manage their emotional reactions, rather than allowing depression to take over.

Working With Belief Systems

Solution-focused scales can also be used to attack particularly troublesome belief systems. For instance, if a client thinks, "My life is meaningless," which often accompanies depression, the way to work with this cognition is, first, to anchor the negative belief at 1 and the opposite, more functional belief at 10. Clients usually have not considered the formulation of more positive and realistic beliefs, and so they might need some help with constructing an anchor at 10. Perhaps in this example, the functional belief is identified as "My life has value and meaning." A benefit of this conceptualization of beliefs as a continuum is the aforementioned tendency for people to become polarized or dichotomized in their thinking, which is a source of many cognitive distortions. (See Chapter 3 for some common cognitive distortions.)

The anchored belief at 10 is made concrete by asking the client to name behaviors that accompany such a belief. A focus on concrete behaviors at 10 shows people they have control over some aspects of how they feel. If they are able to make small steps in behavior changes and thoughts, then the assumption in both solution-focused and cognitive-behavioral therapy is that these are easier to control than are feelings and will also lead to shifts in painful affects.

Cognitive distortions are further challenged during the next part of the scaling intervention, which asks clients to rank-order themselves in relation to 10. Clients often place themselves at a number implying change has already occurred, which allows them to see that their problems are not as all-encompassing as they previously believed. In the event clients place themselves at a 1 on the scale, the helper can inquire when the client feels "just slightly better" or "not as badly," or "how you have stopped things from getting even worse."

Relationship questions—questions about where others may perceive the client—are also asked ("Where would your supervisor place you on the scale?"). Very often clients suffering from cognitive distortions view themselves differently from how others experience them. Getting clients to perceive themselves through the perspective of other people may help them see themselves more realistically. They may also become more able to free themselves from a self-limiting perspective and generate more options and possibilities.

Timothy Green was a 26-year-old White male who reported he was very depressed and felt that his life was meaningless. He believed himself to be trapped in a dead-end job as an auto mechanic, with no other options because he had dropped out of high school. His longtime girlfriend told him last week that if they didn't get married within the month, she would leave him and begin dating other people. Timothy told the clinician that both of his older brothers were successful businessmen with happy families and that he felt he was worthless.

The clinician asked Timothy what his best friend would say about him being worthless. At first, Timothy said his friend just needed him around to have someone to talk to but that he could find another friend. The clinician reminded Timothy that his friend could choose to have someone else for his best friend now but chose Timothy, so there must be a reason. Timothy eventually stated that his best friend had often told him how much Timothy meant to him and how helpful Timothy was when his friend had problems at work or when his car was not running. The clinician also asked Timothy to think about the reasons his girlfriend was giving him an ultimatum. He said that she had wanted to marry him for a long time and often told him how much she cared for him. He said, "I guess if she really wanted to leave, she would have left already. Maybe she just wants me to make up my mind."

The clinician asked Timothy what his supervisor or customers would say about him and he smiled. "They really like me. Some of my customers won't let anyone but me work on their cars." The clinician followed this questioning by asking Timothy what he believed would make his life more meaningful. He replied that he would like to run his own auto repair business. When asked what it would take to accomplish this, Timothy was able to outline a strategy and began to see how he could put it into place.

A decisional balance from motivational interviewing can also be conducted with beliefs that are rated at a 1 or that are experienced as intractable. Clients can be asked, "What are the advantages of holding this belief?" and "What are the disadvantages of having this belief?" By partaking in this exercise, clients begin to get a sense that beliefs and cognitions are not as fixed as they once thought, and the very process of exploring beliefs allows their thinking to become more flexible.

The practitioner in the following case did a decisional balance with James, a 32-year-old White man, who had the common depressed person's belief that his life had no meaning. He reacted with surprise to the idea of examining the advantages and disadvantages of his beliefs and having the practitioner write them down, but he agreed to do so. At first, he said, "There isn't anything I get out of it."

PRACTITIONER: We all get something out of our behavior or our beliefs; otherwise, we wouldn't have them. Most people, for example, feel at least comfortable with their beliefs. They are safe and familiar and would take work to change.

JAMES: Okay, then I guess that's one of them.

PRACTITIONER: We can get back to some of the advantages in a moment. What are some of the disadvantages?

JAMES: Well, I don't feel good. I don't see the use of living sometimes because there's no meaning.

PRACTITIONER: Okay, so that's a real disadvantage. What else?

JAMES: Well, because there's no meaning, then I don't take on anything important. I mean, I keep getting jobs and not sticking with anything, because what's the point?

PRACTITIONER: So you don't make a commitment to a career.

JAMES: Yeah, that pretty much sums it up. And I spend my free time drinking and watching TV and smoking dope, because, hey, why not?

PRACTITIONER: So you don't spend your free time doing anything meaningful. Okay, now let's come back to the advantages.

JAMES [considers]: Maybe it's a good excuse not to do anything. I don't have to figure out the career thing. I can just fool around and smoke dope. I don't have to get involved in a relationship because there's no meaning to that either.

The practitioner went over the list with James and asked him for his reaction. He noted that there were more disadvantages than advantages to the belief, but it made more sense to him now why he held it. The practitioner then asked what he could believe instead as an alternative possibility. With the practitioner's help, he eventually came up with "My life has meaning and is worth something." Then he described some behaviors that would match having that belief, such as going back to college, selecting a major, and sticking with it. He said that would mean he couldn't spend as much time just hanging out with his friends, drinking beer, and smoking dope. He would have to be studying and working to pay for tuition. As the example illustrates, the decisional balance is a way to help people scrutinize their beliefs and see them as more malleable than they previously believed. It also provides a process for people to consider more functional beliefs and behaviors.

Goal Setting Through Scaling Interventions

Depressed people tend to project from their current painful state into the past (they have always felt this way) and into the future (that they will always feel that way) (Young et al., 2001). When people come in for help with depression, they are often overwhelmed and experience their depression as all-encompassing and pervasive. It is very difficult for people in the midst of depression to orient themselves toward different possibilities for the future. Scaling interventions are a concrete way for clients to mobilize a sense of hopefulness. Creating a 1 to 10 scale and asking clients to detail behaviorally what they will be doing at 10 when they are no longer plagued by their depression is, for some, a first glimpse toward a depression-free existence. For example, will they socialize more, exercise, read their favorite type of books, or get back to gardening? Asking questions about what 10 will constitute shifts the focus from a perception that everything is bad and wrong to one where there is some possibility of enjoyment and pleasure.

In the strengths-and-skills-building model, clients are further asked to anchor their cognitions at 10: "Things seem to be looking up." "I am having fun and experiencing pleasure." "I can handle what comes my way." "The day is worth facing." "I may not like this job, but at least it pays the bills for now." "My children are the best thing I have going so I might as well enjoy them." Note how in these examples the emphasis is on the presence of positive behavior and cognitions rather than their absence. If clients persist in answering by focusing on the negative, the practitioner can push for the converse. For example, if a client says she will be "not spending her time alone" or "not staying in bed," the practitioner can ask, "What will you be doing instead of spending time alone or staying in bed?"

It must be noted that 10 should be realistic and achievable within a brief time frame, rather than "when everything is perfect." The solution-focused approach assumes that small changes occurring within a short time frame reverberate in a systemic way. A small difference makes a client feel slightly better with increased optimism, setting up the expectation that other change will occur, which, in turn, spirals into further change. This assumption is similar to the notion of positive and negative spirals as discussed by cognitive-behavioral theorists in relation to depression (Clarke et al., 1990). An example of a negative spiral is as follows: Person feels down; thought is "I don't feel like doing anything. I'm just going to sit around by myself"; isolation leads to further negative thoughts like "Nobody likes me" and "I'm lazy"; mood becomes worse. Positive spirals work the opposite way: Although mood is poor, "I'm going to call my friend anyway"; positive social interaction leads to improved mood and thoughts, such as "Some people must like me. Maybe I am okay."

An orientation toward a future without depression is assisted by introducing the scaling intervention even at an early stage in the helping process. In this way, the client starts to develop a vision about what a depression-free life might look like and recognizes that some of those things are currently in existence. Manageable steps are broken down so that 10 is achieved.

Taking Action

Part of taking action involves task setting, which can be formulated from the solution-focused scale. Clients are called upon to determine how they will move up one rank order from one session to the next. Asking clients to come up with their own answers is seen as more empowering than relying solely on the education or training model of cognitive-behavioral therapy, in which the helper prescribes information or a task.

When tasks are difficult to formulate or when barriers are present, the problem-solving process can be used to keep clients moving up the scale. For clients to experience success from tasks, it may also be necessary to bring in the cognitive-behavioral method of behaviorally rehearsing agreed-upon strategies. Any skill deficits that might impede progress are identified and corrected with some brief training and perhaps modeling from the practitioner.

LaWanda Johnson, a 44-year-old African American woman, sought out the services of the practitioner because "people walk all over me." She complained that her sister was living with her and not paying any of the bills she had promised to pay. And now, on top of everything else, La-Wanda received a notice from her bank the day before that she had insufficient funds to cover several checks she had written. "I just want to give up. I'll never get enough money to pay all the fees! I didn't even know it happened. My job was supposed to deposit my check, and they didn't. I called my boss and he said he'll make sure it gets deposited next week, but I'll be in jail by then."

The practitioner asked LaWanda what she thought to be the problem, but LaWanda only started crying.

LaWANDA: I don't know.
PRACTITIONER: Well, it sounds like the problem is you don't have enough money in the bank right now to cover the checks and overdraft fees.
LaWANDA: But there's more. My rent is due and my sister owes me money and if I go to jail, I'll lose my job.

The practitioner encouraged LaWanda to focus on one problem at a time, so LaWanda agreed that the problem with the bank was probably the most urgent. Together, LaWanda and the worker brainstormed possible solutions and generated a variety of ideas, some of them plausible and some of them ridiculous—the notion being to open oneself to thinking differently and to stimulate ideas. The worker instructed LaWanda to write down every solution before deciding on the ones that would be most useful. LaWanda produced the following ideas with the worker's input:

- She could take out a loan to pay the fees.
- She could close the account and move out of her apartment, so the bank couldn't find her.
- She could ask her ex-husband for the money.
- She could go back to the places where she wrote the checks and explain what happened with her paycheck and see if they'd let her pay them next week.
- She could tell the bank manager what happened and see if he'd cancel the fees and hold the checks until her money is there.

At this point, the worker suggested they evaluate each of the solutions that had been generated.

PRACTITIONER: What are the advantages and disadvantages of taking out a loan to pay the fees?

LaWANDA: Well, obviously, an advantage is that I'd have money in the bank, but the disadvantage is that I'd be deeper in debt.

PRACTITIONER: Okay, what about closing the account and moving?

LaWANDA: The advantage is that I couldn't write any more "hot checks," but there are lots more disadvantages: I'd have to find a place to move, come up with the down payment, pack my stuff, get someone to help me move, and then I'd always be worrying about getting caught.

PRACTITIONER: What are the advantages and disadvantages of going to the places where you wrote the checks to explain the situation?

LaWANDA: An advantage is that they might not make me pay their fees plus they might wait to get the money until next week. But I see a lot of disadvantages. I'm embarrassed that this happened, and I don't want to tell a lot of people. I don't remember how to get to one of the stores where I was. If they see me, they may want me to pay them right now.

PRACTITIONER: How about your idea of talking to the bank manager?

LaWANDA: The advantage is that I know him and he may be nice about this; I've never "bounced" a single check before. He has the power to waive the fees and hold the checks until next week. One disadvantage I see, though, is that I'll be embarrassed.

After addressing all the solutions that were generated, LaWanda decided she would talk to the bank manager about the situation. She and the worker role-played the scenario, and LaWanda left the office feeling empowered and optimistic.

Medication Use

Taking action might also involve working with medication. Meta-analyses have shown the importance of medication for treating depression (e.g., Anderson, 2000). Kok and Leskela (1996) discuss that medication, although stemming from a medical model of treatment, is not incompatible with a solution-focused approach, and that taking medication can be seen as one solution. However, Bertolino and O'Hanlon (2002) caution that people should still be empowered to see the part that they take in change rather than attributing it all to the effects of medication.

- "You mentioned that you think the medication you're taking is helping. How are you working with the medication to better your life?"
- "In your mind, what does the medication you're taking allow you to do that you might not otherwise be able to do?"
- "What percentage of the change you've experienced is a result of the medication and what percentage do you think is your own doing?"
- "What are you able to do as a result of feeling better from taking medication?"

Claudia Adams, a 39-year-old African American woman with an extensive history of physical and sexual abuse in childhood, had recently been demoted at work as a result of poor attendance. She had struggled with depression intermittently for years. Subsequent to the demotion at work, her depression had become profound and led to a suicide attempt. Following the suicide attempt, she was prescribed antidepressants and believed that they were responsible for lessening her depressive symptoms. The clinician helped Claudia recognize her overt contributions to the improvement in her depression.

The clinician asked Claudia how she was able to work with the medication to improve her life. Claudia replied that she was able to get out of bed more easily in the mornings, and she had more energy throughout the day. She went on to say that she used the medicine to make herself get out of bed in the mornings; she kept it in the kitchen and had to go there to take it. The clinician then asked Claudia what she was able to do differently as a result of taking the medication. Claudia replied that one of the biggest changes she was making was to focus on her present life, working toward current goals rather than ruminating about past abuse. She was able to acknowledge that this took active effort on her part and was not simply due to taking medication.

Termination

Termination questions ask clients how they will maintain and amplify treatment changes, as well as how they will handle triggers and difficult circumstances (see Chapter 5). Particular to the problem of depression, the reemergence of depressed feelings, rather than being viewed negatively ("What's the use? I'm always going to be this way"), can be reframed as a signal that the client may need to take proactive behaviors. For instance, Alisa identified in treatment that when people were disrespectful to her or let her down, her pattern was to feel depressed. The positive side of her depression was that it told her when she needed to handle a situation more assertively.

Termination can also involve the practitioner writing a letter (see Chapter 5) that compliments the client, summarizes progress, and highlights resources and strengths. Such a letter is reproduced here from a practitioner who worked in an inpatient hospital:

Dear Don:
It has been a pleasure working with you over the past several weeks. You demonstrated great fortitude in the midst of very difficult circumstances, and your persistence in pursuing treatment for your depression is to be commended.

You have made tremendous progress in the goals you identified—finding a job you enjoy and coping with the stress of dealing of your ex-wife. During the last weeks, you've addressed your thinking patterns and been diligent about completing homework assignments. I appreciate your consistency in doing these exercises and your feedback that they were helpful to you.

I encourage you to focus on those times you described when you felt a little bit better. As you recall, you mentioned that you spent time with friends, played the guitar, and listened to music. Continue with those very positive activities.

While I was disappointed to hear you left the hospital prior to our final session, you are the one who knows what you need. If that includes continuing treatment on an outpatient basis, that is available to you. Please let me know if I can be of further help to you. I wish you good success.

Sincerely,
Barbara

The practitioner and the client did not have the opportunity to have a last session before he left the hospital. Therefore, the letter served as a tangible reminder of this client's strengths, dwelling on the expert role the client holds in his own life. For instance, he was the one to decide if outpatient treatment is what he needed, rather than making the assumption that it is something he must do. The letter summarizes, in a concrete way, the exceptions that have been forged and the strategies that have worked. In this way, client resources are both identified and strengthened.

References

Anderson, I. (2000). Selective serotonin reuptake inhibitors versus tricyclic antidepressants: A meta-analysis of efficacy and tolerability. *Journal of Affective Disorders, 58,* 19–36.

Andrews, J., & Clark, D. (1996). In the case of a depressed woman: Solution-focused or narrative therapy approaches. *The Family Journal: Counseling and Therapy for Couples and Families, 4,* 243–250.

Bass, E. (1994). *The courage to heal: A guide for women survivors of child sexual abuse.* New York: HarperCollins.

Beach, S., Sandeen, E., & O'Leary, K. (1990). *Depression in marriage: A model for etiology and treatment.* New York: Guilford.

Bertolino, B., & O'Hanlon, B. (2002). *Collaborative, competency-based counseling and therapy.* Boston: Allyn & Bacon.

Clarke, G., Lewinsohn, P., & Hops, H. (1990). *The adolescent coping with depression course: A psychoeducational intervention for unipolar depression in high school students.* Eugene, OR: Castalia.

DeRubeis, R., Gelfand, L., Tang, T., & Simons, A. (1999). Medications versus cognitive behavior therapy for severely depressed outpatients: Mega-analysis of four randomized comparisons. *American Journal of Psychiatry, 156,* 1007–1013.

Dolan, Y. (1991). *Resolving sexual abuse.* New York: W. W. Norton.

Hepworth, D. H., Rooney, R., & Larsen, J. (2002). *Direct social work practice: Theory and skills* (6th ed.). Belmont, CA.: Brooks/Cole.

Johnson, L., & Miller, S. (1994). Modification of depression risk factors: A solution-focused approach. *Psychotherapy, 31,* 244–253.

Kalil, A., Born, C., Kunz, J., & Caudill, P. (2001). Life stressors, social support, and depressive symptoms among first-time welfare recipients. *American Journal of Community Psychology, 29,* 355–369.

Kok, C., & Leskela, J. (1996). Solution-focused therapy in a psychiatric hospital. *Journal of Marital and Family Therapy, 22,* 397–406.

Lee, M. Y., Greene, G., Mentzer, R., Pinnell, S., & Niles, D. (2001). Solution-focused brief therapy and the treatment of depression: A pilot study. *Journal of Brief Therapy, 1,* 33–49.

Louden, J. (1992). *The woman's comfort book: A self-nurturing guide for restoring balance in your life.* San Francisco: Harper.

Miller, W., & Rollnick, S. (2002). *Motivational interviewing: Preparing people to change addictive behavior* (2nd ed.). New York: Guilford.

Murphy, J. (1997). *Solution-focused counseling in middle and high schools.* Alexandria, VA: American Counseling Association.

National Institute of Mental Health (NIMH). (2001). Depression. Retrieved January 16, 2002, from http://www.nimh.nih.gov/publicat/depression.cfm.

O'Hanlon, W. H. (1993). Take two people and call them in the morning: Brief solution-oriented therapy with depression. In S. Friedman (Ed.), *The new language of change: Constructive collaboration in psychotherapy* (pp. 50–84). New York: Guilford.

Rollnick, S., Mason, P., & Butler, C. (1999). *Health behavior change: A guide for practitioners*. New York: Churchill Livingstone.

Seligman, M. (1990). *Learned optimism*. New York: Knopf.

Skaersaeter, I., Agren, H., & Dencker, K. (2002). Subjective lack of social support and presence of dependent stressful life events characterize patients suffering from major depression compared with healthy volunteers. *Journal of Psychiatric and Mental Health Nursing, 8*, 107–114.

Softas-Nall, B. C., & Francis, P. C. (1998). A solution-focused approach to suicide assessment and intervention with families. *The Family Journal: Counseling and Therapy for Couples and Families, 6*(1), 64–66.

Sommers-Flanagan, J., & Sommers-Flanagan, R. (1995). Intake interviewing with suicidal patients: A systematic approach. *Professional Psychology: Research and Practice, 26*, 41–47.

Surgeon General. (2002). *Mental health: A report of the surgeon general*. Retrieved December 17, 2002, from http://www.surgeongeneral.gov/library/mentalhealth/home.html.

Trautman, P. (2000). The keys to the pharmacy: Integrating solution-focused brief therapy and psychopharmacological treatment. *Journal of Systemic Therapies, 19*(1), 100–110.

Weiner, B. (1995). *Judgments of responsibility: A foundation for a theory of social conduct*. New York: Guilford.

Wildes, J., Harkness, K., & Simons, A. (2002). Life events, number of social relationships, and twelve-month naturalistic course of major depression in a community sample of women. *Depression and Anxiety, 16*, 104–113.

Young, J., Beck, A., & Weinberger, A. (2001). Depression. In D. Barlow (Ed.), *Clinical handbook of psychological disorders: A step-by-step treatment manual* (2nd ed.). New York: Guilford.

9   Substance Abuse

HOLLY C. MATTO

Individuals struggling with substance abuse often demonstrate pronounced deficits in relationship development, emotional management, and ability to cope with daily life stressors. Drug addiction affects the biopsychosocial and spiritual aspects of the person and can, without treatment, produce intense and sustained losses, entrenching the individual into a cycle of repeated and prolonged use.

Traditionally, treatment for substance abuse has been grounded in the disease paradigm that conceptualizes addiction as a physical illness that must be managed and monitored through patient compliance to a treatment regimen (Sheehan & Owen, 1999). The disease model focuses on patient "denial" and "resistance," with patient responsibility as the key to treatment success, positing addiction as a chronic and progressive illness process that will ultimately lead to death if left untreated (Allen & Litten, 1999). Although this addiction model continues to be the most prevalent in current treatment programs (Allen & Litten, 1999), leaders in the addiction field have called for the development and evaluation of more strengths-based and empowering practice strategies (Hall, Carswell, Walsh, Huber, & Jampoler, 2002; Miller, 1996; Miller, Zweben, DiClemente, & Rychtarik, 1992; Okundaye, Smith, & Lawrence-Webb, 2001), and such efforts are beginning to make their way into the treatment literature.

One well-developed strengths-based substance abuse treatment model is motivational interviewing (MI), also referred to as motivational enhancement therapy. MI incorporates empathy and client choice and utilizes non-confrontational strategies to help support client self-efficacy and goal attainment (Miller et al., 1992; Yahne & Miller, 1999). Miller and Sanchez (1994) discuss components for effective brief motivational intervention, including providing feedback to the client in an empathic environment, emphasizing client responsibility and individual choice, offering advice and supportive recommendations with a menu of options, and bolstering client self-efficacy. The motivational approach has demonstrated effectiveness in treating both alcohol and drug addiction (Bien, Miller, & Tonigan, 1993; Burke, Arkowitz, & Dunn, 2002; Dunn, Deroo, & Rivara, 2001; Miller, 1996).

Cognitive-behavioral therapy (CBT) and solution-focused treatment (SFT) strategies have also been successfully employed with this population (Carroll, 1998; Hall et al., 2002; Marlatt & Gordon, 1985). CBT techniques include functional analyses to identify antecedents and consequences of drug use (Carroll, 1998), such as internal (emotional, cognitive) and external (environmental, relational) triggers or cues, and to explore how these relate to positive and negative behavioral consequences. Treatment sessions focus on previous client functioning, skills training, and future planning (Carroll, 1998). CBT has been shown to be one of the most effective treatments for several substance abuse disorders (DeRubeis & Crits-Christoph, 1998); research suggests that it is most effective when couched within a comprehensive and multidimensional treatment package that targets physical, psychological, and social domains (Longabaugh & Morgenstern, 1999; O'Malley et al., 1992).

Solution-focused treatment uses exception-finding strategies to build on past successes, scaling techniques to quantify observed change, and "miracle questions" that serve to stimulate clients' imaginative capacities related to future change possibilities (De Jong & Berg, 2001). Practitioners take a curiosity stance, questioning with intent and direction, yet endorsing clients' own expectations and perceived realities (De Jong & Berg, 2001).

Berg and colleagues (Berg & Miller, 1992; Berg & Reuss, 1998) have applied SFT to problem drinking and have developed a treatment manual (Berg & Reuss, 1998). In addition, Hall et al. (2002) demonstrated how solution-focused techniques can be incorporated into substance abuse case management models. The client is viewed as "expert" in calling on previous knowledge and abilities, while the practitioner serves as "advocate," working in collaboration with the client to change the existing problem orientation and help the client take on "case manager" responsibilities (Hall et al., 2002).

Integrated Model: A Strengths-and-Skills-Building Approach

The integrated brief treatment model combines core practice principles and techniques from motivational enhancement, solution-focused, and cognitive-behavioral therapies that may be useful with the substance abuse population. SFT and MI offer a style of working with clients that facilitates the client-practitioner engagement process, emphasizing choice, with clients viewed as their own authority. MI, particularly, works toward the enhancement of client commitment to treatment. The practitioner maintains positive expectations toward change, as successful outcomes are associated with both client and provider expectations (Yahne & Miller, 1999). SFT and CBT are action-oriented therapies that offer a set of specific techniques to meet treatment objectives. As in SFT, practitioners employing CBT take on the role of consultant or collaborator, facilitating a therapeutic alliance so that the client feels safe to learn new strategies (Carroll, 1998).

Combined, the three brief therapies support a collaborative and exploratory style of therapeutic interaction, with goals oriented toward change by identifying, mobilizing, and building on client strengths. A future orientation is emphasized; the practitioner facilitates dialogue that directs the client to new possibilities in interpreting events, feeling states, and behaviors. Overall, treatment is used to enhance the natural process of change by helping clients work through initial ambivalence and fear (Sobell & Sobell, 1993). Motivational enhancement strategies help increase client commitment to changing substance-abusing behaviors, solution-focused interviewing focuses on strengths finding, and cognitive-behavioral practice principles target skills building. Clients are seen as agents of change, and practitioners use language that implies and encourages change.

A critical element, different from more traditional substance abuse treatment approaches, is a substantial emphasis on engaging, encouraging, and reinforcing client commitment to change *throughout* the treatment process. Treatment phases exist as constructive parameters that serve to define activities and direct focus but are not rigidly sequenced as separate or distinct treatment units. Assessment is not relegated to intake but is ongoing, treatment goals may change or be revisited and modified, and client motivation can naturally be expected to wax and wane across the treatment trajectory. Problem-exploration and solution-finding opportunities are not necessarily linear; rather, strengths are identified and solution pathways constructed at all points in the process.

One way of operationalizing this integrated treatment model and increasing practice utility is to employ art therapy methods across treatment stages. Art therapy techniques are compatible with this model's tenets, such as using a nonconfrontational approach to relationship development, encouraging emotional expression, and validating the client's construction of the problem (Malchiodi, 2003; Rubin, 2001; Wadeson, 2000). Art therapy emphasizes collaborative work in which the client is seen as the expert on his or her own life and process. The client's own creations can express a unique personal perspective. Problems can be externalized: The art *product* affords both the client and practitioner relationship to the problem that is literally separated from the person, encouraging direct, interactive engagement with such material (Riley & Malchiodi, 2003). Thus, the problem, as expressed in the art product, can be viewed from multiple perspectives and reframed for its implicit strengths. Clients can walk around the art piece, hang it on the wall, or hold it up for viewing as they engage on cognitive, emotional, and behavioral levels. The art experience promotes the construction and reconstruction of client narratives and the new perspective taking that is so critical to SFT, MI, and CBT change strategies.

This chapter demonstrates how such an integrated brief treatment model, incorporating SFT and CBT techniques with MI practice principles, may facilitate client readiness for change, assist the practitioner in understanding the client's perception of problem scope, identify and mobilize client strengths and resources, and help clients recognize and implement change strategies.

The strengths-and-skills-building model is applied, along with art therapy techniques, to the following case example in a short-term inpatient substance abuse treatment facility. Model application is not limited to inpatient substance abuse treatment; rather, this case illustration offers one example of how it can be applied within a specific treatment setting. Typically, inpatient substance abuse treatment program goals are geared toward stabilizing clients in crisis and preparing them for transitional services that connect clients to a lesser level of care upon completion of the program. Specific program goals along these lines include emotional management, self-identity exploration and development, relapse prevention, improving relational functioning, and strengthening clients' social support network (Allen & Litten, 1999; Quigley & Marlatt, 1999). Integrated treatment works toward these goals in a climate of empathic expression, support for developing client self-efficacy, and avoidance of direct client confrontation. Client ambivalence during this process is seen as critical to change, and "resistance" is not seen as client pathology but as an indication that treatment providers need to reassess their change strategies (Yahne & Miller, 1999). The application of these principles is organized by treatment stage: (a) engagement, (b) problem exploration, (c) solution exploration, (d) goal setting, and (e) taking action.

Case Example

Marcos is a 39-year-old White man admitted to an inpatient treatment facility for repeated and prolonged polysubstance abuse. Having dropped out of school in the ninth grade at the urging of his mother, who thought a better use of his time would be to get a job and help support the large family, Marcos has limited formal education. As the oldest of five children, he felt obligated to offer this support. Marcos obtained gainful and stable employment as a laborer, mostly working hard and long days in construction. He accrued a reliable work record and was recognized by his employers as a hard worker. However, over time, Marcos developed severe and persistent back problems. Currently, his back problems are so severe that, even if he could afford surgery, doctors have told him that no medical procedure will permanently alleviate the physical suffering. Marcos has an 18-year-old daughter from his first marriage who "wants nothing to do with him." He also has two small children, a 7-year-old daughter and a 10-year-old son by his second ex-wife. Marcos has strained relationships with both of his ex-wives but a good relationship with his 10-year-old son. Marcos becomes quite passionate and filled with wide-ranging emotion when talking about his son. He expresses pride about his son's consistency on the honor roll and describes him as a "good kid who loves basketball." At the same time, Marcos feels significant guilt and shame related to his functional and relational incapacities, brought on by his addiction, that have affected his relationship with his children. Although he feels guilt and shame associated with not fulfilling his responsibilities as a parent to his children, he still appreciates the strength in his relationship with his son.

Engagement

In the engagement phase, practitioners seek to establish a working alliance with the client by demonstrating support and empathy, and they assess initial client motivation for treatment by asking questions such as "What brings you into treatment right now in your life?" and "What would you like to see different as a result of being here?" Practitioners might take a "wondering aloud" approach, conveying a nonjudgmental attitude, remarking on positive attributes such as clients' courage to come back into treatment so quickly after a recent relapse, or punctuating clients' ability to contain the fear they must be experiencing in order to ask for help.

However, some clients, particularly in the substance abuse population, may initially find a practitioner's "nonjudgmental attitude" so disparate from their experiences and expectations of how others *should* relate to them and their addiction that they question the practitioner's expertise and genuineness. Treatment providers can often preserve genuineness by clarifying the difference between respecting the client as a person in need of help and openly recognizing and directly acknowledging the very real destructive behaviors that must change.

For example, Marcos initially presented himself to the clinical program staff as guarded and focusing exclusively on his physical suffering, which he felt was a more legitimate and less shameful reason for seeking professional assistance. The intake worker helped to validate this emotional pain and legitimate his assistance seeking, while still providing direction and structure, by saying, "Yes, I can see that there's a lot of pain in your life right now—and you are right where you need to be."

It is important to initially honor the client's potential deep sense of shame and despair by constraining SFT future-oriented change questions in this early part of the treatment process. The client may not feel heard if a practitioner moves too quickly toward soliciting change opportunities and strengths without first offering a space that recognizes the client's current desperation. Therefore, thoughtfully gauging client response to such questioning is critical to treatment alliance development.

For example, if the intake worker asks Marcos what he is willing to do to stop his addiction from getting out of control, this question might exacerbate his existing shame and create greater distance, rather than strengthening the alliance between worker and client. In this case, the worker would be moving too quickly toward soliciting change strategies, while the client is still mired in painful emotions (particularly self-blame) that leave him at risk of loosening his commitment to treatment.

Problem Exploration

In reading Marcos's brief story, it is easy to become drawn to the deficits that characterize his narrative. Indeed, many individuals struggling with addiction who enter an inpatient treatment program are stuck in problem-saturated narratives. Continued negative feedback from family, friends, and employers who have lost faith in the person's ability to achieve sobriety often reinforce clients' behavioral paralysis or "stuckness."

Therefore, the problem exploration phase is a risky time for maintaining client engagement and treatment retention, as clients enter into the painful process of drug withdrawal and are simultaneously forced to confront the physical, psychological, and socioenvironmental challenges that the drug use has both masked and precipitated. Not only are clients charged with confronting old problems left unattended during active substance use but also, typically, financial, family, and legal problems have multiplied as a result of the drug-using behaviors themselves, reinforcing the desire to avoid these consequences through continued substance use.

The traditional medical model, undergirding the 12-step self-help program (AA, NA), educates that surrendering to the disease by accepting powerlessness is a necessary first step to recovery. However, "accepting powerlessness" can be an overwhelming process to clients as they begin to recognize the power of the addiction. They may feel ill equipped to confront the magnitude of losses the addiction has produced while still struggling with the urge to use, and these feelings can pose a significant risk to treatment engagement in the earliest stages of recovery. Therefore, practitioners need to facilitate continued treatment engagement and motivation by empathically supporting the client and emphasizing strengths.

Exploring Clients' Concerns About Changing and Not Changing

One aspect of problem exploration involves encouraging the client to explore the multiple losses associated with the substance abuse problem and the potential new losses associated with change. Often clients are able to acknowledge the severity of the problem and express an overt desire to change the drinking or drugging behaviors yet feel immobilized by fear of loss (e.g., loss of freedom from family responsibilities, loss of a reliable coping method, loss of immunity to feelings). Rather than narrowly conceptualizing this ambivalent motivation as "client resistance," exploration reveals a more specific understanding of client concerns about changing versus not changing.

During this process, clients are encouraged to speak from multiple viewpoints about the addiction. For example, in one early treatment group Marcos drew a picture of himself holding what he said was "the world" on his shoulders, with his body hunched over and appearing severely strained, and his face hanging down at the neck. Marcos and the group were invited to entertain new perspectives on the image through focused reflection.

Upon closer inspection of the drawing, the group remarked that it appeared Marcos had actually drawn a transparent balloon, not "the world." This revelation facilitated a climate of curiosity in the group about the discrepancies between perceived and actual strains in Marcos's life. One interpretation was that the load he is carrying is seen by others as lighter than it currently feels to Marcos: having his back turned on the problem (i.e., his addiction) only magnifies its weightiness and pressure, while others who have a more distanced perspective can see the problem in more manageable terms. One group member emphasized that if Marcos would turn to confront the problem, it would become clear that it was really just a balloon. Without the confrontation, the burden would only continue to become heavier.

This initial discussion stimulated another group member's interpretation—that Marcos's severe back pain is a significant burden and barrier in his life and that others have not recognized the full extent to which he is affected by this physical limitation. In fact, the burden is exacerbated by the perception that others "just don't understand."

To continue building on past strengths identified in Marcos's case history, the practitioner intervened in dialogue with Marcos about his drawing. The practitioner reflected to Marcos the reality of his youth, where he had taken on the responsibility of providing for his younger siblings at an early age. She emphasized the strengths he had drawn upon to achieve this. Marcos was then invited to think about putting aside some of the earlier burdens he had assumed at a young age and to acknowledge and accept his own self-care needs now.

This example demonstrates how multiple viewpoints can lead to perspectives on the problem that the client has yet to consider. Rather than figuring out what is "truth," the client is allowed to consider new interpretations of the problem. Entrenched positions are challenged—not through confrontation but by siding with the client in mutual exploration.

Decisional Balance

Exploration tends to uncover client ambivalence about the problem. A motivational interviewing technique that can be used to help clients concretely analyze the cost and benefits and the gains and losses, associated with drug use as precipitant to change, is the decisional balance (Carroll, 1998; Miller, 1995). Specifically, clients may be asked to identify costs and benefits related to self and others and to clarify factors contributing to current ambivalence (Yahne & Miller, 1999). In service of the decisional balance, practitioners might ask clients to write down all thoughts, feelings, and sensations that come to mind on recalling "what it is like to be under the influence of drugs" and, conversely, "what it is [or will be] like to be sober." Clients can likewise consider "How has substance abuse affected your life?" and "How will recovery affect your life?" Wadeson (2000) suggests that these same questions can be translated into drawing or collaging directives for clients who may not readily engage in writing exercises.

Marcos participated in an expressive decisional balance exercise that asked him to illustrate both the positive aspects of sobriety and the negative aspects of substance use, using magazines photos, words, sentences from poems, colors, shapes, drawn images, or lines as symbols. Some of Marcos's affirming recovery-related symbols included swimming in a pool "with clear eyes and more control," a hope chest representing the importance of optimism and encouraging individuals to "take what you need for the day and leave the rest for later," and a nature scene that represented "peace, serenity, freedom, inspiration, and connection to a higher power."

As Marcos shared his affirming symbols, the group noticed that he did not include people in any of his representations. The group suggested that while Marcos has progressed in recognizing the importance of utilizing a strong social support network in navigating early recovery, he did not visually represent that as a critical factor in attaining sobriety. After sharing these symbols with the group, Marcos was encouraged to transfer the two most significant affirming symbols to a small card that he pledged to keep with him as a tangible reminder of his commitment to sobriety. Marcos added two people to his nature scene and pasted the scene on the small card.

Amplifying Discrepancy

Another motivational interviewing intervention asks clients to explore perceived discrepancies between their own values, goals, and problem behaviors. Specifically, clients are asked how their behaviors uphold or undermine their values and goals. For example, the practitioner initiated the following conversation with Marcos:

PRACTITIONER: Marcos, when you think about things that have been affected by your drinking, what comes to mind for you?

MARCOS: A lot, I guess. I mean, mostly what it's done to my relationship with my family . . . my son.

PRACTITIONER: It sounds like your relationship with your son is very important to you—something you really value that you feel has been short-changed by the effects of your drinking behaviors. Is that right?

MARCOS: Yes, he really looks up to me, like a role model or something. We both like sports and the outdoors. That's when I'm not drinking, of course.

PRACTITIONER: If you think for a minute here, when is the most recent time that you and your son had a good time together?

MARCOS: The last time I was clean and not using—about a year ago after I left the detox program at the hospital. I know that my drinking is ruining our relationship.

PRACTITIONER: And if you go back to that time right now—the time when you were clean—what does it feel like for you?

MARCOS [looking down at the floor and seeming to be holding back tears]: It's tough to think about because I know I've disappointed him. I mean he really looks up to me. But it also feels good, you know.

PRACTITIONER: And what feelings do you have right now, thinking about your son looking up to you, when you're with him sober?

MARCOS: I'm proud of him . . . we're laughing together . . . he always asks to go fishing. [trails off]

PRACTITIONER: It sounds like it's important for you to go back to those good times with your son. Let's think about what made it possible for you to be with him then, during the time when you were not drinking.

Often, examining values and behaviors is met with an initial inability to identify any values at all. If this occurs, the practitioner should focus on exploring the circumstances around the lack of attention to values—that is, helping clients challenge the belief that they do not value any aspect of their lives.

Amplified reflection—intentional exaggeration of a client statement—is used to bring out the side of the client that recognizes the need for change. For example, Marcos has told the practitioner at one point that "he feels trapped, that nothing will ever get better." She intentionally amplified the statement by responding, "So there's nothing that can be beneficial to you right now?" Marcos then objected to the response and qualified his previous statement, saying that he knows he did the right thing by coming into treatment despite his shame and "personal shortcomings."

This discussion led Marcos into identifying that he does have a sponsor who would agree that he is "doing the right thing"; however, Marcos believes he has disappointed his sponsor and therefore is planning to avoid any further contact. The practitioner reflected back to Marcos that feeling "disappointed" indicates that he cares about what his sponsor would think about his behavior; this suggests that his sponsor is a valued person to Marcos and that he cares about Marcos's well-being. At this point, the practitioner redirected the dialogue to additional strengths that Marcos had overlooked, such as having previous periods of sobriety with consistent 12-step attendance.

Functional Analysis

Another part of problem exploration is a functional analysis to examine specific thoughts, feelings, and behaviors associated with the problem. Clients are asked to create a chart of their thoughts, feelings, and resulting behavioral consequences related to a drinking or drugging event to help them recognize the antecedents and consequences of their drug use. Some clients, like Marcos, may find it more helpful to use more nonverbal and expressive functional analysis methods.

Marcos was challenged to construct a "time-sequenced incident drawing" that represented a drug-using event. The purpose of this technique is to help clients see the event as a *process* by illuminating its constituent parts: before, during, and after. Clients are then directed to dialogue about what the people or objects in each of the three time dimensions are thinking, feeling, and doing (Landgarten, 1993).

The "incident" upon which Marcos chose to reflect was a recent argument with his daughter, Monique, after Marcos failed to make good on his promise to attend the baptismal ceremony of her new baby. As directed, Marcos drew three pictures representing his thoughts and feelings before, during, and after this event. In the first ("before") picture, Marcos created a collage of magazine photos on construction paper depicting a rowboat on a stormy sea headed toward a cliff, where he said his family stood. Marcos identified strongly with the turbulence of the water, the unpredictability of nature's consequences, and violence as the potential outcome in the picture. Marcos said he felt "powerless," "out of control," and "fearful" of his surroundings in his attempt to reach safety. Of interest was the position his family took in the picture: They were in a cluster together on top of a steep cliff, far from the violence of the storm, yet still represented in the picture. Marcos was isolated and alone in his own storm, characteristic of how he felt in his struggle with the unpredictability and powerful chaos of his addiction that left him estranged from his family.

The middle ("during") drawing was created by using markers on white paper and depicted a man swimming directly into a bottle away from a shark's open jaws. In relation to this drawing, Marcos identified his urge to escape the pain of seeing his daughter, his ex-wife, and other family members at the baptism and to avoid the intense guilt that would be intolerable. In addition, he felt he did not deserve to participate in his family's joyful celebration. His recourse was to "escape into the bottle" and to "deal with the consequences later." Indeed, he missed the baptism and proceeded into a 2-week drinking binge when he managed to entirely evade family contact and responsibilities. This revelation led Marcos to talk about his fears and the lack of courage that paralyzed him from being able to feel deserving of recovery.

The last ("after") picture was a picture drawn with markers of a man chained to the bottom of the sea. Marcos shared that he felt "trapped" and that he was "suffocating" and "drowning in a sea of pain," with no ready escape from his situation. The picture revealed a stick figure submerged in blue water. However, the water was just over the man's head, and the chain, although attached securely to the man's ankle, was not visibly secured to anything on the sea floor. There were no sharks in sight.

While he clearly felt trapped and depleted, the picture offered an opportunity for Marcos to become more flexible in interpreting his circumstances. From a new vantage point, Marcos recognized that the water surface actually was quite close to the man's head, and the chain (representing his addiction) was freed at one end. The picture suggested that if assistance was rendered, the man could be released from his own suffocation. Indeed, suffocation would continue only if he remained trapped in his own mind, without noticing that the chain was not attached to any constraint except his own ankle and that the water was not very deep. In remaining alone and isolated, Marcos's perception of feeling trapped would continue. In being open to assistance and help, Marcos could alter the narrative's theme from one of suffocation to one of liberation and new breath—but only through taking action and being open to receiving assistance.

Solution Exploration

After the client's current reality is expressed, attended to, and validated, the practitioner can move toward externalizing the problem and identifying exceptions to the problem, as well as exploring alternative constructions.

Externalizing

The SFT externalization technique may be implemented during this stage, when the person is separated from the problem enough to allow the client and practitioner to collaboratively rally around the problem (White & Epston, 1990). In doing so, practitioners gain more comprehensive information about problem parameters, while building in opportunities to explore the capacities that clients bring to their struggle by "siding with the client" against the problem. In this way, externalizing can serve as a bridge between problem exploration and solution finding.

For example, Marcos struggles with enormous physical pain. To validate Marcos's current reality of feeling powerless over his body and to explore his construction of physical pain, Marcos was asked to cut out five pictures of people from magazines that illustrated how he felt physically and to assemble these pictures into a "body collage." Marcos was slow and deliberate, careful and calculated in his exploration. Marcos's collage contained only four pictures; he asserted that he needed to "stop looking now."

The largest picture, placed in the center of the page, was of a rescue worker using a power saw to cut through the top of an overturned red car at a crash site. Above this picture, Marcos wrote, "constant agonizing nightmare." The second picture was not a whole figure but a frozen open hand reaching out of the ice and snow, cut off at the forearm. Marcos found the magazine phrase "after all those years of quantity drinking" and pasted this sentence next to the arm.

The third picture was of a skeleton slumped in a chair, over which Marcos had pasted the word *betrayed*. The fourth and smallest picture, located in the bottom right of the collage, was of a man on his hands and knees in a large room filled with books and papers. The man was frantically looking around; Marcos wrote, "The cravings are unbearable." Just above this picture he glued a quote from a magazine: "My whole body is shaking, but I'm not sure if that's because I'm cold, nervous, or about to die."

Marcos externalized his relationship to the physical pain through the magazine photo collage technique. He explored the duality of being in the rescuer role all of his life and currently feeling the "crash" and destruction that have resulted from these life experiences. Marcos discussed feeling stuck; the hand in the snow reaches out for help, needing to "thaw out" and get healthy. He was able to identify feelings such as betrayal, fear, shame, and desperation but acknowledged his desire for help and change.

As a result of these creative art experiences, the practitioner gained important information about the client's relationship to the physical pain, as well as helping Marcos identify and label specific feelings he was currently experiencing. The image of being trapped was reframed into a more workable definition—feeling exasperated, disappointed, and depleted—but not helplessly paralyzed. Once the imagery was translated into feeling terms, the problem became more manageable, as feelings (e.g., exasperation, disappointment, depletion) are temporary and pliable, whereas "trapped" connotes an inability to find alternatives. Marcos was also referred to a pain management group at the treatment center, facilitated by a specialist from the local community hospital, that employed a CBT-based "healthy living" curriculum focusing on relaxation training and self-care techniques. Marcos participated in the group as part of his treatment program.

Exception-Finding

Here the practitioner expanded on one of Marcos's identified strengths: his ability to work hard and persevere through difficulties in the face of pain, which had previously been demonstrated in his work history. The following dialogue demonstrates how the practitioner worked with Marcos around identifying exceptions and applying them to the problem situation.

PRACTITIONER: Your ability to hold down a job even during all the problems you have talked about is pretty remarkable. When else were you able to make good choices in your life, even when times were hard?

MARCOS: Well, when I left the detox program last year, I kept getting calls from this collection agency about some overdue bills. I owed a lot of money I didn't have. I guess I typically would have used right away, but I didn't that time.

PRACTITIONER: So what did you choose to do instead?

MARCOS: I called my sponsor right away. He helped me make an appointment with a credit counselor who deals with debt management.

PRACTITIONER: That sounds like an important alternative you chose. So how might this ability you have to make good choices, even when things are pretty rough, help you stay sober now?

MARCOS: I think I need to remember that there are other ways to handle a problem besides drinking. And to not let my fears get the best of me.

PRACTITIONER: Yes, it sounds like when you had those fears you did something different than drinking. You reached out for help from someone close to you.

Another strength the practitioner illuminated was Marcos's positive view of his son by asking Marcos what has worked well for him in his relationships in the past: "Marcos, you exhibit such passion for your son. It is clear how much he means to you. How have you been able to keep that relationship intact during your drinking and drugging episodes?"

Practitioners may need to keep the client focused on strengths searching if the client circumvents the opportunity. Conceivably, Marcos might discount the practitioner's comment in favor of globalizing the negative interactions his son has experienced because of Marcos's drinking and drugging behaviors. The practitioner might refocus by initiating the following dialogue.

PRACTITIONER: Certainly you've had some very hard times with your son, and that brings up sad feelings for you. I'm asking you to think, now, about those times over the past year when you were able to have a good time with your son.

MARCOS: I don't know. It's hard to think of those times, I guess.

PRACTITIONER: Well, you've told me that your son is really excelling in school and loves basketball. Can you tell me more about this and the part you played in it?

By engaging in this dialogue, Marcos acknowledges that some parts of his life have indeed remained intact. For example, Marcos seems to have a much better relationship with his son than with his other children at the present time. The practitioner continues with strengths finding related to Marcos's relationship with his son.

PRACTITIONER: You seem to have a strong relationship with your son. I wonder what you learned from your earlier parenting experiences that helps you now in building a good relationship with your son.

MARCOS: I don't think that my parenting is any better. It's just that my daughter is at an age where she can reject me. My son is still so young.

PRACTITIONER: And when your daughter was your son's age, what was your relationship like?

MARCOS: I guess pretty bad. I wasn't around. I didn't relate.

PRACTITIONER: So one thing you've learned over the years and that you recognize now is your desire to be around—to be there for your kids?

MARCOS: Yes, that's what I want.

PRACTITIONER: It does sound like your daughter is very angry right now. And it sounds like you are wanting to have a better relationship with her at some point, but that right now we can focus on the relationship with your son. What will the relationship with your son be like when you stop drinking?

Marcos replied that he can see himself going to his son's basketball game as a sober father. Marcos described the game: "I am in the stands yelling for my son. He knows I'm there and he's playing really well. I'm proud of him." The practitioner responded: "And what feelings does your son have about you, as a sober father in the stands?" Marcos replied: "He's probably pretty surprised. But also happy."

This dialogue continues to build on Marcos's motivation by expanding on this identified strength, reinforcing the possibility of change, and helping him recognize that he needs to stop drinking to improve his relationship with his son.

In addition to exploring these historical patterns in the service of drawing out current strengths, the practitioner also collects in vivo data, identifying how clients are applying themselves to the treatment process and how they respond to difficulty, challenge, and the frustrations that arise. For example, a practitioner might note how Marcos responds to mini-opportunities for change within the session itself, such as avoidance or engagement in dialogue or group activities, willingness to risk exposure to rejection (e.g., sharing of self with others), taking responsibility for his own behaviors, expressing concern for aftercare arrangements, accepting feedback from other inpatient community members, and demonstrating an ability to differentiate between a "need" and a "want."

Goal Setting and Taking Action

In this phase, goal setting and action planning are treatment targets. Marcos and the practitioner identified three treatment goals: (a) develop self-efficacy and empowerment to make changes; (b) develop skills in confronting, expressing, and managing painful emotions; and (c) increase social supports and improve family relations.

In order to construct a future vision, clients should be challenged to respond to behaviorally based questions: "How will your life look different when you achieve these goals?" "What will your son notice when things begin to get better for you?" "How can we work together to make those changes happen?" The following dialogue illustrates Marcos's response to what he believes his son will notice about him when he is sober.

MARCOS: Well, he won't be waiting around for me to never show up.
PRACTITIONER: And, if he won't be waiting around, what will he be doing?
MARCOS: He'll be with me.
PRACTITIONER: And when you're both together, what does he notice is different about you?

MARCOS: I'm smiling, not mad and grouchy. We joke around together; we're enjoying the outdoors, like we used to.

When Marcos became ready to move toward learning new strategies associated with maintaining sobriety, CBT action-oriented skills-building techniques were implemented. Strategies might include role-playing activities that teach drug refusal skills, relapse prevention strategies, coping skills for cravings management, and interpersonal relationship skills (e.g., conflict resolution, productive communication, effective emotional expression and management). With progress, new concrete skills-building opportunities can be added to the treatment protocol, based on client ability to tolerate new information.

One specific target skill, related to the goal of developing a social support network, was to help Marcos communicate his feelings more effectively to his son. Marcos started by writing a "good-bye letter" to substances as a way of confronting and expressing the shame and disconnections caused by his drug use.

Dear Mr. Alcohol:
With your help I have lost it all—my health, my family, my self-respect. You helped my pain for so long. But I didn't realize how much more pain you would cause. I no longer want anything to do with you.

Marcos read the letter to the treatment group to behaviorally rehearse saying it aloud in the presence of supportive members. The group positively reinforced his experience and affirmed his courage to commit to recovery. During visitation with his son, Marcos shared his good-bye letter, as he had practiced in the group. The reading of the letter served to focus their initial interaction and facilitated a collaborative father–son engagement around the letter and its contents. This created an opportunity to externalize the problem (addiction) and, thereby, begin relationship development between the two family members.

In addition, the treatment team continued to help Marcos prepare emotionally for family visitation days, when he would have several hours at the facility to spend with his son. The client and treatment community, together, debriefed after each visitation, which helped Marcos in expressing feelings and receiving feedback from others based on their experiences with their own family members.

Marcos began to show greater comfort in accepting feedback from the treatment community as related to the behavioral rehearsal work, and he reported more self-confidence before visitation with his son. Marcos found that looking at pictures of his son and thinking about some of their positive interactions (e.g., their fishing trips when Marcos was not actively using) helped to build his motivation and decrease his anxiety about upcoming interactions.

As was revealed through Marcos's individual and group work, treatment continued to focus on the goals of building a stronger social support network and developing coping skills to effectively express and manage distressing emotions, as functionally related to the overarching treatment goal of maintaining sobriety and preventing relapse. CBT strategies were employed to help Marcos better understand thought patterns associated with emotional consequences. Marcos ultimately left treatment, agreeing to transition into a less intense outpatient substance abuse program that offered him a continued support network and opportunities to further develop the coping skills he needed to remain sober. In addition, Marcos continued with his pain management classes and agreed to look into acupuncture treatment to help him gain control over his physical pain.

Summary

The strengths-and-skills-building model, integrated with art therapy techniques, utilizes language and metaphor that imply and encourage change, amplify client metaphors that draw out strengths, and help clients expand their repertoire of change possibilities. Treatment consists of a collaborative process that helps clients link emotional states with behavior and build new skills (CBT). It applies solution-focused scaling techniques and future-oriented questioning to help clients move to a place where they are willing to modify the problem in the service of finding solutions. This application of the strengths-and-skills-building model allows practitioners to work with clients at their present stage of change and to gently help clients find change opportunities and take credit for growth.

References

Allen, J. P., & Litten, R. Z. (1999). Treatment of drug and alcohol abuse: An overview of major strategies and effectiveness. In B. S. McCrady & E. E. Epstein (Eds.), *Addictions: A comprehensive guidebook* (pp. 385–395). New York: Oxford University Press.

Berg, I. K., & Miller, S. (1992). *Working with the problem drinker.* New York: W. W. Norton.

Berg, I. K., & Reuss, N. H. (1998). *Solutions step by step: A substance abuse treatment manual.* New York: W. W. Norton.

Bien, T. H., Miller, W. R., & Tonigan, J. S. (1993). Brief intervention for alcohol problems: A review. *Addiction, 88,* 315–335.

Burke, B., Arkowitz, H., & Dunn, C. (2002). The efficacy of motivational interviewing and its adaptations: What we know so far. In W. R. Miller & S. Rollnick (Eds.), *Motivational interviewing* (2nd ed., pp. 217–250). New York: Guilford.

Carroll, K. M. (1998). Behavioral and cognitive behavioral treatments. In B.S. McCrady & E. E. Epstein (Eds.), *Addictions: A comprehensive guidebook* (pp. 250–267). New York: Oxford University Press.

De Jong, P., & Berg, I. K. (2001). Co-constructing cooperation with mandated clients. *Social Work, 46*(4), 361–374.

DeRubeis, R. J., & Crits-Christoph, P. (1998). Empirically-supported individual and group psychological treatments for adult mental disorders. *Journal of Consulting and Clinical Psychology, 66,* 37–52.

Dunn, C., Deroo, L., & Rivara, F. (2001). The use of brief interventions adapted from motivational interviewing across behavioral domains: A systematic review. *Addiction, 96,* 1725–1742.

Hall, J. A., Carswell, C., Walsh, E., Huber, D. L., & Jampoler, J. S. (2002). Iowa case management: Innovative social casework. *Social Work, 47*(2), 132–141.

Landgarten, H. B. (1993). *Magazine photo collage.* New York: Brunner/Mazel.

Longabaugh, R., & Morgenstern, J. (1999). Cognitive-behavioral coping skills therapy for alcohol dependence: Current status and future directions. *Alcohol Research and Health, 23,* 78–85.

Malchiodi, C. A. (2003). *Handbook of art therapy.* New York: Guilford.

Marlatt, G. A., & Gordon, J. R. (1985). *Relapse prevention: Maintenance strategies in the treatment of addictive behaviors.* New York: Guilford.

Miller, W. R. (1995). Increasing motivation for change. In R. K. Heister & W. R. Miller (Eds.), *Handbook of alcoholism treatment approaches* (pp. 89–104). Needham Heights, MA: Allyn & Bacon.

Miller, W. R. (1996). Motivational interviewing: Research, practice, and puzzles. *Addictive Behaviors, 21*(6), 835–842.

Miller, W. R., & Sanchez, V. C. (1994). Motivating young adults for treatment and lifestyle change. In G. Howard & P. E. Nathan (Eds.), *Alcohol use and misuse by young adults* (pp. 55–81). Notre Dame, IN: University of Notre Dame Press.

Miller, W. R., Zweben, A., DiClemente, C. C., & Rychtarik, R. G. (1992). *Motivational enhancement therapy manual: A clinical tool for therapists treating individuals with alcohol abuse and dependence.* Project MATCH Monograph Series 2. Rockville, MD: U.S. Department of Health and Human Services and National Institute on Alcohol Abuse and Alcoholism.

Okundaye, J. N., Smith, P., & Lawrence-Webb, C. (2001). Incorporating spirituality and the strengths perspective into social work practice with addicted individuals. *Journal of Social Work Practice in the Addictions, 1*(1), 65–82.

O'Malley, S., Jaffe, A., Chang, G., Schottenfeld, R., Meyer, R., & Rounsaville, B. (1992). Naltrexone and coping skills therapy for alcohol dependence: A controlled study. *Archives of General Psychiatry, 49,* 881–887.

Quigley, L. A., & Marlatt, G. A. (1999). Relapse prevention: Maintenance of change after initial treatment. In B. S. McCrady & E. E. Epstein (Eds.),

Addictions: A comprehensive guidebook (pp. 370–384). New York: Oxford University Press.

Riley, S., & Malchiodi, C. A. (2003). Solution-focused and narrative approaches. In C. A. Malchiodi (Ed.), *Handbook of art therapy* (pp. 82–92). New York: Guilford.

Rubin, J. A. (2001). *Approaches to art therapy*. Philadelphia: Brunner-Routledge.

Sheehan, T., & Owen, P. (1999). The disease model. In B. S. McCrady & E. E. Epstein (Eds.), *Addictions: A comprehensive guidebook* (pp. 268–286). New York: Oxford University Press.

Sobell, M. B., & Sobell, L. C. (1993). *Problem drinkers: Guided self-change treatment*. New York: Guilford.

Wadeson, H. (2000). *Art therapy practice*. New York: Wiley.

White, M., & Epston, D. (1990). *Narrative means to therapeutic ends*. New York: Norton.

Yahne, C. E., & Miller, W. R. (1999). Enhancing motivation for treatment and change. In B. S. McCrady & E. E. Epstein (Eds.), *Addictions: A comprehensive guidebook* (pp. 235–249). New York: Oxford University Press.

10 The Integration of Solution-Focused and Behavioral Marital Therapies

Application to an Elderly Couple With Anxiety

CARRIE BECKER, JACQUELINE CORCORAN, AND KRISTIN A. GARELL

Case Example

William Rutledge is a 68-year-old veteran who was diagnosed with an anxiety disorder 30 years ago. He began collecting disability 2 years later, after unsuccessfully attempting to work at a variety of manual labor jobs. In each position he held, he was able to sustain full-time work for only a few months before he became increasingly agitated and unable to perform daily tasks. His functioning would decline rapidly, and each time he would end up admitted to the local psychiatric hospital for treatment of anxiety. William's disorder manifests as constant visible agitation; he experiences muscle tension and skittishness, such as clenching and unclenching his fists and rapidly turning his head in response to everyday noises. He also engages in ritualistic behaviors, such as walking the neighborhood and collecting trash and buying scratch-off tickets at the local convenience store, in an effort to distract himself from his "nerves." He is a chronic smoker, consuming two to three packs of cigarettes a day.

His wife of 40 years, Helen, worked full-time as a bookkeeper until she retired at age 62. They have no children. Helen managed to save a small amount of money to augment her Social Security income during her retirement. William never returned to work and receives only his disability income, which Helen manages, along with her Social Security, her savings, and their outstanding bills.

William has been the recipient of ongoing mental health services since his diagnosis, including psychiatric care and social service interventions, with the goal of preventing long-term institutionalization. He has been receiving supportive home visits for the past 7 years. He is prescribed alprazolam (0.25 mg twice/day), venlafaxine (150 mg once/day), and buspirone (10 mg twice/day) to counteract his anxiety and diphenhydramine (25 mg twice/day) as a sleep aid. He is inconsistent with his dosing, sometimes taking none of his medications for weeks at a time and at other periods eliminating some prescriptions from the regimen because he does not feel they are effective. Helen expresses frustration at William's approach to his medication. She reports that he is more agitated, as well as more easily angered, when he is not taking his medications as prescribed. Helen has taken on the responsibility of monitoring William's medication intake and prompting him to comply in order to ensure he is consistently following the regimen.

Earlier this year, Helen left William for the first time in their marriage. At that point, the practitioner had been working with William for almost 7 months, performing supportive weekly home visits. Upon his wife's departure from their home, William began to express a commitment to "doing whatever it takes to bring her home." Prior services had been directed at working with William only to maintain his functioning, but Helen's abrupt decision to leave the relationship jarred the practitioner into realizing that a more active approach might be needed. At this juncture, the practitioner decided to approach the weekly sessions with a combined solution-focused and behavioral family-focused intervention.

Helen returned to the home after only 4 days. During her absence, William appeared to maintain his functioning and was also preparing his own meals. He did not, however, clean or pay any bills. He continually expressed his desire for Helen to return, stating that he didn't believe he could survive without her. Helen came back after speaking to William on the phone and eliciting a verbal agreement from him to participate in treatment for their marital issues.

This chapter uses an integration of solution-focused and behavioral marital therapy with the Rutledges. Motivational interviewing can be used in a couples format when partners are ambivalent about staying in the relationship, attending counseling, or following through with skills taught in couples therapy. In this case example, however, little ambivalence was encountered, and solution-focused and cognitive-behavioral approaches were sufficient. In this chapter, these approaches to couples work are described, followed by their integration and then the application to the case study.

Solution-Focused Therapy

The solution-focused assumption is that the context of a behavior is more salient and amenable to change than individual personality traits. Given this assumption, the approach lends itself to couples and family work and indeed evolved out of the field of family therapy. In solution-focused couples work, there is an emphasis on "video talk," which means focusing on specific behavioral descriptors rather than couples' interpretations of each other and their problems. These interpretations are often negative and are seen as unhelpful in determining the way to solutions (Hudson & O'Hanlon, 1993).

Solution-focused therapy is directed at empowering the couple to make changes in problem behaviors based on their demonstrated strengths and resources (Ziegler & Hiller, 2001). By first establishing rapport through the use of joining techniques, the practitioner can assess the partners' perception of the situation and their relationship to intervention. The practitioner can then help the clients identify and amplify exceptions to their problem by reinforcing coping skills and strengths. For entrenched coercive cycles, pattern interventions are used to modify or add interactions to disrupt the pattern.

Solution-focused therapy has been applied conceptually to a range of couples' problems (Hudson & O'Hanlon, 1993; Ziegler & Hiller, 2001), including one study concerning marital distress (Schindler, Zimmerman, Prest, & Wetzel, 1997). The authors used nonrandom assignment of 72 couples to either a couples group treatment format or a control group. Couples reported improved marital adjustment after the 6-week approach, whereas couples in the control group did not.

Behavioral Marital Therapy

Behavioral marital therapy is a skill-building approach following the principles of social learning, cognitive techniques, and behavioral exchange. Partners are taught specific skills to enhance marital support and intimacy and to reduce marital stress and negative expectancies (Jacobson & Margolin, 1979). Behavioral marital therapy addresses the reinforcement patterns of couples so that they can reinforce positive behaviors and either ignore negative behaviors or make behavior change requests that will get the partner to change his or her behavior. The behavioral marital therapist views negative interactions, such as criticism, withdrawal, verbal abuse, and complaining, as punishing responses that create ill feeling between couples and escalate coercive responses. Treatment concentrates on teaching couples to reward the behavior of their partners by complimenting and to create an atmosphere of positive feelings by encouraging pleasant pastimes and coming up with behavior exchange activities that the partners can do for the other each day to increase their satisfaction with the relationship (Jacobson & Margolin, 1979). Couples are taught communication skills, such as "I" messages, reflecting feelings, and making behavior change requests, and problem-solving and negotiating skills through didactic instruction, modeling, and rehearsal.

Behavioral marital therapy has been subject to extensive empirical testing and has proven efficacy (Dunn & Schwebel, 1995). Behavioral marital therapy has also been described as a treatment approach for a range of individual problems, such as depression (Banawan, O'Mahen, Beach, & Jackson, 2002; Beach & Jones, 2002), and anxiety disorders, such as agoraphobia and obsessive-compulsive disorder (for a review, see Baucom, Shoham, Mueser, Daiuto, & Stickle, 1998).

Despite evidence of its success, Jacobson and colleagues (e.g., Christensen, Jacobson, & Babcock, 1995; Wheeler, Christensen, & Jacobson, 2001) modified the behavioral marital model to include a focus on emotional acceptance of the partner with the purpose of inducing a collaborative set in which partners are desirous of accommodating, compromising, and working together to solve problems (Clark-Stager, 1999). Prior to this integration, the behavioral marital therapist assumed couples were already ready to work collaboratively and to follow a fairly structured and programmed approach to changing behavior.

Rationale for Integration

Clark-Stager (1999) has written conceptually on how behavioral marital therapy and solution-focused therapy can be integrated as an approach to couples work. The rationale involves some of the criticisms of solution-focused therapy and behavioral marital therapy. For instance, solution-focused therapy ignores the fact that some couples lack the skills to communicate or problem-solve (Clark-Stager, 1999). Also, behavioral marital therapy suggests that skills have to be taught in a prescribed fashion, rather than taking into account the individual needs and circumstances of the couple. It also ignores the strengths and resources that couples may bring to resolve their own problems.

Both behavioral therapy and solution-focused therapy address the interaction patterns of couples, although techniques differ. In behavioral marital therapy, skills and techniques to change interaction patterns are taught, such as complimenting, building pleasant activities, behavior exchange, and communication and problem-solving skills. In solution-focused therapy, clients are asked questions that focus them on the positive aspects of their partner's behavior and the small steps that need to be taken to indicate improvement in the relationship. A focus on the exceptions is thought to create a changed view of the other person, which can lead to a partner acting differently toward the spouse as a result and then escalate into further positive change. As a result, partners feel more hopeful and optimistic that the relationship will meet their needs.

Both behavioral and solution-focused approaches also center on specific behaviors rather than interpretations partners make of each other, which are often negative attributions of the partner's intent. Such negative attributions can be reframed to reflect a more positive intent in both models. Solution-focused therapy further directs conversations about the past, which is seen as impossible to change, into concrete behaviors that clients desire for the future. Similarly, behavioral marital therapy teaches partners the skills to make behavioral requests that are specific and stated in the positive.

Both modified behavioral approaches and solution-focused therapy emphasize the optimism the practitioner brings about the possibility of success from couples work. Often, when partners have sought a helper for their problems, they feel discouraged and hopeless about the relationship working out. The practitioner, to indicate enthusiasm, compliments the couples on their strengths and helps them find exceptions to problems (Clark-Stager, 1999).

Application

The integration of solution-focused therapy and behavioral marital therapy is demonstrated with the case example of William and Helen Rutledge. In the couples work, the practitioner used various techniques drawn from solution-focused therapy and behavioral marital therapy, building on the strengths of each model to help the couple achieve change in their relationship.

In the first session after Helen returned home, the practitioner enlarged the focus of the work to include Helen rather than just attending to William, the pattern of many years of intervention. Rather than feeling blamed for playing a role in the marital discord, Helen responded with eagerness; she had never before been given the opportunity to participate in the supportive services provided to William and his disorder. Given the significant impact of the disorder on her life, she expressed relief at finally being considered. This change involved redirecting the focus from the individual (William) and his pathology (his anxiety) to the systemic context of the behaviors.

Client needs dictate the choice of techniques, and in this case the processes were the following: developing collaboration between the partners to work on their problems together, problem exploration, exception finding, reinforcing the couple's strengths, using scaling interventions to set goals and formulate tasks, using solution-focused and cognitive-behavioral strategies to help William cope with his anxiety, teaching communication skills, pattern interruption, and scheduling pleasurable activities that the partners could enjoy separately and together.

Engagement

The integration of solution-focused and behavioral marital therapy emphasizes partners working together collaboratively to solve their problems. Part of this process involves assessing the relationship of the partners to the change process and using strategies that will engage them. In couples work, individuals usually present with the complainant type of relationship in which partners blame the other person for their current difficulties; what they would most like is for the other person to change (Clark-Stager, 1999).

Despite Helen's desire to be involved in the counseling, she clearly established that the "problem" was with her husband and that she was not interested in changing her own behavior. In solution-focused terms, she had a complainant type of orientation to the change process. William, on the other hand, waffled in his stance toward change. He consistently stated he was willing to do whatever it would take to keep Helen from leaving again. However, he also tended to view his illness as the culprit for his actions and blamed Helen for not sufficiently understanding his illness. He occasionally displayed the characteristics of the visitor, the involuntary client mandated to attend treatment by an outside person or entity. In this case, the outside entity was Helen, who refused to come home until William agreed to participate in treatment.

In the integration of the models, the tendency of each partner to blame the other was addressed by asking William and Helen to identify how they each contributed to their relationship problems. William quickly acknowledged his deficiencies. Helen, after some thought, stated she was partly responsibly for her husband's behavior; she had enabled him over the 40 years of their marriage to act as he did without addressing it as a problem or communicating her expectations for him to do more. Partners were complimented for being able to see the role they played in their difficulties and for being able to verbalize those roles in front of the other person.

Problem Exploration

After initial exploration of the problem, it became apparent that the couple has some established coping skills, because of their 40-year success in the partnership of their marriage. However, William and Helen were in need of some focus and direction to help them better recognize and build on their strengths to improve their interpersonal relationship. Many of the problems seemed to revolve around both partners' perception of William's lack of competence. William, for instance, said he "can't remember" or he "can't do" chores successfully. Helen believed that William was unable to perform chores up to her standard. She belittled his attempts, which impeded his willingness to continue making an effort, and thus a negative cycle was perpetuated.

This cycle can be discussed in terms of both solution-focused therapy and behavioral marital therapy. In behavioral terms, Helen reinforced William's inability to monitor his own medications by taking care of them herself; she punished his attempts to help with the housework by criticizing his efforts. Treatment involved modifying these reinforcement patterns; that is, Helen was taught to reward William's housekeeping efforts through complimenting and to extinguish her "taking care of his medications" behaviors so that he was pushed to do these for himself. In solution-focused terms, this negative cycle can be upturned by a focus on exceptions, times when William was able to perform chores to at least an adequate level or when he monitored his own medication. The assumption is that when the partners focus on these efforts, these behaviors will expand.

Solution Exploration

The practitioner moved to center on the couple's exceptions to complaints. When Helen was asked to talk about a time when the "problem" wasn't presenting itself, she referred to the earlier days of their marriage, when she was still working and William took responsibility for some of the chores at home. He would sometimes cook for himself, take out the trash, and do the dishes. She had fewer responsibilities at home when she was employed and was able to relax more. She felt she worked harder since retirement than before because William was no longer participating in household chores and tasks. When asked to consider the reason she thought William used to do more around the house, she said, "Because I was too tired, and I didn't do it myself."

Throughout the dialogue, William did not deny or negate any of Helen's statements and periodically nodded in agreement. He was aware that he had stopped helping because "she does it all herself." William further said that he could never do anything to Helen's standard, so he didn't bother to try. Helen then said, "I don't see the reason in doing something if you aren't going to do it right. Why would you mow the lawn or trim the bushes, William, if you're just going to leave the clippings sitting on the lawn?" At this point, the practitioner refocused on the exception finding by summarizing for Helen, "So, the times when you recall the problem being absent were when you were able to share the household workload with your husband?" to which Helen answered affirmatively.

Throughout the process of change, the practitioner should offer positive feedback and praise to help couples maintain an optimistic stance, enlist their cooperation and participation, and encourage their hard work. For example, the practitioner praised Helen for relinquishing control and sharing tasks prior to her retirement. The practitioner then used the solution-focused technique of the indirect compliment, asking Helen a question that would allow her to find the resources she had drawn upon: "How were you able to do this?" After thinking for a moment, Helen said that she was just too tired after working all day and needed to have some time to relax in the evenings so she could recharge for the next day at work. The practitioner complimented her on knowing her limits and being able to take care of herself. She further emphasized that Helen was clearly a woman of enormous strength and capability, as she had cared for her husband and their home all by herself since her retirement 13 years prior. Given these strengths, the practitioner stated her confidence in Helen's ability to share household responsibilities with her husband again.

The practitioner then asked William, indirectly complimenting him: How was he able to spend almost 15 years performing tasks around the house? He was amazed himself that it had been that long and said, "I used to do that, didn't I?" He paused but then said, "But now I couldn't do them to Helen's liking, so why bother even to try?" Still working toward exceptions, the practitioner asked William what he could recall specifically about the time period when he was self-sufficient with his medications. He recalled that he used to have a system involving a watch alarm and a daily chart. The chart indicated the pills to take at each alarm setting, which allowed him to take his medications without Helen's assistance. But once Helen retired and was home to remind him, he stopped wearing the watch.

Goal Setting

Now that the parameters of the problem and some of the exceptions had been identified, the practitioner decided the couple was ready to set goals. During the next visit at the couple's house, she introduced the idea of a scale numbered 1 to 10, with 1 being when Helen left William the week prior and 10 being that the practitioner wouldn't need to see them as a couple anymore; they would be managing just fine on their own. When William was asked where he would place himself on the scale, he said, "Ten! Now that she is back, I have everything I want!" To further engage him in understanding that his behavior was integral to the process, the question was rephrased, "Well, then, what will you be doing when Helen is also at a 10?" William stated with a grin, "Oh, I suppose I'll be doing chores regularly around the house, like taking out the garbage and mowing the lawn without her asking me to." Helen was then asked where she would place William on the scale to help him understand their different perspectives. She said, "A 3 or 4," because he spent more time indulging in rituals to calm his nerves than in productive tasks around the house.

Helen was then asked to describe what would constitute a 10. She said a 10 would be when she was committed to staying with William and no longer entertained the idea of leaving him. Pressed further, she reiterated what William had specified for his involvement in the housework and added that she wanted him to take more responsibility for his medication, so she didn't have to keep up with it all the time. Wanting more concrete details, the practitioner asked Helen to create a picture of what it would be like at 10 as far as William completing chores. The practitioner worked with Helen to define a schedule of chores and times for their completion. She decided that it would be sufficient for him to mow the lawn and rake the clippings once a week and to take the trash to the bin and bring it down to the curb for the weekly garbage collection. She said that he would also be dosing his own medication without her having to remind him. Asked what she would be doing once William was performing the chores she set forth, Helen said she would be spending time each day reading the paper and working on her puzzle collection.

When asked where Helen would place herself on the scale, she hesitated and then said, "Oh, a 5, I suppose." The practitioner praised her for already being halfway to her ultimate goal and asked how she had managed that. Helen responded that while things were not as good as she wanted them to be, she also knew they could be a lot worse. When asked to clarify, she responded with a sigh, stating she was grateful that William was not verbally or physically aggressive, he avoided trouble with the law, and he was mostly able to maintain enough functioning to stay at home without being institutionalized. Her answer was reframed as the following,

"So, you appreciate a lot of William's qualities and what he has been able to accomplish despite his illness." Helen agreed with this appraisal and also elaborated on it, saying she was pleased William was willing to make changes on long-standing behaviors and working in a couples context to make this happen.

Taking Action

Behavioral marital therapy relies heavily on homework tasks for its success so that couples can actually implement the skills learned with each other. Although solution-focused homework tends to be more suggestive (Ziegler & Hiller, 2001), solution-focused marital therapy as described by Hudson and O'Hanlon (1993) also tends to center on the assignment of tasks for couples.

From the goals the couple constructed, the practitioner worked to formulate tasks specifically, so one incremental movement could be made on the scale for the following week. The couple decided that William would take out the trash and that they would go to Kmart together to buy a watch with an alarm for William to regulate his medication.

The practitioner began the next session by asking Helen where she would place herself on the scale. She said, "Oh, I don't feel so good today—kind of depressed—probably a 6." The practitioner told Helen that she was very pleased to hear that, because they were only working toward one point change a session, and she had accomplished that. However, when the practitioner asked William and Helen the outcome of their tasks, they reported being unable to complete them. "We never had time to get to the discount store this week," Helen explained. "I feel badly about it now, but I felt too busy with other things to be able to get out there. Last night I was upset with myself for not doing it, so I wrote up a daily chart that tells William which medicines to take at what time of the day—just like the one he used back when I was working. Until we get the watch, I thought that at least he could perhaps begin to use the chart to take the medicine himself. Of course, I still had to remind him this morning, because he didn't even bother to look at it. But I only said it was time to take something—I made him look at the chart to know what to take." The practitioner congratulated Helen on taking these steps and then asked William about his reaction to the chart. "Very helpful," he said, but then went on to add that until he had the watch alarm to remind him to look at it, he didn't think he'd be able to remember on his own. He asked if Helen could be responsible for reminding him; then he could just use the chart to know which medicines to take. Frustrated, Helen said, "I don't think so, William. I don't want to have to remind you at all. That is the point of the watch—I don't want you relying on me for any part of your medication schedule."

William, flustered by having upset Helen, said, "Oh, I know. I just meant until we could get the watch. Maybe we should go get it today or tomorrow." Helen calmed down, appearing relieved to hear William recommit to the watch idea. The practitioner concluded the medication discussion by reinforcing William's suggestion to purchase the watch soon. The discussion was useful for emphasizing the importance of the tasks that the couple had agreed to undertake.

The practitioner then addressed the other tasks that had been assigned the previous week. Although William had attempted to assist by bringing the trash bin back in after collection, he did it too early, and the trash had not been picked up. As a result, Helen took it upon herself to bring it back to the curb.

When William was asked about his task accomplishment, he said he was pleased with himself for taking the initiative to do the chore and then following through with the first part of it. He then became visibly upset, recalling how Helen had reprimanded him for doing the chore at the wrong time, leaving her with more work than she would have had otherwise. When asked how he and Helen could have better resolved the situation, he thought Helen could have thanked him for the effort and then informed him of his error so he could fix the mistake himself. He also admitted that a lot of the problem would be solved if he simply performed the chore correctly. The practitioner then worked with him more closely to help him overcome the barriers to chore completion.

Building Coping Skills

The primary presenting problem for William was his anxiety disorder. He continually blamed his "nerves" for why he couldn't concentrate long enough to perform a task to completion. Whether he gambled away $50 in less than an hour, failed to take the trash out, mowed only half the lawn and then left the clippings in a pile, or collected trash from the neighborhood that he left in the living room, William defended his actions by blaming his "nerves" for causing him to feel agitated, which he relieved by either abandoning his chore or indulging himself with his hobbies (namely, gambling with scratch-off tickets or wandering the neighborhood collecting trash). The practitioner used two methods to help with his nerves. The first involved the solution-focused intervention of externalizing, and the second used cognitive restructuring and self-talk from cognitive-behavioral therapy.

Externalizing

Externalizing uses language to separate the presenting problem from the person (e.g., Berg, 1994; Bertolino & O'Hanlon, 2002; White & Epston, 1990). Instead of the problem being one of personal dynamics and an inherent quality, it is seen as an external entity. In line with this intervention, the practitioner asked William to recall experiences when he was able to engage in thoughts or behaviors that were contradictory to what his illness might encourage him to do. He quickly came up with many scenarios during which he engaged in behavior that was not typical to how his illness "made" him behave, such as periodic episodes of mowing the lawn, taking out the trash, and doing the dishes. When asked what was different about the times when he initiated and completed these chores, he insisted they were just sporadic moments when he felt restless and the task essentially "presented itself" to him. The practitioner gave William credit for over-riding his nerves and engaging in industrious tasks, which diverted him from his illness's controlling nature.

The practitioner then pursued externalizing interventions with the couple, asking William and Helen to think of a time they were able to work together to keep William's disorder from determining how they lived. Both recounted their joint effort to ensure that William attended his doctors' appointments, each taking responsibility to ready themselves for the long trips to the veterans' hospital where William was treated for both his disorder and various minor physical ailments that were the result of his age and chronic smoking.

Talking about this topic allowed the couple to recall another important exception in their mutual history. Helen was diagnosed with breast cancer in the early 1980s, which led to a complete mastectomy. During her week-long stay in the hospital, William took care of all the chores at home, and he visited Helen every day as well. The practitioner said to William, "Wow, how were you able to do that—take care of yourself during that whole time?" He replied that it was important that he take care of himself so that Helen wouldn't worry about him and thus hinder her recovery. The practitioner then asked William how he was able to help take care of Helen while she was in the hospital. He quickly stated that he didn't help "care" for her, as that was the doctor's job, but that he wanted to be there to keep her company so that she wouldn't be scared or lonely. The practitioner complimented the couple for being able to pull together as a team for such important events, emphasizing that they each helped to meet the other's needs during these stressful situations.

Cognitive Restructuring

As it is the cognitive-behavioral assumption that thoughts guide action, the practitioner asked William to summarize his thoughts whenever faced with a task or chore. He identified his immediate assumption that he would fail to do the task completely or correctly. The practitioner commended him on his insight and explored this further. William believed that to attempt the chore and fail would demonstrate that he was a failure and that the best way to avoid such a label was to do nothing. Therefore, he was most successful with task completion during the times that he spontaneously engaged in a chore without a request from Helen or when the job was not already assigned as his.

Working toward the replacement of his negative thoughts with more constructive self-talk, the practitioner asked William what he could say to himself when faced with a chore that would help him with task completion. When William was unable to do this, the practitioner eventually provided a suggestion: "I know I'm afraid to disappoint Helen, but I have successfully done this in the past, and I believe I can accomplish it again right now." William experienced great difficulty in repeating this statement aloud. He kept interrupting himself to express doubt that he would be able to do the chore. The practitioner role-played Helen, asking William to please complete a given task. William would then audibly recite the agreed-upon phrase until he appeared comfortable with the content.

The practitioner discussed with William how to reinforce himself for successfully accomplishing a task. William was most interested in praise from his wife, which the practitioner said they would continue to work on. However, it was also important that William become engaged in the process for his own satisfaction, and so she asked him to come up with his own self-praise. He settled on rewarding himself with the statement, "I am proud of myself for what I have accomplished." Again, it took some practice for him to become comfortable with the statement.

Communication Training

In integrating solution-focused and behavioral marital therapy, it is not seen as necessary to teach all the communication skills that behavioral couples therapists would usually prescribe, such as reflective listening, making validating statements, formulating "I" statements, making behavioral requests, and problem-solving skills training. Instead, only those that are essential to the couple's improved functioning would be taught. The practitioner, in this case, centered on complimenting and making behavior requests.

In behavioral theory, the central operating principle is reinforcement, and in marital therapy, complimenting is the prime way partners reinforce each other for desired behaviors. In solution-focused therapy, centering on the exceptions to partner problem behavior allows spouses to note the changes they see in each other, which spurs further positive exchanges (Clark-Stager, 1999). The practitioner offered guidelines for complimenting, which included being specific about the behaviors that are being complimented and separating complimenting from criticizing (Beach, Sandeen, & O'Leary, 1990). Helen had some difficulty with the latter guideline. For example, when William took the trash out to the curb but then neglected to return later to bring the empty bin back to the garage, she started by saying, "Thank you for helping me with that chore. It was very thoughtful of you to remember to do that today," but then finished with, "But how can you just leave the empty bin standing there? What do you expect it to do—walk back in on its own?" The practitioner modeled the complimenting by repeating the first portion of Helen's statement while leaving the last half of the sentence out of the exchange. Despite a need for more coaching to refine her tone and choice of wording, Helen demonstrated significant improvement in minimizing her belittling comments and demonstrating praise to William.

Another communication skill the practitioner worked on with this couple was how to make behavioral requests. She offered the following guidelines:

- Make the request specific ("I want you to take care of your medications this morning") versus global ("Why can't you do anything for yourself?").
- Make the request measurable ("On Wednesday night, I want you to take the garbage out, and on Thursday night, I want you to bring the bin back into the garage").
- State the presence of positive behaviors rather than the absence of negative behaviors ("Pick up the litter you have scattered on the living room floor" rather than "Don't be such a slob").

Following these guidelines, Helen practiced making behavioral requests and was successful in doing so, although the practitioner had to remind her at times throughout their work how to phrase requests to William more constructively.

Pattern Interruption

Many homework assignments involve pattern interruption, which is helping couples to do something different—adding or otherwise modifying interactions—than their negative patterned behavior (Hudson & O'Hanlon, 1993). In this case, the practitioner asked William and Helen to decide on a homework assignment for the upcoming week. However, she included the pattern-interrupting requirement that the task must be a joint one, whereby one partner accomplishes the first half, and the other completes the second half. Surprised at the twist, William and Helen responded with a mixture of suspicion and interest. After a brief conversation, William and Helen agreed to continue to work on the task of taking out the trash. They divided the chore as follows: Helen would tell William when the day arrived that the trash was to be picked up; William would then take the full trash bins out to the curb before pickup time, without further reminding from Helen; Helen would then complete the task by bringing the empty bins back in after the garbage truck left.

During the next session, William and Helen were both eager to inform the practitioner of their success. William cheerfully recounted feeling very proud to have done his part without prompting from his wife. Helen was generous in her praise of her husband, which visibly pleased William. Checking in on the scale, William still defined himself as a 10; his general level of agitation had decreased because Helen was not "nagging" him to help out. Helen placed him at a 6 or 7 because he had worked with her to get a chore accomplished. Helen did not hesitate to place herself at a 7, without any of the accompanying feelings of depression she had experienced in the past. Helen reported feeling less stress and that she was able to read the daily paper and dedicate more time to her puzzle collection.

Scheduling Pleasurable Activities

In behavioral marital therapy, one of the components to building marital cohesion is to schedule pleasant events, so that the relationship becomes associated with enjoyment and pleasure rather than coercion and dissatisfaction (Beach et al., 1990). However, when the practitioner said, "What kinds of things do you like to do together?" Mr. and Mrs. Rutledge initially rebelled against the notion of spending more time together because they were already in the house together for hours each day. The practitioner explained that simply being in the same room engaged in different activities did not necessarily constitute quality time. The practitioner asked them to make a list of activities they might enjoy and then to pick one to do in the upcoming week. The couple settled on going out to dinner at a local restaurant because it was something they did not ever do. Because they were on a limited budget, they didn't want to commit to this activity on a weekly basis, and it became a monthly goal instead. Returning to their initial list of possible activities, they agreed on a walk around the neighborhood one afternoon a week.

Hearing the couple's concern about already spending so much time together, the practitioner explored with the partners individual activities they could pursue to experience more enjoyment in their everyday lives. William expressed his desire for more social interaction, so the practitioner said she would research day programs for him to attend. This would have the added benefit, she explained, of channeling William's "energy" more constructively. Such a program might also enable Helen to have more relaxation time to herself at home.

The next time the practitioner met with the couple, she presented William with a program that would pick him up every morning, Monday through Friday, and then bring him home again in the late afternoon. He could go every weekday, or pick 2 or 3 days that appealed to him. The facility provided activities, as well as counseling opportunities, to community individuals with mental health disorders. Although worried about leaving Helen for the whole day, William agreed to try the program for a week. At the next session, he reported he was enjoying the program and was glad to get out of the house and make new friends; he decided to commit to it for 3 days each week.

Summary

The intervention extended for 3 more weeks, during which time William and Helen continued to work toward defining team roles for various household chores. At the end of this period, they agreed that they were able to manage the relationship on their own and that they no longer needed the practitioner's intervention. William had more control over his symptoms, and, more important to Helen, William was pitching in to complete chores and taking care of his medication through the chart, giving her more time to relax and enjoy herself.

As demonstrated with William and Helen, using a combination of approaches, such as scaling to focus couples in a positive direction, exception finding to build on preexisting strengths, and skill building in areas that are needed, can result in small cognitive and behavioral changes that have a significant impact on the clients' quality of life. The practitioner used these various techniques in a flexible fashion, incorporating client input into what was needed. The integration of practice theories allows the practitioner to build on the strengths of each model to help couples achieve change in their relationship.

References

Banawan, S., O'Mahen, H., Beach, S., & Jackson, M. (2002). The empirical underpinnings of marital therapy for depression. In J. Harvey & A. Wenzel (Eds.), *A clinician's guide to maintaining and enhancing close relationships* (pp. 133–155). Mahwah, NJ: Erlbaum.

Baucom, D., Shoham, V., Mueser, K., Daiuto, A., & Stickle, T. (1998). Empirically supported couple and family interventions for marital distress and adult mental health problems. *Journal of Consulting and Clinical Psychology, 66,* 53–88.

Beach, S., & Jones, D. (2002). Marital and family therapy for depression in adults. In I. Gotlib & C. Hammen (Eds.), *Handbook of depression* (pp. 422–440). New York: Guilford.

Beach, S., Sandeen, E., & O'Leary, K. (1990). *Depression in marriage: A model for etiology and treatment.* New York: Guilford.

Berg, I. K. (1994). *Family-based services: A solution-focused approach.* New York: W. W. Norton.

Bertolino, B., & O'Hanlon, B. (2002). *Collaborative, competency-based counseling and therapy.* Boston: Allyn & Bacon.

Christensen, A., Jacobson, N., & Babcock, J. (1995). Integrative behavioral couple therapy. In N. S. Jacobson & A. S. Gurman (Eds.), *Clinical handbook of couple therapy* (pp. 31–64). New York: Guilford.

Clark-Stager, W. 1999. Using solution-focused therapy within an integrative behavioral couple framework: An integrative model. *Journal of Family Psychotherapy, 10*(3), 27–47.

Dunn, R., & Schwebel, A. (1995). Meta-analytic review of marital therapy outcome research. *Journal of Family Psychology, 9,* 58–68.

Hudson, P. O., & O'Hanlon, W. H. (1993). *Rewriting love stories: Brief marital therapy.* New York: W. W. Norton.

Jacobson, N., & Margolin, G. (1979). *Marital therapy: Strategies based on social learning and behavior exchange principles.* New York: Brunner/Mazel.

Schindler, K., Zimmerman, T. S., Prest, L. A., & Wetzel, B. E. (1997). Solution-focused couples therapy groups: An empirical study. *Journal of Family Therapy, 19,* 125–144.

Wheeler, J. G., Christensen, A., & Jacobson, N. (2001). Couple distress. In D. Barlow (Ed.), *Clinical handbook of psychological disorders: A step-by-step treatment manual* (3rd ed.). New York: Guilford.

White, M., & Epston, D. (1990). *Narrative means to therapeutic ends.* New York: W. W. Norton.

Ziegler, P., & Hiller, T. (2001). *Recreating partnership.* New York: W. W. Norton.

PART III

Family Violence

11 The Strengths-and-Skills-Building Model
Application to Women in Violent Relationships

JACQUELINE CORCORAN AND HOLLY BELL

In the United States, lifetime rates of sexual and/or physical assault by an intimate partner are nearly 25% for women and 7.5% for men. About 1.5 million women and 834,732 men are sexually and/or physically assaulted by an intimate partner every year (Tjaden & Thoennes, 2000). In addition to physical well-being and safety, violence by intimate partners poses severe risks to mental health in terms of depression and anxiety disorders, particularly posttraumatic stress disorder (PTSD; Cascardi, O'Leary, & Schlee, 1999; Golding, 1999; Roberts, Williams, Lawrence, & Raphael, 1998) and low self-esteem (Sleutel, 1998).

Since women are the primary victims of intimate partner violence, this chapter will focus on female victims. Much of the public discussion about domestic violence focuses on the question "Why doesn't she leave?" However, there are a number of reasons that women do not do so, including threats by the batterer to kill the woman, her children, or any family or friends who assist her; the lack of shelter beds; the woman's desire to keep her family intact; her belief in the batterer when he says he has changed; and the reality of many women's inability to keep their family out of poverty on their income and resources alone (Stout & McPhail, 1998). Further, leaving the relationship does not always mean the violence will end. Davis and Kraham (1995; cited in Chanley & Alozie, 2001) found that divorced and separated women reported being battered 14 times as often as women still living with their partners. Leaving the relationship and ending the violence are two separate processes, and the period of separation may actually increase the violence.

Mahoney (1994) has argued that the question "Why doesn't she leave?" obscures all the other ways in which women try to protect themselves and their children. It makes invisible the women who manage to negotiate a relationship free of violence. Further complicating the picture is that many women leave their abusers, only to return. Whereas some have suggested that the tendency for battered women to return to their abusers numerous times prior to permanently leaving is evidence of pathological dependency, others have argued that it indicates the women's willingness to work through relationship problems (Mahoney, Williams, & West, 2001). It is therefore important to see leaving and becoming free of violence as a process for women (Campbell, Rose, Kub, & Nedd, 1998; Sleutel, 1998), one that involves factors over which they often have little control, such as the actions of the batterer and access to resources (child care, housing, income, social services, legal protection).

▰▰▰ Feminist Perspectives on Woman Battering

Because most practitioners will work with women who are in the process of cycling in and out of a relationship with a batterer, an understanding of the dynamics of battering is critical to keeping the woman safe. Much of our current understanding of the problem is based on a feminist perspective, which conceptualizes battering as a tactic of coercive control to maintain male power (Yllö, 1993). The feminist perspective holds that the context of abuse, the power and control by the man, is as important as the violence itself. Individual acts of violence are embedded in a web of controlling behaviors illustrated in the power and control wheel (Pence & Paymar, 1993). These controlling behaviors include emotional abuse, isolation, coercion and threats, minimizing, denying, and blaming the woman for the violence, as well as using the children as a means of control, preventing the woman from gaining or keeping a job, and treating her like a servant. As Pressman (1989) writes: "Only by understanding the social context, gender roles, and socialized traits can therapists begin to comprehend why men abuse their partners, why women remain in battering relationships, and why women feel powerless, helpless and less competent than men to take charge of their own lives" (p. 42).

Other feminist contributions include the cycle of violence and learned helplessness, both developed by Walker (1989). Walker described a three-phase cycle of abuse in relationships, starting with a tension-building phase, followed by a period of inevitability, during which the violence occurs, and ending with a period of loving contrition, when the batterer expresses remorse for the abuse he has inflicted and tries to make amends and woo his partner back into the relationship with courtship-like behavior. Without a change in the dynamics of the relationship, the cycle begins again. The Jekyll and Hyde nature of the batterer during different phases of this cycle makes it difficult for a woman to focus solely on the negative and abusive aspects of the relationship because they are so often followed by loving courtship behavior.

Walker (1989) also applied the concept of learned helplessness, first developed by Seligman (1975), to battered women. This model provides additional explanation for why some battered women stay in abusive relationships. When a woman's efforts to either stop the abuse or escape from the dangerous situation have been repeatedly ineffective, either because of the abuser's greater strength and desire to control or because of the lack of outside resources to help her, a battered woman may increasingly choose actions that have the highest probability of success in assuring her survival. They often involve staying with the batterer and trying to accommodate his demands and insulate herself against the abuse rather than risking increased injury or death by attempting to leave. Although there is not universal agreement about the application of learned helplessness to battered women (e.g., see Applewhite, 1996; Gondolf & Fisher, 1998), the model does provide some additional explanation for why some women stay in abusive relationships.

Feminist theory does not prescribe a series of specific techniques but rather a perspective from which to view the problem (Pressman, 1989). However, feminist thought makes a number of unique contributions to practice with battered women. First is the focus on the violence in the woman's relationship. Her safety is the primary therapeutic goal (Stout & McPhail, 1998; Waites, 1993; Walker, 1989). Second, it attempts to understand the violence in the context of socially sanctioned and gendered power and control (Pence & Paymar, 1993; Pressman, 1989; Yllö, 1993). Third, it stresses the importance of eliminating the traditional authoritarian relationship between the battered woman and the practitioner (Walker, 1989) and of empowering the woman to see herself as capable, with choices available to her (Stout & McPhail, 1998; Walker, 1989). The goal of intervention is empowerment, rather than adjustment, and validation of women's perceptions (Davies, Lyon, & Monti-Catania, 1998; Walker, 1989). In contrast to traditional psychotherapy, which attempts to maintain a value-free stance, the practitioner working with battered women must act as an advocate for the woman.

Historically, there has been tension between the feminist principles of the battered women's movement and the field of mental health, whose practitioners also provide services to battered women. Gondolf and Fisher (1998) surveyed state domestic violence coalitions in 1994 and found that more than half of the domestic violence advocates felt that mental health professionals failed to understand the issues of woman battering. Tensions arise from the different perspectives on human problems and the locus of intervention. Although the battered women's movement is built on a sociopolitical model that views power, control, and patriarchal attitudes as the foundation of woman battering (Yllö, 1993), most mental health strategies define the problem more narrowly and focus on the presenting problems of the individual: often a woman's depression, anxiety, paranoia, and dependency (Gondolf & Fisher, 1998; Stout & McPhail, 1998). However, these symptoms are often the result of abuse and not the cause (Stout & McPhail, 1998). Focusing on these individual characteristics can lead to a subtle blaming of the battered woman for her situation and a dangerous minimization of the violence. In particular, most writing from a feminist perspective takes issue with both psychodynamic and family system models of domestic violence and discourages couples treatment for partners in which battering occurs (Pressman, 1989; Stout & McPhail, 1998; Walker, 1989; Yllö, 1993).

Despite their differences, feminist practice and traditional psychotherapy also share common ground. Both traditional and feminist therapies focus on trauma and PTSD, recognition of the role of social factors in mental disorders, and the utility of social support as an intervention (Gondolf & Fisher, 1998).

There have been a number of attempts to apply feminist principles to more traditional therapeutic models, such as the ecological model (Dwyer, Smokowski, Bricout, & Wodarski, 1996) and the barriers model (Grigsby & Hartman, 1997). However, these models tend to be theoretical in nature and lack specification of techniques. In this chapter, the strengths-and-skills-building model is applied to working with women in violent relationships. The strengths-and-skills-building model offers a well-defined and articulated process, a wide array of specific techniques for working with women in violent relationships, and principles that can incorporate feminist perspectives. More specifically, a woman's ambivalence about the violent relationship is targeted, and the woman's readiness to take action toward leaving the relationship is assessed through motivational interviewing techniques. The model empowers women by focusing on strengths and coping capacities that they bring. Skills and capacities are further built by employing cognitive-behavioral techniques, particularly when there is distorted thinking about the acceptability of violence or attributions of blame toward the self. Most important, the role of the helper in the strengths-and-skills-building model is collaborative rather than confrontive or authoritative in nature.

Literature Review on Components of the Strengths-and-Skills-Building Model

Previous work with the individual treatment approaches—solution-focused therapy, cognitive-behavioral therapy, and motivational interviewing—comprising the strengths-and-skills-building model is scant. Greene, Lee, Mentzer, Pinnell, and Niles (1998) discussed a solution-focused approach to crisis intervention and used examples of how to apply the model to different types of crisis situations, including domestic violence. Although cognitive-behavioral treatment has been used as part of batterer intervention programs, cognitive-behavioral treatment has been discussed as an aspect of women's treatment in only the most peripheral way (Abel, 2000). Wahab (2004) recently built an argument for the use of motivational interviewing with family violence victims. MI is both client-centered and empowering to women. It also guides the service provider's interventions in a way that takes the burden of change off the helper.

Brown (1997) and Burke, Gielen, McDonnell, O'Campo, and Maman (2001) have also discussed the broader framework of the stages of change model with battered women. Brown (1997) described that in the first stage of change, precontemplation, the individual lacks awareness of a problem. A woman in this stage may accept the perpetrator's denial of a problem and her blame. In the second stage, contemplation, the woman thinks about changing her situation. She is more open to information about how to go about this but is not yet ready for action. Ambivalent about the feasibility and costs of changing the behavior, she may remain in contemplation for years. In determination, a decision has been made to take action and change, perhaps within the next month. If a woman decides to leave, she may use this time to figure out how she will manage the break and establish independence. She will work out the details of a plan and build up financial support and emotional resources. Some small steps may be taken to ready her family, such as putting away or borrowing money to leave and exploring alternative places to stay. In the action stage, the woman has undertaken a strong measure of action, such as leaving the perpetrator. Consistent change for 6 months leads individuals into the maintenance stage; however, it is also possible that relapse occurs, and the woman returns to the relationship. A strengths orientation is taken regarding relapse; it is seen as a way for individuals to reenter the change process with more knowledge of their vulnerabilities and ways to circumvent them.

Burke et al. (2001) conducted a qualitative study of 78 women who either were in an abusive relationship or had recently ended one and found that the stages of change model was a useful heuristic for how women leave violent relationships. The stages of change framework provides a foundation for the strengths-and-skills-building model, which is applied in this chapter. It must be acknowledged, however, that violence against women occurs within the context of a relationship, and the stages of change model and motivational interviewing have focused on behaviors over which individuals have control, such as substance abuse and overeating (Brown, 1997; Wahab, 2004). Women in violent relationships have choice over their own behaviors but cannot "make" their partners change their behaviors. Service providers can, therefore, work with women around the following menu of topics: safety planning, substance use, child discipline, self-care, and observance of program policies (Wahab, 2004).

▆▆▆▆ Application of the Strengths-and-Skills-Building Model

The phases of the model as applied to battered women—engagement, exploring the problem, exploring the solution, goal setting, and taking action—are discussed in this chapter, along with case examples. The practitioner need not work through the list of techniques in a rigid fashion; rather, clinical judgment dictates the selection of strategies and their particular order. The main guidelines are that the practitioner should start where the client is in terms of her assessment of danger and her readiness to change. The practitioner's efforts should be geared toward matching change strategies to the client's motivation and by examining the belief systems and resource barriers that prevent a woman from taking action to protect herself. The practitioner shows respect for the client's worldview and uniqueness by helping her to tap into the resources that have worked well in the past. In a collaborative manner, the practitioner educates the client on aspects of family violence and helps the woman build skills in needed areas. The relationship between client and practitioner empowers the woman to move toward safety for herself and her children. Davies et al. (1998) label this woman-defined advocacy, where the battered woman's views and information about her situation are valued equally with those of the advocate, as opposed to service-defined advocacy, where the focus is on getting the battered woman to utilize the available services, such as shelter or protective orders, regardless of how the woman assesses her risks and the possible benefits of those services. Such woman-defined advocacy is particularly important with battered women, so that the therapeutic relationship does not mirror in any way the battering relationship.

Engagement

The process of engaging with a client in a violent relationship involves assessing the safety of the victim, providing empathy and validation, and recognizing the client's relationship with the change process. Often the practitioner's contact with a battered woman takes place in crisis situations, such as at the scene of domestic violence or when a woman is calling a shelter, victim service, or assistance agency after an argument or physical violence. At the home of a victim, typically the police secure the scene before the helper becomes involved, so that immediate safety needs are addressed. If a woman telephones for assistance or a worker makes an outreach call, the worker should assess whether the violent partner is present and whether the woman is available to talk.

The safety of the battered woman is a primary concern (Waites, 1993). Risk assessment needs to include consideration of the risks posed by the batterer to the woman's physical and psychological safety, to her financial well-being, to her children, and to the safety of her friends and family. It also includes assessment of life-generated risks, such as the woman's financial limitations as a single parent, where she will live, her own physical and mental health issues, and the response of social institutions to the woman's needs (Davies et al., 1998). It is important in risk assessment to look at both specific incidents and the pattern of abuse across time, including severity, frequency, type of abuse, duration, and the cycles of abuse. Further, the worker and the client must examine the range of risks the woman faces, her perception of how staying in the relationship or trying to leave will increase or decrease those risks, and the meaning each risk presents to the woman. Many workers find it challenging to discover that some women do not see their partners' violence as their greatest risk and therefore do not view leaving the relationship as the most viable plan (Davies et al., 1998). Safety planning will, of necessity, include strategies for leaving the relationship for some women and, for others, strategies for staying in the relationship while increasing her and her children's safety.

After assessing immediate safety, rapport building is the next step so that the practitioner understands what the client is seeking and what she is motivated to do. The practitioner's job at this point is to create a supportive atmosphere and listen with empathy (Miller & Rollnick, 1991): "You're really hurt that your husband would say or do those things." "You're confused about what to do now." "You're worried about the future of your family." "You're afraid of what might happen when he returns." Reflecting back the content and feelings of the client's messages, including the ambivalence that is inherent in the change process, is crucial ("On one hand, you are very upset about what your boyfriend did last night; on the other hand, you really love him and were hoping to get married"). The practitioner avoids arguing with the client ("Do you know what's going to happen with you if you don't make a change? You might be killed!") or giving advice about legal options, filing charges, and calling the police. Premature advice giving might have the effect of polarizing the client from the practitioner's position. The woman may not be receptive to such advice or ready to take action. Although time might be limited in such scenarios, and the practitioner might feel some urgency in conveying information about family violence dynamics, the criminal justice system, procedures for filing charges and protective orders, and accessing resources (such as financial benefits, housing assistance, child care, and legal aid), first the practitioner must understand the individual's situation and what it is the client seeks. When information is given to suit the individual situation, it is much more likely to be used.

At the same time, concerns for the woman's safety are paramount. A helper does not want to support a woman's remaining in a dangerous situation. Although concern for a woman's safety and the risks involved in staying in an abusive relationship should be conveyed, this should not drive a wedge between the worker and the client. The worker should avoid insisting that the only option for the woman is to leave; otherwise, the client is placed in the position of either following the worker's directive or not pursuing the contact further. As Stout and McPhail (1998) warn, the helper working with a battered woman must not attempt to save the client against her will. Instead, the rapport built and the understanding conveyed for the woman's dilemma (she loves him, but he sometimes hurts her; she is financially dependent, but she is afraid of what he might do), as well as taking seriously her assessment of both batterer-generated and life-generated risks, may increase the possibility that the woman will seek further services and support rather than being alienated from them. The clinician must help the woman plan for her safety at the level on which the woman is willing to engage and in a way that makes sense to her.

Assessment of Relationship to the Change Process

From a solution-focused perspective, women who are involved in a violent relationship typically present as either the complainant or the visitor type of relationship to the helping process. (See Chapter 1 for more information on these terms.) The woman in the complainant relationship, while motivated to no longer have violence in the relationship, believes the route to change is through her partner's actions rather than her own choices ("I just want him to get help or get counseling"). Although a feminist perspective on woman battering places the responsibility for the violence on the perpetrator, it does acknowledge that victims must make choices to protect themselves.

The woman who is a visitor to the change process does not admit to others (and perhaps not even to herself) that there is a problem with the relationship: "Nothing's wrong." "It's not that big a deal." She is more interested at this point in getting helpers, law enforcement, or the court system to leave her and the relationship alone. Strategies for assisting women in each of these types of relationships are discussed next.

Complainant Relationship

Techniques for engaging with the woman who is most interested in her partner changing and who may not see all the choices she has available to her include normalizing, asking coping questions, and reframing. These techniques are discussed next, with case illustrations.

Normalizing

Normalizing involves validating the symptoms of distress, such as depression and anxiety, that a woman may feel while in a violent relationship (Cascardi et al., 1999; Golding, 1999; Roberts et al., 1998) and providing information about the dynamics of family violence that the woman may also be experiencing.

CLIENT: Lately, my boyfriend has been mistreating me. He has been distant, pushes me around, and he is seeing another woman. The whole thing is so depressing; it's hard to talk about it. [trying to hold back tears]

PRACTITIONER: It's very normal to feel sad and hurt in a situation when your boyfriend isn't treating you well and seeing someone else.

CLIENT: Really? Because he tells me it's crazy that I'm crying so much and asking him all these questions about where he's been. He tells me I'm crazy, and that's why he loses his temper and hits me.

PRACTITIONER: That often happens in a relationship in which there is physical violence. The physically abusive partner blames the other person for his behavior and doesn't take responsibility for it himself.

In this example, the woman started to at least partially believe her partner's accusation that she is "crazy" for becoming so upset about his behaviors. The practitioner validates her experience, that she has a right to painful emotions due to living in an abusive situation. The practitioner then proceeds to link the woman's experience to information about typical battering behaviors.

Reframing

Reframing, in which a positive spin is offered on behaviors previously viewed as negative, can also be used with women in the complainant type of relationship.

CLIENT: I'm so confused. I feel like I'm split in half. Part of me thinks I should leave him, the other feels like I want to stay. I don't know why I'm so weak and indecisive.

WORKER: You're the type of person who likes to weigh her decisions carefully and to think things through.

In this example, a reframe is offered on the client's ambivalence, with the recognition that the decision to terminate a relationship is a difficult one.

CLIENT: All I do is think about this, especially after he goes off. He did that last week, and I just don't know how much more I can take.

WORKER: You have a bottom line about what you're willing to take in terms of living with violence.

The reframe here involves taking the client's feelings of being overwhelmed with the stress of living with violence and translating it into "a bottom line," which offers the client a more decisive stance.

Reframing can be used specifically with women's attempts at help seeking, as the following example illustrates.

CLIENT: I was in the waiting room and almost got up to go home. I don't know why I'm here. I should be able to handle this on my own.

WORKER: So you're a person who has the courage to face what's going on and seek help.

In this example, the client sees herself as weak for getting help, but the worker reframes her actions as "courageous." In this way, the client's view of herself is altered. The worker follows the reframe with an indirect compliment to further plumb the client's resources that help her act courageously.

Reframes can also be used for a more strategic purpose—when clients' arguments against change can be used in the service of change. Many women, for example, say that they are unwilling to leave their partners; their desire instead is for the partner to get help. The helper can then inform the particular woman that most men who are violent do not seek treatment voluntarily. If they do initially agree, it's usually under a sense of coercion when their partner has left them, and they often drop out after the crisis in the relationship is over. In addition, both men who are voluntary and men who drop out are more likely to assault again than men who are mandated to complete treatment (Gondolf, 1997). Most men who are violent have to be court-ordered to attend treatment, and typically men are offered treatment as a way to avoid worse legal consequences.[1] Further, batterer treatment programs seem to have more effect on physical abuse than on verbal abuse and controlling behavior (Gondolf, 1997), and it is psychological abuse that appears to incur the most harm in terms of low self-esteem, PTSD, fear, and depression (Dutton, Goodman, & Bennett, 1999; Sackett & Saunders, 1999; Sleutal, 1998).

Another reframe can be used for a strategic purpose when women say they do not want to separate from their partners because of the possible negative effects on children of not having a father present. This concern can certainly be validated, but it also can be reframed: A woman has to weigh the effect of father absence against the impact of children witnessing violence, which includes a higher risk of being in violent relationships as adults themselves (McNeal & Amato, 1998).

Coping Questions

Women living in a violent relationship have often drawn on different resources to cope. Coping questions validate the difficulties that have been endured but also ask clients to reflect on the resources they have used to manage their struggles. Some examples of answers to coping questions from battered women include calling battered women's hotlines, talking to friends and family about the situation, keeping busy, focusing on the children rather than the relationship, finding spiritual solace in church going or prayer, and performing self-care activities, such as getting nails and hair done, baths, hot showers, and exercising. A further use of coping questions is to target possible strengths for exception building. For example, if a woman seeks support from either formal (calling a hotline) or informal (friends and family) means, the worker might explore how she could continue to use support seeking as a way to build her resources.

In working with family violence victims, the practitioner must employ the technique of asking coping questions strategically, however, so that staying in an unsafe situation is not encouraged. One prime example is the use of what has been called the coping technique of making "downward comparisons," which means comparing oneself to someone in a hypothetical worse situation and, as a result, viewing one's own situation as acceptable (Koss & Burkhart, 1989; Wills, 1981). For certain problems (e.g., breast cancer), this coping mechanism is positively associated with adjust-

---

1. Stuart and Holtzworth-Munroe (1995) caution, however, that for men who have a history of chronic violence and substance abuse, both within and outside the intimate relationship, treatment will probably not be effective; rather, punishment through sentencing is usually the best recourse. In these instances, treatment may offer a false sense of security and hope about the possibility of the relationship changing and might put a woman into further danger.

ment and recovery. Unfortunately, making downward comparisons may not be adaptive for battered women, who are often in relationships where their partners minimize the damage the violence inflicts. Herbert, Silver, and Ellard (1991) studied, among other coping mechanisms, the use of downward comparison with women who had suffered violence in relationships. Women who compared themselves with hypothetical others who were faring worse ("Other women are getting hospitalized from violence by their husbands; I'm only being pushed around") perceived their own situation, as a result, as more positive and acceptable than it could have been ("It's really not so bad"), and this practice was associated with staying rather than leaving the relationship.

The various techniques that have been discussed in this section—normalizing, reframing, and coping questions—can also be used with the woman who is in a visitor relationship to the change process. Other engagement strategies for this kind of relationship are discussed below.

Visitor

For the woman who is unwilling, at this point, to change her situation and who insists, at least to outsiders, that there is not a problem, strategies include asking future-oriented questions about actions that could be taken to get referral sources "off her back" ("What needs to happen so that the police are no longer concerned about your safety?") or using motivational questions that get the client to argue for her own change. Not only can asking motivational questions engage the person who is defensive about the problem but also it is a way to explore the problem in a productive way that may be used whenever a client is unable to see her capacity to make changes that will increase her safety. Examples of how to elicit self-motivational statements are demonstrated in the next section, followed by other motivational techniques to handle women's fears about change.

Eliciting Self-Motivational Statements

A part of the problem exploration process involves building the client's motivation by exploring the client's perception of the advantages and disadvantages of change. Table 2.2 has a complete list of questions that elicit self-motivational statements. This exploration can be useful for a woman who does not believe there is a problem and also for those who are just "contemplating" change and are as yet ambivalent about taking definitive action. Again, this process helps the woman experiencing domestic violence to assess the unique batterer-generated and life-generated risks that are germane for her, so that pertinent strategies are formulated to promote her and her children's safety (Davies et al., 1998).

Motivational interviewing is first demonstrated with the woman discussed previously who is ambivalent about staying with or leaving her boyfriend.

CLIENT: He criticizes everything I do. He calls me names and curses me and shoves me away. I feel hurt and stupid when he treats me that way. I heard him talking to another woman on the phone. I've confronted him. He responds with more abuse. I have no peace at home any more. When he comes home after staying out all night, he usually starts an argument and blames me for it.

PRACTITIONER: How is this affecting you and your son? [problem recognition]

CLIENT: I can't sleep at night. My thoughts are constantly on him and these problems. I've lost my appetite and cry a lot. My son whines and cries more, too.

PRACTITIONER: What effects will this situation have if it continues?

This open-ended question may encourage the determination of the client to change if she finds that the impact of the current situation will only worsen over time. Answering these questions for herself is more powerful than having the practitioner advise her on what will happen if she fails to act.

CLIENT: I worry a lot but don't know what to do. I left Jose once and stayed with a friend for a while. It felt peaceful then. I've thought more about getting help since then. That's why I'm here.

PRACTITIONER: When you left him before, you were successful in gaining a sense of peace and freedom for a while. What changes will need to be made for you to have continued peace?

This solution-focused statement orients the client toward contemplation of the changes she may potentially enact.

CLIENT: My son and I stayed with my friend for 2 weeks and returned because my boyfriend said he missed me. But for change to happen, he will have to stop abusing me and stop seeing other women, or I'll have to do something.

PRACTITIONER: What do you think you will have to do?

This statement encourages the client to produce some answers for herself, rather than the practitioner simply telling her what she must do.

Handling Women's Fears About Change
Another category of motivational techniques can be applied to women's fears about change (Miller & Rollnick, 1991), which include denial ("He doesn't hurt me"), minimization ("It's only every once in a while"), ration-

alization ("I'm really hard to live with; I don't blame him for losing his temper every once in a while"), and hopelessness ("What's the use? It'll never change"). These responses need to be understood in the context of the battered woman's experience of violence, as well as her life context. Many of these responses echo what the batterer has told her and reinforced with violence. What may be underneath the battered woman's "resistance" toward change is fear for her safety and her family's. When encountering resistance in clients, Miller and Rollnick (1991) advise that the worker should consider it a signal that the client is in a different stage of change than the worker assumes and should adjust strategies to the client's level of motivation. This may involve further exploration of the client's safety needs and environmental resources or motivational techniques such as simple reflection, double-sided reflection, or amplified reflection, as the following examples illustrate.

CLIENT: I don't know what to do. I suppose I need to leave him for the sake of my son, but I can't afford to raise him by myself.
PRACTITIONER: You're concerned about how you'd be able to manage financially without him. [simple reflection]
CLIENT: I want to deal with my problems, but sometimes I think it would be easier not to bother.
PRACTITIONER: On one hand you don't want to be here, and, on the other hand, you want help for your problems. [double-sided reflection]

Reflecting the ambivalence involved with change is helpful so that people can hear for themselves the often contradictory pulls that influence them. Women attempting to leave violent relationships have concerns about their safety and financial security, as well as emotional ties to the batterer, that will need to be addressed before they will be motivated to leave.

Amplified reflection and agreement with a twist are demonstrated with another client who has received an outreach call from a worker at a victim assistance unit of a police department.

CLIENT: My husband is a decent man.
WORKER: Your husband would never hurt you. [amplified reflection]
CLIENT: I wouldn't say "never." But he feels bad when he does it.
WORKER: Your husband hurts you.

In this example, the worker in the first part exaggerates the client's response. The result of this technique is for the client to back away from the original position and counter the worker's remark. The worker responds in turn with a reflection of the client's statement that violence sometimes does occur, selectively emphasizing the part that argues that change should occur.

CLIENT: It's only every once in awhile and out of the blue.
WORKER: So you can't even see it coming. That must be very difficult.

The client here explains that the violence is intermittent, and she minimizes its effects. By her statement, the worker allows the client to see the risks involved with this particular pattern of violence. Understanding the context and function of a woman's fears about changing can help the counselor ally with the woman in her efforts to protect herself, rather than further diminishing her self-esteem by pathologizing her. It can also help to address environmental risks, such as fears of poverty or loss of help with childrearing, that may be keeping the woman in a violent relationship.

The following case example shows how a combination of solution-focused, motivational interviewing, and cognitive-behavioral techniques are used with Ronnie, a 38-year-old woman. Ronnie was initially angry with the police after her boyfriend was arrested for bruising her arm and possibly wrenching it as well (she held it gingerly but refused medical care). She admitted they had been arguing but insisted that there was no need for police involvement (a neighbor called 911). However, the police department had a pro-arrest policy; therefore, if police arrived at a domestic scene where violence had occurred, an arrest was mandated. Ronnie's boyfriend was arrested, and a victim services worker was called to the scene.

The worker has just heard Ronnie's story about the events that occurred that evening, listening with empathy and support.

CRISIS WORKER: How much is your boyfriend's violence a problem for you? [a problem recognition question to elicit motivation]
RONNIE: Violence is too hard a word.
CRISIS WORKER: What do you want to call it? [looking for idiosyncratic phrasing]
RONNIE: Sometimes he pushes me around—but only when he was been drinking.
CRISIS WORKER: He pushes you around when he drinks. [simple reflection] How much of a problem is that for you? [repeating problem recognition statement]
RONNIE: Most of the time it's not. It just happens every once in a while, and not every time he drinks.
CRISIS WORKER: So sometimes it's hard to predict when it's going to happen? [While the lack of predictability has not been stated, the worker states the implicit message.]
RONNIE: I guess so.
CRISIS WORKER: It must be very difficult, not knowing when he's going to start pushing you around. [simple reflection]
RONNIE: I can tell, most of the time. He has usually drunk at least a 12-pack, and he's starting to think about stuff that's pissed him off.

CRISIS WORKER: Then what happens? [open-ended question to explore the problem]

RONNIE: I guess you would say he's frustrated because he's not further along, money-wise, than he thought he would be at this stage in his life. He's mad at his boss for not giving him a raise when he gave another guy one, who my boyfriend says is a lazy son of a bitch. Anyway, you get the picture.

CRISIS WORKER: So he's frustrated with his job, people he works with, and possibly himself. [simple reflection]

RONNIE: Yeah, he has a lot on his mind.

CRISIS WORKER: Then what happens? [open-ended question to explore the problem]

RONNIE: He starts getting pissed at me. I tell him, don't take this out on me. I want you to be making more money, too.

CRISIS WORKER: Has he done this kind of thing at work where he pushes someone around, and it's gotten him into trouble? [The worker tries to establish whether he has a problem in other contexts or whether his anger is targeted at her.]

RONNIE: Well, it's never gotten to the stage where he's hit someone, but he's lost his temper, got in people's faces, and stormed off jobs before.

CRISIS WORKER: So he's had some problems controlling his anger on the job, too, and it's caused some problems for him. [simple reflection]

RONNIE: Yeah, I've told him, you can't do that. You can't just lose it.

CRISIS WORKER: Somehow, though, he seems able to control his anger at work so it doesn't get to the shoving and pushing stage. With you, though, he doesn't. Some men have an easier time pushing around the women they live with rather than other men. [Reframing: The worker here takes the woman's statement and argues for the opposite side, that Ronnie's boyfriend has a propensity to hit a woman rather than men who are his physical equals.]

RONNIE: In his younger days, he did beat up on other men, but he's past that now.

CRISIS WORKER: How has he not been able to get past that with you, his partner?

RONNIE [tears glisten for the first time]: He says he will. He's so sorry later. He says he doesn't even remember; he's blacked out the whole thing. But he promises, and then he does it again the next time.

CRISIS WORKER: You're really hurting when he says he'll stop, and it keeps happening. [simple reflection]

RONNIE: At work, he wants to keep making money, but for me, who cares?

CRISIS WORKER: So what do you think his getting arrested tonight will tell him?

[Ronnie pauses for a moment.]

RONNIE: It was so embarrassing. All my neighbors saw.

CRISIS WORKER: What did you do to be embarrassed about? [Socratic questioning so the client will deduce for herself the reason the police arrested her husband]

RONNIE: Well, I was screaming and yelling, too.

CRISIS WORKER: So you were screaming and yelling. [simple reflection]

RONNIE: But I was only doing that because he was being such an asshole and backing me up into the wall.

CRISIS WORKER: So he was threatening you and intimidating you physically? That's why you were screaming. [simple reflection]

RONNIE: He was grabbing me and shaking me. My arm still hurts.

CRISIS WORKER: Do you think you need to get that arm checked out?

RONNIE: I'll be okay.

CRISIS WORKER: Then what happened?

RONNIE: The police came and took my husband away in handcuffs.

CRISIS WORKER: And what was the reason they did that? [deductive questioning]

RONNIE: Because he put a bruise on me.

CRISIS WORKER: Because of something he did. [simple reflection]

[Ronnie is silent for a moment as she seems to contemplate this.]

RONNIE: I'm not leaving him. I'm telling you that right now.

CRISIS WORKER: We are not anywhere to that point. I am, however, concerned about this happening again. [Rather than getting into a debate about why Ronnie should leave him, the worker shifts the focus of the conversation.]

RONNIE: I bet he will stop now. He's never been arrested before. Well, for a PI [public intoxication], but nothing like this.

CRISIS WORKER: I hope so, but just in case, I'd like to make sure you're safe. Can we take some time now and draw up what we call a safety plan?

This example illustrates how to use the strengths-and-skills-building model so that a woman who is, at least initially, resentful of intervention that she perceives as being pushed on her starts to consider that violence has occurred and that she might take some steps to prevent it from happening again.

Problem Exploration

Exploration of the problem can proceed in a productive way by asking the woman about previous problem-solving attempts and having her explore the advantages and disadvantages of leaving versus staying.

Problem-Solving Attempts

Asking a woman how she has tried to protect herself and her children from violence and to get the violence to end gets at important information. Such a discussion not only helps to identify resources that have been employed but also gives the woman credit for being actively engaged in trying to keep herself and her children safe. When a woman is discouraged that she has left her partner half a dozen times but still has not ended the relationship or the violence, the practitioner can emphasize that the change process can be viewed like a positive spiral. It may feel to the woman like she is going round and round, stuck in the same impasse, but actually she is moving forward incrementally and learning more about what needs to be done for the next time around. Research shows that many women have to leave their abusive partners multiple times before they are actually able to leave permanently (Okun, 1986). Each time around, she is learning more and building skills to navigate the situation more successfully.

Sometimes past problem-solving attempts (for example, a woman leaving a partner briefly after an episode of violence) may help her get in touch with what can be used effectively again. Answers to these questions can give the practitioner and the client ideas on where future interventions may need to be applied.

Questioning about problem-solving attempts can also pinpoint why efforts have not been more successful. For example, 27-year-old Anita mentioned that she left her boyfriend and went to stay with her aunt after he had kicked her in the ribs during an argument. He had called repeatedly, his messages becoming increasingly apologetic and despondent until he seemed close to suicidal. Anita said she felt sorry for her boyfriend then and called him. The worker talked with her about extinction bursts, first illustrating the information with a child behavior example because Anita had a 5-year-old boy. The crisis worker used the example of a child throwing a tantrum to get his way. If the tantrum was ignored, first the parent would experience an "extinction burst" when the child's behavior escalated out of proportion to what had been done before. Rather than giving in to this extravagant display, which Anita could see was only training the child to use tantrums even more aggressively, the parent should take this behavior as a sign that the ignoring process was starting to work. If the parent continues ignoring through this process, the behavior eventually stops. In the same way with her ex-boyfriend, if Anita kept ignoring his calls to the point where he said he was suicidal, she could see that responding to his call would result only in a further escalation of his behavior to get her back.

The worker next took Anita through the process of how she could handle repeated calls from her boyfriend in the future. Potential strategies included leaving the phone off the hook, allowing the answering machine to pick up the calls and then deleting the messages without listening to them, enlisting the support of someone else to screen the calls, changing her number temporarily or permanently, relying only on a cell phone, leaving the house when he called, and keeping busy. The worker also helped Anita deal with feeling responsible for her boyfriend's suicidal threats and consider other ways to handle this rather than answering his calls (for example, asking one of his friends or family members to check on him). The worker further pointed out that threatening suicide is often used as a tactic by batterers to get their partners back. Anita could also apply for a protective order so that his alleged suicidality would not be turned against her.

Questions about past problem-solving attempts are also important so the practitioner avoids repeating the same tactics that have already been tried. For example, Anita attended a support group for battered women and found listening to other women's stories of violent incidents painful and depressing. Rather than feeling empowered, she felt even more hopeless about the prospect of change. The worker would then not suggest attending this group to Anita but engage her on some other possibilities for seeking support.

Decisional Balance

Exploration of the relative advantages and disadvantages of leaving a violent relationship involves the motivational technique of the decisional balance. The decisional balance reveals considerable information about the specific factors that need to be addressed before the woman is ready to change her situation. As much as possible, the woman should come up with the benefits and costs herself, although prompting can involve asking relationship questions, pushing her to respond from the perspective of another: "What would your mother say is a benefit of leaving?" "What would your sister say about staying?" After prompting has exhausted her replies, the worker is allowed to add in other benefits and costs the woman may not have yet considered. See Table 11.1 for a delineation of some of the reasons that may be involved.

Usually, women can see the many advantages of ending a violent relationship, although the disadvantages to changing and the advantages to remaining in the relationship exert a tremendous pull. If a woman is with a violent partner, there are certain gains she experiences from the relationship, whether companionship, financial support, the feeling of being needed, acting in alignment with religious values, concern about the impact of divorce on children, lack of housing options, and so on. This process of change has been established empirically in a study, using social exchange as its theoretical framework, of battered women residing in a shelter (Applewhite, 1996). Women who had left their partners perceived they were losing more from the relationship in terms of physical and psychological

Table 11.1

Sample Decisional Balance for Leaving an Abusive Relationship

Benefits of continuing to stay in the relationship	Costs of continuing to stay in the relationship	Benefits of leaving the relationship	Costs of leaving the relationship
Gets love, attention, affection, and companionship	Physical injury	Increased self-esteem and self-respect	Loneliness
Obtains financial support	Emotional problems	Physical safety	Fear of the unknown
Has a father figure for the children	Feels worse about self	Focus on parenting rather than the relationship	Fear of retaliation
Only happens periodically, combined with loving, contrite behavior at other times (Fernandez, Iwamoto, & Muscat, 1997)	Poor role modeling for children	Gain respect of children	Lack of financial support
If abuser is the father of children, there will be continuous contact anyway for the sake of the children (Fernandez et al., 1997)	Lack of stability/ security in home	Build a better social support network	Give up house/ residence
He might follow through on his promises to change	Possible intergenerational cycle of abuse		Have to find/ maintain a place to stay
No other place to stay	Isolation (hiding the effects of the abuse, shame)		

Note. For simplicity, only one side of the decisional balance may be completed (i.e., the benefits of staying in the relationship versus the costs of staying in *or* the benefits of leaving the relationship versus the costs of leaving the relationship).

abuse and loss of self-esteem than what they received in terms of love and financial resources from their partners. In the Applewhite study (1996), these factors were described as naturally occurring processes, whereas in motivational interviewing the advantages and disadvantages are targeted for change directly.

The practitioner, therefore, is advised to put efforts toward selecting the advantages that have the most influence in terms of keeping the problem in place. For instance, if financial support presents the foremost reason for remaining in the relationship, then working on financial options, such as referrals to social services for financial assistance, job training, employment, and access to child care, might be the first line of intervention. In this way, the work on the decisional balance will aid the practitioner and the client in discovering the priority goals that should be targeted.

Solution Exploration

Solution-focused therapy concerns itself with the resources individuals use to manage their problems. This focus empowers the client to resolve her difficulties rather than having to receive "expert" advice, which puts the helper in the role of expert and the woman in a position of a person with deficits that someone else will correct for her. Again, this reinforces to the woman that she, rather than the batterer, is the problem. Therefore, considerable time should be spent on gleaning client resources and strengths and amplifying them.

Miracle Question or Dream Question

To help people turn from a problem-focused view to one in which change is possible, the miracle question, one of the signature techniques of solution-focused therapy, can be employed. However, to further empower battered women, a variant of the miracle question, the dream question formulated by Greene and associates (1998), should be used. The dream question is as follows:

> Suppose that tonight while you are sleeping you have a dream. In this dream you discover the answers and resources you need to solve the problem that you are concerned about right now. When you wake up tomorrow, you may or may not remember your dream, but you do notice you are different. As you go about starting your day, how will you know that you discovered or developed the skills and resources necessary to solve your problem? What will be the first small bit of evidence that you did this? . . . Who will be the first person to notice that you have and are using some of the resources you discovered in your dream? What will they be noticing about you that will be evidence to them that you have and are using some of these resources? (Greene et al., 1998, p. 397)

As opposed to the miracle question, the dream sequence asks clients to tap into their own internal resources (the answer to the problem you came here for) rather than the external event of a "miracle." Whenever possible, women in violent relationships need to be empowered. One warning with the miracle question is that some women answer this in terms of their partners magically being transformed. A woman can be validated for such a response ("wouldn't that be nice") and then directed to a response that is within her power to affect.

Yolande, an African American woman with three children, answered in the following way:

> In the morning when I wake up, I will feel a sense of relief, and there'll be no worrying about what will set my husband off. I won't be tiptoeing around. I will be relaxed, living on my own in a nice apartment with my three children, who will be happy and energetic, not sulking and trying not to make their dad mad. My daughter comes in to wish me good morning. She is smiling and relaxed, too, not worried about me anymore. The bedroom is decorated the way I want, not the way he wants it to be. I will shower, dress, and help my children do the same before we all go into the kitchen and prepare breakfast together. My children and I will sit around the table and eat breakfast and discuss the upcoming day. I will walk my children to the bus stop. I enjoy being with my children in the morning. I return home and get ready for work. Now I can take my time in the morning. I'm no longer tense and stressed out. Then I leave for my job.

As with many women, Yolande was initially mired in hopelessness with her current situation. The miracle question or dream question allows women who have been stuck in difficult circumstances see some possibilities for the future they had yet to consider. Developing a view of life without the problem gives women hope and sometimes gives them the accompanying energy to make some changes in the present in accordance with a view of the future without violence.

Exception Finding

Through the use of other solution-focused techniques previously named— coping questions, finding out about previous problem-solving attempts, the dream sequence—the worker has already discovered many of the resources and strengths that clients bring. Exception finding continues along this track. However, caution must be advised that with battered women, techniques must be applied strategically and focused on the woman's own efforts. For instance, exceptions related to when her partner was acting "nice" or when she placated her partner and "walked on eggshells" are not encouraged.

Following is an example of a worker addressing the client's feelings of low self-esteem with exception finding.

CLIENT: I just feel so stupid and useless.

WORKER: Let's see . . . you say you feel stupid and useless. However, aren't you working two jobs, one as the bookkeeper for your husband's business, raising your two children, and taking care of your mother since she got out of the hospital? That doesn't sound very useless or stupid to me.

CLIENT: Well, I guess when you put it that way, I'm not.

The worker then continues to probe so that the client explores the strengths she uses to manage all these responsibilities.

Here is another example in which the worker uses exception finding to address the client's feeling that she had no control over her boyfriend's erratic behavior:

CLIENT: When he gets like that, I just feel so helpless. I just want to crawl under the covers and not come out.

WORKER: Sound like your boyfriend is pretty scary when he's upset and has been drinking.

CLIENT: Yes, and if it goes on for very long, eventually he comes after me.

WORKER: Can you think of a situation where your boyfriend was drinking and upset that didn't wind up with him hitting you?

CLIENT: Well, one night I was getting real nervous because he had been drinking for several hours. The TV was broken, and he was mad about that. I heard some of our neighbors outside on the stairs of our apartment. My boyfriend likes them, so I impulsively opened the door and started talking with them. I invited them in for a beer. I don't really like to have those guys in my house, but I knew that they would distract him and keep him drinking. He won't hit me in front of other people. Eventually, he passed out. In the meantime, I went to bed. Once he passes out, I'm not too worried.

WORKER: Well, that sounds like a very clever way to protect yourself in that situation. It sounds like you're not as helpless as you feel to take care of yourself.

Following is another example with a woman named Carla, who has been married to her husband for 14 years with two children by him. She said that she stopped her husband from hitting her when her children were around.

CARLA: I don't like them to see him hurting me. I remember how I used to feel when my mother got hit. I used to think she deserved it. I don't want my children thinking that way of me.

Here, the worker might congratulate Carla on being such a caring and attentive mother. The worker is ever vigilant for strengths that can be enlarged on to build solutions in problem areas. Carla's concern for her children, for example, might be used to galvanize her to action. The worker explores with Carla how she handles the situation differently when her children are present.

CARLA: If he shoves me down, I say, "Stop it, Steven! Not in front of the children!" Sometimes he backs off. Not always, but sometimes. Then he'll just throw stuff around instead.

Because even having the children around may be to some extent outside Carla's control, the worker asks the client what she is doing differently at those times.

WORKER: Great! So you're able to tell him to stop, and he does. He listens because you tell him in such a firm way. How can you do that when the children are not around?

CARLA: I guess I could do that. Usually, I just don't say anything. I just want it to be over as quickly as possible.

WORKER: How could you tell him like you mean business?

CARLA: I guess I could say it loud and firm, like when I'm telling the kids no.

WORKER: How do you think he will react when you are loud and firm like that?

CARLA: He'd be shocked, I bet, that I finally stood up for myself.

The narrative influence on solution-focused therapy is illustrated in this scenario with the use of presuppositional language. "How do you think he *will* react *when* you are loud and firm like that?" Words like *when* and *will* convey the certainty that change will occur rather than tentative phrasing—words like *if* and *would*.

The client, at the conclusion of this contact, considers standing up to her husband and calling the police if violence recurs. Although these might seem like tiny steps toward progress, they have been generated from the client and, hence, have more lasting and empowering value than if the worker had just lectured her on what she should do.

Goal Setting

Goals may differ according to the woman's readiness to change. Many women do not begin the help-seeking process with the goal of leaving their partners. They are likely to be more motivated toward goals that lessen the violence but keep the relationship intact. The worker must be sensitive to what the woman wants at this stage, while keeping the woman's safety a primary focus. This may involve helping the woman make short-term safety plans, such as going to her mother's house for the weekend or staying at a friend's house overnight in case of violent episodes. Regardless of the woman's stated goals, the worker can help her more effectively turn goals into actions. For example, after several months in a help-seeking relationship, a woman states that her goal is to "leave my husband." More discussion might reveal that to do this, she will have to make some major accomplishments, such as "living on her own," "being financially independent," and "developing a social support system." However, each of these could stand as a goal on its own or could justifiably be delineated even further. For example, a common goal might be "finding a job." However, this, in turn, might have some very large subgoals: finding child care and reliable transportation and obtaining adequate job skills, for instance. Each of these perhaps deserves its own scale, depending on where the woman is starting out, as the following example demonstrates. LaTisha's priority goal was to find appropriate child care, so that her two children are taken care of on the days she works. On a scale for this goal, LaTisha currently ranks herself at a 4: She has been relying on her family and friends to look after her children and has begun to gather references for other child care providers. Exception-finding questions about how she was able to get to this point are a source of inquiry. In the next section on taking action, task setting is explored, along with problem solving, delivering information collaboratively, working with belief systems, and helping women loosen their attachment to the batterer.

Taking Action

Task setting involves planning with clients how they will take one incremental step toward their goal. In the example with LaTisha, the helper and LaTisha spent time devising a list of questions that LaTisha could use for screening child care providers, such as names of references, their licensure status, fees, their experience level, the amount of space they have, and what neighborhood they live in.

Problem Solving

To devise a task, the woman might sometimes need to go through the problem-solving process: defining a specific problem, brainstorming, considering pros and cons of viable options, and figuring out how to implement feasible options. Many times, financial problems block a woman's exit from a violent relationship. A crisis worker went through the problem-solving process for a woman named Vicki, who had recently left her husband and was now undergoing financial strain. When they went through the process of developing alternatives, Vicki said her foremost priority was to apply for a job. In the meantime, she could also complete a welfare assistance application. She is preparing to speak with child support enforcement about garnishing wages from her ex-husband to ensure that her children are financially secure. Vicki commented that she recently received a letter from her union, stating that she was inappropriately terminated from her position. She thought maybe there was some action the union might take on her behalf, either to regain her job or to compensate her with money, but that she would have to call the number on the letter to find out. Another option was to examine the client's monthly expenses, to determine what areas she might reduce spending.

After brainstorming, the worker and Vicki together evaluated the possible outcomes of each proposed solution. Vicki has already completed several job applications, and she was scheduled for an interview the same afternoon. She would also be eligible for health benefits if she were employed full-time, and her grandmother could once again care for her children at a reduced fee. Vicki was also motivated to reapply for public assistance. Previously, she was ineligible because of her income, but because she was now unemployed and not currently receiving child support, she could qualify for benefits. Although assistance would be limited once she began receiving support for her child, it could help make ends meet while she is unemployed and her child's father is uncooperative. Vicki does not understand what plans her union is making or if any steps can be taken legally, and she will try to get more information about this option. As for the last option, to reduce her monthly expenses, Vicki has already been successful in limiting her monthly expenses by maintaining Section 8 housing, obtaining food stamps, and relying on her grandfather for transportation. Therefore, she does not believe she can reduce her costs considerably further without disconnecting her telephone, electricity, or gas, which were the only monthly expenses remaining. Based on the evaluation of each of the possible solutions, Vicki developed the following plan: to look for employment, to complete an income application, and to seek legal action to obtain child support.

In another example, a woman named Lourdes had the goal of "protecting herself from violence." She produced the following list of options: (a) engage in the usual arguments with her husband, alternatively allowing him to rant at her with her crying, or screaming insults back to him; (b) remain in the bedroom, continuing to ignore his insults, and occasionally repeating that she does not want him to talk to her in that way; (c) leave the house under a guise (grocery shopping or running an errand); (d) call the police; and (e) leave the house forcefully, hitting back, and screaming at him.

In the next step of the problem-solving process, the client and the worker critiqued some of the viable options they had uncovered in Step 2. For a delineation of this example, see Table 11.2. In appraising the alternatives, Lourdes selected the option of leaving the room and refusing to engage in an argument with him.

Table 11.2

Weighing Options as Part of the Problem-Solving Process With Lourdes

Advantages	Disadvantages
Option 1: Engaging in the usual argument	
1. Don't have to try any new behaviors.	1. Not helpful for her self-esteem to hear these insults.
2. Don't have to deal with the potential for escalation if she tries anything new.	2. Gives him the message that it's okay.
Option 2: Leaving the room and refusing to engage in an argument with him	
1. She would be proud of her behavior, not going down to his level.	1. He might try to escalate and it would be difficult to remain calm in the face of this.
2. He might stop insulting her and leaving her alone.	2. He might escalate into physical abuse when verbal abuse is getting no effect.
Option 3: Leaving forcefully	
1. Gets the message across that she won't stand for this behavior.	1. She might get hurt as he restrains her leaving.
2. She doesn't have to listen to this.	
Option 4: Calling the police if physical violence happens	
1. He gets arrested and removed from the situation.	1. He might be even angrier after he gets out and hurt her worse.
2. She relays a strong message to him that she will no longer put up with this.	2. He doesn't work when he is arrested, and his lawyer's fees will eat up more of their money.
3. He may be mandated into a counseling program.	
4. Men who are employed are deterred from future violence by arrest.	
Option 5: Leaving the house under a guise (grocery shopping or running an errand)	
1. She doesn't have to listen to his abuse.	1. He might prevent her from leaving.
2. She is safe from further escalation.	2. Where will she go and when will she come back?
	3. He might be even angrier when she returns.

When the client comes up with an action step, the practitioner's responsibility is to help the client plan and perhaps rehearse what has been agreed upon. Usually, barriers to implementation need to be resolved before the plan can proceed more successfully. The process for discussing tasks is illustrated with the previous case involving Lourdes.

PRACTITIONER: What will it take for you to leave the room? What specifically will you do? [using definitive phrasing and trying to elicit the details of the plan]

CLIENT: I can just leave. I can say, "I don't need to listen to this bullshit."

PRACTITIONER: It sounds like a good idea to leave the room. What might happen if you say it to him in that way? [assessing some of the possible barriers to plan implementation]

CLIENT: I guess he would be mad.

PRACTITIONER: What's another way to say it that might not have that effect? [empowering the client to come up with her own answers]

CLIENT: Just leave, I guess.

These responses from Lourdes allow the practitioner to provide some information from communication skills training on how to handle the situation: that profanity might be inflammatory and to remain calm but firm, refusing to engage in defending herself or making counterattacks. The practitioner may then have to role-play the situation with the client, modeling how to take proactive steps when a situation seems volatile.

Delivering Information Collaboratively

In the stages of change model, consciousness raising (providing education about the problem) is seen as a part of helping clients move through the change process. Exposure to feminist principles of domestic violence can provide a powerful shift in perspective and motivation for an abused woman. Helping her see that her partner hits her, not because she deserves it, but because he believes he has a right to, may lift her out of disempowering self-blame. Learning that many violent relationships follow a predictable pattern may also give the woman additional tools to understand what is happening to her and to protect herself against it.

To name a prime example, when a woman talks about the violence occurring in a cyclical fashion ("He's okay for awhile. Then he starts getting mad and finally blows up. Afterwards, he's real sorry and nice, and says it won't happen again. It won't be for a while, but then he does it again"), it can be tremendously reassuring to hear about the "cycle of violence," described earlier (Walker, 1989). However, the information needs to be delivered so that an individual's reactions and experiences are processed and made meaningful to her particular situation (Carroll, 1998). There are several specific ways the helper can achieve this:

- Ask clients what they already know on a certain topic: "What do you know about resources for women in your situation?" "What do you know about family violence?"
- Elicit clients' reactions to the material: "Does this seem to fit what going on with you and your boyfriend?"
- Ask clients to provide concrete examples from their own experiences on how material applies: "Can you think of a time when that happened?"
- Pay attention to clients' verbal and nonverbal cues, such as lack of eye contact, one-word responses, and yawning: "I notice that you haven't said much in a while, and I'm wondering what your thoughts are on what we're talking about today."

For instance, Marian, a 34-year-old White woman, didn't think the cycle of violence (a tension-building stage, leading to violence, and then apologies from the batterer, and a honeymoon period until the tension built again into violence) as particularly descriptive of the pattern of violence she endured. She said it often happened "out of the blue": "Sometimes he seems like he's in an okay mood, and then one thing will get to him, and he'll pop me one. Other times, I'll make a mistake or do something stupid, and he'll say, 'That's okay, honey,' and not even be mad."

Discussing how nonviolent behaviors by their partners may contribute to battering may also be helpful. Many women respond to the wheel of power and control (Pence & Paymar, 1993) with recognition. They are surprised to see how the perpetrator uses all of the mechanisms as ways to exert power and control. Some have said they never before realized it all boiled down to power and control. They can relate to other aspects of the abuse, such as the intimidation, emotional abuse, isolation, blaming, and threats to take the children.

There may also be different cultural responses, but again, each individual needs to be considered for herself, not just as a carrier of culture. DeJong and Berg (2001) note that in working with people of color and immigrants one should not make assumptions but rather explore what the problem and methods of solution mean to them. For example, when LaTrice, a 28-year-old African American woman with a 6-year-old daughter, hears the information on how male privilege is thought to underlie violence toward women, dismisses it. The man who perpetrated violence against LaTrice, her boyfriend, doesn't work, whereas she has a part-time job as a cashier in a gas station. She says, "I'm not about to give him money. Huh, male privilege. He was too high to make any decisions anyway. I was the one always telling him what to do." These illustrations indicate that education must be delivered in a way that is sensitive to the individual's situation, not as global assumptions about all battered women and violent relationships.

A similar collaborative process is suggested when the practitioner provides clients with referrals. A lot of work with battered women involves educating them on local laws and community resources. Rather than just giving information and referrals—to call the police, to obtain a protective order, and to file charges—and then assuming the job is done, the practitioner is advised to discover how the information has been processed. Many of the responses to domestic violence—calling the police, going to a shelter—involve dramatic upheavals in the client's life. Successful referral making includes attending to the client's emotional processing of information. For example, the practitioner may say, "I have just covered a lot of information about the court process. Just to make sure I've been clear, could you summarize what you have heard?" or "How would you feel about taking your children to the shelter?"

Whenever possible, the practitioner ought to have accurate and up-to-date information about local processes and services, as well as some hands-on experience with the service referred to. Concrete information about the process may allay a client's fears about pursuing a certain course of action. It will also help prevent a referral from backfiring when client's expectations are not met. Doing a thorough job of knowing the services available and referring appropriately can build and maintain a client's trust in the change process.

It is also important to find out clients' reactions to receiving the information and validating concerns, as well as their previous experiences and what they have heard from others: "I can understand you would be shocked that this whole process takes so long and that you were wanting answers before then about what to do with your relationship." Finally, advice and information should be followed by exploring with the client her perceived barriers to implementation of the options named. Some of the following types of questions can be helpful in this regard:

- What thoughts come to mind when you think about calling the police [filing charges, calling the battered women's shelter]?
- What barriers come up for you?
- Does this seem relevant to you right now?

If the helper doesn't explore clients' reactions to information, some women might agree to take information and referrals without any intention of following through, just to get the practitioner "off their backs" or because they want to please the worker.

Occasionally, the worker has to advocate for a woman within another service. Women in crisis are not always able to advocate for themselves well, particularly when the systems involved are complex. For this reason, they are not always able to access the information and services they need and for which they are eligible. With the client's permission, a respectful call from a therapist or worker to another agency may help smooth the way for the client to get what she needs. This call can be used as an opportunity for modeling and discussing how to effectively access resources. Another strategy may be for the worker to role-play with the woman ways to successfully ask for what she needs. The purpose is to empower the woman to advocate on her and her children's behalf.

Examining Belief Systems

Many women who have been both psychologically and physically abused have come to believe some of the statements their partners make about them. Indeed, psychological abuse, in terms of criticizing, ignoring, ridiculing, and controlling behavior, apart from physical abuse, is associated with low self-esteem (Sleutel, 1998), PTSD (Arias & Pape, 1999; Street & Arias, 2001), fear (Sackett & Saunders, 1999), and depression (Dutton et al., 1999).

The cognitive aspect of the strengths-and-skills-building model involves working with women on their distorted beliefs—that they deserve the abuse, that they won't be able to survive on their own, religious beliefs that tolerate violent behavior against women, and the belief that a woman is a failure if she gets a divorce. When the batterer tells her these things in concert with the ongoing terror and social isolation that may also be part of the batterer's effort to control her, these distorted beliefs are particularly insidious. Distorted beliefs may emerge at any point but may become especially apparent during the process of completing the decisional balance, when the reasons for staying in the relationship or leaving it are made explicit.

When examining belief systems, it is important to target a woman's attributions for the violence. Andrews and Brewin (1990) studied 70 women who had experienced marital violence and found that women who were still with their spouses had high rates of self-blame. In contrast, women who had left their partners reported a significant change, from a pattern of self-blame to one in which they blamed the husband for the abuse. Taking into account that women who leave a relationship may now have a new perspective on the blame factor, it still seems worthwhile to understand a woman's stance toward self-blame versus partner blame in explaining the violence and in predicting whether she will continue to remain in an unsafe situation. Belief systems that allow a woman to expose herself to violence can be targeted by (a) deductive reasoning, (b) scaling questions, and (c) a decisional balance.

Deductive Reasoning

Deductive questioning can get clients to examine the validity of their beliefs. Rather than just having cognitive distortions pointed out, this process allows women to think through the evidence at each juncture and come to their own conclusions. This process is demonstrated with a typical cognitive distortion: excusing violent behavior due to a partner's alcohol abuse.

CLIENT: It's not that bad. It's only every once in a while. And only when he drinks.
WORKER: So you're saying that it's only every once in a while, but when he drinks, he can be violent with you?

The client agrees with this appraisal.

WORKER: What kind of conversations have you had about his drinking?
CLIENT: I've told him he drinks too much, that he gets mean. I said he should go to AA or something.
WORKER: What does he say?
CLIENT: He says he doesn't have a problem with alcohol, and that I don't have any right to tell him what to do.
WORKER: If he doesn't see a problem with his drinking and doesn't see the connection between his alcohol use and his pattern of violence, how do you see the violence being taken care of?
CLIENT: Hmm, I don't know. I guess it won't.

Going through the process of deductive questioning allows the woman to formulate her own answers rather than accept persuading and advice giving. Women who have lived with violence have often been controlled and demeaned and need encouragement to come to their own conclusions. In this way, the practitioner avoids taking over the controlling role of the batterer.

Scaling Questions

Scaling questions constructed around a particular belief that is keeping the woman in her relationship ("I deserve the abuse") can make the belief explicit and subject to logical examination. The visual display of a scale numbered from 1 (the negative belief) to 10 (the opposite, positive belief) conveys the notion of a continuum rather than the dichotomous thinking that underlies so many cognitive distortions. The process of developing the positive belief ("I deserve to be treated well") orients clients toward the changes they want rather than focusing on their negative thoughts. Anchoring the belief to specific behaviors reinforces the interconnection between thoughts, feelings, and behaviors and focuses on small, manageable steps the client can take to operationalizing a more positive belief.

The following case example shows how the scaling interventions can be used to counteract negative beliefs.

WORKER: On a scale of 1 to 10, where 1 is it's totally true what he's saying and 10 is it's totally not true, where would you put yourself on a scale of 1 to 10?

(The worker could also have chosen at this point to focus on anchoring 10 behaviorally, which implies the relationship between thoughts and behaviors.)

CLIENT: Three, I guess.

WORKER: Great, so you haven't bought into—what do you want to call it, those things he says about you?

CLIENT: The bullshit.

WORKER: What stops you from not giving in to the bullshit?

Here the worker externalizes these beliefs, to cast them outside the client, so she is freed up to view them with a different perspective. She also compliments the client on being a 3 and seeks to find out why she ranks herself at this number.

CLIENT: I can't be that worthless because he stays with me.

WORKER: So if you were that worthless, why would he be with you?

The worker reflects back the client's statement to check that the worker is hearing her accurately and to ensure that the client hears her own remarks, reinforcing them.

CLIENT: Right.

WORKER: What else is part of the bullshit?

CLIENT: When he says no one else would have me if he left.

WORKER: How do you stand up to that one?

The worker continues the externalizing process, implying that the client has power over the belief.

CLIENT: He gets really jealous of me. He always wants to know where I'm going, and who I talked to. If he's that jealous, he must think that someone else would want me.

WORKER: How were you able to figure that out?

The worker provides an indirect compliment so that the client is pushed to reveal the resources she used to figure this out.

CLIENT: I just came up with it. I never thought of it before when he's saying those things. I guess I'm just too mad then to think straight.

WORKER: So when you're calm, you can realize that some of the things he is saying don't make sense. [reframing the client's statement] How else do you stand up to the bullshit? [continuing to externalize]

CLIENT: It's hard when he says I'm fat and ugly because I really am overweight.

WORKER: How helpful is his making derogatory remarks to you in your efforts to lose weight? [deductive questioning]

CLIENT: It's not. In fact, I eat more when he talks to me like that. I don't know if it's because I want to get back at him or because I feel bad.

WORKER: You have some good insight into some of the effects his comments have on you. [complimenting]

CLIENT: And I'm not lazy. That's another thing he says about me. I take care of our three children, and his sister's kids when she works. That's not lazy. Just because I'm not out there painting like he is, he thinks I'm not working. But he'd go crazy doing what I do all day.

WORKER: That's hard work taking care of children all day.

After their discussion, the worker again asked the client to rank her belief in her husband's verbal abuse. She now said she was at a 6. The worker pursued how the client would be able to maintain this ranking in light of her husband's comments. She said she would remind herself of the conversation she'd had with the worker, and that this would be helpful to her. Although scaling questions were the frame for the intervention, deductive questioning, externalizing, exception finding, complimenting, and reframing were also used. These techniques allowed the client to explore these beliefs and arrive at a new perspective.

Decisional Balance

Another way of addressing beliefs is through a decisional balance, in which people are asked the advantages and disadvantages of holding a particular belief. This intervention helps people see that their beliefs are more malleable than they previously thought and can be modified with practice so they can feel better and act more productively. An example of the process is described with the client discussed in the previous instance.

CLIENT: I don't think I'm getting anything out of it. I hate that he does this.

WORKER: We'll put that under the disadvantages. What specifically do you hate about it?

CLIENT: Well, it's just plain mean. He shouldn't be saying those things about me. I'm his wife. And he says them in front of the children, too.

WORKER: Okay, so he isn't treating you with the respect you, as his wife, deserve. And you are concerned about the effects it has on your children. What effects have you noticed?

CLIENT: Well, sometimes my oldest, Brian, says the same thing to me. I tell him, "I'm your mom. You can't talk to me that way."

WORKER: So your oldest boy is learning from his father how to treat you. I wonder what he is learning about how to treat women.

Rather than supplying this information, the worker offers an opportunity for the client to draw the conclusion for herself.

CLIENT: Probably not good—that they can be insulted and kicked around.

WORKER: And what might your girls be learning?

CLIENT: That's what they deserve as girls. They don't deserve no better than their mom.

When the worker probes for more disadvantages, the client reveals that over the years, her self-confidence has diminished. The client is still unable to produce any advantages, so the worker tentatively presents, "Well, usually our beliefs are comfortable in some ways even though they may not be helpful for how we act or feel. Perhaps staying in this relationship was the only way you could imagine you could take care of your children. Changing these beliefs might take some effort over a period of time."

The client agreed that this was probably operating. She also agreed with the worker's statement that if she didn't believe this anymore, then she would have to take a much stronger stance with her husband, perhaps even to the point of leaving him. And she was fearful about having to take such action.

This section has demonstrated different ways that the practitioner can address clients' belief systems that may keep them trapped in a violent situation. In the examples, the beliefs this woman had internalized from the verbal abuse she had endured were examined and deconstructed, so that new perspectives could be introduced.

How to Loosen Attachment for the Batterer

One of the reasons that women stay in violent relationships is their stated love for the abuser (e.g., Applewhite, 1996). Because the violence in most battering relationships is cyclical, most of these relationships have periods of calm and companionship, when the woman feels loved and connected. Women must therefore weigh what they are giving up in order to leave an abusive relationship. Feelings of love in deciding whether to proceed with the relationship and dealing with longing if she decides to leave need to be addressed, as these are salient factors.

When women talk about loving their partners as a reason to stay in the relationship, they can be asked about their meaning of love and how, more specifically, it is tied to their partners' behaviors. For example, when one client was asked to behaviorally describe love, she said that it was when both partners did nice things for each other, were respectful of each other, and had good sex. She was asked on a scale of 1 to 10 how loving her partner was toward her. She said because he was "nice sometimes" and they were "good in bed together," she gave him a 5. However, she could see that was only half of what she wanted from him. The behavioral indicators are important because the strengths-and-skills-building model emphasizes the reciprocal relationships between feelings, thoughts, and behaviors.

The worker might offer that feelings of love are powerful, intense, and not usually under voluntary control. However, working with thoughts and behaviors, which are more amenable to control, can, over time, have an impact on feelings. The woman may indeed never stop loving her abusive partner, and that was acceptable, but she can consider whether the other disadvantages of being in a violent relationship far outweigh her love. She might just have to accept these feelings in herself, while simultaneously continuing to take action to protect herself.

Sometimes women go back with violent partners because they experience overwhelming feelings of longing for or missing the abuser. Because the feelings are so intense, the woman might give in to them. However, if this phenomenon is understood and anticipated, these feelings can be managed more effectively. The information in the substance abuse literature on handling craving (e.g., Carroll, 1998) can inform women who are trying to leave a violent relationship and are having a difficult time with breaking ties.

Cues for longing might include times of the day (e.g., going to bed alone at night), experiencing a setback in a new lifestyle (e.g., not getting a job one has interviewed for), feeling lonely, and seeing other couples. The practitioner can help the client identify these cues and convey the time-limited nature of longing—that it peaks and dissipates, if not acted on. After identifying the woman's most problematic cues, the practitioner should explore the degree to which some of these can be avoided. For example, can she change routes going to work or to the children's school and avoid places where she might meet the abuser, his friends, or his relatives? Obviously, many battered women have children with their perpetrators, and avoidance of all contact is unrealistic. However, even in these cases, contact can be restricted and managed. Strategies can be developed by asking solution-focused questions about times in the past when a woman had experienced intense longing for the partner and had coped rather than succumbed.

Strategies for coping with craving (adapted from the substance abuse literature) include distraction, talking about craving, "going with" the craving, recalling the negative consequences of being in the relationship, and self-talk (Carroll, 1998). Distraction involves keeping busy and engaging in enjoyable and relaxing activities. Talking about the craving is conversing with supportive people about the feelings. In "going with the craving," Carroll (1998) explains: "The idea behind this technique is to let cravings occur, peak, and pass; in other words, to experience them without fighting or giving into them. Clients should be told that the purpose is not to make the cravings disappear, but to experience them in a different way that makes them feel less anxiety provoking and dangerous and thus easier to ride out." The steps summarized in Box 11.1 should be practiced within sessions or at home before craving occurs.

Another technique to help clients manage longing for their mates is to recall the negative consequences of being in the relationship. When experiencing craving, many people tend to remember only the positive aspects of the relationship; they often forget the deleterious consequences. Thus, when experiencing craving, it is often effective for women to remind themselves of the benefits of staying away from the relationship and the negative consequences of staying in it.

Self-talk may be a strategy for women to use for coping with feelings of longing for their partner (adapted from Carroll, 1998). Automatic thoughts associated with craving often have a sense of urgency and exaggerated dire consequences (e.g., "I have to see him now" or "I'll die if I'm not with him"). In coping with craving, the client needs to both recognize the automatic thoughts and counter them effectively. To help clients recognize their automatic thoughts, practitioners can point out cognitive distortions that occur during sessions (e.g., "A few times today you've said you need to talk to him, see how he's doing. Are you aware of those

---

Box 11.1

Steps for "Going With the Craving"

1. Find someplace safe to let oneself experience craving (e.g., a comfortable and quiet place at home).
2. Relax and focus on the experience of craving itself—where it occurs in the body or mind and how intense it is.
3. Focus on the area where the craving occurs. This involves paying attention to all the somatic and affective signals and trying to put them into words. What is the feeling like? Where is it? How strong is it? Does it move or change? Where else does it occur?

Note. Adapted from A Cognitive-Behavioral Approach: Treating Cocaine Addiction, by K. Carroll, 1998, retrieved August 28, 2001, from http://www.drugabuse.gov/TXManuals/CBT/CBT1.html

thoughts when you have them?"). Another strategy is to help clients "slow down the tape" to recognize cognitions: "When you decided to go back with Jonathan last time, you said you really weren't aware of what he might say to you if you called him. But I'll bet if we go back and try to remember what the night was like, sort of play it back like a movie in slow motion, we could find a couple of examples of things you said to yourself, maybe without even realizing it, that led to you going back with him. Can you sort of play last night back for us now?"

Once automatic thoughts are identified, it becomes much easier to counter or confront them, using positive rather than negative self-talk. This includes cognitions, such as challenging the thought (e.g., "I won't really die if I don't have him in my life") and normalizing the feeling (e.g., "Craving is uncomfortable, but a lot of people have it, and it's something I can deal with without going back to a dangerous situation"). If strategies are in place and have been rehearsed, a woman is much less vulnerable to the powerful feelings of longing that may assail her.

Summary

The strengths-and-skills-building model provides a framework and a number of specific techniques useful for working with women in violent relationships. Although the model focuses on work with the individual woman, it is flexible enough to incorporate and draw on the strengths of the feminist perspective. The strengths-and-skills-building framework can incorporate information about the dynamics of battering, address some of the social underpinnings of this problem within the context of a therapeutic model, and incorporate the necessary risk assessment and safety planning required with women in abusive relationships. Because the model builds on a woman's strengths, it can provide a form of empowerment for her. The focus on collaboration between client and worker can also provide an antidote to the authoritarian relationship the woman has had with her batterer. Thus, it combines some of the strengths of both feminist and mental health perspectives on domestic violence: a focus on educating women about the social context of battering, while empowering them with concrete, definable skills, within a collaborative and supportive therapeutic relationship to promote the woman's safety.

References

Abel, E. (2000). Psychosocial treatments for battered women: A review of empirical research. *Research on Social Work Practice, 10,* 55–77.

Andrews, B., & Brewin, C. (1990). Attributions of blame for marital violence:

A study of antecedents and consequences. *Journal of Marriage & the Family, 52,* 757–767.

Applewhite, M. (1996). *A social exchange model of the decision-making process of women in abusive relationships.* Doctoral dissertation. University of Texas at Arlington.

Arias, I., & Pape, K. (1999). Psychological abuse: Implications for adjustment and commitment to leave violent partners. *Violence and Victims, 14,* 55–67.

Brown, J. (1997). Working toward freedom from violence: The process of change in battered women. *Violence against Women, 3,* 5–26.

Burke, J., Gielen, A., McDonnell, K., O'Campo, P., & Maman, S. (2001). The process of ending abuse in intimate relationships: A qualitative exploration of the transtheoretical model. *Violence Against Women, 7,* 1144–1163.

Campbell, J., Rose, L., Kub, J., & Nedd, D. 1998. Voices of strength and resistance: A contextual and longitudinal analysis of women's responses to battering. *Journal of Interpersonal Violence, 13*(6), 743–762.

Carroll, K. (1998). *A cognitive-behavioral approach: Treating cocaine addiction.* Retrieved August 28, 2001, from http://www.drugabuse.gov/TXManuals/CBT/CBT1.html.

Cascardi, M., O'Leary, K., & Schlee, K. (1999). Co-occurrence and correlates of posttraumatic stress disorder and major depression in physically abused women. *Journal of Family Violence, 14*(3), 227–249.

Chanley, S. A., & Alozie, N. O. (2001). Policy for the "deserving," but politically weak: The 1996 welfare reform act and battered women. *Policy Studies Review, 18*(2), 1–25.

Davies, J., Lyon, E., & Monti-Catania, D. (1998). *Safety planning with battered women: Complex lives, difficult choices.* Thousand Oaks, CA: Sage.

DeJong, P., & Berg, I. K. (2001). *Interviewing for solutions* (2nd ed.). Pacific Grove, CA: Brooks/Cole.

Dutton, M., Goodman, L., & Bennett, L. (1999). Court-involved battered women's responses to violence: The role of psychological, physical, and sexual abuse. *Violence and Victims, 14* (1), 89.

Dwyer, D. C., Smokowski, P. R., Bricout, J. C., & Wodarski, J. S. (1996). Domestic violence and woman battering: Theories and practice implications. In A. R. Roberts (Ed.), *Helping battered women: New perspectives and remedies* (pp. 67–82). New York: Oxford University Press.

Fernandez, M., Iwamoto, K., & Muscat, B. (1997). Dependency and severity of abuse: Impact on women's persistence in utilizing the court system as protection against domestic violence. *Women and Criminal Justice, 9,* 39–63.

Golding, J. M. (1999). Intimate partner violence as a risk factor for mental disorders: A meta-analysis. *Journal of Family Violence, 14*(2), 99–132.

Gondolf, E. (1997). Patterns of reassault in batterer programs. *Violence and Victims, 12*(4), 373–383.

Gondolf, E. W., & Fisher, E. R. (1998). *Assessing woman battering in mental health settings.* Thousand Oaks, CA: Sage.

Greene, G., Lee, M. Y., Mentzer, R., Pinnell, S., & Niles, D. (1998). Miracles, dreams, and empowerment: A brief therapy practice note. *Families in Society, 79,* 395–399.

Grigsby, N., & Hartman, B. R. (1997). The barriers model: An integrated strategy intervention with battered women. *Psychotherapy, 34*(4), 485–497.

Herbert, T., Silver, R., & Ellard, J. (1991). Coping with an abusive relationship. *Journal of Marriage and Family, 53,* 311–325.

Koss, M., & Burkhart, B. (1989). A conceptual analysis of rape victimization. *Psychology of Women Quarterly, 13,* 27–40.

Mahoney, M. R. (1994). Victimization or oppression? Women's lives, violence, and agency. In M. A. Fineman & R. Mykitiuk (Eds.), *The public nature of private violence: The discovery of domestic abuse* (pp. 59–92). New York: Routledge.

Mahoney, P., Williams, L. M., & West, C. M. (2001). Violence against women by intimate relationship partners. In C. M. Renzetti, J. L. Edleson, & R. K. Bergen (Eds.), *Sourcebook on violence against women* (pp. 143–192). Thousand Oaks, CA: Sage.

McNeal, C., & Amato, P. (1998). Parents' marital violence: Long term consequences for children. *Journal of Family Issues, 19,* 123–139.

Miller, W., & Rollnick, S. (1991). *Motivational interviewing* (2nd ed.). New York: Guilford.

Okun, L. (1986). *Woman abuse: Facts replacing myths.* Albany: State University of New York Press.

Pence, E., & Paymar, M. (1993). *Education groups for men who batter: The Duluth model.* New York: Springer.

Pressman, B. (1989). Treatment of wife abuse: The case for feminist therapy. In B. Pressman, G. Cameron, & M. Rothery (Eds.), *Intervening with assaulted women: Current theory, research, and practice* (pp. 21–45). Hillsdale, NJ: Erlbaum.

Roberts, G., Williams, G., Lawrence, J., & Raphael, B. (1998). How does domestic violence affect women's mental health? *Women Health, 28,* 118–129.

Sackett, L. A., & Saunders, D. G. (1999). The impact of different forms of psychological abuse on battered women. *Violence and Victims, 14,* 105–117.

Seligman, M. E. (1975). *Helplessness: On depression, development, and death.* New York: Wiley.

Sleutel, M. (1998). Women's experiences of abuse: A review of qualitative research. *Issues in Mental Health Nursing, 19,* 525–539.

Stout, K. D., & McPhail, B. (1998). *Confronting sexism and violence against women: A challenge for social work.* New York: Longman.

Street, A., & Arias, I. (2001). Psychological abuse and posttraumatic stress disorder in battered women: Examining the roles of shame and guilt. *Violence and Victims, 16,* 65–78.

Stuart, G., & Holtzworth-Munroe, A. (1995). Identifying subtypes of maritally violent men: Descriptive dimensions, correlates and causes of violence and treatment implications. In S. M. Stith & M. A Strauss (Eds.), *Understanding partner violence: Prevalence, causes, consequences, and solutions* (pp. 162–172). Minneapolis: National Council on Family Relations.

Tjaden, P., & Thoennes, N. (2000). Extent, nature, and consequences of intimate partner violence. National Institute of Justice and the Centers for Disease Control and Prevention. Retrieved April 22, 2004, from http://ncjrs.org/txtfiles1/nij/181867.txt.

Wahab, S. (2004). Motivational interviewing: Moving away from a "one size fits all" approach to intimate partner violence. Manuscript submitted for publication.

Waites, E. (1993). *Trauma & survival: Post traumatic and dissociative disorders in women.* New York: W. W. Norton.

Walker, L. E. A. (1989). Psychology and violence against women. *American Psychologist, 44*(4), 695–702.

Wills, T. A. (1981). Downward comparison principles in social psychology. *Psychological Bulletin, 90,* 245–271.

Yllö, K. A. (1993). Through a feminist lens: Gender, power, and violence. In R. J. Gelles & D. R. Loseke (Eds.), *Current controversies in family violence* (pp. 47–62). Newbury Park, CA: Sage.

12 Enhancing Motivation, Strengths, and Skills of Parents in the Child Welfare System

MELINDA HOHMAN, CHRISTINE
KLEINPETER, AND HILDA LOUGHRAN

Child maltreatment continues to be a major concern in our society. In the United States in 1999, almost 3 million referrals or reports of suspected abuse or neglect were received by county child protective services (CPS) agencies. Of these referrals, 29.2% were substantiated, meaning that abuse or neglect had actually occurred. In that same year, 1,563,000 children received CPS attention to prevent further maltreatment (U.S. Department of Health and Human Services, 2002). Those who work in the CPS system are responsible for quickly assessing child safety and the risk of further child maltreatment, providing an intervention plan for those whose cases are substantiated, and overseeing implementation of that plan through the provision of case management services (Brown, 2002).

In the application of the strengths-and-skills-building model to work with child welfare clients, several key aspects of child welfare practice must be recognized for their impact on the helping process. Common to both child welfare and those who work in the court system is the issue of the workers' dual roles. CPS workers are expected to act as policing agents,

The authors would like to thank Michelle Panzarella and Ron Dailey, County of San Diego Health and Human Services Agency, Children's Services, for their help with this chapter.

first assessing for possible child abuse or neglect and later determining compliance with case plans. On the other hand, workers need to establish helping relationships that focus on engagement and collaboration to foster parental behavior change (Dawson & Berry, 2002). Workers are expected to do both policing and engagement tasks quickly because of the implementation of the Adoption and Safe Families Act of 1997, which mandates family improvement to occur within 12 months. If families do not comply with court-ordered intervention plans, the court may proceed to terminate parental rights and remove the child from the home (Johnson, Baker, & Maceira, 2001).

Another concern of CPS workers is having "dual clients." The main client of the CPS system is the child whose safety is at stake. But for this safety to be assured, it is the parent who has to make the behavioral changes. Workers must assess the risk to the child by understanding the concerns of parents, whose problems may include substance abuse, domestic violence, anger, lack of parenting skills, and poverty (Dawson & Berry, 2002). Although the child is the main client, workers interact with the parent to create a case plan of what services must be accessed and behavioral changes made. If the child has already been removed from the family, parents may vent their anger on the CPS worker, making it extremely difficult for the worker to engage in a helping relationship. CPS workers are also accountable to both the judicial system and to the public. Many work under the pressure that a "mistake" in assessment could result in a dead child and the resulting media attention.

Our experiences in training CPS workers (and others who work with mandated clients) in motivational interviewing and solution-focused therapy have indicated that workers are interested in different styles of interacting with clients. In the past, the worker's role focused on "policing," emphasizing risks with little acknowledgment of strengths, and resulted in telling clients what they need to do; their experiences suggest that this is not effective. Child welfare workers have expressed concern to us that it may be very difficult to interact with clients in the manner prescribed by these models and worry that it borders on "therapy," which they perceive is not part of their role. First, they are concerned about the amount of time careful interviewing seems to take. For example, spending valuable time reflecting thoughts and feelings, many believe, may preclude gathering the information needed to complete risk assessments. This type of interviewing, we reassure workers, is a style of interacting with clients to promote more positive communication and, it is hoped, outcomes. Insofar as CPS workers aim to work with clients to improve the quality of their lives, all interactions with clients should be therapeutic in nature.

Second, a change in interaction approaches with clients may not be supported by other workers or supervisors in agencies. Using these models is a paradigm shift from the notion of the worker being "the expert" who tells parents what they need to do, to the worker acting as a "collaborator," working on identifying and addressing concerns and solutions together (Bell, 1999). This shift is clearly situated within the theoretical framework of social constructionism (see Chapter 4). The adoption of these new approaches demands both support for CPS workers within the structures of their agencies and a willingness on the part of workers to champion the client's perspective.

Third, clients are so overburdened with multiple problems that it is hard to imagine change occurring, by both the parent and the CPS worker, especially from the viewpoint of the traditional "deficit model," instead of from the strengths perspective that both motivational interviewing (MI) and solution-focused therapy (SFT) emphasize (Christensen, Todahl, & Barrett, 1999). Clients may also be viewed as not wanting to change, as child welfare workers sometimes see themselves as uninvited guests into the lives of clients, who are angry at the presence of CPS.

Compatibility of the Strengths-and-Skills-Building Model With Child Welfare Work

Integrative models of interventions have been receiving more attention and empirical support over the past several years. Most of the work has focused on integrating MI or motivational strategies with cognitive-behavioral interventions for those with substance dependence or mental disorders (Barrowclough et al., 2001; Bauer, Kivlahan, & Donovan, 1999; COMBINE Study Research Group, in press; Dolder, Lacro, & Jeste, 2002). Although the strengths-and-skills-building model has not been empirically tested, a review of the literature regarding best practices in child welfare work has indicated at least four areas where the strengths-and-skills-building model is especially compatible.

The first area is the relationship between the CPS worker and the family. If the family is approached in an empathic, nonjudgmental, cooperative manner, which is highly congruent with MI and SFT, they are more likely to participate and engage in the interaction with the worker (Tohn & Oshlag, 1996). Second, instead of goals being decided by the "expert" (CPS worker), joint decision making and goal setting, by both the worker and the family, appears to have more positive outcomes. Parents are more likely to be invested in changes they have identified as necessary (Hubberstey, 2001; Littell & Tajima, 2000; Rooney, 1992). Both MI and SFT models view this as critical to work with clients, especially those who are mandated to treatment (Ginsburg, Mann, Rotgers, & Weekes, 2002; Tohn & Oshlag, 1996).

Third, jointly developed case plans must be individualized and relevant to the particular situation, instead of "standardized" plans, such as all domestic violence problems mean anger management classes, child abuse incidents mean parenting classes, and so on (Besharov, 1998; Christensen et al., 1999). Fourth, interventions for parents in the CPS system should focus on concrete skill development, the hallmark of CBT. Insight-oriented therapy has been found to be less useful by CPS parents (Dawson & Berry, 2002; Sun, 2000). Other factors that have been found to produce positive outcomes in CPS clients include other types of services not included in the strengths-and-skills-building model specifically, such as in-home services, the provision of concrete services, early childhood programs, and strengthened social support (Dawson & Berry, 2002). However, the strengths-and-skills-building model is seen as compatible with these services. For example, the model can be delivered as part of in-home services. In addition, interventions can center around empowering individuals to follow through with services and strengthening social support.

Solution-Focused Therapy in Child Welfare

Few studies have empirically examined the use of SFT in child welfare settings, but several authors have applied SFT conceptually to child welfare work (Berg & Kelly, 2000; Corcoran, 1999; Corcoran & Franklin, 1998; DeJong & Berg, 2001; Rosenberg, 2000; Walsh, 1997). Variations of SFT have also been applied conceptually to child welfare practice, including a strengths-based model (Noble, Perkins, & Fatout, 2000) and a solution-based casework model (Christensen et al., 1999). In the United Kingdom and Australia, the practical application of solution-focused ideas has resulted in a shift in emphasis away from exclusively risk assessment to incorporate the much broader assessment of strengths and resources in clients. This dual assessment values risk assessment and also building signs of safety (Turnell & Edwards, 1997, 1999).

Empirical studies of SFT in problems relevant to CPS include the areas of substance abuse, domestic violence, and child behavior problems. High rates of domestic violence co-occur with child abuse and neglect. CPS caseloads with confirmed child maltreatment have reported violence between adult partners ranging from 32% (Hangen as cited in Edleson, 1999) to 51% (Magen & Conroy, 1997). Sirles, Lipchick, and Kowalski (1993) applied a solution-focused intervention with court-mandated batterers. Of the male partners, 54% stated that the intervention was successful in providing them with skills to control their drinking, arguing, and violence; 23% of the men stated that they had experienced some success. Female partners, in general, were more favorable toward the intervention, with 84% reporting positive results.

As well as domestic violence, substance abuse also tends to co-occur with child maltreatment. According to a 1996 Child Welfare League survey, 67% of parents involved with the child protective services system require substance abuse treatment (Petit & Curtis, 1997). Children with substance-abusing parents in the child protective services system are twice as likely as children whose parents are not chemically addicted to be placed in foster care, and they tend to stay in foster care longer (U.S. Department of Health and Human Services, 1999). A program evaluation of SFT with substance-abusing CPS clients showed high satisfaction and treatment adherence (Pichot, 2001).

There is also considerable overlap between child maltreatment and behavior problems in children (Howing, Wodarski, Kurtz, Gaudin, & Herbst, 1990; Kaufman & Rudy, 1991). Specifically, the triggering event for physical abuse by parents often involves a child's act of disobedience or aggression (Gelardo & Sanford, 1987). For parents experiencing conflict with their adolescents, Zimmerman, Jacobsen, MacIntyre, and Watson (1996) examined the use of SFT in a group setting. Compared with a randomized waitlist control group, SFT participants reported significant improvements on certain subscales of the Parenting Skills Inventory, including role image, communication, limit-setting, and rapport. Corcoran (2004; Corcoran & Stephenson, 2000) has also studied the effect of solution-focused family therapy for child behavior problems in an outpatient clinic. Both the SFT and the treatment-as-usual conditions showed improvement on parent ratings of child behavior in four to six sessions, although SFT produced better treatment engagement.

Motivational Interviewing in Child Welfare

Motivational interviewing was initially developed to work with alcohol and other substance abusers (Miller & Rollnick, 2002). Outcome studies have, for the most part, shown positive results with clients with addiction problems. Clients who have received motivation interviewing interventions include pregnant drinkers (Handmaker, Miller, & Manicke, 1999), substance abusers mandated into treatment (Lincourt, Kuettel, & Bombardier, 2002), marijuana users (Stephens, Roffman, & Curtin, 2000), cocaine users (Stotts, Schmitz, Rhoades, & Grabowski, 2001), and alcohol users (Sellman, Sullivan, Dore, Adamson, & MacEwan, 2001). MI in these studies was used as an addition to treatment as usual or as a stand-alone intervention of usually one to four sessions.

Similar to SFT, most of the work in applying MI to CPS has been on a conceptual basis (Action for Child Protection, n.d.; Hohman, 1998). Conceptual use of MI has been applied to work with criminal offenders (Ginsburg et al., 2002), including sexual offenders (Mann, 1996; Mann, Ginsburg, & Weekes, 2002) and domestic violence offenders (Easton, Swan, & Sinha, 2000). One outcome study applied MI to substance-abusing parents who were referred for substance abuse treatment by CPS workers. Participants were randomly assigned to a standard assessment interview or to an assessment interview that utilized MI. Those who received the MI interview were more likely to attend one additional treatment session after the assessment (Carroll, Libby, Sheehan, & Hyland, 2001).

Other outcome studies have utilized MI with similar populations to child welfare: low-income urban women to reduce high-risk sexual behavior (Carey et al., 2000), probation clients (Harper & Hardy, 2000), and high-risk families (community sample of parents of preteens with behavioral problems) (Rao, 1999). These populations are similar in that clients were at high risk for abuse or neglect problems or were under court supervision. All of these studies used random assignment to an MI intervention or to a treatment as usual or waitlist control group and showed positive outcomes, which included decreases in the targeted negative behaviors, for those in the MI groups.

Cognitive-Behavioral Therapy in Child Welfare

Child abuse and neglect, it has been proposed, results because parents lack the absolute minimum levels of skills required to sustain a family, not from their lack of altruism for children (Brandon, 2001). Cognitive-behavioral approaches have been used in many modalities of treatment with abusing parents. Parental skill building has been found to be an important component in intensive family preservation programs (Kinney, Haapala, & Booth, 1991). Models of skill building with child welfare parents that have had positive outcomes include bibliotherapeutic aids (Bourke, 1995), small group training in self-control and child management skills (Barth, Schinke, Schilling, & Blythe, 1983; Brunk, Henggeler, & Whelan, 1987; Wolfe & Haddy, 2001), and family therapy with a focus on parenting (DeMaria, 1986). Other types of skill-building work with child welfare clients have included problem-solving skills, anger management, and communication (Acton & During, 1992; Kolko & Swenson, 2002; Schinke et al., 1986; Whiteman, Fanshel, & Grundy, 1987). For a review of cognitive-behavioral interventions with parents in the child welfare system, see Corcoran (2000).

Integrating parental skill building into substance abuse treatment for women has been suggested (Yaffe, Jenson, & Howard, 1995). A study of cocaine-dependent mothers found that providing psychosocial enhancement services that included parenting skills classes, individual therapy sessions, and vocational training improved treatment outcomes over a control group that received case management–oriented outpatient services (Volpicelli, Monterosso, Filing, O'Brien, & Markman, 2000). A pre–post examination of self-esteem and parenting knowledge and attitudes found positive increases in these areas for women who had participated in parenting skills classes in two urban residential treatment programs for substance use (Camp & Finkelstein, 1997).

Because so many clients involved in the child welfare system also have substance-related disorders (Marcenko, Larson, & Kemp, 2000), they may be able to benefit from substance use relapse-prevention skill building (Larimer, Palmer, & Marlatt, 1999; Marlatt & Gordon, 1985). Cognitive-behavioral methods, including relapse prevention, have been found to be particularly effective with cocaine and methamphetamine users (Ling, 2000; Obert et al., 2000). The goals of relapse prevention are to prevent a return to substance use or, if this occurs, to successfully manage relapse episodes. Rather than viewing those who experience relapse as "treatment failures," the relapse-prevention approach views such episodes as temporary setbacks that might be expected from someone who is in the process of learning new coping behaviors. Using cognitive-behavioral methods, an individual is taught skills and strategies to recognize and successfully navigate situations that may have led to relapse in the past. Other types of skill building that may be included in relapse prevention are communication and assertion skills, job training skills, and problem-solving skills (Monti, Rohsenow, Colby, & Abrams, 1995).

In summary, the cognitive-behavioral conceptualization of addictive behavior is that abusive drinking and drug use are learned behaviors that can be modified. A number of these approaches have been found to be effective. Parents in the child welfare system who are struggling with addiction may benefit from treatments that are comprehensive in nature, including parenting skills, social skills, and job-related skills, as well as addressing relapse prevention.

Application of the Integrated Model to the Case Example

At the heart of the assessment in cases of child abuse and neglect is the issue of whether parenting is adequate. The CPS worker must decide (a) whether the allegation is justified; (b) whether it is necessary to take the child into protective custody; (c) if, when, where, and under what conditions parents will be allowed to visit children who are taken into custody;

(d) whether the family is making incremental progress in correcting the circumstances that required state intervention; and (e) whether progress is sufficient to enable the family to remain intact (Greene & Kilili, 1998). When a call is placed to a child abuse hotline, the seriousness of the allegations is evaluated, and a CPS worker may be sent to the home or school to interview the parents and children.

Using the strengths-and-skills-building model, the CPS worker also works to join with the parents and children to explore the strengths and solutions within the family. The initial assessment may focus on the parents' perspectives about what, if anything, needs to change and their readiness to address these changes. Working in a collaborative fashion, the worker contextualizes the situation for clients by describing the expectations of the child welfare system and the likely consequences of noncompliance. Motivational interviewing provides a basis for helping clients discuss their ambivalence regarding concerns and for harnessing their commitment to change. For ongoing work with parents in the CPS system, skills training is offered so parents can manage their children without resorting to physical abuse or neglect.

As with any model of intervention, no one model is applicable to all situations. Children's safety is the priority of CPS workers, and workers must gather the pertinent information to make a risk assessment, when applicable. Thus various models of intervention and communication may be used. We believe the strengths-and-skills-building model offers an excellent integrative guide for work with clients in many situations.

In this chapter, a case example centers on a client who has substance abuse problems and whose children suffer neglect as a consequence. It illustrates how the CPS workers in this case implemented the phases of the helping process: engagement, problem exploration, solution-exploration, and goal setting. It follows how the client put her plan into action, as well as how she coped with substance-related and other difficulties in this plan before she was terminated from services. Chapter 13 focuses on other kinds of problems families experience that put them at risk for involvement in the CPS system. Chapter 14 centers on work with mothers who come to the attention of the CPS system for the sexual abuse of their children.

Case Example

Scene I

A call was placed to the CPS hotline by a woman who stated that her neighbor's two children were wandering the street about 9 P.M. several nights ago. The children were ages 5 and 7. When the neighbor took them back to their home, she heard loud fighting from the house. The children appeared unkempt and frightened. Their mother's boyfriend stormed out of the house and took off in his car when the neighbor knocked on the door. The neighbor added that she thought there might be drug dealing going on at the home, as strangers frequently came and went. She didn't call the police right away because she was afraid that the boyfriend would come back and know she had reported him. She called the hotline anonymously a few days later.

An emergency response CPS worker was sent to the home. Angela Adams, the mother, was home alone. Her two boys were at school. The CPS worker discovered that Angela is a 28-year-old woman who lives with a man not the father of her children. She is unemployed. The worker observed her to be extremely thin and nervous. The house was cluttered, with piles of clothing on the living room floor, stacks of papers and magazines strewn around, dirty dishes in the sink, and rotten food on the kitchen counter with many flies buzzing around. Bongs like those used to smoke marijuana and glass pipes to smoke methamphetamine were observed on the bottom portion of the living room coffee table.

CPS WORKER: Hello, Mrs. Adams. I am _____, CPS worker, from Children's Services. We have received information from a concerned person that your children were wandering on the street last week, after 9 P.M., and that fighting was heard coming from your home. It's my job to discuss this situation with you and see if we can figure out what's going on and if there is some way we can help.

ANGELA: Who turned me in? Did that nosey neighbor call you? She is always getting into my business.

CPSW: Mrs. Adams, I can appreciate that this is difficult for you, that you feel that others are interfering in your business. When we get an anonymous phone call to the hotline, legally the caller's identity is protected so we don't ask them to tell us who they are.

ANGELA: So anyone can call and say what they like about me?

CPSW: You're actually right, that's the way the system works. I know that it seems unfair to you, but sometimes these callers help us get in touch with families who need our help. You said that someone must've "turned you in." Tell me what happened the night your boys were in the street by themselves.

ANGELA: This is crazy! All that happened was my boyfriend and I had a fight, the kids went outside to get away from the noise, that's all! I knew where they were the whole time.

CPSW: It made sense to you that they would want to get away from the noisy fighting.

ANGELA: Yeah, when we fight, we get loud and maybe they get upset. They don't understand what is going on, they're just kids.

CPSW: It sounds like you and your boyfriend have been having some problems and that you are very aware that the kids don't understand and may be getting scared at times.

ANGELA: Well, I wouldn't say we are having problems, but yeah, we do have fights like anyone else. I try to explain it to the kids, but they don't really like Joe [her boyfriend] so they don't really listen.

CPSW: It sounds like you are in a bit of a bind. On the one hand, you are trying to make your relationship with Joe work, but on the other hand, the kids don't like it, they get scared when you argue, and last week they even ran out of the house.

ANGELA: Well, I haven't looked at it that way, but I suppose you are right.

CPSW: You have been trying to make things right for the kids, but sometimes being with Joe gets in the way. How have you been managing this?

ANGELA: I try to keep them out of Joe's way as much as I can. He doesn't really "get" kids and they're not his, so you know what that's like. But it's not like he's mean or hits them or anything. He just yells and gets upset.

CPSW: So one of the things you found helpful is to keep them out of his way. How does that work?

ANGELA: Well, they have a TV in their room, and when Joe is around with his friends, I make sure they stay in there.

CPSW: What else works?

ANGELA: I send them over to my mother's, or I take them to the park for a few hours.

CPSW: It sounds like you have several plans that you use.

ANGELA: I've even left Joe before once or twice, but it's hard, there's no room for me at my mother's house, and since I don't work, I can't afford rent anywhere else. So back we come.

CPSW: You have given the kids a lot of thought, haven't you? Even though you are under a great deal of pressure, you are still determined to do the best you can to keep your family together. I'm just wondering what happens when your boys do get in Joe's way.

ANGELA: It's not so bad when Joe's on his own, like just around the house, and it's not like he hits them or anything, but if the guys are here that can be tense.

CPSW: You've mentioned Joe's friends a couple of times. It seems like when they are around, you get more concerned about the boys.

ANGELA: Don't get me wrong. Joe is pretty good to the kids, really, but sometimes he just likes to party with the guys, and since this is his house, there isn't much I can say.

CPSW: You are not happy for the boys to be around when Joe is partying with his friends.

ANGELA: Well, of course they are usually in bed and it's okay then, but yes, I do think about it. What if something happened, like the other night, somebody just decides to call and complain about nothing? I don't want Children's Services involved with my family.

CPSW: I can see from what we have been talking about that you really want to make things right for the boys. You have some clear plans about how to keep them out of Joe's way, and you use support from your mother when you think that will help. Now we need to talk about something a bit different. You know that I have seen the drug paraphernalia around the living room. Of course you don't want Children's Services to get involved, and I understand that. But you do see that drug use might be a problem for your family. I have to ask what that is about.

ANGELA: This is Joe's friend's stuff. He leaves it here. Joe smokes a little weed [marijuana] and crank [methamphetamine] with him sometimes.

CPSW: It's hard for many people to be around drugs, especially when everyone else is using, and not use it yourself.

ANGELA: Well, I only use a little bit. And not too often. And only when the boys are in bed. I smoke some crank and then some weed to help bring me down. But my boys don't know anything about it.

CPSW: Can you tell me what you like about smoking crank? What are the good things?

ANGELA: The good things? Well, I never thought of it that way. I guess I like it because it makes me feel good, gives me energy. I feel like I can get more done. It's something to do with Joe and helps me cope with him better. He's always bugging me to learn how to cook it [make it at home] but I tell him, "No way!" We may use a little bit, sometimes he sells a little bit, but no way are we going to get into *that*.

CPSW: It sounds like you have set some limits around what you will and will not do with crank. So the good things you like about it are that it gives you energy, relieves your stress, and it is something you can do with Joe. What are the not-so-good things about your smoking crank?

ANGELA: I know I shouldn't do it, that it makes me nervous sometimes, and then I have to smoke some weed to calm down. And I do more than I should, and then I get paranoid and edgy. And when I crash, I don't feel like doing anything around the house. I've tried to quit, but it is hard to do.

CPSW: So on the one hand, the good things about crank are that it gives you energy and makes you feel good, but the not-so-good things are that you don't like how you feel after you've used for a while, it makes you paranoid, you then need to smoke marijuana to calm down. It is hard to come down from it, and you tend to forget about taking care of stuff around the house. And it is difficult for you to quit. Is that accurate?

ANGELA: Yes.

Angela and the CPS worker then proceeded to discuss in more detail her drug use and her understanding of its effects on her boys. They discussed her attempts to quit. In this aspect of the discussion, the worker focused on what attempts to stop or use less have worked, even for a short time. These exceptions are the foundation of the solutions to the problem. Identifying what the client is already doing that is helpful and doing more of what works are central to the solution focus of this model.

The final aspect of the approach, even at the initial interview stage, is to establish goals for the future. The agreed goals must reflect both the hopes and wishes of the client and the demands for signs of safety from children's services.

CPSW: It's been helpful for me to get a better picture of what has been going on in your life. I appreciate your honesty, and in particular I admire the lengths that you have already gone to, to try to make sure that your boys are safe. In our discussion, some issues came up that are of concern to you and that would also concern Children's Services. You mentioned your drug use, the state of your house, and, in particular, Joe's dealing drugs and your concern about his friends. I know that you don't want Children's Services getting involved in your life, but right now they are. What do you think needs to happen next so that you can get on with things and get Children's Services out of your life?

ANGELA: Well, I guess since you've made such a big thing about my drug use, I'm going to have to do something to deal with that. Maybe quit, get some help.

CPSW: That sounds like a good start. What else?

ANGELA: Maybe I could clean some of this stuff up, throw out stuff, clean up the house.

CPSW: It sounds like you are willing to tackle your drug use and do something about the house. Would you be willing to work with a worker in our voluntary services program? This is where you would set up a contract, work on it, and then if you complete it all, have Children's Services close your case, without having to ever go to court. The CPS worker would give you support and help you with those ideas you mentioned, like help you get into some kind of drug treatment.

ANGELA: I'll give it a try.

Commentary

The aim of this initial meeting was to assess the situation of this family. Using the strengths-and-skills-building model involves reviewing risk and ascertaining strengths and resources. The CPS worker clarified her role and began the process of engaging with Angela to establish a collaborative relationship. The worker rolled with resistance by reflecting Angela's anger at the anonymous report but moved on to help her voice her own concerns and to identify Angela's strengths in dealing with the situation. Using double-sided reflections, the CPS worker amplified the client's ambivalence regarding the fighting and her own drug use. The process also involved reframing her parenting skills, normalizing her difficulty with drug use, validating her concerns, and exploring her previous attempts to take care of her children. This discussion facilitated Angela's move from precontemplation to contemplation, and she began to think about a plan for change. The worker took her to the point of wanting to make some goals, setting the stage for the client's work with her next worker.

Not all of the concerns identified in this initial interview were incorporated into the change plan at the end of the session. Achieving a commitment to change and satisfying safety and risk issues formed the key aspects of the interview, not necessarily developing a comprehensive strategy. With this in mind, the CPS worker was able to explore signs of safety around Joe's presence without tackling Angel's ambivalence toward her relationship with him. As it happened, the situation with Joe took an unexpected turn when the worker discovered that there was a warrant out for his arrest for a parole violation. He was subsequently arrested and sent to prison.

Scene 2

The voluntary services CPS worker arrived to work with Angela on setting up her voluntary contract. Angela admitted to feeling "bad" that Joe was arrested but admitted also to feeling relieved that he was out of the house. She had already taken steps toward cleaning up the house and announced that she had been clean for a week. There was no sign of any drug paraphernalia.

CPSW: Hi, Mrs. Adams, I'm _____, the CPS worker from Voluntary Services. I'm here today because you decided to get involved in setting up a contract regarding the concerns that you spoke about with [the emergency response CPS worker]. She gave me the information you agreed on in your meeting.

ANGELA: Yes, come in, I was expecting you.

CPSW: How have things been going so far?

ANGELA: Well, if you look around, you can see that I have straightened up the house. Of course, with Joe not being here to bug me, it was a little easier. You did hear that he was arrested, right? [CPS worker nods yes.] Well, I feel bad that he got picked up because of the whole business with Children's Services, but it does make things easier that he is gone. Sort of. I will have to figure out how I am going to pay the rent while he is in prison. I feel a little better, too, as I have been clean for a week. That has been hard, too. I threw out all the drug stuff once Joe was arrested, but I keep thinking of using.

CPSW: Sounds like you have had some big adjustments to make already, with figuring out how you are going to support your family and dealing with trying to stay clean.

ANGELA: Yeah, well, this is no picnic.

CPSW: Part of what we need to do today is to figure out what you want to do. Your ideas are really important if we are going to make this work. I'm guessing that with all that has been happening, it has been hard for you to think about the future. Let me ask you this. Supposing you went to sleep tonight and when you woke up in the morning, you found that something happened and all your problems were sorted out. What would your life be like?

ANGELA: Wow! That's a tough question! Well, for one thing, I'd be clean and I wouldn't even think about using, you know? I wouldn't have any cravings, and if anyone were to ask me to use, I could walk away from it easily. It would be no big deal for me.

CPSW: What else?

ANGELA: I would have a job, and my own place to live, just myself and my boys. It would be a place where they were proud to live and bring their friends. And their friends' mothers would let them come to play. My boys would be really happy.

CPSW: What about your relationship with Joe?

ANGELA: That's a little harder to think about, cause I can't really imagine everything else going so well if he were to still be using and bringing his stupid friends around. So I guess he would either be out of my life, or he would be clean, too, and be staying away from his using friends and dealing.

CPSW: You can't imagine everything else going well unless he is clean or if he is out of your life. Let's think for a minute about the things you have talked about changing—your use, your relationship with Joe, your employment situation, your housing. Which one of these would make the most difference to you?

ANGELA: I guess my drug use.

CPSW: Have you ever quit using drugs before?

ANGELA: I have quit before, several times.

CPSW: What did you do that worked?

ANGELA: I would get fed up with it all, and throw everything away, just like I did this time. I would go to NA [Narcotics Anonymous] meetings and hang out with some people from there. I even had a sponsor once for a while. I stopped going by the bar where I would sometimes drink and use with some people. I left the boys' dad—he's a drug addict in prison, too. But I would get lonely, it would be hard to say no to people, and back to using I would go.

CPSW: You have been strong in the past in leaving the boys' dad when you were unhappy with that situation. It sounds like you liked feeling good about being clean, avoided some using friends and places, and went to NA. But sometimes you would get lonely and find yourself back around using friends or in a relationship. Let me ask you this: On a scale from 1 to 10, with 1 being you feel lonely and want to use and 10 is staying clean and feeling supported, where would you place yourself right now?

ANGELA: I'd give myself a 5.

CPSW: Great! Why is it a 5?

ANGELA: Well, I feel pretty good, and I think it will help having Joe out of the house. I haven't been to any meetings or anything, but I am feeling pretty strong.

CPSW: And are there other things that help you stay at 5?

ANGELA: I tell myself that I don't want to be involved with Children's Services and I want to keep my kids. I know that I can be a good mom to my boys. I want to give them a good home. So I just remind myself that working with you all will help me keep them and get the things I want. And I've got to stay clean if I want to do any of this.

CPSW: That's great. What do you think a 6 would look like?

ANGELA: I guess just doing it, maybe going to some meetings. I'm really pretty shy. Maybe some kind of counseling could help me work on that so that I am not so nervous when I talk with people at NA.

CPSW: What else?

ANGELA: If I went to counseling, I would like it to be some kind of a small group, just for women. I think it would be easier for me to talk about myself in something like that. Maybe women who are in similar situations as myself.

CPSW: Many women feel the same way you do about counseling—they would like to be with other women in counseling. It really sounds like you have done a lot of thinking about this! You have described many options here. You talked about feeling better and really focusing on the things that are important to you, namely, being a mother and providing a good home for your boys. You also mentioned that you could get into drug treatment, spend time with others who are clean, and attend some NA meetings. Of the things you mentioned, which of these do you think will work best for you? A step forward would be. . . .

ANGELA: I think most of them will work. I've never been to counseling; that might be what I need to move ahead. Maybe I need to go to some drug counseling every week, meet other clean women, and also start attending NA. And I need to not see my using friends.

CPSW: This seems like a good plan and a lot to do. How will this fit into your schedule?

ANGELA: I don't know when counseling groups meet. I would like to go when the boys are in school. There are some NA meetings in the morning for women and a big Sunday morning meeting you can take kids to. I've been to that one before.

CPSW: That sounds like it would work for you. I will get information for you on different drug counseling programs and when they meet. You indicated that seeing using friends is a red flag for relapse for you. What might be some ways you can handle them if you happen to run into them?

ANGELA: I'll have to tell them that I am clean, and if I start using again, CPS will take my kids. They'll respect that and leave me alone. And if they don't, I'll just walk away. Maybe go call somebody from NA.

CPSW: It sounds like you have thought this through. Let's talk about your job situation now. How would you know you that you have gotten a handle on this?

The worker and Angela went on to discuss employment possibilities and where she has succeeded in getting employment in the past. Her housing and financial situation were also discussed. The final voluntary contract that was drawn up specified that Angela attend an intensive outpatient drug counseling program while her boys were in school. This program also provides various social services that include employment counseling and assertiveness training. Angela agreed to seek work after she had completed the first 3 months of counseling; she also agreed to random drug testing and to begin to seek alternative housing once she became employed.

Commentary

The purpose of this interview was to complete a voluntary contract. As in many CPS systems, the investigative worker was different from the ongoing worker. The ongoing worker wanted to maintain the positive connection with Angela that the emergency response worker had made. This worker helped Angela more clearly define her goals, which, in this case, meant attending a substance abuse treatment program and remaining away from a boyfriend who also had a problem with substances. To determine Angela's overall goals, the worker asked Angela the "miracle question" about how her life would look if she woke up and found all her problems resolved. Adaptations of the miracle question may be used by CPS workers to enable a client to identify and invest in a preferred future (Walsh, 1997). In this case, the CPS worker established that Angela wanted to be drug-free, employed, and in a place of her own. Using a scaling question, the worker was able to elicit "change talk" (see Chapter 5) regarding how she saw herself achieving these goals.

Once Angela identified these goals, it was fairly easy to put them into a measurable contract or implementation plan. The worker also utilized some cognitive behavioral methods by focusing on Angela's "red flags" (thoughts, feelings, or behaviors) that may occur before substance use. Angela identified ways that she might handle seeing using friends. The worker could also discuss how Angela might deal with cravings to use or with feelings of loneliness. A comprehensive drug treatment program would further focus on relapse prevention planning, as well as job and parenting skills. In an actual interview, the CPS worker would go into greater detail regarding all the different areas before the contract was drawn up. In-depth discussions of the various areas are to highlight the client's goals and to learn her motivations to achieve them.

Scene 3

During the third week of outpatient treatment, Angela reported to her treatment program that she had a "slip" (relapse). She described to her drug counselor that she received a call from her boyfriend from jail and he was pressuring her to get back together after his release. She told him no but was so upset afterward that she went to the local bar to find some old friends and had some drinks with them. When she reported the slip to her counselor, she was placed on probation status at her treatment program. She had already missed some sessions because of her children's illnesses. The counselor worked with Angela on identifying personal triggers around her use, which included feeling guilty for not giving in to her boyfriend, feeling lonely for not having anyone in her life, and hopelessness about achieving sobriety. Together they discussed alternative strategies for these high-risk feelings and their accompanying behaviors (such as going to see old friends) and rehearsed coping behaviors. Angela subsequently described these rehearsal activities when she met with the social worker, who had been notified of the relapse. The CPS worker reinforced the intervention strategy and affirmed Angela for her willingness to "hang in there" and do "what it takes."

In Angela's sixth month of the voluntary contract, the CPS worker met with her to review her case. Angela had been clean since her slip, has attended most of her drug treatment groups, and has secured part-time work as a waitress in a coffee shop. She has moved her family into an apartment near the school, and it is somewhat neat. Prior to this meeting, the worker met with Angela's two sons at school. Both boys appeared to be groomed and to have attended school daily. Angela has recently learned that her boyfriend, who still calls her, is due to be released from prison and wants to live with her. She is ambivalent about this.

CPSW: Hi, Angela, good to see you. Today we need to discuss the progress you have made, which has been great. Can you bring me up to date with what has been going on with you?

ANGELA: As you know, I have been clean since that slip I had. I have been going to the drug counseling, and I attend about two or three NA meetings a week. My work is going okay, and I like having my own place. The boys love it!

CPSW: I know one of the biggest things you have worked on is making friends with other people who are clean and sober, because you talked about loneliness as being a red flag for your relapse. How is that going?

ANGELA: The women I have met have been nice. Many have kids, and we do stuff together with the kids. I have a sponsor; she's about my mother's age and easy to talk to, though she can be tough, too. So I think I have made some good friends. I still get lonely for a relationship, though. As a matter of fact, last night Joe called and said he is getting out of prison. He wants to come back to me and live here. He said he lost his place when I moved out, and he has nowhere to go.

CPSW: What are your thoughts on this?

ANGELA: I don't know. I feel really mixed up. He might still be using, even though he got treatment in prison and says he is clean. I miss him and if he's clean, maybe it could work. I don't know how to tell him he can't come here if he is still using. He's pretty hard to say no to!

CPSW: It sounds like you feel two ways about this. On the one hand, you miss his company, but on the other hand, you are unsure if he is sincere about being clean and realize that if he were to come here to live, and was still using, this might be risky for you.

ANGELA: Yes, it would be risky because I don't know if I could stay clean if drugs were in the house and he was using. I feel pretty strong but not that strong. And I don't want my boys around that behavior anyway.

CPSW: How, in the past, were you able to protect your boys—and yourself—from their father's drug use?

ANGELA: Well, he was really tough to stand up to, so I didn't do it too often. There was one time when I just told him that if he wanted to use, to go do it somewhere else. That I didn't want that stuff in my house. So he took me seriously and left, and I pitched everything out, like I did with Joe.

CPSW: It sounds like in the past you were able to be assertive and set limits, and he knew you meant it. I'm wondering, what do you think was different about that time that you could stand up to him and not be talked out of it?

ANGELA: I don't know, I guess I was angry enough, had had enough. I was trying to quit myself. But once I get over being mad, then I give in to whoever it is, and let them back in.

CPSW: So, one of the things that helped you in the past was to get angry. You got angry trying to protect your sobriety and your children.

ANGELA: I get so mad when I am trying hard and I get no support.

CPSW: In this situation with Joe, however, you don't sound angry, just really clear about what you think is best for you and your family. Would you like to try practicing how you might talk to Joe about all this, but with me [playing Joe]? Practicing different things you could say might prepare you to have this conversation with Joe, especially when you are doing it when you are calm and composed.

ANGELA [laughs]: Well, I guess we could try it! Okay. Joe, I've been clean for 5 months now, you know, and have been going to drug counseling, and I have to report to a CPS worker. I have my own job and my own place. I can't have drugs around here because I don't want to lose my clean time and risk the kids and my job.

CPSW [as Joe]: C'mon, Angela, you know I have no place else to go. If I want to use, and I'm not saying that I will, I can just do it somewhere else. A little bit of crank every now and then won't get in the way of what you're doing.

ANGELA [responding to Joe]: If you are using at all, I don't want you here.

CPSW: That's a clear message, Angela. Good job. How does that fit for you? Can you picture yourself saying this to Joe?

ANGELA: It's always been hard for me not to give in to Joe.

CPSW: What kinds of things could you tell yourself if you were talking to him and found yourself wanting to give in?

ANGELA: If I can just remember how hard it was to get this far and remind myself how important my kids are to me, I think it would be easier to say no to Joe.

CPSW: So if you tell yourself, my kids come first and my clean time is important, this might help you say no.

ANGELA: Yeah, I think I could try that. Having Joe live here will just mess up everything I have worked for.

CPSW: What other kinds of things could you do that will keep you from feeling bad and giving in to him?

A: Hmmm. I could call my sponsor, she would give me an earful! I could go talk to one of my friends who knows what he's all about.

CPSW: You've made tremendous progress in staying clean, going to meetings, getting a job, and a place of your own. You are really a strong and determined woman. You have identified some thoughts and behaviors you can use when you start feeling lonely and are at risk for relapse.

Commentary

The purpose of this session was to review Angela's progress. The strengths- and skills-building model encourages CPS workers to help the client identify and discuss in detail her progress. Typically, this would involve spending more time reviewing these details. During this meeting, however, the worker learned that Angela had a difficult situation looming, namely, the return of her boyfriend. This seemed to be her primary concern at this time. As motivation can fluctuate over time, the worker wanted to focus on *why* Angela was committed to staying sober (motivation) and *how* she could continue to maintain this behavioral change (skills) (Bauer et al., 1999). Using reflective listening, the CPS worker enabled Angela to discuss her ambivalence about her boyfriend's possible return to her home. She used the solution-focused model to ask an "exception question" regarding how Angela had successfully handled the boys' father's drug use in the past in order to acknowledge and support the skills Angela already has. The worker reframed that this situation was different, in that Angela was calm, not dealing with Joe in the heat of the moment. She then proceeded into cognitive-behavioral and skills work by asking Angela to role-play a conversation with Joe. This allowed Angela to practice saying no to Joe and to identify thoughts and behaviors that would assist her.

The use of a cognitive intervention is helpful to imagine phrases that can be recalled during a stressful confrontation. Behavioral rehearsal makes it more likely that a client will be able to use the skill in an actual situation. If the client cannot imagine how to respond in a given situation, the CPS worker can model the behavior first and then have the client try it (see

Chapter 3). Using the strengths-and-skills-building model, the worker may teach new skills but prefers to draw on the strengths and resources of the client, as the CPS worker did in this scene. Depending on the client's concern, CBT work could focus on a variety of topics, including anger management, parenting and discipline, dealing with cravings to use drugs, and facing a difficult relationship, as in this situation. The CPS worker will continue to monitor Angela's case for a period of time to determine how she handles this situation with Joe's release and begin to work on termination. Termination could include affirmations of Angela's progress and her handling of difficult situations, with a focus on how she could continue to do so in the future.

Summary

The strengths-and-skills-building model allows CPS workers and other professionals involved with CPS clients to utilize different types of interventions, depending on the goal of the interview and the needs of the client. Motivational interviewing engages involuntary clients by tapping into their internal motivation to change. Solution-focused techniques highlight clients' strengths and resources, helping them envision their preferred future and determine their goals. Cognitive-behavioral work helps clients identify high-risk situations and practice skills they can use to cope with them. In this way, workers can build collaborative relationships that rely on the capacities parents bring, as well as enhancing their skills so that child safety is protected.

References

Action for Child Protection. (n.d.). *Change-based CPS intervention*. Charlotte, NC: Author.

Acton, R., & During, S. (1992). Preliminary results of aggression management training for aggressive parents. *Journal of Interpersonal Violence, 7*, 410–417.

Barrowclough, C., Haddock, G., Tarrier, N., Lewis, S. W., Moring, J., O'Brien, R., et al. (2001). Randomized controlled trial of motivational interviewing, cognitive behavior therapy, and family intervention for patients with comorbid schizophrenia and substance use disorders. *American Journal of Psychiatry, 158*(10), 1706–1713.

Barth, R., Schinke, S., Schilling, R., & Blythe, B. (1983). Self-control training with maltreating parents. *Child Welfare, 62*(4), 313–324.

Bauer, J. S., Kivlahan, D. R., & Donovan, D. M. (1999). Integrating skills training and motivational therapies: Implications for the treatment of substance dependence. *Journal of Substance Abuse Treatment, 17*(1–2), 15–23.

Bell, M. (1999). Working in partnership in child protection: The conflicts. *British Journal of Social Work, 29*(3), 437–455.

Berg, I. K., & Kelly, S. (2000). *Building solutions in child protection*. New York: Norton.

Besharov, D. (1998). Four commentaries: How we can better protect children from abuse and neglect. *Protecting Children from Abuse and Neglect, 8*(1), 120–132.

Bourke, M. (1995). Parent training: Getting the most effective help for the most children. *Journal of Psychological Practice, 1*(3), 142–173.

Brandon, P. (2001). State intervention in imperfect families. *Rationality and Society, 13*(3), 285–303.

Brown, V. A. (2002). *Child welfare: Case studies*. Boston: Allyn & Bacon.

Brunk, M., Henggeler, S., & Whelan, J. (1987). Comparison of multisystemic therapy and parent training in the brief treatment of child abuse and neglect. *Journal of Consulting and Clinical Psychology, 55*, 171–178.

Camp, J. M., & Finkelstein, N. (1997). Parenting training for women in residential substance abuse treatment: Results of a demonstration project. *Journal of Substance Abuse Treatment, 14*(5), 411–422.

Carey, M. P., Braaten, L. S., Maisto, S. A., Gleason, J. R., Forsyth, A. D., Durant, L. E., et al. (2000). Using information, motivational enhancement, and skills training to reduce risk of HIV infection for low-income urban women: A second randomized clinical trial. *Health Psychology, 19*, 3–11.

Carroll, K. M., Libby, B., Sheehan, J., & Hyland, N. (2001). Motivational interviewing to enhance initiation in substance abusers: An effectiveness study. *American Journal of Addictions, 10*(4), 335–339.

Christensen, D. N., Todahl, J., & Barrett, W. C. (1999). *Solution-based casework*. New York: Aldine de Gruyter.

COMBINE Study Research Group. (in press). Testing combined pharmacotherapies and behavioral interventions for alcohol dependence: Rationale and methods. *Alcoholism: Clinical and Experimental Research*.

Corcoran, J. (1999). Solution-focused interviewing with child protective services clients. *Child Welfare, 78*(4), 461–479.

Corcoran, J. (2000). Family interventions with child physical abuse and neglect: A critical review. *Children and Youth Services Review, 22*, 563–591.

Corcoran, J. (2004). A comparison group outcome study of solution-focused therapy versus treatment-as-usual. Manuscript submitted for publication.

Corcoran, J., & Franklin, C. (1998). A solution-focused approach to physical abuse. *Journal of Family Psychotherapy, 9*(1), 69–73.

Corcoran, J., & Stephenson, M. (2000). The effectiveness of solution-focused therapy with child behavior problems: A preliminary report. *Families in Society: The Journal of Contemporary Human Services, 81*(5), 468–474.

Dawson, K., & Berry, M. (2002). Engaging families in child welfare services: An evidence-based approach to best practice. *Child Welfare, 81*(2), 293–317.

DeJong, P., & Berg, I. K. (2001). Co-constructing cooperation with mandated clients. *Social Work, 46*(1), 361–374.

DeMaria, R. (1986). Family therapy and child welfare. *Family Therapy Networker, 10*(1), 45–49.

Dolder, C. R., Lacro, J. P., & Jeste, D. V. (2002). *Medication adherence therapy: Individual inpatient therapy for antipsychotics*. San Diego: Geriatric Psychiatry, VA San Diego Healthcare System.

Easton, C., Swan, S., & Sinha, R. (2000). Motivation to change substance use among offenders of domestic violence. *Journal of Substance Abuse Treatment, 19,* 1–5.

Edleson, J. L. (1999). Introduction to special issue. *Child Maltreatment, 4,* 91–92.

Gelardo, M., & Sanford, E. (1987). Child abuse and neglect: A review of the literature. *School Psychology Review, 16,* 137–155.

Ginsburg, J. I. D., Mann, R. E., Rotgers, F., & Weekes, J. R. (2002). Motivational interviewing with criminal justice populations. In W. R. Miller & S. Rollnick (Eds.), *Motivational interviewing* (2nd ed., pp. 333–346). New York: Guilford.

Greene, B. F., & Kilili, S. (1998). How good does a parent have to be? Issues and examples associated with empirical assessments of parenting adequacy in cases of child abuse and neglect. In J. R. Lutsker (Ed.), *Handbook of child abuse research and treatment* (pp. 53–72). New York: Plenum.

Handmaker, N. S., Miller, W. R., & Manicke, M. (1999). Findings of a pilot study of motivational interviewing with pregnant drinkers. *Journals of Studies on Alcohol, 60*(2), 285–287.

Harper, R., & Hardy, S. (2000). An evaluation of motivational interviewing as a method of intervention with clients in a probation setting. *British Journal of Social Work, 30,* 393–400.

Hohman, M. M. (1998). Motivational interviewing: An intervention tool for child welfare workers working with substance abusing parents. *Child Welfare, 77*(3), 275–289.

Howing, P., Wodarski, J., Kurtz, P., Gaudin, J., & Herbst, E. (1990). Child abuse and delinquency: The empirical and theoretical links. *Social Work, 35,* 244–249.

Hubberstey, C. (2001). Client involvement as a key element of integrated case management. *Child and Youth Care Forum, 30*(2), 83–97.

Johnson, M. B., Baker, C., & Maceira, A. (2001). The 1997 Adoption and Safe Families Act and parental rights termination. *American Journal of Forensic Psychology, 19*(3), 15–28.

Kaufman, K., & Rudy, L. (1991). Future directions in the treatment of physical child abuse. *Criminal Justice and Behavior, 18,* 82–97.

Kinney, J., Haapala, D. A, & Booth, C. (1991). *Keeping families together: The homebuilders model.* Hawthorne, NY: Aldine de Gruyter.

Kolko, D. J., & Swenson, C. C. (2002). *Assessing and treating physically abused children and their families: A cognitive-behavioral approach.* Thousand Oaks, CA: Sage.

Larimer, M., Palmer, R. S., & Marlatt, G. A. (1999). Relapse prevention: An overview of Marlatt's cognitive-behavioral model. *Alcohol Health and Research World, 23*(2), 151–160.

Lincourt, P., Kuettel, T. J., & Bombardier, C. H. (2002). Motivational interviewing in a group setting with mandated clients: A pilot study. *Addictive Behaviors, 27,* 381–391.

Ling, W. (2000). Methamphetamine and cocaine abusers: Differences in characteristics and treatment retention. *Journal of Psychoactive Drugs, 32*(2), 233–238.

Littell, J. H., & Tajima, E. A. (2000). A multilevel model of client participation in intensive family preservation services. *Social Service Review, 74,* 405–435.

Magen, R., & Conroy, K. (1997, June). *Screening for woman abuse in child welfare settings.* Presentation at the fifth International Family Violence Conference, University of New Hampshire, Durham.

Mann, R. E. (1996). *Motivational interviewing with sex offenders: A practice manual.* Hull, England: National Organisation for the Treatment of Abusers.

Mann, R. E., Ginsburg, J. I. D., & Weekes, J. (2002). Motivational interviewing with offenders. In M. McMurran (Ed.), *Motivating offenders to change: A guide to enhancing engagement in therapy.* Chichester, England: Wiley.

Marcenko, M., Larson, N., & Kemp, S. (2000). Childhood experiences of abuse, later substance use, and parenting outcomes among low-income mothers. *American Journal of Orthopsychiatry, 70*(3), 316–326.

Marlatt, G. A., & Gordon, J. R. (Eds.). (1985). *Relapse prevention: Maintenance strategies in the treatment of addictive behaviors.* New York: Guilford.

Miller, W. R., & Rollnick, S. (2002). *Motivational interviewing* (2nd ed.). New York: Guilford.

Monti, P., Rohsenow, D., Colby, S., & Abrams, D. (1995). Coping and social skills training. In R. K. Hester & W. R. Miller (Eds.), *Handbook of alcoholism treatment approaches: Effective alternatives* (pp. 221–241). Boston: Allyn & Bacon.

Noble, D. N., Perkins, K., & Fatout, M. (2000). On being a strength coach: Child welfare and the strengths model. *Child and Adolescent Social Work Journal, 17*(2), 141–153.

Obert, J. L., McCann, M. J., Marinelli-Casey, P., Weiner, A., Minsky, S., Brethen, P., et al. (1997). *Child abuse and neglect: A look at the states: 1997 CWLA stat book.* Washington, DC: CWLA Press.

Petit, M., & Curtis, P. (1997). *Child abuse and neglect: A look at the states: 1997 CWLA Stat Book.* Washington, DC: CWLA Press.

Pichot, T. (2001). Co-creating solutions for substance abuse. *Journal of Systemic Therapies, 20*(2), 1–23.

Rao, S. A. (1999). The short-term impact of the family check-up: A brief motivational intervention for at-risk families. *Dissertation Abstracts International, 59,* 3710.

Rooney, R. H. (1992). *Strategies for work with involuntary clients.* New York: Columbia University Press.

Rosenberg, B. (2000). Mandated clients and solution focused therapy: "It's not my miracle." *Journal of Systemic Therapies, 19*(1), 90–99.

Schinke, S., Schilling, R., Kirkham, M., Gilchrist, L., Barth, R., & Blythe, B. (1986). Stress management skills for parents. *Journal of Child and Adolescent Psychotherapy, 3,* 293–298.

Sellman, J. D., Sullivan, P. F., Dore, G. M., Adamson, S. J., & MacEwan, I. (2001). A randomized controlled trial of motivational enhancement therapy (MET) for mild to moderate alcohol dependence. *Journal of Studies on Alcohol, 62*(3), 389–396.

Sirles, E., Lipchick, E., & Kowalski, K. (1993). A consumer's perspective on domestic violence interventions. *Journal of Family Violence, 8,* 267–276.

Stephens, R. S., Roffman, R. A., & Curtin, L. (2000). Comparison of extended versus brief treatments for marijuana use. *Journal of Consulting and Clinical Psychology, 68,* 898–908.

Stotts, A., Schmitz, J. M., Rhoades, H. M., & Grabowski, J. (2001). Motivational interviewing with cocaine-dependent patients: A pilot study. *Journal of Consulting and Clinical Psychology, 69*(5), 858–862.

Sun, A.-P. (2000). Helping substance-abusing mothers in the child welfare system: Turning crisis into opportunity. *Families in Society: The Journal of Contemporary Human Services, 81*(2), 142–151.

Tohn, S. L., & Oshlag, J. A. (1996). Solution-focused therapy with mandated clients. In S. D. Miller, M. A. Hubble, & B. L. Duncan (Eds.), *Handbook of solution-focused brief therapy* (pp. 152–183). San Francisco: Jossey-Bass.

Turnell, A., & Edwards, S. (1997). Aspiring to partnership: The signs of safety approach to child protection. *Child Abuse Review, 6,* 179–190.

Turnell, A., & Edwards, S. (1999). *Signs of safety: A solution and safety oriented approach to child protection.* New York: W. W. Norton.

U.S. Department of Health and Human Services. (1999). *Blending perspectives and building common ground. A report to Congress on substance abuse and child protection.* Washington, DC: U.S. Government Printing Office.

U.S. Department of Health and Human Services. (2002). *Highlights of findings.* Retrieved November 8, 2003, from http://www.acf.dhhs.gov/programs/cb/publications/cm99/high.htm

Volpicelli, J., Monterosso, J., Filing, J., O'Brien, C., & Markman, I. (2000). Psychosocially enhanced treatment for cocaine-dependent mothers: Evidence of efficacy. *Journal of Substance Abuse Treatment, 18*(1), 41–49.

Walsh, T. (1997). *Solution focused child protection: Towards a positive frame for social work practice.* Dublin, Ireland: Trinity College, Department of Social Studies.

Whiteman, M., Fanshel, D., & Grundy, J. (1987). Cognitive-behavioral interventions aimed at anger of parents at risk of child abuse. *Social Work, 32,* 469–474.

Wolfe, R. B., & Haddy, L. (2001). A qualitative examination of parents' education groups. *Early Child Development and Care, 167,* 877–887.

Yaffe, J., Jenson, J. M., & Howard, M. O. (1995). Women and substance abuse: Implications for treatment. *Alcoholism Treatment Quarterly, 13*(2), 1–15.

Zimmerman, T. S., Jacobsen, R. B., MacIntyre, M., & Watson, C. (1996). Solution focused parenting groups: An empirical study. *Journal of Systemic Therapies, 15*(4), 12–25.

13 Working With Physical Abuse and Neglect

JACQUELINE CORCORAN, AUDREY JONES, AND CHRISTINE ANKERSTJERNE

This chapter continues to explore the topic of working with parents in the child welfare system. Three case examples, integrated throughout the chapter, illustrate techniques at the various stages of the helping process: engagement, exploring the problem, exploring the solution, goal setting and developing case plans, and taking action toward goals.

Case Study 1

In the spring of the previous year, three girls—Andrea (15), Katelynn (14), and Kathleen (13)—were removed from their single-parent mother, Ms. Jackson, because of a physical abuse incident and a years-long history of domestic violence between the children and their mother. The mother has been court-ordered to work with the ongoing child protective services worker to meet the goal of reuniting her with her children. The caseworker has made telephone calls and mailed letters to Ms. Jackson's home but has received no response. She has also visited Ms. Jackson's home in an attempt to set up an appointment, but until now Ms. Jackson has offered reasons as to why she could not meet with the caseworker.

Engagement

No matter what the role of the child protective services (CPS) worker—investigator, ongoing worker, or foster care worker—a collaborative relationship must be set up with the client in which concern, empathy, respect, and acceptance of the individual are conveyed, even when the worker does not agree with or condone the previous behaviors of the client (DePanfilis, 2000). When faced with CPS involvement, parents typically feel judged and blamed. They resent the intrusion into their privacy and the strangers who are telling them how to raise their children. At the same time, some of their hostility may be fueled by unspoken shame that they have been unable to manage their home lives without outside involvement. Parents are also deeply fearful about the consequences to their families, which might include the loss of their children. If children are taken away to foster care or other placement, tremendous grief may result. Understanding the perspective of clients is essential to the joining process and to building a mutual working relationship.

In the example involving Ms. Jackson and her three teenage daughters who have been taken into care, Ms. Jackson has been, until now, avoiding her appointments with the caseworker—ignoring phone calls, letters, and a home visit. She is now at the caseworker's office, although she is reluctant to enter.

The caseworker greets Ms. Jackson with a warm smile and compliments her on her punctuality. Ms. Jackson enters and responds by saying that she thought she better not be late because the court has ordered her to be here. The caseworker reframes her comment by saying that it is nice to know that she takes court orders seriously, as some people do not.

As well as showing acceptance and warmth, specific techniques can also enhance engagement with CPS clients, who are usually mandated to participate in the helping process. These include asking relationship questions, aligning with the client against an external entity, focusing on future positive behavior rather than on past negative behavior, asking coping questions, reframing, and normalizing. These are discussed and illustrated in the following sections.

Although an investigative interview requires an understanding of the inciting reason behind the referral, routinely asking clients to detail the reasons they are involved with the CPS system may arouse defensiveness: "Professionals often assume that services can not be productive until perpetrators overtly admit guilt and accept responsibility. . . . However, an admission of wrongful behavior is difficult for anyone" (Christensen, Todahl, & Barrett, 1999, p. 69). Insistence on its occurrence may lead to an impasse in progress. Therefore, in the example with Ms. Jackson, questions about the original incident are avoided, particularly at the beginning of the interview, when she might be expecting accusation.

Instead, we see in the following exchange that the caseworker orients Ms. Jackson toward what action she can take in the future by asking a relationship question. By asking the client to relate what needs to happen from the perspective of another person or entity that is interested in the client's change, the caseworker can sidestep the client's possible unwillingness to admit that she needs to change. In the process of asking relationship questions, the caseworker also aligns herself with the client against the external entity, in this case, the court system:

CASEWORKER: So it was the court's idea that you come here?
CLIENT: Yes, they think I need help with my kids because I tried to keep one of them from hurting herself and accidentally bruised her arms.
CASEWORKER: What does the court need to see so you don't have to come here anymore?
CLIENT: I guess they need to see me handling my kids without leaving bruises on them.
CASEWORKER: When you say handling your kids, what do you mean?
CLIENT: Well, when they act up, the court thinks I need to discipline them without leaving bruises on them. It is just so hard to have three teenage girls in one house. They all have mood swings and get angry, I just don't know what to do. Sometimes I feel like throwing up my hands and letting someone else try for a while.

After validating the client's difficulties, the caseworker decides not to inquire further about the problems Ms. Jackson currently experiences with her daughters. Instead, she works with Ms. Jackson to behaviorally describe what she wants to see change in her household. For instance, the caseworker asks her, "What would I see happening if I was filming on videotape?" The caseworker helps the client develop a vision of a positive future, asking for the presence of positive behaviors rather than the absence of negatives (e.g., "What will you be doing instead of arguing and screaming?"). Ms. Jackson eventually imagines the following scenario:

CLIENT: Okay, instead of the police coming to my house, we would take time away from one another, then sit down and talk about the problem. We wouldn't be cursing and yelling—we would just be talking in normal voices.

By asking Ms. Jackson what she must do to show that she is ready to have her children, the caseworker emphasizes what Ms. Jackson can do in the future rather than what she has done in the past. These questions also indicate to Ms. Jackson that the caseworker is invested in helping her end the treatment process as quickly as possible. As Ms. Jackson is reluctant to attend, this should come as a relief to her and might motivate her to take action.

Another way to engage with clients is to explore the circumstances that give rise to the problematic behavior. For example, if a mother left her children alone, was it because she had to go to work or be fired? Was her regular baby-sitter sick? Did she feel she had no other option? Expressing understanding of the difficult situations in which clients are embroiled often decreases their defensiveness. Reframing can then follow, which emphasizes the positive intention behind behaviors rather than the dangerous behaviors themselves.

For example, Ms. Jackson relates the inciting incident for her children entering foster care.

CLIENT: Andrea wouldn't go to her anger management class and started yelling and cursing. Kathleen joined in, telling Andrea how she needs help with her anger, and the girls started screaming at each other. Kathleen got so upset that she grabbed her bottle of antidepressants and said she was going to overdose on them. I was just trying to get the bottle away from her, and I accidentally bruised her arm.

The positive intention behind the violent behavior was that Ms. Jackson, concerned with Kathleen's safety, wanted to keep her from overdosing.

The use of reframing does not have to be limited to engagement and can come into play throughout the helping process. One ideal situation in which to use reframing is when parents attribute their children's misbehavior to dispositional qualities. For example, a mother might say, "These kids are just hardheaded like their father. That's why they won't listen." The caseworker reframes her attribution of her children as "hardheaded" (a fixed and inherent quality of her children that has been inherited from their father) to one involving more temporary and changeable circumstances: "I wonder if they are just tired at that time of night and are cranky as a result." Another way to reframe parents' attributions of their children's negative behaviors as being due to dispositional qualities is by offering an alternative view that is compatible with the available data (D'Zurilla & Nezu, 2001): "It seems like your child is more likely to push the other kids when the classroom is full, and the children have to share a lot."

Another way that reframing can be used throughout the helping process is from motivational interviewing. Here, a client's arguments against change are used instead to argue for change. For instance, if a parent who is physically abusive says that the only way she can get her children to obey is to hit them, the caseworker can reframe this statement and explain that if parents resort to physical punishment, they train their children to disobey until physical punishment is used.

In addition to reframing, another way to promote client engagement is coping questions. Clients involved with the CPS system are often caught up in very difficult life experiences. Coping questions can be one way to validate these circumstances and discover the resources clients have used to manage them.

For instance, at times in her conversation with the caseworker, Ms. Jackson becomes overwhelmed by hopelessness and has trouble seeing her situation differently. The caseworker turns to coping questions, recognizing that unless some of her struggles are validated, Ms. Jackson will not readily engage in solution talk.

CASEWORKER: Sounds like things have been difficult for you for a while. How have you managed to keep things from getting worse?

CLIENT: Well, my sister is close by, and sometimes I just call her and complain about the kids. That helps a little.

CASEWORKER: How is that helpful for you?

CLIENT: Well, I just had to call somebody because the kids were out of control, and I needed somebody to talk to. My sister or my boyfriend sometimes would give me some things to say to the girls to get them to calm down. That was good because I'd run out of things to say to them.

CASEWORKER: What types of things would they suggest?

CLIENT: They would tell me to send one of the girls to her room until she calmed down. Or sometimes they told me to take the phone outside. They'd help me calm down by talking to me about what was going on.

CASEWORKER: Sounds like they have been quite helpful in times of stress.

CLIENT: Sometimes my boyfriend will take one of the girls outside or to town with him when they get upset. They like doing that because their dad has not been around since they were small. He is the only father figure they've ever had.

CASEWORKER: Sounds like he can be a good support for you and your kids. So you have used your sister and your boyfriend as supports. I'm wondering what you do when these supportive people aren't around.

CLIENT: I always try to do what is best for my children. I didn't mean to hurt Kathleen, but she would not put down the pill bottle.

CASEWORKER: What is it that keeps you going?

CLIENT: Well, I've got my kids, and I don't want anything to happen to them.

CASEWORKER: Sounds to me that you care very much for your children and want to do what is right.

In this situation, asking coping questions elicited many different resources that Ms. Jackson had used. She had used informal support from her sister and boyfriend, and she identified strategies that they invoked that were helpful, such as sending the girls to their rooms, going outside to calm down, and having other activities for the girls to do when they became upset. Ms. Jackson was also resourceful in the past by calling on the police to assist, even though she perceives this option as no longer plausible. The coping questions also elicited from Ms. Jackson the deep sense of caring she has for her girls.

Another way to invoke cooperation rather than defensiveness from clients involves normalizing, which is a solution-focused technique that de-pathologizes people's concerns and presents them instead as normal life difficulties (Bertolino & O'Hanlon, 2002; O'Hanlon & Weiner-Davis, 1989). Parents who are abusive and neglectful often believe that children should be able to achieve developmental milestones that exceed what is appropriate for their age. Parents become frustrated with their children when these expectations are not met (Azar, Barnes, & Twentyman, 1988). Part of the helping process may therefore involve increasing parents' knowledge of developmental norms and creating realistic appraisals of children's abilities.

Christensen et al. (1999) also discuss normalizing the frustrations of everyday tasks associated with typical life stages. For parents of young children, difficulties may center on dealing with crying and children's inability to communicate and reason, setting and maintaining eating and sleeping schedules, toilet training, and keeping children from harm. For families with school-age children, routines around getting ready for school and bedtime; setting expectations for school behavior and achievement; managing contact with the school; coordinating children's extracurricular activities, homework, and chore completion; and discipline and supervision issues can be challenging. For teenagers, there are the added stressors associated with their increased freedoms, such as more time spent with peers and away from the family, driving, and possible experimentation with alcohol and drugs. Normalizing the difficulties associated with managing these different tasks (though not the harmful behavior that resulted in the maltreatment) can help parents feel understood and can get them to focus on how to better manage these life stressors with which most families struggle (Christensen et al., 1999).

Normalizing can further center on the particular life challenges some families face, such as single parenthood, as the following example illustrates:

CASEWORKER [to Ms. Jackson]: Adolescence is a difficult time to get through. Teenagers are caught in this in-between stage of not being a child but not yet being an adult. They are struggling for their independence and, at the same time, still need their mom to be there for them. It can be difficult for both teenagers and their parents. And at the same time that your girls are going through these difficult changes, you have to deal with being a single parent. That is also stressful in itself. Being a single parent is challenging, and having three teenage girls only magnifies that challenge. All single parents have to deal with trying to play two roles for their children—both mom and dad—and that can be overwhelming at times.

CLIENT: You sure are right about that. Being a single parent is not easy, and it seems to be getting harder as the girls get older. I thought they required a lot of attention when they were younger, but now they need even more. Sometimes I just want to throw up my hands and leave.

As in this instance, normalizing can reassure parents that their struggles are natural, given their circumstances. This can help them feel validated and better prepared to face the reality of the situation, rather than pathologizing and escalating it to greater extremes.

Exploring the Problem

Exploring the problem entails assessing, building motivation, and tracking problem sequences so that parents gain awareness of the patterns and context of their maltreatment.

Assessing Motivation

A client will not change his or her behavior unless motivated to do so. Therefore, the practitioner should take ample time to assess a client's level of motivation and then use techniques that build motivation and enhance confidence, thus increasing the client's abilities to make desired changes and manage obstacles to success (Miller & Rollnick, 2002).

In the conversation between the caseworker and Ms. Jackson that follows, the caseworker seeks to assess Ms. Jackson's readiness to take action toward getting her girls back by using a scaling intervention to measure her motivation.

CASEWORKER: Let's say 1 represents the way you feel when you are ready to throw up your hands and give up on your girls, and 10 represents how you will feel when you are completely prepared to have them come back. Where do you see yourself on the scale?

CLIENT: I think I am around a 6, because I know there are things that I have to do before I am ready to get the girls back.

CASEWORKER: Tell me what places you at this number. How have you come so far?

CLIENT: The girls have been visiting on the weekends, and they have been doing pretty good. We didn't have any major fights the last couple of weeks.

CASEWORKER: Okay, it sounds like you are motivated to get the girls back. Now let's take a look at how confident you are that you can do something different to change things for the girls. We'll use the same type of scale that we used for your motivation: 1 will be when the girls came into foster care, and 10 is when you're confident you can have them back, and you can manage conflict and disagreement calmly without screaming or coming to blows. Where would you say that you are on that scale?

CLIENT: I am around a 6 there, too, because I recognize that the girls are a handful when they come home for weekend visits. They wear me out. But we don't argue and yell quite as much as we did before.

CASEWORKER: Great! Then it looks like your motivation and confidence are at the same level, and you are ready to move forward toward getting your girls back.

The caseworker takes this as a sign to progress with exploring the problem behavior and finding exceptions that Ms. Jackson can build upon (as addressed in the section entitled Exception Finding).

Another technique from motivational interviewing, the decisional balance, assesses the advantages versus the disadvantages of the problem. Not only can this help the client to see that disadvantages of a problem behavior may outweigh the advantages but also it is useful as an assessment tool to uncover the reasons the client keeps the problem in place. Efforts can then be targeted toward making these reasons less salient.

A decisional balance is helpful with a parent like Ms. Jackson who physically abuses her children. By asking the parent to detail the advantages of such behavior, she is allowed to express how well it works for her, and the caseworker hears her point of view. Then the caseworker explores the other side—the "not so good things" about using physical punishment. Going through this process helps parents see that while there may be some advantages from their point of view, there are also drawbacks. As a result, they often become more willing to consider a change in their behavior. Table 13.1 offers a sample decisional balance involving the typical advantages and disadvantages to physical punishment. Across from the "advantages" section are some ways caseworkers can address these points. However, it is important that clients are allowed to express the advantages they

Table 13.1

Typical Decisional Balance for Parents Who Are Physically Abusive

Advantages to abusive behavior	Possible responses to these arguments
Children obey	Explain that abusive behavior trains children to disobey until they are physically punished.
Feels good to release anger	Work on developing awareness of when anger builds, on how to circumvent escalation, and on taking time-outs.
Children know who's in charge and respect parent	Affirm the goal of authoritative parenting, which involves having and enforcing clear and consistent rules and monitoring children's whereabouts and activities.
Want children to succeed in life, to be tough against adversity	Authoritative parenting (having clear and consistent rules and monitoring children's whereabouts and activities) has been consistently related to positive outcomes in low-income children and adolescents (Steinberg, 2000).
	The effects of physical punishment don't carry over to situations where it is not applied; for instance, the child might eventually comply at home but not at school where physical punishment is not used.
Their own parents physically punished them, so it must be right	Explore the subsequent result on the relationship between parent and child from physical punishment/ how the parent feels about his or her own parent. Discuss changes in society's attitudes about physical punishment.
Parent insists that they were physically punished, and they turned out fine	Ask: "How would you like things to be different for your children?"

Disadvantages to abusive behavior

Consequences to parents:
Possible trouble with the legal system
Outsiders get involved in family life

Consequences to children:
Children may feel negatively toward the person enacting the punishment and toward the source of the behaviors for which they are being punished (e.g., homework, other siblings).
Teaches children aggression by modeling aggression.
Teaches children what they shouldn't do but not what they should do.

(continued)

Table 13.1 (continued)
Typical Decisional Balance for Parents Who Are Physically Abusive

Disadvantages to abusive behavior

Research findings indicate physical abuse is correlated for children with (a) aggression/
behavior problems, (b) poor impulse control, (c) social skills deficits, (d) cognitive
deficits in terms of language and IQ academic problems, (e) trauma-related symptoms,
such as anxiety and depression (Kolko, 2002).

Adolescents physically abused as children exhibit more externalizing behaviors and violent
criminal offending than their non–physically abused counterparts (Malinosky-Rummell &
Hansen, 1993).

Longer-term consequences for adults include the following (Malinosky-Rummell &
Hansen, 1993): among men, increased rates of violence, including criminal offenses;
among women, internalizing problems, such as self-abuse, suicidality, dissociation,
somatization, depression, and anxiety.

see before the caseworker educates them on other possibilities. As always,
when offering information, the caseworker is advised to proceed tentatively, processing information as it is given by using the skills outlined in
a later section.

Rather than just focusing on problem behavior, the decisional balance
can also be used to motivate a client toward taking action toward a specific
goal, as the following example demonstrates.

Case Study 2

Jamie is a 17-year-old White female who has been living in a foster home
for 2 years. She was removed from her home because of her aggressiveness
at home and at school, which included chasing family members with a
knife. Child protective services found that her mother was not able to keep
Jamie safe and, therefore, removed Jamie from the home. Her mother has
been diagnosed with Parkinson's disease, and Jamie's father died of a heart
attack a few years ago. Jamie has to leave the foster home when she turns
18 and graduates from high school; this makes developing independent
living skills a high priority. Although there are a lot of subgoals under
independent living, such as applying to colleges and learning how to run
a household, Jamie has chosen obtaining a driver's license as her priority.

CASEWORKER: Jamie, I am hearing from you that you would like to work
on obtaining your driver's license, is that correct?
JAMIE: Yes, I think so.

CASEWORKER: You think so, but you are still not sure?

JAMIE: Well, I know that I need to get it but. . . .

CASEWORKER: What do you think is holding you back?

JAMIE: I'm not really sure. Mostly that I don't want to take on another responsibility, having to get insurance and all those other things.

CASEWORKER: So, getting your driver's license seems like a big responsibility to you, one you are not sure you are ready for?

JAMIE: Yeah, but I know that I need to get it.

CASEWORKER: You have stated to me several times that you know you need to get it. Let's look at some of those reasons. I'd also like to make a list of all of the pros and all of the cons of getting your driver's license. What do you think about that?

JAMIE: I think my list of pros will be bigger than the cons.

CASEWORKER: Well, let's see. I will write the list as you talk. Let's start with the pros. What are some of the good or helpful reasons for you to get your driver's license?

JAMIE: Well, first I'd be able to drive myself around and not have to rely on my foster mom and worry about her forgetting to pick me up like she did last week. I'd be able to drive to school and to get stuff that I need. Also, when I go to visit my real mom, I'd be able to help her out and drive her to do her errands, and we wouldn't have to take a taxi all over the place. Mostly I would just be able to take myself to all of the places I need and want to go.

CASEWORKER: That is a great list, Jamie. Let's look at the other side. What are some of the disadvantages of getting your license?

JAMIE: All the added responsibility. Like I have to get insurance, and because it's her car, I think my foster mom would make me do everything for her, running here and there all of the time. I wouldn't like that part of it.

CASEWORKER: Are you worried that she might take advantage of you being able to drive independently and have you run all of her errands? Is that what you are saying?

JAMIE: Yes!

CASEWORKER: I think that is something that we could probably work through. We could come up with some compromises with your foster mom so that you don't feel overwhelmed. What do you think of trying to work something out with her?

JAMIE: You mean like coming up with a coupon book or something where she has to give me coupons to run errands for her, and she only gets so many per day or week?

CASEWORKER: Excellent idea! That's a very creative way of possibly dealing with the issue with your foster mom.

JAMIE: Really? I was kind of kidding about that.

CASEWORKER: I think it's a great idea and something that may work for both of you. How are you feeling about things right now?

JAMIE: Well, I know I need to get my license, and I think I'm ready to start.

CASEWORKER: That is great, Jamie. I'm glad to hear it.

In this example, initially the client was not yet ready to move forward on the goal of obtaining a driver's license. By processing through the decisional balance, the caseworker discovered the salient reason for Jamie's hesitancy—her fear that her foster mother would use her for errands. Jamie originally expressed this in vague terms as a "fear of responsibility," but the process of applying a decisional balance helped clarify the issue for both the client and the caseworker. The caseworker could then work with Jamie on addressing this specific concern—helping her negotiate with the foster mother.

Tracking Problem Sequences

When people are in the contemplation stage of change (when they are ready to consider change), the caseworker can help them deconstruct the problem sequences into the specific behaviors they contain. (For more information on the Stages of Change model, see Chapter 2.) Typically, parents who maltreat children have little understanding of what triggers their children's behaviors, how they contribute to escalating the behavior, and the consequences of their actions (Christensen et al., 1999). Often parents say, "It just happened," implying that they have no control over the problem behavior. The worker's task is to slowly take the client through an incident and figure out the antecedents, the behaviors, and the consequences. Figure 13.1 is a

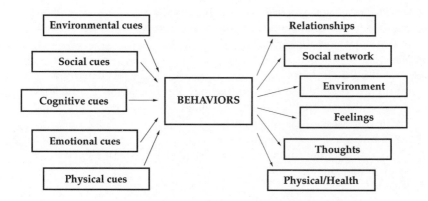

Figure 13.1. The Antecedents and Consequences of Behaviors

diagram of cues and consequences that can help clients gain awareness of the different areas—social, environmental, emotional, cognitive, and physical—that may both contribute to and be affected by problem behaviors.

Using the example of an incident of physical abuse to uncover antecedents, the following questions can be asked: What seems to trigger "losing it"? Is it something your children say? Are there situations that make you more prone to have a fit? Where do they occur? Who is there? At what time of day and on what days of the week do the incidents occur? What feelings and thoughts do you have right before a fit? What bodily reactions are you having?

To discover consequences, the following inquiry can be made: What happens after your fits? How do you react? What do you say and do? How long do these reactions last? What do you do after your fits? How do you feel? What thoughts run through your mind? How do your children react? What does that do to your relationship with them?

Then there are questions for tracking the specific behavior problems themselves (Spiegler, 1993): When you say you "lose it," what do you do? How do you feel? What are you thinking? What bodily reactions do you experience?

Once the caseworker and client identify specific behaviors, cues, and consequences, they can proceed as partners to find solutions (discussed in the next section) and develop a case plan individualized to the client's situation. Table 13.2 shows cognitive-behavioral techniques that, for example, address some of the antecedent conditions behind maltreatment.

Exploring the Solution

As discussed throughout the book, finding and amplifying strengths is a critical piece of the strengths-and-skills-building model. Even parents who have been abusive or neglectful have shown plenty of examples of appropriate parenting behavior (Berg, 1994; Berg & Kelly, 2000). CPS clients are more likely to comply and be motivated toward services when practitioners reinforce and build on already existing resources. It is also easier to build on strengths than to teach parents entirely new skills (Bertolino & O'Hanlon, 2002).

Miracle Questions

Miracle questions ask clients to cast themselves into a future position and advise themselves from that perspective on what steps they should take to solve their problem. A problem-ridden present can be sidestepped so that a more promising future can be considered (Christensen et al., 1999). In this way, hope and a positive expectation for change can be developed.

Table 13.2

How to Manage Cues for Maltreatment by Using Cognitive-Behavioral Techniques

Cue	Cognitive-behavioral technique	Example
Social cue	Avoidance	A parent who is prone to neglecting her children when she drinks or uses drugs with a certain set of friends is taught how to avoid friends with whom she "parties."
	Self-coping statements	"My children come first. If I see [drug-using friend], I know that I will end up buying drugs. I am not going to go there. I am making the right choice."
	Communication skills	How to be assertive with friends who use substances
	For unavoidable situations, relaxation training, coping self-statements	A parent who lives in a high-crime, drug-infested neighborhood has to cope with living in that environment ("I'm just going to walk by that house, even though I know I can buy drugs there. It's not worth it. I can do this. My children come first. I want to stay out of trouble. I want to show them the right way to live.")
	Problem-solving skills	What are other options for raising income or tapping into other resources so I can live in a different neighborhood?
Environmental cues (e.g., running out of money, child noncompliance)	For child noncompliance, behavioral management techniques	Child won't go to bed: Use extinction to put up with child protest until he is trained to stay in bed.
	For child noncompliance, communication skills	Child is misbehaving after his father has left the home: Listen to his feelings and reflect them back.
	For environmental stress (e.g. short on money), budgeting	Determining the amount of money coming in through child support and government support and the amount needed to pay rent, utilities, food, clothing, and so on.
	Problem-solving skills	How can income be increased?

(continued)

Table 13.2 (continued)

How to Manage Cues for Maltreatment by Using Cognitive-Behavioral Techniques

Cue	Cognitive-behavioral technique	Example
	Communication skills	Negotiating with people to whom money is owed; obtain needed services (e.g., landlord fixing heat vent so that the electric bill is lower) and required benefits.
Emotional cues	Identification of feelings; feeling expression and management	A parent who is depressed is prone to sleeping in and not getting the children up for school.
	Problem solving	How to handle difficult mood states.
	Communication skills	Communicating to people about feelings and making behavior requests.
Cognitive cues	Challenging negative thoughts, replacing with more positive thoughts	Parent views children as malicious and "out to get me." ("How do you know that's what your child is thinking?" "How do you feel when you think that?" "How do you act toward your child?" "What are some other ways to view this? Maybe she is just tired, hungry, or used to misbehaving until she is hit.")
Physical cues (e.g., restlessness, tension, pain, cravings)	Relaxation training, breathing exercises, other self-care activities	A parent gets tense being cooped up with her three young children each day. She arranges to have a neighbor look after them for an hour (and she does the same for the neighbor) while she takes a walk and then a bath.

▮▮▮▮ Case Study 3

The miracle question is demonstrated in the case study of Tanya, a 25-year-old African American woman with a 4-year-old daughter, Lynne. Tanya has been reported to child protective services (CPS) by Lynne's day care provider. The teacher reported that Lynne often came to school hungry. When the children were fed, Lynne ate her portion voraciously and then tried to grab food from the other children. She also looked thin and mal-nourished.

The main purpose of the CPS worker's investigative interview was to inform the mother of the basis of the report and to receive her response to the allegation. In the interview, Tanya explained that she had just lost her job. She was living temporarily in her mother's home with her mother, her daughter, and her brother. Her mother was being evicted for nonpayment of rent for 6 months, and Tanya would have to move out in less than 2 weeks. Tanya was upset with her mother because the money that she and her brother had given her for rent had been spent on alcohol.

Tanya explained her tenuous relationship with Lynne's father, saying that they dated "on and off" for the last 4 years. His financial assistance was sporadic and could not be counted on. Tanya admitted that her daughter was not getting enough to eat at home. Tanya has been out of work for a few weeks and is low on money. To stretch what she had, she gave her daughter small portions. Tanya sometimes did not eat at all to make sure that her daughter had something.

The following dialogue begins as Tanya, after providing the preceding information, reveals that sometimes she feels like giving up.

CASEWORKER: Well, Tanya, it sounds like you are really overwhelmed. You have a lot going on right now.

TANYA: Yeah, I mean when it rains it pours, you know? Nothing seems to be going right. And now this. I do the best I can for my child, but my ends don't seem to meet lately.

CASEWORKER: It sounds like things have gotten difficult just recently. Let me ask you this: If you woke up tomorrow and all your problems were solved, what would be different? What would your day be like?

TANYA: Well, I would wake up in the morning, and I would have plenty of food in the refrigerator. I would make me and Lynne breakfast.

CASEWORKER: What else would happen?

TANYA: Me and Lynne would have a home to wake up in, in the first place, otherwise where would I make breakfast?

CASEWORKER: Okay, what else would your day be like?

TANYA: I would take her to the day care. I would be all paid up with the day care. Of course, all this money would come from my new job. Maybe I would get along better with Lynne's dad.

CASEWORKER: What would you and Lynne's dad be doing when you are getting along better?

TANYA: We would argue less.

CASEWORKER: What else would be different?

TANYA: Well, my mom wouldn't drink so much. But I guess I can't really do anything about that. Maybe me and Lynne's dad would get along better, even if we're not living together. For Lynne's sake, you know.

CASEWORKER: It sounds like you have a pretty good idea of what you want things to be like for you.

TANYA: Yeah, I know I would feel better, because all these problems make me frustrated, so I have an attitude all the time.

CASEWORKER: What would it be like for you not to be so frustrated and have an attitude all the time?

TANYA: Well, it would be wonderful! I don't want to be negative. If my problems were solved, it would be easy to enjoy myself and play with my daughter. I would be able to feed her as much food as she needs without worrying if I'll have enough money for our food the next week. I wouldn't feel so bad when she is hungry, and I can't afford food or milk.

Tanya's responses made it possible to bypass her current challenging circumstances by describing a comprehensive picture of what she wanted her future to look like. Tanya began to experience a greater sense of energy and hopefulness about resolving her present situation. The caseworker then used this opportunity to lead into exception finding.

Exception Finding

The strengths-and-skills-building approach seeks to identify and enhance the successful parenting practices the client has used in the past. A caseworker can validate a client's sense of parental competency by asking what he or she has done to solve the problems that have been going on in the home. Then the parent's successful efforts can be mined for long-term solutions, and skills can be taught that enable the parent to put these solutions into practice.

The caseworker and Tanya's dialogue continues. Tanya has just answered the miracle question.

CASEWORKER: Tell me about a time in the past that is like what you're describing.

TANYA: Well, yeah, a month or so ago, I was working at a department store, and I had a stable living arrangement with my mom. I would get paid every week. I paid her rent every month. We always had food in the house. We could get any food that we needed. Lynne's dad would come over most evenings. He would bring me money whenever he had it. I seemed to be in a better mood most of the time.

CASEWORKER: How did you make all of that happen?

TANYA: I stayed home at night instead of going out with my friends. So I got a good night's rest. I was able to get up and get myself and Lynne ready, and take her to the day care, and still be at work on time.

CASEWORKER: How were you able to stay home at night instead of going out with your friends?

TANYA: I just decided that I needed to be home with my daughter sometimes instead of leaving Lynne with my mother or brother. I guess I started to go out more with my friends when me and Lynne's dad broke up a month ago.

CASEWORKER: Tanya, that must have felt good for you to be able to get your daughter to day care and make it to work on time as well. I see that you've had success in the past with preparing yourself in the evening to get enough sleep in order to get to work on time.

TANYA: Yeah, nobody else is gonna do it for me. I have to take care of my daughter. I love her so much. I want the best for her. I gotta do what's best for her. And I've done a pretty good job of it the last 3 years. This is the first time things have gotten this bad. I've been so busy feeling sorry for myself. I just need to get myself together so I can take care of my child.

This exception-finding example illustrates that Tanya recently had a period of time when things were going well for her. She identified clearly some of the things she had done in the past to make her life better for her and her child: working steadily, staying in at nights so she could get enough sleep, spending time with her daughter, and paying her mother rent.

We return at this point to Ms. Jackson and her situation with her daughters in foster care to provide another example of exception finding.

CASEWORKER: Let's focus a little more on what has been successful for you in dealing with your daughters' behavior. I'd like to hear about a recent situation where you were successful in getting one of your daughters to calm down when she was upset.

MS. JACKSON: Well, the other day Kathleen was upset about not getting to go to the local fair because money is tight, and I told her that I would borrow the money for her to go if she would stay out of trouble for the rest of the week in the foster home. See, her sister is there with her, and they argue a lot.

CASEWORKER: Sounds like you were able to give Kathleen clear guidelines for getting a ticket to the fair. How did she respond?

MS. JACKSON: Well, she didn't argue with her sister for the rest of the week, and I borrowed the money from my sister for her to go to the fair.

CASEWORKER: Wow! So that was a success?

MS. JACKSON: Yeah, I guess it was a success. [A faint smile crosses Ms. Jackson's face.]

At this point the caseworker capitalizes on the client's realization that change can happen. The caseworker explores with Ms. Jackson how she coordinated with the foster parent in order to make this happen. The caseworker continues in this vein with Ms. Jackson, helping her apply the solution—that is, setting a clear guideline for her daughter and then rewarding appropriate behavior.

The caseworker then continues to probe for exceptions—this time for the type of communication Ms. Jackson had identified she wanted for the family.

MS. JACKSON: One time a couple of weeks ago when the girls were home for the weekend, I was able to get them to sit down in the living room and tell me without yelling what was going on.

CASEWORKER: What were the children doing when they all sat down with you a couple of weeks ago?

MS. JACKSON: At first they just wanted to yell at each other, but I told them that only one person could talk at a time. So I made them raise their hand—like they were in school—to talk. That seemed to work out pretty well.

CASEWORKER: What did you do differently that time?

MS. JACKSON: I got involved in their argument before they started cursing at each other.

CASEWORKER: So getting involved before they start cursing sounds like it might be important. How did you get them to all sit down together?

MS. JACKSON: Well, at first they didn't want to, but I told them they all had to be in the same room sitting down before we could talk about the problem, and they did. I had to wait a little while, but they all sat down.

CASEWORKER: Sounds like your patience paid off! That's great! Tell me more about how you apply this solution in other situations.

MS. JACKSON: Well, I have been trying in the past month to use this "sit down and talk rule" when the girls come home on the weekends.

CASEWORKER: So you have been using this technique for the past month and have been successful.

In these examples of the exception-finding intervention, the caseworker helped Ms. Jackson identify and explore two methods she can use with her daughters: setting an incentive to promote their appropriate behavior and intervening in an argument before it escalates. The identified exceptions can be built upon when setting goals and developing case plans.

Goal Setting and Developing Case Plans

In child protective services agencies, current practice tends to dictate the goals required of clients. As Christensen et al. (1999) comment, case plans typically involve the rote assignment of interventions to problems identified. For instance, if physical abuse has occurred, parenting classes are assigned; if alcohol use is present, substance abuse counseling is indicated; if domestic violence is involved, a perpetrator group is required. This practice violates a number of guidelines about collaborative goal setting (detailed in Chapter 5). First, the practice of assigning a treatment package that is not tailored to the individual often overwhelms the client. Individuals already experiencing a multitude of life stressors, including poverty, housing problems, neighborhood violence, and so forth, will not be able to scatter their efforts and seek services from numerous agencies in the community at once (Azar & Wolfe, 1998). Focusing on a limited number of goals is critical because the client needs to achieve success and experience some confidence as a result of his or her efforts.

Another problem with selecting goals in a rote fashion is that this leaves out client input. If a goal is not personally important to a client, he or she will not be motivated to pursue it. Goals should be related as much as possible to what a client sees as the problem. Clients who have physically abused their children usually see their children's behavior as the problem. When formulating goals, this viewpoint should be capitalized upon. The goal of good behavior from the parent's children can be supported and validated, and at the same time the parent can be taught that a more effective way to achieve compliance—from young children especially—is to structure the environment in a way that trains children to obey their parents' directions.

An additional problem with assigning treatment packages is that the practice focuses on attending services rather than on what clients should achieve as a result of these services. Goals, in other words, should focus on outcome (Christensen et al., 1999). For instance, rather than going to a perpetrators' group for domestic violence, a goal might be to settle conflict between partners by using time-outs, "I" messages, and behavior change requests. Although the perpetrator group may be a way to achieve this outcome, the focus is not on the journey (which can leave a client with the sense of being endlessly mired in services) but on the destination. Some clients might find the prospect of attending all these classes and services rather daunting. But if their efforts are centered on final results, they might be motivated to attend and participate in services. Alternatively, there might be better ways of achieving outcomes than attending prescribed services.

A further problem with the rote assignment of goals and services is that it assumes that clients are in the action stage of change. However, many CPS clients are in the precontemplation or contemplation stages of change. When clients are unmotivated (precontemplators or visitors), goals should be oriented toward meeting the requirements of the mandate: "Whose idea was it that you come here? What does _____ need to see so you don't have to come here anymore?" Goal setting may also involve working on enhancing the advantages of behavior change and reducing the disadvantages of change. This might mean building coping skills so that clients have alternatives to the problem behavior. It also might mean referral making, so that clients are linked to resources that may improve, for instance, a problematic housing situation that has been causing a lot of stress and endangering the children.

The next section details scaling interventions, a helpful technique not only in developing goals but also in tracking progress and task setting. The following section explores some of the cognitive-behavioral techniques that can be taught as part of the intervention plan.

Scaling Questions

Scaling questions have been detailed throughout the book; therefore, their advantages and the guidelines for formulating scales are not replicated here. Instead, we focus on examples. The first is an investigative interview surrounding Tanya's neglect of her daughter, Lynne; the second revolves around Jamie, the teenager in foster care who has the goal of living independently after she graduates from high school.

With Tanya, the caseworker not only uses scaling interventions for goal setting but also employs them to assess Tanya's willingness to change and her confidence that she will be successful.

CASEWORKER: Let's say we have a scale from 1 to 10, with 1 being further away from what you want, and 10 meaning you have gotten yourself together. What will 10 look like?

TANYA: Having a job, so I can afford to buy food and clothes. Having a nice place for us to live, and being able to continue paying for her to go to day care.

CASEWORKER: Good! Okay, now that we know what you're heading toward, what number would you say you are right now?

TANYA: I would probably be around a 3.

CASEWORKER: You're at a 3 now. How were you able to get from zero to 3?

TANYA: Well, losing my job, my family being evicted, and now somebody has reported me to CPS. All of these things have been like a wakeup call to me. Because the last thing I want to do is lose my child. I know I can provide for her, I've done it for the last 3 years. I guess I just got selfish, hanging out late all the time. But I know I can take care of her. Like I said, I just need to get myself together. I know I can do it.

CASEWORKER: Let me ask you this, Tanya. How hard are you willing to work on getting yourself together so you can provide for Lynne? On a scale from 1 to 10—10 means that you are willing to do whatever is necessary, and 1 means that you are willing to do nothing—where are you on that scale?

TANYA: I'm at a 10.

CASEWORKER: Wow, a 10! Where does all this willingness to work hard come from?

TANYA: I know this is what I should do, what I need to do, what I want to do. So I'm willing to work hard at it. This is my daughter, my baby. I'll do whatever I have to do for her.

CASEWORKER: It sounds like your daughter is very important to you, and that you are committed to working hard. How confident are you that you will be able to solve these problems? On a scale again, 1 means that you have no confidence that you will be able to solve the problem, and 10 means you have every confidence that you will be able to solve the problem. Where on the scale are you?

TANYA: I'm an 8 or 9 on the scale. I have a lot of confidence that I will be able to do it. I've been able to do it in the past.

CASEWORKER: Great! Tanya, it sounds like you feel very capable of solving these problems.

TANYA: Yeah, I know I can do it. It's just a matter of doing it now.

Tanya was able to rate her current situation, her willingness to change, and her confidence that she would be successful in making changes. She had rated her current situation a 3 and compared it with her high motivation to change and her confidence that she could change. Because of Tanya's past capacities and her commitment to making these changes, the caseworker helped Tanya come up with some action steps. These steps are described in sub-section entitled Problem-Solving Skills.

To further demonstrate the use of scaling interventions, we return to the example of 17-year-old Jamie, who has been living in foster care. Jamie had been described by her therapist as "withdrawn, passive, highly anxious, with a fear of success." These descriptors are characterological in nature and seem fixed and unchanging, whereas scaling questions, like many solution-focused interventions, focus on concrete and measurable behaviors. The goal of "getting a driver's license" seems much more achievable than working on Jamie's "passive" and "anxious" qualities. Change is likely to be maximized when specific, concrete behaviors are targeted rather than hypothetical entities (Cade & O'Hanlon, 1993).

CASEWORKER: We're going to use a scale to help us see what you need to do to accomplish your goal, and it will also help us to see what you have done so far. Tell me again what you would like to get done.

JAMIE: I'd like to get my license, actually have it in my hand.

CASEWORKER: Okay, good. So now let's create this scale from 1 to 10, where 10 represents having your license and 1 is on the opposite end, where you have not made any progress. So in order to get to a 10, let's write out what needs to happen.

JAMIE: I need to get behind-the-wheel experience.

CASEWORKER: Okay, that's good. I also want to write down all the steps from the beginning of the process. This may include things you have already done. What are the first things you did?

JAMIE: I had to get my learner's permit, get driving lessons from my foster dad, and take a test. I also took driver's ed in school.

CASEWORKER: So now what do you need to do?

JAMIE: I need to get behind-the-wheel hours from a driving school and then go to the DMV and apply for a license.

CASEWORKER: So now that you know what you need to do in order to be at a 10, where would you place yourself on this scale?

JAMIE: I probably would be at about a 5. I already did all that stuff to get my learner's permit.

CASEWORKER: Wow, Jamie. That's impressive. You're already halfway there. Where do you think your foster dad would place you, since he's the one helping you out?

JAMIE: Probably about a 5 or 6, because I did get my lessons and my permit. I still have the biggest thing to do, though.

CASEWORKER: And what is that?

JAMIE: Get the behind-the-wheel hours. That makes me nervous because I haven't really driven that much.

CASEWORKER: I can see how that might make you scared if you haven't had a lot of experience. Do you have a driving school picked out so you know how much experience they expect you to have?

JAMIE: I have one that is close to my house, and I know child protective services will pay for it, but I don't have any information yet.

CASEWORKER: What can you do to get the information you need?

At this point Jamie identifies that she should call the driving school and ask them questions. Because she seems uncertain how to proceed, the caseworker helps her to write down a list of questions that would be helpful to ask.

After Jamie successfully makes the phone call, she then begins to feel anxious about the behind-the-wheel driving with an instructor. Her first concern is that she does not have enough driving experience yet to make an appointment to start at the driving school.

CASEWORKER: So Jamie, if you feel like you haven't had enough driving experience, what are some things that you can do to help in that area?

JAMIE: Well, my foster dad gave me lessons before, and maybe if I asked him again, he could take me out a few more times before I start the driving school.

CASEWORKER: Do you think that would help you feel a little better about the driving school?

JAMIE: Yes, I'm just not sure I feel comfortable enough driving yet. Getting some more lessons from him could help.

CASEWORKER: I think that sounds like a great plan. Now, what else worries you about starting the driving school?

JAMIE: I don't like the idea of having three other people in the car and that when they come get me, I'm expected to just start driving straight from my house.

CASEWORKER: I can see how those things might be stressful for you. I know that you have experienced other stressful times in your life, not necessarily about driving, but maybe that also. What kinds of things did you do to help deal with the stress?

JAMIE: Sometimes I just avoid doing things that are stressful.

CASEWORKER: Do you think that is going to be helpful for this situation?

JAMIE: No, because I need take these driving lessons, and I can't avoid it.

CASEWORKER: Okay, then let's think about other things you have done.

JAMIE: Well, sometimes I can talk to my therapist, and she helps me. Also my mom sometimes.

CASEWORKER: Those sound like really good ideas. What else helps you to relax when you are feeling stressed out?

JAMIE: Sometimes if I just take a break and read a book, then I can go back and finish something. Maybe I could read and relax before starting the driving lessons.

The caseworker asked the client to detail her progress toward her goal of getting her driver's license. This allowed Jamie to identify the next steps that needed to be taken: first, calling the driving school and, second, getting more driving experience. The caseworker asked her to remember her coping strategies during other stressful times, and Jamie produced ideas on how she could overcome her nerves during the driving practice with other students. The caseworker empowered the client to identify the steps she needed to take to continue moving toward her goal. The client, rather than being passive and withdrawn, as her therapist had described her, took an active role in what she needed to do to get her license.

Now let's look at how Ms. Jackson is encouraged to take an active role in progress toward her goal. Ms. Jackson had already identified the goal of communicating with her daughters and ranked her progress toward this goal at a 4. The caseworker asks how Ms. Jackson can move up one number to a 5.

MS. JACKSON: Well, I can probably work harder at communicating with the girls. I know that sometimes I get so stressed out that I am just about to lose it with them.

CASEWORKER: Okay, what specifically can you do to communicate better with the girls?

MS. JACKSON: I guess if I was more involved with their teachers, then we could talk about school.

CASEWORKER: Good. So getting to know their teachers would help with communication. What specifically could you do to get more involved with their teachers?

MS. JACKSON: I could go to the meetings they have, since all my girls are in special education classes. They always invite me to come, but I don't usually go. Oh, and they also have parent–teacher conferences at the end of the 9 weeks. I could go to those.

CASEWORKER: Okay, what would be your first step in getting to know your daughters' teachers?

MS. JACKSON: The 9 weeks end next week, so I could call the school and ask when the next parent–teacher conference will be.

CASEWORKER: That sounds like a great start. Research shows that when parents are involved in their kids' school, it really improves school performance.

MS. JACKSON: Well, they all need that.

CASEWORKER: What else can you think of that would improve communication with your girls?

MS. JACKSON: Probably having fun time with all of us together. If we were to spend some time just being together watching a movie, I think that would help.

CASEWORKER: Sounds like you have some good ideas. What success have you had with this type of activity in the past?

MS. JACKSON: It was real successful when they were younger, but now that they are teenagers, they act like they don't want anything to do with me.

CASEWORKER: So what is it that makes you think that this will work now?

MS. JACKSON: Well, now that they are in foster care, they seem to miss me more. If they miss me, then when we are together, they will want to spend time with me.

CASEWORKER: So the girls do tell you that they miss you! Can you tell me how you will suggest to your daughters that you spend some time together the next time they come for a visit?

MS. JACKSON: I'll tell them that I have rented their favorite movie and bought popcorn so that on the weekend we can all watch the movie together.

Now that the client is looking forward to what she can do to improve her relationship with her children, we want to capitalize on her motivation and openness to change to give her some new skills that may increase her ability to successfully communicate with her children. The next section highlights some of the work the caseworker did with the client on communication skill building.

Taking Action

Once gaps in knowledge have been identified, the caseworker and client can concentrate on skill building. Skill building comprises both behavioral management and cognitive-behavioral techniques (Tables 13.2 and 13.3; for the application of cognitive-behavioral interventions with parents in the child welfare system for physical abuse, consult Corcoran, 2003). In the strengths-and-skills-building model, a collaborative approach is taken to skill building; that is, the caseworker delivers information in a way that is attentive to client signals about the level of comprehension and engagement (Webster-Stratton & Herbert, 1993). There are several ways this can be achieved (Carroll, 1998).

- Asking parents to talk about what strategies they are aware of or have tried. ("You've said you've tried time-out. Tell me about what happened when you did that. Walk me through the steps.") This gives parents credit for having tried to solve their problems and acknowledges that they are actively engaged in the process of trying to work on their parenting skills. It also identifies for the worker the gaps in knowledge that need to be addressed. For instance, if a father says that he used time-out by putting his stepchildren behind the couch for 2 hours, the worker can educate him on some of the principles of time-out (that it should last a minute for each year of the child's age and be in a place free from reinforcement).
- Asking clients to provide concrete examples of situations in which strategies or skills can be applied ("Can you think of a time last week when your children did that?")
- Eliciting clients' views on how they might use particular skills ("Now that we've talked about praising and time-out, what do you think would work best for you? Which of these techniques have you used in the past? Is there any other way you've tried to teach your children how to mind?")
- Eliciting clients' reactions to the material ("Does this seem like it's an important issue for us to be working on right now, or do you have something else in mind?")

Table 13.3

Behavior Management Techniques

Technique	Example
Prevention: Taking care of antecedent conditions that set up misbehavior.	Ms. Jackson's daughters have trouble going to different rooms in the house to cool down because the house is so disorganized and cluttered. Therefore, cleaning up the house will help the girls be able to go to their own rooms.
Rewards: Offering an incentive for good behavior. This can be an ordinary activity that children expect to do anyway, such as watching TV or playing outside.	Ms. Jackson decides that before the girls go out with their friends, they will have to complete chores.
Distraction: Instead of confronting misbehavior, children's attention is directed to another activity.	When Ms. Jackson's daughters start to argue, she can ask one of them to take a walk outside with her or go to the store with her.
Extinction: ignoring a behavior so that it is no longer reinforced and eventually stops.	Ms. Jackson's daughters "keep on her" so that she gives in to their demands; she refuses to give in, and they eventually learn that it won't get them what they want.
Time-out: As punishment, the child is removed from activities that he or she finds rewarding. He or she is placed in a neutral area of the house in which no rewards are available for a short period of time.	Ms. Jackson adapted this idea to her teen daughters; they could take a walk outside or listen to music in their room by themselves.
Logical consequence: The punishment is a consequence of the misbehavior.	When Ms. Jackson's daughters destroy property, they have to pay for or fix what they have broken.
Effort-based consequences: Chores are assigned as punishment.	When Ms. Jackson's daughters disobey the rules she has set up, they are assigned to clean the house.

- Asking parents to describe the skill in their own words ("We've talked a lot about having the kids take a time-out when they're misbehaving. Just to make sure you're confident about what you want to do, can you tell me what you plan to do when they are fighting with each other and won't stop?")
- Paying attention to clients' verbal and nonverbal cues—these might include lack of eye contact, one-word responses, or yawning ("I no-

tice that you keep looking out the window and I was wondering what your thoughts are on what we're talking about today.")
- Employing frequent modeling and behavioral rehearsal
- Giving feedback in normative terms ("I have another parent I'm working with. She was waiting all week to give her children their reward, but then she realized that a week was too long, and they were too young to remember what they were working toward"; Azar & Ferraro, 2000)
- Using physical and concrete prompts, such as writing things down or placing signs in high-traffic areas in the home. Ms. Jackson identified that she had several strategies for managing her children, such as sending the girls to their rooms and walking outside to calm down. When she became angry and overwhelmed, however, these emotions clouded her ability to recall strategies. Therefore, the caseworker helped Ms. Jackson design a sign to paste on her refrigerator to remind her of plans she could use.
- Using adult analogies to help parents understand information. ("If you worked all day making a nice dinner for your boyfriend and afterwards he didn't say anything, would you do it again?"; Azar & Ferraro, 2000, p. 438). Selekman (1999) uses an exercise with parents in which they are asked to list the characteristics of their best and worst supervisor. From this exercise, parents often see the importance of praise and reward and the problems with criticism, yelling, and physical punishment.
- Complimenting parents extensively by using both "direct" compliments (praise: "You did a good job" and "I liked the way you said that") and "indirect" compliments (implying something positive about the client but pushing the client to figure out the resources used to achieve success: "How were you able to do that?" and "How did you know that was the right thing to say?").
- Offering rewards to parents for following through with skills (meals at McDonald's, toys for the children, a positive report at the next court date)
- Using deductive questioning so that clients are asked questions that will help them figure out connections between their behaviors and their children's learning. For instance, when Ms. Jackson lapses back into her sense of hopelessness ("Sometimes I give them stuff anyway, even when I tell them they're supposed to be good, and that's how they'll get their reward. When they all get on me like that, I just give up"), the caseworker elicits from Ms. Jackson the consequence of "giving in" when she has set up a reward system for certain behaviors.

Now that the general principles of providing information have been outlined, examples of communication skills and referral making (Ms. Jackson) and problem solving (Tanya) will be illustrated.

Communication Skill Building

Communication and listening skills include constructing "I" messages, reflective listening, validating family members' experiences, and making behavioral change requests. In the first part of communication training, individuals are taught the necessity of being vulnerable with their own feelings rather than accusing and blaming the other person. After building this rationale, the caseworker provides the basic format for giving "I" messages: I feel [a description of my emotional reaction] about what happened [a specific activating event].

Ms. Jackson's caseworker introduces the subject with Ms Jackson, first eliciting from Ms. Jackson what she already knows about the topic:

CASEWORKER: Now maybe we can work on some specific skills you can use with your girls. Have you heard of "I" statements?

MS. JACKSON: Isn't that where you say, "I feel"? [in a therapeutic tone of voice]

CASEWORKER: Yes, I'm impressed. You already know about this?

MS. JACKSON: Yeah, one of the in-home counselors used it with the girls. It worked okay. I just felt funny talking that way.

CASEWORKER: It does feel kind of fake in the beginning, but after you get used to it, you'll get more comfortable. And once you get the hang of it, we can talk about adapting it in a way that works best for you and your family.

MS. JACKSON: Well, I would be willing to give it a try.

CASEWORKER: Okay. Give me an example of what you would say.

MS. JACKSON: I would say, "Kathleen, I need you to listen to me when I'm trying to talk to you. I need you to respect the fact that I have to work for us to have food in the house."

The caseworker commends Ms. Jackson for these statements and then provides some education on feeling identification.

CASEWORKER: There are four main feelings: happy, sad, mad, and scared. What feelings do you have in these situations with your daughters?

With prompting, the client is able to relate the following feelings: *mad* that her daughters won't listen to her even though she is the parent, *sad* that her family life has deteriorated to the point where the girls have been placed in foster care, and *scared* that they would never be returned to her and would live out the rest of their teenage years in placement. The caseworker has her rehearse how she could say this to her daughters, and eventually she is able to come up with the following statements.

MS. JACKSON: I would say, "I would like us to be able to work this out. I feel sad that you girls are in foster care, and I'm scared that I won't get you back. We need to be able to talk to each other so that we can be a family without other people being involved."

The caseworker warmly compliments Ms. Jackson on her efforts, encouraging her to speak in this way to her children on the next weekend visit. She says she will also work with the girls and the family as a whole so that these efforts will be successful.

After discussing skill building with Ms. Jackson, the caseworker segues into making a referral for a parenting group so that the client can further her knowledge and skills, as well as gain information and support from others.

CASEWORKER: I know of a parenting group for parents of teenagers who struggle with some of the same issues that it sounds like you are dealing with. What do you think about the idea?

MS. JACKSON [shifts in her seat]: I don't know. [looks at her watch] What would I have to do?

CASEWORKER [Noticing Ms. Jackson's nonverbal communication when asked about the parenting group, the caseworker asks a few questions to explore her feelings further.]: I notice you seem a little uncomfortable with the idea of attending a parenting group. What are your thoughts on the group?

MS. JACKSON: Well, no offense, but I don't want the whole world knowing that my kids are in foster care. How many people are in this group?

CASEWORKER: Well, there are usually between 7 and 10 people in each session, but it doesn't go over 10.

MS. JACKSON: That's not too bad.

CASEWORKER: Tell me, what do you think you could get out of the group?

MS. JACKSON: Well, if they are all parents of teenagers, then maybe they have some ideas for how I could handle my girls better.

CASEWORKER: I think you're right, and you might have some good ideas for them, too. You would be learning from each other as well as from the group leader.

MS. JACKSON: I could definitely use more support.

CASEWORKER: On a scale of 1 to 10 with 10 being ready to call the group leader tomorrow and sign up, where do you see yourself?

MS. JACKSON: An 8 . . . yes, an 8.

CASEWORKER: So it sounds like you're ready to try it.

MS. JACKSON: I think I just need to think about it, and then next week maybe I can get the number from you.

CASEWORKER: That sounds great! I'll have the name of the group leader next week if you decide that you want more information before making a commitment.

MS. JACKSON: So we will meet at the same time next week?

CASEWORKER: Yes, have a good week.

Problem-Solving Skills

The problem-solving process has been outlined in previous chapters so it is not detailed again here (see Table 3.5 for an outline). The process is illustrated here with a dialogue between Tanya and her caseworker.

The caseworker begins the problem-solving process by asking Tanya to select a priority goal. Tanya chooses finding a place for her and her daughter to live. The caseworker explains the brainstorming process as simply free-associating different ideas in order to come up with as many as possible. At first, Tanya can't think of any place that she could go other than a shelter. When the caseworker prompts her as to whether there are other family members she could stay with, Tanya names Lynne's father as a possibility. The caseworker asks about friends. Tanya says she has a lot of friends that she is close to. The caseworker identifies this to Tanya as a strength, that she seems to have a lot of support. Tanya agrees but says that none of her friends would present a housing option because they live with their parents and they wouldn't have room for her and Lynne. Then Tanya remembers a friend she has kept in touch with since high school. They have known each other several years and are close. The caseworker then offers a suggestion—that Tanya apply for Section 8 housing. Ideally, more options should be generated in a problem-solving session, but the interview is already drawing to a close, and the caseworker needs to make sure Tanya has a plan in place.

The next part of the process involves evaluating the alternatives. Tanya explains that she wouldn't feel very safe in a shelter, but she would go if she had nowhere else. Tanya rules out living with Lynne's father because of the instability of their relationship. She fears that if they argued, he would kick her out of his house. Tanya's friend seems to be the best option because Tanya gets along well with her, and her friend enjoys spending time with Lynne. Her friend also has plenty of room for Tanya and Lynne in her house. Tanya's task is to talk to her friend about her and Lynne coming to stay. Section 8 housing is not an immediate solution because the waiting list is a year long, but it is something Tanya can apply for now and possibly use in the future.

As Tanya is concerned about her finances, the caseworker also helps her brainstorm ways that she could find a job, which include looking in the want ads, applying with a temporary work agency, and filling out applications at department stores at shopping centers and malls. Tanya says she has been in the work force since she graduated from high school—for the past 7 years. The caseworker commends her on all her experience and says that it will help her find a job.

However, Tanya realizes that even if she gets a job, she won't get a paycheck for several weeks. In the meantime, Tanya and Lynne have to eat. The caseworker gives her information about obtaining food stamps and income assistance. Before the caseworker terminates the interview, she asks Tanya if she has enough money to purchase food for her and Lynne. Tanya says she has some cash and that she will get her last check from her old job in a few days. The caseworker sets up a follow-up interview with Tanya. Because she is so motivated to change her situation, Tanya commits to completing three tasks before that time, which comprises the implementation part of the problem-solving process: to talk with her friend about letting her and Lynne stay with her and paying her rent as soon as she is able to get a job, to apply for benefits, and to complete and turn in three applications to employers.

Three weeks later, the caseworker and Tanya evaluate Tanya's plan for implementation. Tanya reports that she and Lynne have moved in with her friend. Tanya's friend enjoys having Tanya and Lynne live with her and says that Tanya can stay there until she gets her own place through the Section 8 program. Tanya's food stamps and income assistance applications have been processed, and she is purchasing sufficient food through emergency food stamps. Tanya has also gotten a job at a clothing store in the local mall.

Summary

This chapter has continued the focus from the previous chapter on applying the strengths-and-skills-building model to families in the child welfare system. To illustrate how the stages of the helping process can be applied, this chapter used three cases: a mother who was physically abusive with her teenage daughters, a mother who was being investigated for neglect, and a teenager in the foster care system. The case examples show that the techniques can be adapted to a wide range of situations; choice of technique depends on the situation, the individual clients involved, and the length of time the helping relationship spans. The main theme of the chapter is that change in the interest of protection of children involves collaborating with parents and engaging and empowering them in the process.

References

Azar, S., Barnes, K., & Twentyman, C. (1988). Developmental outcomes in physically abused children: Consequences of parental abuse or the effects of a more general breakdown in caregiving behaviors? *Behavior Therapist, 11,* 27–32.

Azar, S., & Ferraro, M. (2000). How can parenting be enhanced? In H. Dubowitz & D. DePanfilis (Eds.), *Handbook for child protection practice* (pp. 437–624). Thousand Oaks, CA: Sage.

Azar, S. T., & Wolfe, D. A. (1998). Child abuse and neglect. In E. J. Mash & R. A. Barkley (Eds.), *Treatment of childhood disorders* (2nd ed., pp. 501–544). New York: Guilford.

Berg, I., & Kelly, S. (2000). *Building solutions in child protective services.* New York: W. W. Norton.

Berg, I. K. (1994). *Family-based services: A solution-focused approach.* New York: W. W. Norton.

Bertolino, B., & O'Hanlon, B. (2002). *Collaborative, competency-based counseling and therapy.* Boston: Allyn & Bacon.

Cade, B., & O'Hanlon, W. H. (1993). *A brief guide to brief therapy.* New York: W. W. Norton.

Carroll, K. (1998). *A cognitive-behavioral approach: Treating cocaine addiction.* Retrieved August 28, 2001, from http://www.drugabuse.gov/TXManuals/CBT/CBT1.html.

Christensen, D., Todahl, J., & Barrett, W. (1999). *Solution-based casework: An introduction to clinical and case management skills in casework practice.* New York: Aldine de Gruyter.

Corcoran, J. (2003). *Clinical applications of evidence-based family intervention.* New York: Oxford University Press.

DePanfilis, D. (2000). How do I develop a helping alliance with the family. In H. Dubowitz & D. DePanfilis (Eds.), *Handbook for child protection practice* (pp. 36–40). Thousand Oaks, CA: Sage.

D'Zurilla, T., & Nezu, A. (2001). Problem-solving therapies. In K. Dobson & S. Keith (Eds.), *Handbook of cognitive-behavioral therapies* (2nd ed., pp. 211–245). New York: Guilford.

Kolko, D. (2002). *Assessing and treating physically abused children and their families.* Thousand Oaks, CA: Sage.

Malinosky-Rummell, R., & Hansen, D. (1993). Long-term consequences of childhood physical abuse. *Psychological Bulletin, 114,* 68–79.

Miller, W., & Rollnick, S. (2002). *Motivational interviewing: Preparing people to change addictive behavior* (2nd ed.). New York: Guilford.

O'Hanlon, W. H., & Weiner-Davis, M. (1989). *In search of solutions: A new direction in psychotherapy.* New York: W. W. Norton.

Selekman, M. (1999). The solution-oriented parenting group revisited. *Journal of Systemic Therapies, 18*(1), 5–23.

Spiegler, M. (1993). *Contemporary behavior therapy* (2nd ed.). Belmont, CA: Brooks/Cole.

Steinberg, L. (2000, April 1). *We know some things: Parent–adolescent relations in retrospect and prospect*. Presidential address, Society for Research on Adolescence, Chicago. Retrieved November 8, 2003, from http://astro.temple.edu/lds/sra.htm.

Webster-Stratton, C., & Herbert, M. (1993). What really happens in parent training? *Behavior Modification, 17,* 407–457.

14 Working With Nonoffending Parents of Sexual Abuse Victims

JACQUELINE CORCORAN, DIANNA HART,
KRISTIN A. GARELL, AND JANICE BERRY-
EDWARDS

In North America approximately 30% to 40% of females and 13% of males have been sexually abused (Bolen & Scannapieco, 1999). The possible psychological and emotional damage to victims of sexual abuse, both children and adults who were abused as children (Jumper, 1995; Kendall-Tackett, Williams, & Finkelhor, 1993; Neumann, Houskamp, Pollock, & Briere, 1996), and the potential risk factors for molestation have been documented. Unfortunately, several of these factors, including intrafamilial abuse, multiple offenders, continuing abuse with repeated incidents, forced secrecy and threats, and perpetrator exoneration from charges (Kendall-Tackett et al., 1993; Wolfe & Birt, 1997), entail aspects of the abuse that cannot be altered.

There is, however, one factor, that *can* be changed—maternal support (Kendall-Tackett et al., 1993). Support entails both belief and protection. Belief involves validating the child's account, placing the responsibility on the adult rather than on the child, and conveying an attitude of concern (Corcoran, 1998). Protective action involves behaviors that protect the child from further abuse and aid in recovery, such as cooperating with the child protective services and criminal justice agencies, removing the child from perpetrator access, and seeking counseling (Corcoran, 1998).

Evidence has shown that a mother's support is essential to a child's healing and recovery from sexual abuse (Deblinger, Steer, & Lippmann,

1999). Sadly, the time when a mother's nurturance is most needed is often when she herself is experiencing a great deal of stress; women suffer many negative effects (emotional, economic, and social) when they learn of their child's sexual abuse (Carter, 1993; DeJong, 1988; Elliott & Carnes, 2001; Everson, Hunter, Runyon, Edelsohn, & Coulter, 1989; Newberger, Gremy, Waternaux, & Newberger, 1993).

A review of studies revealed that 65% to 80% of mothers deem their children's stories of abuse as true; however, despite their belief, only 29% to 64% of mothers take protective action (Elliott & Carnes, 2001). Although there is a direct correlation between belief and protective action, one does not necessarily lead to the other. In their recent study of 435 primarily African American mothers, Pintello and Zuravin (2001) discovered that only 42% believed and protected their children, 31% neither believed nor protected, and 28% either believed but did not protect or protected but did not believe.

Given the importance of maternal support to children who have been sexually abused, this chapter focuses on how the strengths-and-skills-building model can be applied to mothers during the initial period of a child's sexual abuse disclosure. This period is often one of extreme crisis for both parent and child. It has been suggested from crisis theory that crises usually resolve within 4 to 8 weeks (Parad & Caplan, 1960). Generally speaking, information on interventions with mothers during this period of time is limited; the majority of research has focused instead on treatment *following* this period. Interventions with nonoffending parents are discussed in the next section.

Interventions for Nonoffending Mothers

Interventions taking place during the sexual abuse disclosure period include crisis theory and social learning. In Corcoran (1995), crisis intervention at a police department victim services program had several components: (a) processing of the victims' and their families' feelings and experiences; (b) providing information about law enforcement and the legal process, victims' compensation, and education on sexual abuse dynamics; (c) helping parents handle talking to their children about the abuse and how to manage symptoms in their children; (d) discussing parents' coping mechanisms; and (e) providing referrals for ongoing counseling. A follow-up survey indicated that 67% of nonoffending parents found victim services "very helpful" and 25% found them "somewhat helpful" (Corcoran, 1995). Most children had attended counseling beyond crisis intervention at the police department (65%), and half of adult caregivers (50%) attended counseling. Unfortunately, there was only a 7.58% response rate to the survey, so results were biased in terms of who responded to the survey.

In the Jinich and Litrownik (1999) study, social learning involved having parents view a 20-minute informational video on how to convey supportiveness to their children. Although parents in the social learning videotape condition did not perceive themselves as being more supportive, behavioral observations showed that they did, in fact, appear to act supportively, and their children reported less distress than the children of parents who watched the "control" video.

As for the treatment literature with nonoffending parents, most of the work is described as cognitive-behavioral in nature. Cognitive-behavioral treatment for sexual abuse focuses on feeling identification and management, coping mechanisms, managing child sexual abuse symptoms through behavioral techniques, handling discussions with children about the sexual abuse, and providing information on sexual abuse dynamics, sex education for children, and sexual abuse prevention (Cohen & Mannarino, 1993; Deblinger & Heflin, 1996). Cohen and Mannarino's treatment is designed for preschool children and their parents; Deblinger and Heflin emphasize the treatment of child posttraumatic stress disorder (PTSD) symptoms. Cognitive-behavioral treatments have produced improved adjustment for both parents and children over control and comparison conditions both at pretest and at follow-up periods (Cohen & Mannarino, 1996, 1997; Deblinger, Lippmann, & Steer, 1996; Deblinger, Stauffer, & Steer, 2001; Stauffer & Deblinger, 1996). (See Corcoran, in press, for a review.)

Principles of the Strengths-and-Skills-Building Model

Typically, when sexual abuse is disclosed and the perpetrator is a family member, the child protective services (CPS) system expects a mother to take in the information and quickly decide whether or not she will support her child. Exploration of a woman's feelings and motivation is critical, so that she does not feel so pressured that she latches onto defense of the perpetrator, a response that may become entrenched. Bernard (1997) indicates that a woman's initial level of supportiveness may not change over time. Although cognitive dissonance is used in motivational interviewing to create discrepancy between values or beliefs and problematic behaviors, cognitive dissonance can also work in an undesirable direction. For example, a woman, pressured into making a decision, may support the perpetrator over her child and then feel forced to defend and maintain this position she has taken.

The way to achieve the priority of children's safety is to develop a collaborative relationship between the helper and the nonoffending parent. A woman's strengths, her coping skills in the midst of a period of intense distress and crisis, and her supportive attitudes and behaviors are amplified through solution-focused techniques, as well as motivational interviewing. Education on sexual abuse dynamics is also critical to help mediate mothers' emotional distress and assist them in gaining more empathy for their children. However, other sources, such as Deblinger and Heflin (1996), provide excellent information on sexual abuse dynamics, so their material is not reproduced here.

Instead, this chapter focuses on the phases of the strengths-and-skills-building model. Engagement is explored first, followed by problem exploration. Although collaboration and strengths are a theme throughout, because of the serious nature of sexual abuse and the priority for child safety during the disclosure process, solution exploration is not discussed as a separate phase. After problem exploration, goal setting—described mainly in terms of helping mothers build supportive attitudes and behaviors and cope with the crisis of disclosure—and taking action toward these goals are discussed.

Engagement

Engagement involves listening and validating a woman's concerns when she learns that her child has been sexually victimized. The worker's initial task, which continues throughout the helping process, is to create a supportive atmosphere for the mother by listening to and validating her concerns. Her reactions may include shock and denial or disbelief ("This isn't happening. This can't be happening. This isn't real." "She [he] can't be telling the truth"), anger (at the perpetrator, at the child, at herself), sadness for what has been lost and the hurt that has been done to the child, disgust or sickness, betrayal, and fear (of losing her child, her partner, her relationships with family members, her home, her freedoms) (Corcoran, 2002). The worker reflects the mother's experiences empathetically ("I know how hard this must be for you," "You don't want this to be true," or "You're furious with your child") and avoids opposing the client with statements such as "You need to take action. Your daughter will be taken away from you if you don't protect her." The mixed feelings and the ambivalence inherent to intrafamilial sexual abuse are validated as normal responses and reflected by the worker ("On one hand, you can't believe that your husband would do something like this, and you also know that your daughter would not make this up if it didn't happen"). During this time, the worker should reinforce any *supportive* statements a mother might make: "I can see you're a very attentive mother." "You really care about your children. You want what's best for them." Although assessment of maternal belief and protective action begins with the moment of first contact, problem exploration will take a more targeted approach.

Problem Exploration

Problem exploration first involves assessing and building the mother's level of support by asking the mother questions to elicit self-motivational statements (see Table 2.2). A more explicit way to discuss the advantages and disadvantages of increasing maternal support is through the decisional balance, which is explored later in this section. Also discussed is a way to assess maternal attributions—that is, whom she holds responsible for the abuse.

Self-Motivational Statements

If the relationship with the mother starts to become polarized, the worker needs to adjust strategies, with what Miller and Rollnick (2002) refer to as reflective and strategic statements (Chapter 2). Techniques for eliciting self-motivational interviewing and making reflective and strategic statements are described in the following example.

Ms. Rhonda Connelly, White, age 29, is the mother of 13-year-old Amy. A CPS report alleges sexual abuse of Amy by her father, Roger James. The report specifies that, 3 days earlier, Mr. James had shown nude pictures of Amy to her friend Meghan, who was visiting in the home that evening. Upset, Meghan informed her mother when she returned home later that evening. Meghan's mother then reported her daughter's experience to the police. Although Mr. James and Ms. Connelly are divorced, they have remained friends over the years. At the time of the incident, Mr. James was staying at the Connelly home to visit with Amy.

Using a search warrant, the police secured the photographs of Amy and arrested Mr. James. In an interview with a police officer, Amy disclosed sexual contact with her father. Since this disclosure was made, Amy has retracted her statement about sexual contact with her father.

While the CPS worker interviewed Amy, Ms. Connelly interrupted to ensure Amy's well-being and to remind Amy that she did not have to talk with the worker unless she wanted to do so. In the interview, Amy maintained her retraction of the alleged sexual contact. Amy acknowledged that the nude photographs of her were taken by Mr. James when she was less than 11 years old but claimed she could recall no other specifics of the incident.

After the interview with Amy, the CPS worker explained the authority, procedures, and goals of CPS to Ms. Connelly.

WORKER: Ms. Connelly, I can see you are very concerned and protective of Amy. [reframing her behavior during Amy's interview] I appreciate your coming in to speak to me and permitting me to interview Amy. From the information I received, you have been through a lot over the past few days. Tell me how these sexual abuse disclosures are affecting you. [eliciting problem recognition]

MS. CONNELLY: What sexual abuse? Meghan is lying. My poor little girl! That police officer scared her—threatened to take her to the hospital for a pelvic exam. Amy told me that she said this about her father because she was afraid to have a pelvic exam. This on top of seeing her father handcuffed and taken away in a police car. Everyone in the neighborhood is talking. And Amy is afraid every one in school is going to talk about her.

WORKER: You sound extremely angry with what Amy experienced as a result of Meghan's disclosure and the police intervention. [simple reflection]

MS. CONNELLY: I am! The police mishandled this whole thing!

WORKER: Tell me more about how this has affected you. [eliciting problem recognition]

MS. CONNELLY: I'm humiliated! I feel so overwhelmed and out of control. Here I am on Saturday afternoon with friends sitting around the living room talking. The police show up and give me this piece of paper and start searching my house. They find those photographs and pass them among themselves. Roger is handcuffed and put in a police car. I mean, there were at least three police cars in front of the house. Then one policeman takes Amy into her bedroom alone and won't let me in or tell me what is going on. Another officer shows me those photographs, asking me to identify Amy and Mr. James. The officer interviewing Amy tells me that Amy told him Mr. James has been having sex with her and told me to get her a medical exam. Then they all leave. Amy is crying and upset. I'm crying and upset.

WORKER: Sounds like a nightmare. You have the police invading your home and taking over. On top of that, they hit you with the pictures and the news of Mr. James having sex with Amy. Then they leave as abruptly as they arrived. [simple reflection]

MS. CONNELLY: It was the worst day of my life.

WORKER: How did you cope with all that? [coping question]

MS. CONNELLY: I was furious and hysterical. I've never been through anything like this. Amy wouldn't talk with me when I tried to find out what she told the police. She wouldn't talk with me about the pictures. Amy locked herself in her bedroom and told me to leave her alone. I called Roger's parents to let them know. On Sunday morning I had to go off for a while to get away from it all. When I got back, Amy came out of her bedroom and told me that she had lied to the police about her father because she was afraid of getting a medical exam. I was so relieved to hear her say Roger hadn't sexually abused her. The police have made a big mistake. I taped Amy saying it wasn't true. Roger's parents asked me to tell his attorney, which I did.

WORKER: So you were upset about the police intervention and eager to clear Mr. James by taping Amy's retraction. [amplified reflection]

MS. CONNELLY: Yes, I'm very angry with the police. I wasn't trying to help Roger, though—I thought the tapes would stop this madness.

WORKER: You wanted the sexual abuse situation to go away. [amplified reflection]

MS. CONNELLY: I made the tape so Amy didn't have to talk with anyone else. I was helping her—protecting her from having to talk about this anymore.

WORKER: I find it admirable that you want to protect Amy. I wonder what needs to be done to protect her from Mr. James's wanting to take pictures of her. [agreement with a twist]

MS. CONNELLY: I can make sure Roger doesn't have another opportunity to take pictures like that.

WORKER: Tell me, what would have been your concerns if Amy had told you about Mr. James having sex with her? [eliciting concern for the problem]

MS. CONNELLY: I don't want to think about it. It's horrible! It's not true, so why should I think about it?

WORKER: It sounds like the thought of Amy having sex with her father is too painful for you to contemplate. [simple reflection] Let's look at this for a second. What would be some reasons for a child to say she is being sexually abused and then say she is lying? [deductive questioning]

MS. CONNELLY: Well, obviously, a child was made to make an untrue statement and wants to correct it.

WORKER: What else?

MS. CONNELLY: She is afraid of what people will think about her. [pauses] I can tell you want me to keep going. A child could think no one believes her or would take care of her if she says she is sexually abused. A child could be afraid of what would happen as a result of telling. I don't see how this is helpful—you heard Amy say that her father did not have sex with her.

WORKER: Good! You seem to have a good grasp on the reasons for a child to retract her sexual abuse allegations. By the way, has Amy had contact with her father since his arrest? [shifting focus]

MS. CONNELLY: Amy hasn't seen him, although Roger has asked me to bring her to the jail.

WORKER: So you've spoken to Mr. James. Has Amy spoken to him?

MS. CONNELLY: Well, she took a message from him when I was away from the house Sunday morning.

WORKER: I see, so Amy had contact with Mr. James. How much does it concern you that Mr. James spoke to Amy over the telephone? [eliciting concern for the problem]

MS. CONNELLY: Not much. Oh, I see. You think Roger talked Amy into retracting her statement. But Amy says she lied because the police officer intimidated her. I believe my daughter.

WORKER: I agree that the way the police handled the situation was upsetting, but what caused them to come to the house with a search warrant? [agreement with a twist/deductive questioning]

MS. CONNELLY: Meghan telling them about Roger's pictures.

WORKER: Who was ultimately responsible for the police coming to your door?

MS. CONNELLY: Well, Roger took the pictures and then he showed them to Meghan. Roger shouldn't have shown those pictures. I realize that.

WORKER: I recall you saying Amy won't discuss the pictures with you. What are your concerns about these pictures? [eliciting concern about the problem]

MS. CONNELLY: Roger told me that he took the pictures to document Amy's physical development. I don't know what the big deal is. You know, these pictures would not be considered pornography in any other country.

WORKER: Hey, you've done some of your own investigating, haven't you? Good for you! So you're saying that as long as it's okay in some other country, it makes it okay with you for Mr. James and Amy? [amplified reflection]

MS. CONNELLY: I didn't mean that! Roger should not have taken those pictures of Amy. And he should not have shown them to Meghan.

WORKER: What worries do you have now for Amy regarding Mr. James taking these pictures? [eliciting concern about the problem]

MS. CONNELLY: Well, I'd like to know why she won't talk to me about these pictures. I'm worried that she will be ostracized at school. Amy is such a lovely girl!

WORKER: What are your concerns about Amy's relationship with her father? [eliciting concern about the problem]

MS. CONNELLY: Amy is very close to her father. She talks with him better than she talks with me. It's always been that way. I'm not going to let her be alone with him again. But I don't want to jeopardize their relationship.

WORKER: It sounds like Amy does have a very special relationship with her father. It also sounds like you're left out. This is characteristic of sexually abusive father–daughter relationships. The daughter appears closer to the father, and mother is out in left field somewhere, in the dark about what's going on between the two. [reframing]

[Ms. Connelly appears to consider this information.]

WORKER: How do you think Amy has been affected by these pictures? [eliciting problem recognition]

MS. CONNELLY: Just because Roger took those pictures does not mean he was having sex with Amy. I haven't noticed any problems with Amy during the time since these pictures were taken. What has harmed her is the way the police handled this matter. Since Saturday, Amy has been having nightmares and isn't sleeping well.

WORKER: Having nightmares and difficulty with sleeping are definite indicators that Amy is having trouble handling what has happened to her. What do you think about Amy receiving counseling to help her process what's going on and to help her recover from all her experiences related to this sexual abuse report? [agreement with a twist]

MS. CONNELLY: Amy definitely needs counseling—so do I, for that matter. I'll get in touch with our family doctor to find out what I need to do to arrange for counseling. Even though Amy will go to counseling, I don't think she needs to talk about the sexual abuse issues anymore. I don't even want the counselor to bring it up.

WORKER: If you continue not wanting Amy to talk about her experiences related to the photographs, what do you think will happen? [eliciting concern about the problem]

MS. CONNELLY: Oh, if Amy wants to talk about it, that's okay, but I would rather she be allowed to forget about it. What I'm worried about is Amy being forced to testify in court or talk with any more authorities.

WORKER: Well, I have enough information to keep CPS involved to help you protect Amy and support her recovery from this ordeal. Whether Amy testifies in court depends on what Mr. James decides to do about these photographs. So, in essence, Mr. James will be the one who decides if Amy testifies or not. The prosecutor tries not to have the child testify unless there's no other choice in presenting the evidence to protect the child.

MS. CONNELLY: Roger better not cause Amy to testify! I think he's done enough to hurt Amy already.

WORKER: You sound angry with Mr. James. It sounds like you're considering his role in this matter. [simple reflection]

MS. CONNELLY: Yeah, I feel manipulated and confused. Roger is calling collect from jail and wants to talk to Amy.

WORKER: What do you or Amy see as a reason for concern about these phone calls? [eliciting statements for intention to change]

MS. CONNELLY: You know, that's very strange! Amy didn't seem to care this afternoon when I told her that she missed her father's call. She shrugged her shoulders and went on talking about her day at school.

WORKER: Well, Ms. Connelly, what are you thinking you should do now? [eliciting statements for intention to change]

MS. CONNELLY: I'm not sure. All these years, I see Roger and Amy having this close relationship—then I see those pictures. Fathers don't take pictures like that of their daughters.

WORKER: On one hand you have valued Amy's relationship with her father and, now, you have doubts because the pictures are inappropriate. [double-sided reflection] What do you think needs to be done? [eliciting statements for intention to change]

MS. CONNELLY: Well, I don't think Amy should have contact with her father until he gets a better understanding of what a father is, and he gets out of jail. But how do I go about doing this? There's a visitation order. And Amy and I haven't been very close for a while. I don't want to drive a wedge into what relationship we do have.

WORKER: It sounds like you're concerned about what you're up against if you try to stop contact between Amy and her father. [simple reflection]

MS. CONNELLY: I'm now realizing that Amy does not feel close enough to confide in me. I'm afraid that Amy will hate me if I have to be a heavy and keep her away from Roger.

At this point, the worker explains the legal processes operating to restrict contact between Mr. James and Amy. Ms. Connelly and the worker solidify plans for counseling and contact restrictions.

At the beginning of the interview, Ms. Connelly is angry, argumentative, and in denial about the sexual abuse problem. Ms. Connelly initially viewed the police intervention as the primary problem her family was facing. Through the use of motivational interviewing, Ms. Connelly changed toward more appropriate protective and supportive thoughts, feelings, and plans for action. Ms. Connelly acknowledged the nude photographs of her daughter were inappropriate and placed increased responsibility upon Mr. James for the problem. Ms. Connelly agreed to seek counseling for Amy and herself and recognized the need for contact restrictions.

Decisional Balance

Another motivational technique, the decisional balance, more explicitly lays out the advantages of supporting children versus the disadvantages of doing so. The decisional balance technique is illustrated with the example of Mae, a 31-year-old White woman with two daughters, who is deciding whether to have her husband or her child leave.

Mae is married to Tommy, 44 years old, who has just admitted to the police and CPS to sexually molesting their daughters, Donna (age 12) and Julie (age 10). The CPS worker is discussing with Mae the agency policy for either the victim or the offender to leave the house during the legal and treatment process. This policy is to ensure safety and healing for the involved individuals and the family as a whole. Through motivational interviewing, Mae understands the need to separate Tommy and the girls but is ambivalent about who should leave the home.

MAE: I love them all. I just don't know what to do. I'm angry with Tommy for touching the girls, and I'm angry with the girls for not telling me right away and letting it go on for so long.

WORKER: Your feelings are similar to other mothers in the same situation and very understandable. I know we won't be able to resolve all the issues at once—it will take time—but I can tell from my contact with all of you, there's a lot of love and strength here in your family that will get you through this challenge.

The worker acknowledges Mae's feelings and normalizes them by comparing them with other mothers' reactions. The worker compliments the family and instills hope with her observations of the family members and her reframe of "this challenge."

WORKER: Let's take a look at the pros and cons of your options and see if one stands out more than the other does. Want to give it a try?

MAE: We might as well, because I'm feeling pretty overwhelmed with thoughts spinning around in my head.

The worker labels one sheet of paper with Tommy's name and another with the names of Donna and Julie. The worker draws a dividing line, denoting two sections on each sheet, and labels one section of each sheet "advantages," and the other "disadvantages."

WORKER: Okay, Mae, where do you want to start? With Tommy leaving the home or the girls leaving the home? What is the first thing that comes to mind?

MAE: Well, my thought is that I want my girls with me so I can watch over them. I want to put my arms around them, hold them, and tell them I love them and I'll be there for them no matter what. Then I think that I want Tommy at home so I can talk with him. He's my best friend, and I want him to put his arms around me while I cry on his shoulders.

WORKER: Yes, to comfort your little girls and to be comforted by your best friend. Let's see—we'll list "my daughters could be with me" and "they'll know I love them and I will stick by them no matter what" under advantages for Tommy leaving. Under advantages of the girls leaving, we'll list "Tommy would stay with me" and "I'd have his companionship."

The worker acknowledges Mae's thoughts and feelings on both sides of her ambivalence. At the same time, there is emphasis on "your little girls" to stress their dependency.

The worker continues to work with Mae to identify other advantages and disadvantages of Tommy or the girls leaving until Mae's key concerns are identified.

Advantages of Tommy Leaving the Home
1. My daughters could be with me.
2. They'll know I love them and will stick with them no matter what.
3. I would avoid my family becoming angry with me if I tell them I chose Tommy over the girls.
4. The neighbors won't think badly of me.

Advantages of Donna and Julie Leaving the Home
1. Tommy would be with me.
2. I'd have his companionship.
3. I would have some distance from Donna and Julie's preteen troubles.

Disadvantages of Tommy Leaving the Home
1. I'll have to parent the girls alone.
2. I'll have to become responsible for taking care of the car and Tommy's work around the house.
3. Tommy may decide he doesn't want a wife and family any more and make the separation permanent.
4. I won't have all of Tommy's paycheck available to me.

Disadvantages of Donna and Julie Leaving the Home
1. They might have to live with strangers in foster care.
2. I won't be able to stay on top of what they are doing.
3. They might think I don't love them anymore.
4. They might think I believe it's their fault.
5. Social services would be in my life indefinitely.
6. I might have to pay child support for them.

This example involves a parent who is actively engaged in deliberating about the advantages and disadvantages of each course of action. The main intervention at this stage is to increase the advantages of supporting the child (e.g., support is important for the child's safety and recovery; it reduces long-term CPS involvement) and to decrease the advantages of siding with the perpetrator (e.g., provide mother with referrals to resources and services that may help with housing and finances; connect mother with alternative sources of social support).

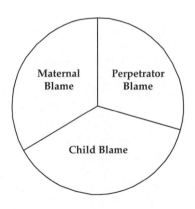

Perpetrator Blame
- "He should never have done that to a child."
- "He took advantage of my child."
- "There is something wrong with him that he would do that to a child."

Maternal Blame
- "I should have been watching."
- "I shouldn't have left him alone with her."
- "I am a bad mother."

Child Blame
- "She should have told me."
- "She shouldn't have let it happen."
- "She shouldn't have gone over there."

Figure 14.1. Pie of Attribution

Assessing Attributions

Mothers may assign responsibility to various parties associated with the abuse. The mother may partly blame herself, the perpetrator, her child, and perhaps others. Berliner (1997) suggests using "a pie of attribution" as an assessment device. In this intervention, a mother divides up the "pie" according to how much responsibility she places on each person connected to the abuse (see Figure 14.1). This gives both her and the caseworker greater clarification when it comes to her thoughts and feelings about the abuse and where further attention is warranted. For example, if a mother is particularly blaming of a child, then presenting information on sexual abuse dynamics in a collaborative way may be necessary. If a mother is blaming of herself, perhaps cognitive restructuring would help her gain a more realistic appraisal of the situation and place responsibility more appropriately on the perpetrator. If she has put her child at risk, ways she can ensure her child's safety are paramount.

Goals

The main goal of work at the stage of disclosure is to build maternal support of a child who has been sexually abused. A secondary goal is to help mothers manage the crisis of disclosure. This is not only to help mothers during this difficult time but also because maternal adjustment affects children's recovery (Deblinger et al., 1999). Although these goals are critical for the safety and well-being of the child who has been sexually abused, individualized goals in service of these overarching objectives can also be negotiated.

Building Maternal Support Through Scaling Questions

Caseworkers typically make a decision about the level of a woman's support in a dichotomous way: Is she supportive or not? However, intrafamilial sexual abuse brings up a host of conflicting feelings and loyalties in parents. Therefore, it is more helpful to consider support on a continuum rather than as an all-or-nothing entity, as there are more possibilities for change and for movement when a mother is assessed in this way.

Scaling questions, detailed in Chapter 5 as a way to formulate and track goals, can also be used as an assessment tool for maternal support. In this intervention, the caseworker anchors 1 as no support and 10 as total support and asks the mother to identify the thoughts and behaviors that would demonstrate her support at 10. This aspect of the intervention not only helps educate mothers about what support entails but also uncovers gaps in knowledge and distorted beliefs about sexual abuse of children (e.g., the child somehow provoked the abuse). A mother is asked to rank herself on this scale, and, if a period of time has elapsed since the disclosure, she is asked to rank herself where she first was. Many times, mothers have made a shift in their level of support over time. They are then asked to account for their change in belief and accompanying behaviors through exception-finding questions.

The following example shows how a caseworker uses a scaling intervention to assist a mother (Renee) in becoming more supportive and protective of her daughter (Terry, age 15). Note how the worker interweaves empathy, exception finding, relationship questions, deductive questioning, and education about sexual abuse in this intervention.

Renee is a 34-year-old White woman married to a man named Frank. Together they have three children. Terry recently revealed that her father had sexually abused her. She was removed from the home and placed in foster care because Frank initially denied the abuse, and Renee could not provide a protective, supportive home at the time. Since then, Frank admitted to the sexual abuse, and Renee revealed that she had been sexually abused by her own father.

WORKER: Renee, you look pretty sad today. What's going on with you?

RENEE: Even with Frank out of the house, foster care won't let Terry come home. They're letting her visit with her sisters and me, but no one is talking about her coming home for good.

WORKER: Sounds like you're pretty confused.

RENEE: I am. I don't know what's going on.

WORKER: What have you been told by foster care about Terry coming home?

RENEE: They tell me that they want to make sure she is protected and gets the support she needs to get over what Frank did to her. But I believe her now. Frank is going to prison and won't be around. Terry can go to therapy from my house, just like she's going from my sister's house. What more do they want?

WORKER: So Frank is out of the house, and you now believe Terry. You are also willing to take her to therapy. Tell me, what was going on between Terry and you when Terry was placed in foster care?

RENEE: Well, after Terry told me about her father, CPS wouldn't let me see her. Terry called me once from the hospital, but it didn't go well. I asked Terry why she was lying about her father and trying to hurt our family. I'm really sorry now I asked her that.

WORKER: It sounds like you are unhappy with how you talked to Terry that time. What would you like to see for Terry now?

RENEE: I'm her mother. I want to see Terry healthy and happy. But what do I need to do to get my daughter back?

WORKER: We can take a look at where you were when Terry told you that her father had sexually abused her. And then look at what you can do to help Terry become a healthy and happy young woman. Are you willing to work on this?

RENEE: I want to know what I need to do.

WORKER: Let's draw a line. [She does so on a piece of paper.] On one end is 1 and the other is 10. The 1 is not believing or protecting your daughter; 10 represents the thoughts and behaviors you will have when you are showing total support and protection of Terry.

RENEE: Okay, but I think I've done that all along, even though I believed her father at first, rather than her.

WORKER: Renee, believing your daughter involves accepting her disclosure as to what really happened and putting the responsibility for the abuse on her father, the perpetrator, and being committed to whatever is needed to help Terry recover. Being protective is keeping Terry from any further abuse or harm—preventing her from hurting any worse. It includes working with the police and child protective services, and also getting therapy and any other services that would aid Terry's recovery. So, considering this scale we are building, what would you consider as 10? It might be helpful to think about what might have been helpful for you as a child when your father sexually abused you.

RENEE: You're tough! I would want my mother to tell me that the abuse really happened—to talk and act about it like something as real as my own name. [Renee grips her hands in fists, and tears start running down her cheeks.] I would want my mother to tell me she is sorry for not believing me and for hurting me by not believing me. I would want my mother to tell me she loves me no matter what—even knowing what my father made me do. I would want my mother to tell me that the abuse was not, in fact, my fault, and my father was the one who did wrong. I would want my mother to tell me sincerely that she still loves me, even after I get all my anger at her out.

WORKER: Wow! That's a lot of things to do for a 10. When you do all these things, what will you be saying to yourself?

RENEE: Right now I feel really useless, because it appears I knew the whole time what I should have done for Terry. I was just too confused and afraid to think about it. What would I say to myself? I love Terry. I'm going to be a real mother to her now.

WORKER: How are you doing? This exercise is really hitting on some painful issues.

RENEE: Despite the tears, doing this is an eye-opener!

WORKER: Sounds like you're ready for the next step. On this 10-point scale, where do you see yourself right now?

RENEE: I see myself at a 3.

WORKER: A 3. What's that about?

RENEE: Well, I believed Frank sexually abused Terry because he confessed—not because she told. Now I see that I should have believed Terry in the first place. Really believed it! Even though Terry has visited, we have not talked about what happened—we just enjoy being a family for a few hours, and then Terry goes to my sister's. I feel really bad about not being there for her.

WORKER: Where on the scale would your sister place you?

RENEE: Right now, I think my sister would put me at a 5. I'm in therapy, and I believe Terry. I also won't have anything to do with Frank now. My sister likes that.

WORKER: How about your daughters who are still with you, Susie and Lori?

RENEE: I think they would put me around a 6. They are happy to visit with Terry. They see that I now know that Terry has been telling the truth all along. But they don't think I'm doing well with the stress.

WORKER: And where do you think Terry would place you on the scale?

RENEE: I keep thinking about how lousy a mother I am now. But, thinking over what we have been through, I would think Terry puts me at 5 because I do believe her now.

WORKER: You've placed yourself at 3. What would 4 look like? What would you be doing and saying?

RENEE: I want to work through this with Terry in therapy. I have a lot to talk with her about, but I don't know how to say it.

WORKER: Going to mother—daughter counseling looks like something you could do that would move you one step. How would you put this plan in place?

RENEE: I think I'll call the foster care worker to find out what I need to do to have counseling with Terry.

The worker and Renee finalize details of this plan, such as deciding when she would make the call and rehearsing what she would say to the foster care worker. The scaling interventions help this mother see the changes she has already made. Relationship questions—asking Renee questions from the perspectives of other people—give her different views on how she comes across. Getting her to think about moving one number up the scale means that she will continue to progress toward greater belief and support.

Building Maternal Coping Skills Through Scaling Questions

Scaling interventions are also helpful when mothers are anxious, depressed, and feeling overwhelmed by the circumstances of disclosure. The concrete nature of scales makes such experiences somewhat more manageable, as the following example demonstrates.

Betty's husband, Rob, was recently jailed for sexually abusing their 11-year-old daughter, Samantha. Betty now has full responsibility for caring for her four children. She also has a medical problem with her legs, which is aggravated by a job that requires her to stand for hours at a time.

BETTY: I've been doing a lot of crying. I'm not getting enough sleep. And I have to have people repeat themselves to me at work. I can't concentrate.

WORKER: Anything else?

BETTY: I'm doing a lot of "what if" thinking—what am I going to do if Rob doesn't give us any money after he gets out of jail? What if the therapy doesn't help, and Samantha continues acting out and gets in real trouble? I'm always worrying, especially at night when I'm trying to go to sleep.

WORKER: What you're describing is a normal reaction to the disruptions in your life. Would you like to take a closer look at what's happening so you can manage this reaction and get some relief?

BETTY: I don't know if that's possible—but I need to get a handle on this before I lose it altogether.

WORKER: Okay, Renee, let's look at the stress reaction you're handling and develop a 10-point scale to address where you want to be. What will it look like when you're at a 10?

BETTY: You mean, like I would be sleeping through the night or going back to sleep without a problem if I happen to wake up for any reason?

WORKER: That's good! What else?

BETTY: I would stop this constant thinking and worrying. Or I would be able to think about something less bothersome or be able to pay attention to what I'm doing, instead of worrying.

WORKER: You'd be able to exercise some control over what you're thinking when you find yourself worrying. What kind of things would you be saying or thinking to yourself if you were at this point—at this 10?

BETTY: Saying to myself? What do you mean?

WORKER: Well, right now, you told me that you keep thinking about the "what-ifs." When you're having these thoughts, what are you saying to yourself?

BETTY: Oh, I see. I'm telling myself that I can't handle everything.

WORKER: Okay, if you were at this 10, what would you be telling yourself?

BETTY: I would like to be able to tell myself, "I don't like what's happened, but my kids and I are going to make it. Like we always do."

WORKER: That's a great way to talk to yourself. Next we need to place where you think you are at on this 10-point scale we're making. If 1 is "losing it," where would you put yourself right now?

BETTY: I don't know—3 maybe.

WORKER: A 3? That's pretty good! What have you been doing to get to a 3?

BETTY: I get up, get the kids going, go to work—the routine stuff.

WORKER: What else is going on to give yourself a score of 3?

BETTY: Well, I cry a lot.

WORKER: Tell me about the crying.

BETTY: Well, I'll break down crying when Samantha is ugly toward me, or when my 3-year-old asks where his dad is. And I'm not sleeping a whole lot. Maybe 3 hours right now—max. I'm just so tired. I feel like I'm walking through molasses.

WORKER: So you're having a tough time right now managing work and the kids' needs without enough sleep. We'll talk more about what you can do about that. First, let's talk about where on the scale others would place you. Where on the scale do you think Samantha would place you and why?

BETTY: Samantha would put me at 7. She is so busy being Samantha—and also trying not to show me how she feels—she doesn't see a lot of what I'm doing. She sees me pushing her like I always do—getting her up for school, making her do her homework—despite all her remarks.

WORKER: What about Detective Smith?

BETTY: Oh, Detective Smith? He thinks I'm great. I've done everything that's been asked of me. Who knows? He probably puts me at an 8.

WORKER: How about your mother?

BETTY: Mom? That's tough! She would see me at a 6. I've been talking to Mom—and crying on her shoulder. Mom keeps telling me that she has seen me go through hard times before, and I've come through with only a little wear and tear. And that's what she keeps telling me.

WORKER: It looks like others think you're doing better than you think you are. Tell me what needs to happen to move you to a 4 on the scale.

BETTY: Getting more sleep! I know I could think more clearly, and I would have more energy.

Scaling questions allow Renee to develop a more realistic appraisal of herself when she ranks herself according how others see her. The intervention also helps her center on a tangible, salient concern, her sleeplessness, rather than being overwhelmed with everything she is going through. To cope with her worries, the caseworker can further teach Betty cognitive restructuring and problem-solving skills, which are addressed in the next section.

Taking Action

As applied to work with nonoffending parents of sexual abuse victims, taking action involves enhancing their support of their children and bolstering their coping strategies. The collaborative delivery of information on sexual abuse dynamics and skill building are discussed in this section. Although these interventions are geared toward terminating services after the disclosure period, workers may also need to assess parents' motivation to continue with CPS involvement and/or ongoing counseling.

Delivering Information Collaboratively

Parents often need direction on how belief can be conveyed, which sometimes relates to their understanding of sexual abuse dynamics. This information is best relayed through a collaborative process in which the worker uses deductive questioning, adult analogies, and normalizing of parents' concerns. The following example demonstrates this process with a mother who questions her child's account, a behavior that tends to indicate an attitude of nonbelief. After the example, a discussion on helping mothers believe when perpetrators deny is presented.

Cathleen, who is White, is the 34-year-old mother of Ginger, age 12. Ginger has disclosed sexual abuse by Greg, the husband of Cathleen's best friend, Sally, while she was spending the night with Sally's daughter. Ginger had given a statement describing the sexual abuse to a CPS worker and a police detective but had not told her mother beforehand. After the CPS worker had informed Cathleen of Ginger's allegations, Cathleen would not accept the worker's review of Ginger's statement and questioned Ginger in depth when Ginger came home from school, despite the worker's caution not to do this.

The next day the guidance counselor at Ginger's school contacted the CPS worker. Ginger had come to the counselor that morning, crying, wanting to "take back her statement" because her mother "is angry and doesn't believe her." The CPS worker had visited Ginger at her school to reassure her, and then the worker went to see her mother at the home.

WORKER: Cathleen, I'm concerned about Ginger and how upset she is by your questioning her over the details of the abuse.

CATHLEEN: I know I had agreed not to question Ginger, but Sally's my best friend. I didn't want her husband to be accused of something he didn't do. I wanted to make sure Ginger was telling the truth. I have a lot of doubts because she just could not tell me the specific weekend each time something happened, and she couldn't tell me what his penis looked like. Anyway, I've been having trouble with her telling me stories lately to get herself out of trouble.

WORKER: Cathleen, I hear you are concerned for your friend and her family. But, tell me, what do you think are the reasons I asked you not to get into heavy questioning with Ginger?

CATHLEEN: Well, maybe because Ginger was already upset and my questioning her got her even more upset.

WORKER: Good. What else?

CATHLEEN: If a kid does tell about being sexually molested, she needs support—not a lot of hassle.

WORKER [observing Cathleen lighting a fresh cigarette from her last]: Let's say, Cathleen, you were mugged at the convenience store where you went out late to get a pack of cigarettes. You make a police report and go through the interviews with the police by yourself because Stan can't leave the children unattended to be with you. When you get home, Stan does not hug you and check if you're all right. Instead, he launches into a third degree, questioning you about what happened, insisting you describe the assailant, and repeatedly asking if you were sure that the assailant had a gun. I could go on, but I think you get the general idea. How would you feel?

CATHLEEN: I would be devastated. I know I would want to cry on Stan's shoulder and have him tell me I'm okay. With all those questions, I might think I was at fault. You know, I would think he didn't believe me. Okay, I see why you didn't want me to question her.

WORKER: What would have been a more supportive, caring way of handling Ginger last night?

CATHLEEN: I guess giving her a hug and asking her to tell me how she was feeling. Maybe I could have told her what you had told me about the molestation and then let her know she can talk with me about anything—that I love her. I am, however, still concerned that she is telling the truth—these are serious accusations.

WORKER: Okay, you did mention she had been telling stories. What kind of stories has she been telling?

CATHLEEN: Ginger's been lying about having homework so she can watch TV or talk on the phone.

WORKER: So how are these two types of lies different?

CATHLEEN: Different? Oh, lying about her homework is kind of self-serving. Telling on Greg is—well, it isn't self-serving—Ginger doesn't get any benefit from telling.

WORKER: Well, what do you think?

CATHLEEN: When you look at it like that—there is a difference. I guess I'm angry that she did not come to me when it first happened. I have told her over and over again to tell me if anyone touches her like this.

WORKER: It's been my experience that children usually don't tell anyone right away. And when they do, they tell someone else—a friend or someone at school like a guidance counselor or teacher. Just like you, their parents have told them to come to them immediately when something like this happens. What do you think is going on that the kids don't tell their parents?

CATHLEEN: Ginger told me that she was afraid to tell—afraid I'd get angry and upset with her because she didn't tell right away and because she didn't make it stop. Ginger also said she didn't think I would believe her.

WORKER: Well?

CATHLEEN: I got my answer. I guess Ginger read me right. I feel so bad. I wouldn't tell me anything either if I was in her shoes.

WORKER: When Ginger gets home from school this afternoon, how will things be different?

CATHLEEN: I think right now, Ginger would probably like a big hug, an "I love you," and an "I'm sorry" from me when she gets home.

This example shows how the caseworker used deductive questioning ("What do you think are the reasons I asked you not to get into heavy-duty questioning with Ginger?" "What would have been a more supportive, caring way of handling Ginger last night?"), adult analogies (using the example of the mother being a crime victim and her husband acting in a nonsupportive way), and education about how children have difficulty telling their parents about the abuse to help this mother gain empathy for her daughter's position. Delay in telling their parents is a common reason for mothers' frustration with their children at disclosure. Therefore, it is important for parents to understand the many possible reasons children do not tell: The perpetrator threatens the child; the child does not want to get the offender in trouble; fear that the child will be blamed and/or punished if the abuse is discovered; loyalty to the perpetrator; fear for the effect on the family; shame and embarrassment; and confusion and helplessness (Deblinger & Heflin, 1996).

Mothers also often find it difficult to believe their children when the perpetrator denies the abuse. Indeed, a majority of offenders, at least initially, fail to admit to the abuse (Sirles & Franke, 1989). This may confuse some nonoffending parents and pose a dilemma about whom to believe: their partners or abusive relatives, on the one hand, or their children on the other. It is helpful if caseworkers discuss this phenomenon with mothers in normative terms ("What are the reasons offenders might lie about having been sexually abusive?"). Mothers usually can see that offenders have a lot to lose by admitting to their behavior: arrest, possible prison time, probation, mandated treatment, and loss of family. These consequences are tangible and practical. The practitioner may also encourage mothers to consider the psychological factors behind offenders not admitting to sexual abuse. To this end, the practitioner could ask the mother to share how the offender has coped with wrongdoings in the past. A mother may report that the offender has difficulty admitting when he is wrong. The offender may have become ashamed and stopped speaking with persons he may have offended in other ways in the past. Other reasons identified may be the offender's fears of losing control in his life, reinforcement of preexisting self-esteem problems, and loss of support from relatives and friends. Some individuals holding high social status become severely depressed and suicidal when anticipating the loss of esteem from family and friends. Other offenders are fearful or are reluctant to give up their perception of their special relationship with their child victim. A conversation in which mothers discuss reasons why perpetrators in general might deny helps mothers understand the many possible reasons the offender in her particular case might also fail to admit the abuse.

Many other dynamics of sexual abuse may confuse a parent, including why children's accounts of the abuse might change and how the perpetrator is able to engage the child in sexual abuse. A caseworker may follow a similar process for explaining information in these situations.

Skill Building

This section focuses on helping mothers handle the distress they experience when they learn of their child's sexual abuse. Cognitive coping, problem solving, and communication skill building are some techniques that may be applied.

Cognitive Coping

Cognitive interventions can be especially helpful to women undergoing the trauma of the sexual abuse disclosure (Deblinger & Heflin, 1996). For example, if a woman continues to hear in her mind the perpetrator's accusations of her child's deception, she may oppose these statements with positive self-talk, such as "Children wouldn't make up such a thing, especially when they are as young as my child." If a mother is not confident in her ability to take care of herself and her child, she may counter these doubts with positive assertions, such as "I didn't think I could handle this, but so far, I've survived—I will get through this. I have a strong social support system if I need help."

In cases of sexual abuse, parents may hold erroneous beliefs about the nature of sexual abuse or are excessively self-blaming about the occurrence of the abuse. Cognitive restructuring—disputing irrational or unhelpful beliefs in a systematic way—may be a helpful technique to employ in these types of situations.

Cognitive restructuring is illustrated with Melanie, whose 12-year-old daughter, Jenny, was sexually abused by Don, Melanie's husband and Jenny's stepfather.

MELANIE: I remember the day Jenny is talking about. I was home recuperating from a tubal ligation. Friends invited us over for the evening, and Don insisted that we go, even though I had been instructed to take it easy. You're filled with air to perform the procedure, and there's a lot of pain and swelling. Anyway, I give in and go to the party with Don. I have some drinks on top of the painkillers. I know that's a bad combination, but Don insisted. When we get home, Don is full of himself and wants to have sex. I just couldn't. I had just had surgery, and I was passing out from the alcohol and painkillers. Don gets mad and leaves the room. I don't remember a thing after that until the next day. I feel responsible for Don abusing Jenny.

WORKER: It sounds like that day was pretty rough on both Jenny and you. You feel responsible for the abuse. Tell me specifically what feelings you're having about the abuse. [identify the feeling]

MELANIE: I feel guilty and depressed. I'm furious with myself.

WORKER: You have mentioned that you feel responsible. What thoughts are behind these feelings? [identify the underlying thoughts]

MELANIE: I think I caused Don to go to Jenny for sex when I wouldn't have sex with him that night.

WORKER: If it's okay with you, let's take a look at how you caused Don to abuse Jenny.

[The worker begins the process here of challenging the inaccuracy.]

MELANIE [doubtfully]: Okay.

WORKER: Was this the first time in your relationship with Don that you weren't able or willing to have sex with him?

MELANIE: No.

WORKER: How did Don deal with it in the past?

MELANIE: He would go on to sleep or watch television.

WORKER: And Jenny has been in the house during these times?

MELANIE: Of course, Jenny has always been with me.

WORKER: Has Jenny reported or disclosed any other incidents of sexual contact with Don before this occasion?

MELANIE: No! Up until this time, Jenny and Don have gotten along wonderfully. There's many a night that I've gone on to bed and left the two of them up watching a movie. You've spoken with Jenny—has she mentioned anything before this one night? She hasn't to me.

WORKER: No, Jenny hasn't. What are some givens? Don knows Jenny is 12 years old. Don knows he is Jenny's stepfather. Don seems to have average intelligence and has been reared in the United States. So he has an understanding that 38-year-old men do not have sex with their 12-year-old daughters.

MELANIE: That's not a given for me. When I was 11, my mother's boyfriend raped me.

WORKER: Do you blame your mother?

MELANIE: Yes, because when I told her, Mom said I was lying and that it was my fault—if I hadn't been so friendly toward him, it wouldn't have happened. Mom did nothing to get rid of the guy, and it continued until I ran away.

WORKER: So the message you got from your mother was what?

MELANIE: That I caused that man to abuse me, and I was responsible for stopping him.

WORKER: Do you think what Don did to Jenny was her fault?

MELANIE: Of course not! She's just a little girl. She loves Don. He was the father she never had. They had a great relationship until this happened. Jenny trusted him.

WORKER: Who went into Jenny's bedroom and sexually touched her?

MELANIE: Don did.

WORKER: Did you tell Don, "Leave me alone—let Jenny take care of you"?

MELANIE: No, I most certainly did not.

WORKER: When Jenny told you about the abuse by Don, how did you react?

MELANIE: I cried with Jenny. I told her I loved her, and I believed her.

WORKER: Melanie, did you make Don sexually abuse Jenny?

[The worker starts the process of constructing alternative thoughts.]

MELANIE: No.

WORKER: What thoughts could you put in place of the ones that tell you you're responsible for Don abusing Jenny?

MELANIE: I didn't make Don abuse Jenny. I had surgery that day and could not have sex. Most husbands accept this and get over it. Don should have. Don had no right to touch Jenny. Jenny trusted him. I trusted him. Don betrayed both Jenny and me. Once I found out, I have made sure Don couldn't do it again.

WORKER: How do you feel now?

MELANIE: A whole lot better. Relieved. I'm angry with Don. I'm also eager to do what needs to be done to take care of Jenny. Because of what I went through, I'm going to make sure Jenny gets all the help and support she deserves.

Problem-Solving Skills

The material on cognitive restructuring segues to problem solving, because sometimes in order to debunk negative thinking, a mother might have to come up with alternatives she has not yet tried. Problem-solving skills are taught so that when mothers encounter an unfamiliar situation, instead of resorting to hopeless thinking ("I can't do anything about this," "I'm powerless"), they work to generate alternatives. The problem-solving process involves the following steps (D'Zurilla & Nezu, 2001): (a) define the problem, (b) brainstorm options, (c) weigh the pros and cons of various options, (d) select the best alternative and implement it, and (e) evaluate the implementation.

This intervention is illustrated with Ruth, who is attending a support group for mothers whose children have been sexually abused. Even though Wes, Ruth's husband, is out of the home, Ruth brings him dinner every night and does his laundry. Wes talks to her at length about what he is going through by telephone or when she drops off his dinner. Ruth states she is exhausted after working all day and ends up having little time for Sherry, the daughter Wes molested.

The practitioner asks the group to help Ruth define the problem: Ruth is so busy taking care of Wes that she has little time to take care of Sherry and herself. The practitioner asks the group to brainstorm options to solve the problem while Ruth writes up the ideas generated by the group and herself. The suggestions include hanging up on Wes when he calls, getting an answering machine and deleting or choosing when she will pick up Wes's messages, telling Wes that she is too tired to take care of his dinner and laundry and that she will no longer do these jobs for him, limiting his calls to 15 minutes or specific times of the week, and working it out in couples therapy.

The group then names the advantages and disadvantages of each viable course of action. Ruth was not comfortable with hanging up on Wes. Ruth also felt unable to tell Wes on her own that she was going to stop cooking and doing laundry for him. Ruth decided that the answering machine gave her some control over the timing of the calls without directly confronting Wes.

When Ruth acknowledged that she needed to stop cooking and doing laundry as soon as possible, the group brainstormed again how Ruth could address this particular issue. Judy, another group member, offered that she and her husband could meet with Ruth and Wes for coffee. Judy's husband is also a sexual abuse offender who is further along in therapy and group work. With the help of Judy's husband, they could engage Wes in a discussion about taking care of himself and allowing Ruth the opportunity to restore herself and take care of Sherry.

Ruth chooses to purchase an answering machine and accepts Judy and her husband's offer of assistance to approach Wes about taking care of his own cooking and laundry. With an answering machine, Ruth can screen calls and control when she would talk with Wes. The coffee with Judy and her husband would give Wes the advice and support of another man who has "been there" and has learned new independent living skills, providing a model to Wes of someone who shares similar circumstances and has made significant progress.

Communication Skill Building

The caseworker can also talk to mothers during the period of disclosure about their communication skills, so that they can better handle pressure from the offender and other family members, build appropriate support systems, and discuss with their children topics related to the abuse. Mothers must learn to communicate self-assertively (expressing one's own feelings and needs while considering the rights of others) instead of passively (avoiding expression of needs) or aggressively (expressing feelings and needs without considering those of others). They must also learn that assertive communication involves three key components: emotion ("I feel), action ("what happened"), and need (desire for behavioral change).

To illustrate, the group facilitator contrasts the three different ways to handle a situation by using Ruth, the mother who has been entangled with her husband, Wes. Passivity involves Ruth not saying anything at all and letting Wes talk at length to her each night. As a result, Ruth does not have time for Sherry and herself. An assertive response uses the "I" position: "I am very tired, Wes, and don't have time or energy to give you my full attention. If there's any business I need to know about, tell me quickly so I can get back to Sherry and our dinner [homework, etc.]." The third way is to be aggressive: Ruth yells at Wes, "Stop calling me! I'm sick and tired of listening to your whining and demands. Do your own laundry! I don't care if you starve to death." Then Ruth hangs up the phone on him.

The group members discuss possible reactions Wes may have to the different messages. Although some group members feel that Ruth is justified in speaking harshly because Wes hurt Sherry and Ruth, they could see that such an exchange might result in Wes taking repercussions, such as withdrawing financial support or his guilty plea or requiring Sherry to testify to the abuse. In contrast, if Ruth makes her request politely without hostility, she might end the telephone conversation quickly and get back to whatever she is doing with minimal emotional distress. Teaching mothers these communication skills helps them gain confidence that they can manage their families without the perpetrator's involvement.

Parents also often experience difficulty with communicating to their children about sexual abuse. However, parents, unlike professionals, spend the most time with their children. Therefore, if they are trained in appropriate responses, they can help their children handle the abuse experience. Despite the rationale given, parents may demonstrate some resistance about talking to the child about sexual abuse. In Table 14.1, the various reasons named by parents are posed, along with responses to reassure them. The practitioner can stress that the parent need not always have the answers; the skill of reflective listening conveys acceptance of the child's concerns (Deblinger & Heflin, 1996). Reflective listening is paraphrasing back to the speaker the gist of his or her message with the following format: "What I hear you saying is . . ." or "You feel . . . [feeling word]." Listening reflectively to children is beneficial because it helps them feel understood by and close to their parents. It also gives them the words to express their own feelings and thoughts. When this communication is internalized, the child is more self-aware and has more self-control (Deblinger & Heflin, 1996).

Another critical aspect to parents' communications to their children is that they assure them that in no way was the abuse their fault. For a variety of reasons, children have a tendency to assume responsibility for the abuse with potential damaging consequences to beliefs about themselves (see James, 1989).

Summary

This chapter has covered how the integrative strengths-and-skills-building model can be used with nonoffending parents whose children have recently disclosed sexual abuse. The approach works toward bolstering strengths,

Table 14.1

Addressing Parents' Concerns About Talking to Their Children About Sexual Abuse

Parents' concerns	Possible responses

1. Parents worry that they (parents) will get upset.	a. Process the abuse experience in group and/or individual therapy first.
	b. If they do become emotionally upset:
	  • Reassure child not to blame for feelings
	  • Identify feelings for child
	  • Reassure child that parent has other adults she can turn to for support

2. Parents worry that their child will become upset.	a. See this as positive sign that children are expressing their feelings about the abuse. b. Reinforce the child for sharing feelings with parent ("I'm glad you told me about this"). c. Provide reflective listening and comfort for the child.
3. Parents won't know how to respond to children's questions or concerns.	a. Reflectively listen to children's concerns. b. Admit that aspects of the abuse or the disclosure process are difficult to understand. c. Tell the child that parent will seek guidance from group facilitator or individual therapist.
4. Children start to talk about the abuse when parents are busy.	a. Take time out to listen to the child's concerns, if possible. b. If not possible, assure child that parent will come back to the topic later (set a specific time).

maximizing maternal supportiveness, and enhancing skills. This chapter has described specific ways these aims can be operationalized so that parents' and their children's adjustment from sexual abuse will be achieved.

References

Berliner, L. (1997, March). *Child abuse treatment*. University of Texas at Arlington special speaker's series, Arlington, TX.

Bernard, C. (1997). Black mothers' emotional and behavioral responses to the sexual abuse of their children. In G. K. Kantor & J. Jasinski (Eds.), *Out of the darkness: Contemporary perspectives on family violence* (pp. 80–89). Thousand Oaks, CA: Sage.

Bolen, R., & Scannapieco, M. (1999). Prevalence of child sexual abuse: A corrective meta-analysis. *Social Service Review, 73,* 281–301.

Carter, B. (1993). Child sexual abuse: Impact on mothers. *AFFILIA, 8,* 72–90.

Cohen, J. A., & Mannarino, A. P. (1993). A treatment model for sexually abused preschoolers. *Journal of Interpersonal Violence, 8,* 115–131.

Cohen, J. A., & Mannarino, A. P. (1996). A treatment outcome study for sexually abused preschool children: Initial findings. *Journal of the American Academy of Child and Adolescent Psychiatry, 35*, 42–50.

Cohen, J. A., & Mannarino, A. P. (1997). A treatment study for sexually abused preschool children: Outcome during a one-year follow-up. *Journal of the American Academy of Child and Adolescent Psychiatry, 36*, 1228–1235.

Corcoran, J. (1995). Child abuse victim services. *Family Violence and Sexual Assault Bulletin, 11*, 19–23.

Corcoran, J. (1998). In defense of mothers of sexual abuse victims. *Families in Society, 79*, 358–369.

Corcoran, J. (2002). The Transtheoretical Stages of Change Model and Motivational Interviewing for building maternal supportiveness in cases of sexual abuse. *Journal of Child Sexual Abuse, 11*, 1–17.

Corcoran, J. (in press). Treatment outcome research with non-offending caregivers of sexual abuse: A critical review. *Journal of Child Sexual Abuse.*

Deblinger, E., & Heflin, A. H. (1996). *Treating sexually abused children and their nonoffending parents: A cognitive-behavioral approach.* Thousand Oaks, CA: Sage.

Deblinger, E., Lippmann, J., & Steer, R. (1996). Sexually abused children suffering posttraumatic stress symptoms: Initial treatment outcome findings. *Child Maltreatment, 1*, 310–321.

Deblinger, E., Stauffer, L., & Steer, R. (2001). Comparative efficacies of supportive and cognitive behavioral group therapies for young children who have been sexually abused and their nonoffending mothers. *Child Maltreatment, 6*, 332–343.

Deblinger, E., Steer, R., & Lippmann, J. (1999). Maternal factors associated with sexually abused children's psychosocial adjustment. *Child Maltreatment, 4*, 13–20.

DeJong, A. (1988). Maternal responses to the sexual abuse of their children. *Pediatrics, 81*, 14–21.

D'Zurilla, T., & Nezu, A. (2001). Problem-solving therapies. In K. Dobson & S. Keith (Eds.), *Handbook of cognitive-behavioral therapies* (2nd ed., pp. 211–245). New York: Guilford.

Elliott, A., & Carnes, C. (2001). Reactions of nonoffending parents to the sexual abuse of their child: A review of the literature. *Child Maltreatment, 6*, 314–331.

Everson, M. D., Hunter, W. H., Runyon, D. K., Edelsohn, G. A., & Coulter, M. A. (1989). Maternal support following disclosure of incest. *American Journal of Orthopsychiatry, 59*, 197–207.

James, B. (1989). Treating traumatized children: New insights and creative interventions. New York: Free Press.

Jinich, S., & Litrownik, A. (1999). Coping with sexual abuse: Development and evaluation of a videotape intervention for nonoffending parents. *Child Abuse and Neglect, 23*, 175–190.

Jumper, S. A. (1995). A meta-analysis of the relationship of child sexual abuse to adult psychological adjustment. *Child Abuse and Neglect, 19*, 715–728.

Kendall-Tackett, K. A., Williams, L. M., & Finkelhor, D. (1993). Impact of sexual abuse on children: A review and synthesis of recent empirical studies. *Psychological Bulletin, 113,* 164–180.

Miller, W., & Rollnick, S. (2002). *Motivational interviewing: Preparing people to change addictive behavior* (2nd ed.). New York: Guilford.

Neumann, D. A., Houskamp, B. M., Pollock, V. E., & Briere, J. (1996). The long-term sequelae of childhood sexual abuse in women: A meta-analytic review. *Child Maltreatment, 1,* 6–16.

Newberger, C. M., Gremy, I., Waternaux, C. M., & Newberger, E. H. (1993). Mothers of sexually abused children: Trauma and repair in longitudinal perspective. *American Journal of Orthopsychiatry, 63,* 92–102.

Parad, H., & Caplan, G. (1960). A framework for studying families in crisis. *Social Work, 5,* 3–15.

Pintello, D., & Zuravin, S. (2001). Intrafamilial child sexual abuse: Predictors of postdisclosure maternal belief and protective action. *Child Maltreatment, 6,* 344–352.

Sirles, E. A., & Franke, P. J. (1989). Factors influencing mothers' reactions to intrafamily sexual abuse. *Child Abuse and Neglect, 13,* 131–139.

Stauffer, L. B., & Deblinger, E. (1996). Cognitive behavioral groups for nonoffending mothers and their young sexually abused children: A preliminary treatment outcome study. *Child Maltreatment, 1,* 65–76.

Wolfe, V. V., & Birt, J. A. (1997). Child sexual abuse. In E. J. Mash & L. G. Terdal (Eds.), *Assessment of childhood disorders* (pp. 569–623). New York: Guilford.

PART IV

Measurement

15 Measures for Assessment and Accountability in Practice With Families From a Strengths Perspective

THERESA J. EARLY AND
W. SEAN NEWSOME

Traditional assessment of clients often has the intent of arriving at an understanding of the client's problems. In strengths-based interventions, however, assessment seeks to uncover positive aspects of the client's situation and functioning, such as "survival skills, abilities, knowledge, resources, and desires that can be used in some way to help meet client goals" (Early & GlenMaye, 2000, p. 119). Several authors have elaborated the need for human services to include assessment of strengths as part of practice (Early & GlenMaye, 2000; Ronnau & Poertner, 1993; Weick, Rapp, Sullivan, & Kisthardt, 1989). These and several other works describe the dimensions on which strengths should be sought (Cowger & Snively, 2002; DeJong & Miller, 1995; Dunst, Trivette, & Mott, 1994; Rapp, 1997). For instance, Ronnau and Poertner describe a family systems approach to strengths assessment that concentrates on elements such as family functions, subsystems, culture, and life cycle. Dunst, Trivette, and Mott (1994) identify the need for assessment of family strengths in overlapping cognitive, attitudinal, and behavioral components. Cowger and Snively (2002) focus on strengths and deficits at both the client and environmental levels. Several of these works also describe important elements of the process of a strengths assessment, highlighting important aspects of interviewing such as pointing out strengths to family members to enhance the family's confidence that they can change their situation (Ronnau & Poertner, 1993).

As interventions have become more strengths-oriented, practitioners have the additional responsibility to document the outcomes of their interventions. To be successful, practitioners need to base their interventions on research evidence. They also need to assess the progress of clients to judge the effectiveness of these interventions with individuals (Cournoyer & Powers, 2002). However, because traditional assessment looks for problems, few instruments exist to measure strengths.

This chapter, building on an earlier article (Early, 2001), is intended to fill this gap for those who practice from a strengths perspective and need to measure treatment objectives and outcomes. We describe measures that have been designed to elicit strengths with children and families, as well as those that elicit strengths and problems in relatively equal measure. The latter were included because of the small number of instruments that have been constructed exclusively from a strengths perspective. For both types of instruments, the focus is on how to use them in a solution-generating way, even if the measure also identifies problems. We describe measures for families and measures for children separately.

We searched several sources to identify measures, including collections of instruments (Corcoran & Fischer, 2000; McCubbin & Thompson, 1991), recent social work research on measures for families and children (Combs-Orme & Thomas, 1997; Tutty, 1995), and selected practice materials (Dunst, Trivette, & Deal, 1994; Fraser, 1997; Walton, Sandau-Beckler, & Mannes, 2001). Each of the instruments described has acceptable psychometric properties; that is, the authors judge that each one measures what it intends to measure, based on evidence presented by the creator of the measure or other researchers, and each one works the same way time after time. This evidence about validity and reliability is summarized for the reader's information in Tables 15.1, 15.2, and 15.3. Each of the measures described is a self-report measure that captures information from the perspective of one or more individuals in the family. Other measures that reflect a professional's view, for instance, are not included.[1]

At the end of the chapter are some guidelines for administering and using measures with individuals. We also give several examples of how measures can be introduced and employed in the process of a collaborative

1. Gilgun (1999) has provided a set of instruments, developed from a risk and resilience perspective, to document family risks and strengths from a clinician's perspective. Two other measures from the child welfare field gather information from a child welfare worker's perspective, using an ecological understanding of family functioning. These are the North Carolina Family Assessment Scale (Kirk & Reed Ashcraft, 1998) and a revision of the scale called the Strengths and Stressors Tracking Device (Berry, Cash, & Mathieson, in press).

Table 15.1

Strengths-Based Measures for Families

Title and author	What it measures	Scales and subscales	Who completes	Reliability	Validity
Family Resource Scale, Dunst & Leet, 1987	Adequacy of tangible and intangible resources		Parent or other adult family member	Items are reliable and measure is moderately stable over time	Face validity as assessed by authors of this chapter: measure seems to measure what is intended (resources); total scores are correlated with similar measures such as the Personal Well-Being measure and the Commitment to Intervention measure
Family Functioning Style Scale, Deal, Trivette, & Dunst, 1988	Family strengths and capabilities	Interactional Patterns, Family Values, Coping Strategies, Family Commitment, Resource Mobilization	Parent or other adult family member, individual or two or more members complete together	Internal consistency: both split-half and average correlations among the 26 items indicate an internally consistent measure	Criterion validity assessed in relation to Family Hardiness Index: total scores correlated fairly strongly (r = .62). Predictive validity assessed in relation to the Psychological Well-Being Index (PWI) and the Mastery and Health subscale of the Family Inventory of Resources and Management (FIRM): elevated scores were related to a better sense of personal well-being on the PWI and fewer family-related health problems on the FIRM.
Family Support Scale, Dunst, Jenkins, & Trivette, 1984	Social support for families	Informal kinship; Spouse/partner support; Social organization; Formal kinship; Professional services	Parent or other adult family member	Fairly high reliability reported in both internal consistency and split-half methods; quite stable over short-term (1 month, r = .91) and fairly stable longer-term (1 year, r = .50)	Criterion validity assessed in relation to Questionnaire on Resources and Stress: correlations moderate and in the expected direction.

(continued)

Table 15.1 (continued)

Strengths-Based Measures for Families

Title and author	What it measures	Scales and subscales	Who completes	Reliability	Validity
Family Empowerment Scale, Koren, DeChillo, & Friesen, 1992	Empowerment in terms of personal attitudes, knowledge, and behaviors	Family level, Service system, Community/political	Parent or other adult family member	Internal consistency of subscores is strong, ranging from $r = .88$ to $r = .87$. Reliability also reflected in short-term stability over 3–4 weeks	Content validity assessed by classification of items by independent raters and factor analysis to check for agreement with conceptual framework. Both reported to be acceptable. Discriminant validity: Subscores discriminated parents who were behaviorally involved in each type of advocacy activity from those who were not.

Note. Information on reliability and validity is condensed from available studies. Consequently, the measures of reliability and validity vary from measure to measure. Ideally, we would report that same information for each measure so that comparison would be easier. Unfortunately, that is not possible at this time.

Table 15.2

Additional Measures for Families

Title and author	What it measures	Scales and subscales	Who completes	Reliability	Validity
Parental Strengths and Needs Inventory, Strom & Cooledge, 1987	Parenting efficacy	Satisfaction, Success, Teaching/guidance, Parenting Difficulties, Parenting Frustrations, Information Needed	Parent and child (separately)	Internal consistency ranges from $r = .67$ to $r = .93$ for the areas of parenting (satisfaction, difficulties, etc.) and from $r = .88$ to $r = .95$ for the strengths index and needs index	Construct validity assessed by 30 human development graduate students who match responses from original survey to items on instrument; degree of agreement exceeded 91%.
Parent-Adolescent Communication Scale, Olson, McCubbin, Barnes, Larsen, Muxen, & Wilson, 1992	Communication aspect of Circumplex Model of Family Functioning	Open Family Communication, Problems in Family Communication	Parent(s) and adolescent (separately)	Internal consistency assessed in a sample of adolescents and parents. Values were satisfactory for research purposes but a little low for diagnostic use, especially on the Problems in Family Communication subscale	Face validity: assessed by chapter authors as acceptable. Construct validity: factor analysis yielded 3-factor solution. All of the items from one of the factors were contained in the Problems in Family Communication subscale, so the scale authors elected to continue using the two scales described
Parent Perception Inventory, Hazzard, Christensen, & Margolin, 1983	Children's perceptions of positive and negative parental behaviors	Mother Positive, Father Positive, Mother Negative, Father Negative	Child (ages 5–13)	Positive and negative items all significantly correlated with the appropriate scale in a study that examined differences in distressed and nondistressed families. Internal consistency measures also are acceptable.	Convergent validity: assessed by computing correlations between this measure's subscales and a measure of children's self-concept and a parental measure of conduct disorders. Results were in predicted directions with high positive behavior correlated with high self-esteem and negative behavior scores related to scores on the conduct disorder measure.

(continued)

363

Table 15.2 (continued)

Additional Measures for Families

Title and author	What it measures	Scales and subscales	Who completes	Reliability	Validity
Family Assessment Device, Epstein, Baldwin, & Bishop, 1983	Family functioning—the McMaster Model	General functioning, Problem solving, Communication, Roles, Affective responsiveness, Affective involvement, Behavior control	Individual family members (parents, youth)	Scales have strong internal consistency; test–retest reliabilities over 1 week were moderate	Differentiates between healthy and poorly functioning families. Comparisons to the Marlowe–Crown Social Desirability test suggest scores are relatively free of the influence of socially desirable responding.
Family Assessment Measure (FAM-III), Skinner, Steinhauer, & Santa-Barbara, 1995	Family functioning—the McMaster Model, Total family functioning, Individual within family functioning, Functioning of specific dyads	Subscales: Task Accomplishment, Role Performance, Communication, Affective Involvement, Affective Expression, Control, Values and Norms	Individual family members	Reliability of General Scale and Dyadic Relationship Scale are very strong for both adults and children 10 and older. Reliability of Self-Rating Scale is good for both adults and children.	Scores found to significantly differentiate between families involved and not involved in mental health treatment. Two subscales identify response biases: Social Desirability and Defensiveness.

Table 15.3

Strengths-Based Measures for Children

Title and author	What it measures	Scales and subscales	Who completes	Reliability	Validity
Behavioral and Emotional Rating Scale, Epstein & Sharma, 1998	Behavioral and emotional strengths of children ages 5–18	Strengths Quotient and five subscales: Interpersonal Strengths, Family Involvement, Intrapersonal Strengths, School Functioning, Affective Strengths	Parent, teacher, or other adult caregiver	Internal consistency of Strengths Quotient strong, and test–retest reliabilities are also high. Interrater reliability for subscales ranged from $r = .83$ for Interpersonal Strengths to $r = .96$ for Family Involvement, with coefficient for the Strengths Quotient $r = .98$ (in a study that rated males attending an alternative school independently by pairs of special education teachers. Consistency of parent and teacher ratings largely agree.	In development of the instrument, items were deleted if they did not discriminate between children with and without emotional disorders; therefore, content validity is high. Criterion-related validity assessed by comparing ratings to those obtained by established measures of the constructs: Strength Quotient $r = .77$ with the Walker-McConnel Scale of Social Competence and School Adjustment; $r = .57$ with the Scholastic Competence score and $r = .61$ with the Behavioral Conduct score of the Self-Perception Profile for Children.
School Success Profile, Bowen & Richman, 1997	Protective and risk factors for children ages 5–18	Social Environment Profile: Neighborhood, School, Peers, Family dimensions. Individual Adaptation Profile: Support, Self-Confidence, General Well-Being	Youth	Cronbach's alphas: Neighborhood Support = .80 Neighborhood Youth Behavior: .88 Neighborhood Safety: .80 School Satisfaction: .72 Teacher Support: .86 School Safety: .84 Friend Support: .87 Peer Group Acceptance: .79 Friend Behavior: .91 Family Togetherness: .91 Parent Support: .91 Home Academic Environment: .76 Parent Education Support: .75 School Behavior Expectations:	Range of factor loadings for items on each subscale: Neighborhood Support: .34 to .70 Neighborhood Youth Behavior: .60 to .81 Neighborhood Safety: .43 to .67 Teacher Support: .49 to .72 School Safety: .48 to .75 Friend Support: .71 to .86 Peer Group Acceptance: .53 to .76 Friend Behavior: .67 to .82 Family Togetherness: .76 to .84 Parent Support: .79 to .87 Home Academic Environment: .62 to .71 Parent Education Support: .44 to .72 School Behavior Expectations: .54 to

(continued)

Table 15.3 (continued)

Strengths-Based Measures for Children

Title and author	What it measures	Scales and subscales	Who completes	Reliability	Validity
				.83 Social Support: .80 Physical Health: .75 Happiness: .72 Personal Adjustment: .64 Self-Esteem: .84 School Engagement: .79 Trouble Avoidance: .78 Adult Social Capital: .73	.76 Social Support: .50 to .73 Physical Health: .56 to .64 Happiness: .56 to .71 Personal Adjustment: .71 to .84 Self-Esteem: .80 to .84 School Engagement: .82 to .85 Trouble Avoidance: .51 to .74 Adult Social Capital: .73 to .75
Social Skills Rating System, Gresham & Elliott, 1990	Social behaviors of children and youth ages 3–18, in the areas of student cooperation, assertion, responsibility, empathy, self-control	Total Skills, Total Problems, Internalizing Problems, Externalizing Problems, Cooperation, Assertion, Responsibility, Self-Control	Parent, teacher, student (for older youth)	Across all forms and levels, median coefficient alpha is .90; internal consistency estimates range from $r = .83$ to $r = .94$	Standardized on a national sample of 4,000 children and youth ages 3–18, stratified by grade and sex.
Strengths and Difficulties Questionnaire, Goodman, 1997	Positive and negative attributes of behavior of youth ages 3–16	Prosocial behavior, conduct problems, inattention-hyperactivity, emotional symptoms, peer problems	Parent, teacher, or youth (ages 11–16)	Internal consistency of scales had a mean Cronbach alpha of .73. Cross-informant correlation was a mean of $r = .34$. The latter is not exactly a measure of interrater reliability, but rather of agreement among different perspectives (e.g., parent and teacher). Test-retest stability after 4–6 months had a mean of $r = .62$. (Reliability was reported by Goodman, 2001.)	The five-factor structure was confirmed using data from a sample of more 10,000 British youth ages 5–15. SDQ problem scores about the 90th percentile were highly predictive of independently obtained psychiatric diagnoses, with mean odds ratios of 15.7 for parent-completed scales, 15.2 for teacher-completed scales and 6.2 for youth-completed scales.

search for solutions with clients. We draw on our combined experience in mental health, school, and other community settings to provide the examples.

Strengths-Based Measures for Families

One of the primary sources for measurement instruments for strengths-based practice with families is *Supporting and Strengthening Families* (Dunst, Trivette, & Deal, 1994). Collected in this important work in early intervention and family support are three useful measures, all with an explicit strengths focus:

- Family Resource Scale (Dunst & Leet, 1987)
- Family Functioning Style Scale (Deal, Trivette, & Dunst, 1988)
- Family Support Scale (Dunst, Jenkins, & Trivette, 1984)

An additional family measure with an explicit strengths focus was developed by researchers at the federally funded Research and Training Center on Family Support and Children's Mental Health at Portland State University in Oregon:

- Family Empowerment Scale (Koren, DeChillo, & Friesen, 1992)

These measures are each detailed in the following sections.

Family Resource Scale

The Family Resource Scale, developed for use in early intervention programs for children with disabilities, measures tangible and intangible resources that are considered important for families with young children (Dunst & Leet, 1987). A parent or other adult family member completes the instrument, which has 30 items rated on a 5-point scale on the extent to which each resource is adequately met for the family. Higher scores indicate greater adequacy; lower scores indicate needs. Scale items represent a hierarchy of needs, with resources roughly ordered from most to least basic. The resources include major components of both internal and external supports, such as food, shelter, financial resources, transportation, time to be with family and friends, toys for the children, and vacation/leisure.

As part of a strengths assessment, the Family Resource Scale could be used to identify areas in which the family is successfully meeting needs. The Family Resource Scale also could be used to quickly identify areas for intervention targets or goals, as well as to measure outcomes when program goals include families being able to meet their needs. The tone of the measure is consistent with the strengths perspective in that it asks a family member to evaluate, from her or his own perspective, how well various common family needs are met on a month-in, month-out basis. The instrument is readily available, in that it may be copied or reproduced without permission, with proper acknowledgment and citation. (See Table 15.4 for information about accessing the measure.)

Family Functioning Style Scale

The Family Functioning Style Scale, developed from research on strong families, is intended to measure family strengths (Trivette, Dunst, Deal, Hamby, & Sexton, 1994). Its 26 items assess the extent to which an individual family member (or two or more completing the scale together) believes the family is characterized by different strengths and capabilities. Ratings are on a 5-point scale from "not at all like my family" to "almost always like my family." The measure yields five scales: Interactional Patterns, Family Values, Coping Strategies, Family Commitment, and Resource Mobilization.

In practice, the primary use of the Family Functioning Style Scale is assessment, to identify sources of strength the family uses. Interventions, then, could be built on those strengths. The Family Functioning Style Scale also could be used as an outcome measure, as some of the items represent attributes that could be modified, such as interactional patterns and coping strategies. This instrument also may be copied or reproduced without permission, with proper acknowledgment and citation. (See Table 15.4 for information about accessing the measure.)

Family Support Scale

The Family Support Scale is a measure of social support for families. It has 18 items designed to assess the degree to which potential sources of social support have been helpful to families, with a 5-point scale from "not at all helpful" to "extremely helpful." Potential sources of support range from particular family members to various professionals and service providers with whom the family may be involved. As with all of the measures from Dunst, Trivette, and Deal (1994), the perspective obtained is that of a parent or other adult family caregiver. The Family Support Scale captures not only information about what sources of support the family has available but also how *helpful* they have been. Sometimes there is a critical difference between the size of a social network and the value of its support to an individual or family, with the latter having a more positive effect on outcomes. The sources of social support measured are Informal Kinship,

Table 15.4

Resources

Instrument title	Authors	Source
Behavioral and Emotional Rating Scale	Epstein & Sharma, 1998	PRO-ED 8700 Shoal Creek Blvd. Austin, TX 78757 800-897-3202 http://www.proedinc.com
Family Assessment Device	Epstein, Baldwin, & Bishop, 1983	Brown University Family Research Program Rhode Island Hospital Department of Psychiatry 593 Eddy St. Providence, RI 02903 401-444-3534
Family Assessment Measure	Skinner, Steinhauer, & Santa-Barbara, 1995	Multi-Health Systems Inc. P.O. Box 950 North Tonawanda, NY 14120 800-456-3003 www.mhs.com
Family Empowerment Scale	Koren, DeChillo, & Friesen, 1992	Research and Training Center on Family Support and Children's Mental Health P.O. Box 751 Portland, OR 97202 503-725-4040
Family Functioning Style Scale	Deal, Trivette, & Dunst, 1988	*Supporting and Strengthening Families:* *Methods, Strategies, Practices* ISBN 0-914797-94-8 Available from Brookline Books P.O. Box 1046 Cambridge, MA 617-868-0360
Family Resource Scale	Dunst & Leet, 1987	*Supporting and Strengthening Families:* *Methods, Strategies, Practices* ISBN 0-914797-94-8 Available from Brookline Books P.O. Box 1046 Cambridge, MA 617-868-0360

(continued)

Table 15.4 (continued)

Resources

Instrument title	Authors	Source
Family Support Scale	Dunst, Jenkins, & Trivette, 1984	*Supporting and Strengthening Families: Methods, Strategies, Practices* ISBN 0-914797-94-8 Available from Brookline Books P.O. Box 1046 Cambridge, MA 617-868-0360
Parent–Adolescent Communication Scale	Olson, McCubbin, Barnes, Larsen, Muxen, & Wilson, 1992	Family Inventories David H. Olson Life Innovations P.O. Box 190 Minneapolis, MN 55440
Parental Strengths and Needs Inventory	Strom & Cooledge, 1987	Scholastic Testing Service 1-800-642-6787 or www.ststesting.com
Parent Perception Inventory	Hazzard, Christensen, & Margolin, 1983	Andrew Christensen Dept. of Psychology–Clinical University of California, Los Angeles P.O. Box 951563, A326B FH Los Angeles, CA 90095
School Success Profile	Bowen & Richman, 1997	Jordan Institute for Families University of North Carolina at Chapel Hill School of Social Work 301 Pittsboro St. Chapel Hill, NC 27599
Social Skills Rating System	Gresham & Elliott, 1990	American Guidance Service 4201 Woodland Rd. Circle Pines, MN 55014 www.agsnet.com
Strengths and Difficulties Questionnaire	Goodman, 1997	www.sdqinfo.com

Spouse/Partner Support, Social Organization, Formal Kinship, and Professional Services.

The Family Support Scale could potentially be used as an assessment device (to identify major sources of support for a family and untapped, potential sources of support), for intervention planning to increase social support, and as an outcome measure in determining the success of mobilizing formal and informal supports. Additionally, the measure can be used to begin a conversation with family members about how to increase the support available to the family. The Family Support Scale may be copied or reproduced without permission, with proper acknowledgment and citation. (See Table 15.4 for more information about accessing the measure.)

Family Empowerment Scale

The Family Empowerment Scale was developed to measure empowerment in families with children with emotional disorders (Koren et al., 1992). Empowerment is an explicit goal of many collaborative interventions for this population and fits more broadly with the strengths perspective as well in its emphasis on clients being active in their own change efforts and having capacity for competence (Early & GlenMaye, 2000). The Family Empowerment Scale has 34 items designed to reflect three levels of empowerment (family, service system, community/political) in statements about personal attitudes, knowledge, and behaviors. The respondent rates each item on a 5-point scale from "not true at all" to "very true." Examples of the statements include: "I feel my family life is under control," "I make sure that professionals understand my opinions about what services my child needs," and "I know the steps to take when I am concerned my child is receiving poor services."

The Family Empowerment Scale could be used as both an assessment and an outcome measure, especially in programs that have empowerment of family members as a goal. At assessment, responses to the various items could indicate both strengths (knowledge, attitudes, and skills the family member already has) and potential targets for intervention. (See Table 15.4 for information about accessing the measure.)

▧ Case Example: Using Strengths-Oriented Family Measures

The Bowers family consists of Elsie, who is 34 years old and African American, and her two children, 11-year-old Bruce and 5-year-old Jennifer. Two weeks ago, Elsie was arrested on charges of driving under the influence of alcohol and endangering her children, who were with her in the car at the time of her arrest. Her attorney negotiated a plea agreement for her to enter a diversion program for first-time substance abuse offenders in exchange for dropping the endangerment charge, which was a felony.

When Elsie left her parents' home at the age of 20, she married and gave birth to her son Bruce 3 years later. Elsie has been divorced from Bruce's father for about 8 years. Since her divorce, Elsie has had several boyfriends, one of whom is the father of Jennifer. Her children do not have contact with their fathers.

Elsie and her children are to attend the Sober Families, Safe Kids program. Elsie has an appointment to meet with Maria Rivera, a counselor for the children's portion of the program. As Ms. Rivera greets the family, she hands Elsie several questionnaires and explains, "Ms. Bowers, if you could answer the questions on these three forms, the Family Functioning Style Scale, the Family Resource Scale, and the Family Support Scale, it will give me some ideas for planning the time we will spend together. Meanwhile, maybe Jennifer and Bruce can show me how to play one of their favorite games." When Elsie has finished filling out the forms, Ms. Rivera looks each one of them over, counts up responses, and jots down a few notes.

The Family Support Scale assesses the existence and/or helpfulness of various sources of support, including parents, friends, spouse, spouse's friends, coworkers, parent groups, social groups and clubs, church members and minister, family doctor, and various programs or their staff. Ms. Rivera observes that Elsie says she gets helpful support from her parents and probes further, revealing that Elsie's mother provided transportation to the first appointment, since Elsie's license is suspended until she successfully enrolls in the program. Elsie said that her mother helps with other concrete needs, such as child care, but she also provides emotional support; Elsie speaks to her mother at least once a day on the phone, and she and her mother visit each other's houses regularly. Responses to items also show that Elsie has a friend who sometimes helps her with child care, especially for the younger child, so that Elsie can attend doctors' appointments and run errands. Elsie and this friend also provide emotional support and advice to each other, maintaining frequent phone contact. Additionally, Elsie's answers to the Family Support Scale showed that church members and minister have been "not at all helpful" in the past 3 to 6 months (the time frame of the measure). Elsie explained, when Ms. Rivera asked further questions, that after she had an abortion, she did not feel like she could go back to the church. Elsie became emotional when speaking about this and agreed that the pain around the abortion contributed to her substance use. After empathically reflecting the feelings, Ms. Rivera discussed, as a possible goal for Elsie when in the program, that she resolve some of her feelings about the abortion and reconnect with the church.

The Family Resource Scale covers the adequacy of basic resources: housing, food for two meals a day, money to buy necessities, sufficient clothing for family members, heat for the house/apartment, indoor plumbing/water, money to pay monthly bills, good job for self and/or spouse/partner, medical care, public assistance, dependable transportation, time to get enough sleep/rest, furniture, time to be by oneself, time for the family to be together, time to be with children, time to be with spouse/partner or close friend, telephone or access to one, baby-sitting for children, dental care, someone to talk to, time to socialize, time to keep in shape, toys for children, money to buy things for self, money to save, and travel/vacation.

Elsie indicated that most of these are at least "usually adequate" (4 on a 5-point scale), with the exception of having a good job, time to be with a spouse/partner (she doesn't have a partner), money to buy things for her children and herself, money to save, and travel/vacation. She marked "sometimes adequate" when discussing money to pay monthly bills, dental care, and regular day care.

Ms. Rivera complimented Elsie on her ability to take care of the family, acknowledging the challenges involved with single parenting. To discover other strengths, Ms. Rivera inquired about how Elsie made ends meet those times when money was short; Elsie responded that she tried to plan ahead with paper and pencil, figuring out the priorities and what can be done without. She also said that one of the ways she makes ends meet is by helping out her sister's office cleaning crew when it is shorthanded.

On the Family Functioning Scale, Elsie strongly endorsed the following items: "Our family is able to make decisions about what to do when we have problems or concerns," "We try to solve our problems first before asking others to help," and "We find things to do that keep our minds off our worries when something upsetting is beyond our control." As an example of how to explore answers, Ms. Rivera asked further about the last item; Elsie talks about making her children's favorite foods and telling silly stories. Ms. Rivera continues in this line of questioning:

MS. RIVERA: What else do you do to keep your mind off worries when things are beyond your control?

ELSIE: Well, sometimes I play cards with my friends, but I guess I won't do that for a while because there's usually beer [ruefully]

MS. RIVERA: Tell me about times you get together with friends and there isn't alcohol.

ELSIE: When we go play bingo with my friend Jade's grandmother at the nursing home.

MS. RIVERA: That sounds like fun. How often can you do that?

ELSIE: They play on Tuesday and Friday evenings. Jennifer and Bruce like to go visit the grandmas, too.

MS. RIVERA: Does that sound like something you might be able to do in the next week?

In this practice vignette, Ms. Rivera used the three instruments to gather some assessment and baseline information for measuring outcomes. More than that, however, she employed the instruments as a way to open up discussion with Elsie, not about the legal and substance abuse problems that have brought her to the program, but instead about the times when things are going well. Ms Rivera implied through her line of questioning that Elsie already knows what she needs to do to establish a safe and sober lifestyle. Using these instruments has documented sources of support for Elsie (e.g., her mother and her friends), as well as coping resources Elsie uses, such as finding distractions from worry about things that are out of her control. The conversation has identified what Elsie already knows and what she is doing that will improve her situation and increase "sober support."

Other Measures for Families

As previously noted, few measures for families truly represent the strengths perspective in human services practice. For example, the Parent—Adolescent Communication Scale (Olson et al., 1992), the Family Assessment Device (Epstein, Baldwin, & Bishop, 1983), and the Family Assessment Measure (FAM-III) (Skinner, Steinhauer, & Santa-Barbara, 1995) are all developed from models of family functioning that assume that a "normal" or normative family exists (Weick & Saleebey, 1995). This assumption is in contrast to the strengths perspective's assumptions that value strengths in all families (Early & GlenMaye, 2000). Appropriate use of one of these instruments would be based on paying special attention to the more positive attributes of family functioning that the instrument can identify. The practitioner would use the instrument to identify questions to explore with the family, instead of answers about the family. The intervention would build on strengths identified. Areas of family functioning not identified as strengths could be explored as potential areas to target intervention, if the family desires change in one or more of the areas.

In addition, several of the instruments discussed in this section facilitate gathering information from different family members, which can be very useful because different members often have different experiences that need to be explored and honored.

The following measures are discussed in this section:

- Parental Strengths and Needs Inventory (Strom & Cooledge, 1987)
- Parent–Adolescent Communication Scale (Olson et al., 1992)

- Parent Perception Inventory (Hazzard, Christensen, & Margolin, 1983)
- Family Assessment Device (Epstein et al., 1983)
- Family Assessment Measure (FAM-III) (Skinner et al., 1995)

Parental Strengths and Needs Inventory

The Parental Strengths and Needs Inventory is intended to measure parenting efficacy. It was developed from qualitative analysis of responses from 3,000 parents, teachers, and children about various aspects of parenting (Strom & Cooledge, 1987; cited in Combs-Orme & Thomas, 1997, and in Strom & McCalla, 1988). The Parental Strengths and Needs Inventory has 60 items completed separately by both parent and child in the following areas of parenting: satisfaction, success, teaching/guidance, parenting difficulties, parenting frustrations, and information needed. A strengths index is derived from scores on satisfaction, success, and teaching/guidance. A needs (or concerns) index is derived from ratings on parenting difficulties, parenting frustrations, and information needed. The reading level is reported to be grade 5.5. Items are rated on a 4-point scale, with higher scores indicating greater strength and fewer concerns.

This measure could be used in assessment to get a sense of areas of parenting that are strengths and areas for potential intervention. It could also be used as an outcome measure of changes in parenting attitudes and strengths. (See Table 15.4 for information about accessing the measure.)

Parent–Adolescent Communication Scale

The Parent–Adolescent Communication Scale is intended to measure, intergenerationally, the communication dimension of the Circumplex Model of Family Functioning (Olson et al., 1982). The scale compares the separate perceptions of each parent directly with the adolescent's perceptions of each respective parent. Responses to 20 items result in two subscales. The Open Family Communication subscale represents more positive aspects of parent–adolescent communication (free-flowing exchange of factual and emotional information, lack of constraints, degree of understanding, and satisfaction experienced in parent–adolescent interactions). The Problems in Family Communication subscale measures more negative aspects of communication (hesitancy to share, negative styles of interaction, and selectivity and caution in what is shared). An adolescent may complete the measure twice, once rating the mother and once rating the father. All ratings are on a 5-point scale from "strongly disagree" to "strongly agree" for each item.

Although this scale is not a strengths-based measure, it could be used to assess strengths in communication between parents and adolescents, as well as areas of communication to improve. It likewise could be used as an outcome measure, to gauge changes in communication that result from interventions with adolescents, parents, or families. In generating solutions, identifying communication that is going well could allow the youths or parents to see ways they contribute to positive communication. (See Table 15.4 for information about accessing the measure.)

Parent Perception Inventory

The Parent Perception Inventory is an 18-item measure of children's perceptions of positive and negative parental behaviors (Hazzard & Christensen, n.d.; Hazzard et al., 1983). It is intended for use with elementary school-aged children (ages 5–13). The child rates each parent separately on the same items, which are presented in a written or oral manner and rated in a pictorial or written fashion. Half of the items reflect positive behaviors (positive reinforcement, comfort, talk time, involvement in decision making, time together, positive evaluation, allowing independence, assistance, and nonverbal affection). The other half of the items reflect negative behaviors, although a number of them may well be appropriate parenting behaviors, depending on the circumstances (privilege removal, criticism, commands, physical punishment, yelling, threatening, time-out, nagging, and ignoring). The Parent Perception Inventory yields four subscales entitled Mother Positive (9 items), Father Positive (9 items), Mother Negative (9 items), and Father Negative (9 items), with total scores ranging from 0 to 36. Items are scored 0 for "never" to 4 for "a lot."

The Parent Perception Inventory could be used as an assessment measure, to understand a child's perspective on the parenting environment, and as an outcome measure when an intervention intends to change the parenting environment in some way (modifying parental behavior, child's perception, or both). (See Table 15.4 for information about accessing the measure.)

Family Assessment Device

The Family Assessment Device has 60 items that operationalize the Mc-Master Model of Family Functioning (Epstein et al., 1983), which conceptualizes as important a number of instrumental, as well as emotional and psychological, aspects of family functioning. Six subscales correspond to the theoretical dimensions in the model: (a) problem solving, (b) communication, (c) roles, (d) affective responsiveness (the ability of family members to experience appropriate affect over a range of stimuli), (e) affective involvement (the extent to which family members express interest in and value each other's activities), and (f) behavior control (the way the family expresses and maintains standards of behavior). A General Functioning Scale can be used as a global measure of family health or pathology. Items are rated on a 4-point scale regarding the level of agreement with the statement as a description of the family. Items describing unhealthy functioning are reverse scored, so lower scores indicate healthier functioning.

The Family Assessment Device is not a strengths-based measure, but it could be used in assessing family strengths if the worker is careful to pay attention to the positive aspects of functioning identified, as well as the "problem" areas indicating relatively healthier functioning. The instrument could also be used as an outcome measure for interventions that are intended to improve a family's functioning in some way. (See Table 15.4 for information about accessing the measure.)

The Family Assessment Measure (FAM-III)

The Family Assessment Measure (FAM-III) is another instrument that measures the constructs of the McMaster Model of Family Functioning (Skinner et al., 1995). The measure examines the functioning of an individual within the family, as well as total family functioning. The measure produces a General Scale that focuses on the family as a system, a Self-Rating Scale that assesses the functioning of an individual within the family, and a Dyadic Relationship Scale that targets specific family dyads. Each of the scales (General, Self, and Dyadic) has subscales corresponding to the McMaster dimensions of task accomplishment, role performance, communication, affective involvement, affective expression, control, and values and norms.

The FAM-III is intended as an assessment measure. As part of a strengths assessment, the FAM-III could be used to identify areas of family functioning that are strong. When scores are in the weakness range or ratings by different family members vary greatly, further investigation may be warranted to determine whether the family wishes to work on functioning in that dimension. The FAM-III could also be used as an outcome measure, because the dimensions of family functioning measured are amenable to change. (See Table 15.4 for information about accessing the measure.)

Measures for Children

In human services practice with children, as with families, practice is often focused on children's problems; hence, many of the measurement instruments for children are designed to document the range and extent of problems children exhibit. In recent years, however, several different instruments for children have been developed with a greater focus on positive aspects of functioning.

Three of the four instruments for children have the capacity to obtain perspectives of teachers or other professionals who know the children well (the Behavioral and Emotional Rating Scale, Epstein & Sharma, 1998; the Social Skills Rating Scale, Gresham & Elliott, 1990; and the Strengths and Difficulties Questionnaire, Goodman, 1997). Education is a major part of children's social environment, and what happens at school often affects every other aspect of the child's life. All of the measures for children obtain information about the child's school experiences in some way. Additionally, the School Success Profile (Bowen & Richman, 1997) obtains information about the child's experiences beyond family and school to neighborhood and community. The following measures add a great deal to practice in reflecting an ecological perspective:

- Behavioral and Emotional Rating Scale (Epstein & Sharma, 1998)
- School Success Profile (Bowen & Richman, 1997)
- Social Skills Rating System (Gresham & Elliott, 1990)
- Strengths and Difficulties Questionnaire (Goodman, 1997)

The Behavioral and Emotional Rating Scale (Epstein & Sharma, 1998) was developed from an explicit strengths focus to measure children's functioning in the environments of family and school. The School Success Profile was developed from a perspective of risk and resilience, which identifies both risk and protective factors at the individual, family, school, neighborhood, and community levels. The Social Skills Rating System reflects a broad assessment of social behavior, including problem behavior and academic competence. Similarly, the Strengths and Difficulties Questionnaire assessed both problem areas and prosocial behavior.

Behavioral and Emotional Rating Scale

The Behavioral and Emotional Rating Scale measures children's behavioral and emotional strengths from the perspective of a parent, teacher, or other caregiver who knows the child well. The questionnaire has 52 items rated as to the extent to which each behavior is present or absent for the child. Scoring results in an overall Strengths Quotient and five subscales: Interpersonal Strengths, Family Involvement, Intrapersonal Strengths, School Functioning, and Affective Strengths. Comparisons can be made among the subscales to identify relative strengths and weaknesses and to two sets of norms to get a sense of how an individual child's functioning compares with a national sample of children who have emotional and behavioral disorders, as well as a representative sample of children without such disorders.

The Interpersonal Strengths subscale represents the child's ability to control his or her emotions or behavior in social situations. Family Involvement reflects a child's participation in and relationship with his or her family. Intrapersonal Strengths captures a child's perception of his or her competence and accomplishments. School Functioning is a measure of the child's school competence and classroom performance. Affective Strengths measures the extent to which a child accepts affection and expresses feelings.

The Behavioral and Emotional Rating Scale is designed as an assessment instrument. The pro-social nature of the items adapts easily to intervention planning from a strengths perspective, identifying behaviors to be strengthened and strengths present to build on. The Behavioral and Emotional Rating Scale could be used as an outcome measure of change in behaviors described on individual items, scale scores, or the total Strengths Quotient. (See Table 15.4 for information about accessing the measure.)

School Success Profile

The School Success Profile is a questionnaire developed from a risk and resilience perspective for a dropout prevention program used in several states across the country (Richman & Bowen, 1997). Development of the instrument was based on the school success literature, as well as an ecological perspective of risk and protective factors for a variety of challenges faced by youths. The School Success Profile is for use with middle and high school students and is written at the fourth-grade level. A version for younger children is in development.

Protective and risk factors are operationalized in the areas of neighborhood, school, friends, and family, in 220 multiple-choice items. The measure is written in English and Spanish language versions.

Scoring results in two profiles, each with a number of subdimensions. The Social Environment Profile is comprised of Neighborhood (satisfaction, peer culture, safety), School (satisfaction, teacher support, freedom from disruption), Peers (satisfaction, acceptance), and Family (satisfaction, integration, parent support) dimensions (and subdimensions). The Individual Adaptation Profile is comprised of Support (social support, parent school interest, parent school monitoring), Self-Confidence (self-esteem, school resilience, school influence), School Behavior (attendance, avoid problem behaviors, grades), and General Well-Being (physical health, happiness, adjustment). An individual student's score on these dimensions can be compared with peers (at the same school or within a district, for example) or to a national random sample.

The School Success Profile is designed as an assessment and an outcome measure. It is unique in its ecological approach, tapping youths' perspectives on their social environments, as well as their own competencies. (See Table 15.4 for information about accessing the measure.)

Case Example: Using the School Success Profile (SSP)

Marcus is a 14-year-old, African American male in the eighth grade at an urban junior high school. According to some of his teachers, Marcus is an "average" student who has difficulty maintaining peer relationships. Other teachers report Marcus that is a "nice" student who, on occasion, gets "mixed up" in a variety of verbal and physical conflicts with his peers. Most recently, Marcus was involved in a verbal and physical confrontation with another student during lunch period. As a result of his misbehavior, the assistant principal suspended Marcus for 3 days. He was sent to the school counselor upon his return to school for the prevention of further such incidents. The school is located in a high-crime, low-socioeconomic status (SES) neighborhood but has strict policies in the service of providing and enforcing a safe, nonviolent atmosphere.

The following is a first session dialogue. At the conclusion of introductions and the purpose of the meeting, the SSP was utilized as an assessment and intervention tool to help navigate and guide the session. Given the recent issues related to peer conflict, it was determined that the Friends subscale on the SSP would be utilized as a way to identify possible strengths related to the establishment and maintenance of pro-social behavior and the management of conflict with peers.

COUNSELOR: I know that you recently got into a physical confrontation during your lunch period, which resulted in a 3-day suspension from school.

MARCUS: Yes.

COUNSELOR: Tell me about that. What happened?

MARCUS: Well, the kid walked by me in the lunchroom and started talking about me and making comments about my hair and clothes.

COUNSELOR: I see. What were some of his comments?

MARCUS: Oh, things like "Hey, Marcus, look at that big ole 'fro," and "Marcus, why doesn't your mom take you to the store and buy you some new clothes? I hear you guys were spotted at Goodwill."

COUNSELOR: Then what happened?

MARCUS: I got out of my seat and told him to either "shut his mouth," or I would shut it for him.

COUNSELOR: Then what?

MARCUS: We started throwing punches.
COUNSELOR: In looking back on the situation, is there anything perhaps you could have done differently?

Because Marcus was unable to come up with anything he could have done differently, the counselor suggested that he complete the School Success Profile to help Marcus consider some of the things he has done in the past or could do in the future if a similar issue arose.

COUNSELOR: Here is a questionnaire that might help us think about situations like this. It's called the School Success Profile. There are questions in several different areas, such as neighborhood, school, and friends. Could you take a few minutes to answer these questions?

After taking approximately 20 to 25 minutes to complete the SSP, Marcus and the counselor focused on specific questions and responses on the Friends subscale to elicit a conversation about enhancing and maintaining successful peer relationships. The counselor also hoped that Marcus would recognize a more viable approach to handling conflicts with peers.

COUNSELOR: Thanks for completing the questionnaire. I see that when it comes to the statement "I get along well with my friends," you stated that this was a lot like yourself.
MARCUS: Yes.
COUNSELOR: That's great. Can you tell me what it means to get along well with your friends?
MARCUS: Sure. It means having fun playing football and basketball at lunch or after school.
COUNSELOR: Okay, what else is involved in getting along well with friends?
MARCUS: Talking to them and respecting each other, I guess. I also don't fight or argue with my friends because I like hanging out with them.
COUNSELOR: What does talking and respecting each other mean to you?
MARCUS: If they make fun of me or we disagree, I just listen to what they have to say, and then I move on.
COUNSELOR: What if it is someone who is not your friend? Let's say it's someone you just met, and they say something you don't like.
MARCUS: I try to do the same thing.
COUNSELOR: Refresh my memory. What is that?
MARCUS: I listen and either walk away, or I try to change the subject before it gets too heated, or I just "move on."
COUNSELOR: I see! So it sounds like you don't let them get under your skin.
MARCUS: Yes.

COUNSELOR: How are you able to do that?

MARCUS: I usually tell them I don't like what they're saying to me, and I start talking about something else, or I just walk away.

COUNSELOR: Tell me about a time you did this recently.

MARCUS: The other day when I got back from being suspended from school. I was changing classes when this kid came up to me and started laughing.

COUNSELOR: Laughing "at you" or laughing at something you meant to be funny?

MARCUS: *At* me. Our classes are right across the hall from each other, and we both came out of the rooms at about the same time. When we did, the kid started laughing and pointing his finger at me and saying things like "Hey, Marcus, I see you still haven't gotten a haircut," and "Marcus, how long are you going to keep those same clothes."

COUNSELOR: And during this time he's also laughing?

MARCUS: Yeah, the jerk.

COUNSELOR: Was this the same student you got into the fight with?

MARCUS: No, this was one of his friends.

COUNSELOR: I see. So what happened next?

MARCUS: Well, I just kept on walking until I got to my locker, and then I just started talking to my locker partner.

COUNSELOR: So, it sounds like you were able to ignore this person's comments and, as you said earlier, "move on" from the situation so he wasn't able to get under your skin.

MARCUS: Yes.

COUNSELOR: Great! It sounds like you put into practice some of the skills we talked about and that you may have uncovered a new approach to handling some of the conflicts that have occurred here at school.

MARCUS: I guess.

COUNSELOR: Let's look at one other question.

MARCUS: Okay.

COUNSELOR: Under the Friends section where it asked, "How much difficulty do you have making new friends," you stated, "Some difficulty."

MARCUS: Yeah.

COUNSELOR: So it sounds from your answer that there are times when you have no problems making new friends. Can you tell me what's different about those times?

MARCUS: I guess it's easier to make new friends when I start off being nice instead of being mean.

COUNSELOR: And what does "being nice" look like?

MARCUS: What do you mean?

COUNSELOR: How would you act or respond to someone for the first time if you would like to be his or her friend? Think back to when you first met some of your current friends; how did you respond to them?

MARCUS: I smiled and laughed with them. I played some games they wanted to play.

In using the SSP as an assessment and intervention tool to tap into Marcus's strengths, the counselor identified items that helped him and Marcus explore the essential qualities and behaviors that maintain and establish appropriate friendships. Because Marcus lives in a high-crime area, further work explored how he can ignore and avoid physically threatening circumstances in that environment and what situations might be sufficiently dangerous to warrant responding in a conflictual or violent way. Follow-up sessions continued to amplify the strengths uncovered during the initial assessment.

Social Skills Rating System

The Social Skills Rating System is a checklist that provides student (elementary or secondary), parent, and teacher ratings in the areas of cooperation, assertion, responsibility, empathy, and self-control (Gresham & Elliott, 1990). For preschoolers (ages 3 years to 4 years, 11 months), only parent and teacher ratings are obtained. Each version (by respondent and age) contains about 50 items. The questionnaires ask the respondent to rate, for a variety of positively stated behaviors, the frequency (on a 3-point scale from "never" to "very often") and the perceived importance of the behavior (also on a 3-point scale from "not important" to "critical"). Using the parent version as an example, responses are combined to yield social skills subscale scores (Cooperation, Assertion, Responsibility, and Self-Control), a Total Social Skills score, problem subscales (Internalizing and Externalizing), and Total Problems Score. The Total Problems and Total Social Skills scores are converted to standard scores for comparisons with norms.

The Social Skills Rating System is particularly suited to assessment and intervention planning. It evaluates the presence of specific pro-social behaviors and the significance of these behaviors for the rater (parent, teacher, or student). The Social Skills Rating System is also suited as an outcome measure, as it is sensitive to positive changes in the identified behaviors. (See Table 15.4 for information about accessing the measure.)

Case Example: Using the Social Skills Rating System (SSRS)

Tina is a 13-year-old, Hispanic American girl in the seventh grade at an urban junior high school. Tina has been referred to counseling because of her combative and argumentative behavior with adults at home and school. Tina lives with her mother and stepfather. She has an older sister who is in the tenth grade at the nearby high school and a younger half-brother in first grade. Tina and her immediate family have recently moved (within the last 6 months) to the area in hope of seeking employment for her mother and stepfather. School records indicate that Tina is bilingual in Spanish and English but that her current academic ability is in the below-average range. Before arriving in junior high school, Tina attended elementary school in a rural setting, where she received average grades in core academic areas. According to her current teachers, Tina has made few friends at her new school. In addition, many of Tina's teachers report her as having difficulty in adjusting to her new surroundings. Although there are other Hispanics in the area, they are primarily recent immigrants from Mexico, and Tina's family is Puerto Rican.

The following is a first session dialogue. At the conclusion of introductions, the counselor used the Social Skills Rating System instrument as an assessment and intervention tool to help navigate and guide the first treatment session.

COUNSELOR: Hi, Tina, thanks for coming down to see me.
TINA: Who are you? [stated with a frown and puzzled look on her face]
COUNSELOR: My name is Mr. S. My job here at school is to talk with students and to find out how things are going.
TINA: So what does that have to do with me?
COUNSELOR: Well, I thought that since you were new here at school, we might be able to talk about how things are going for you.
TINA: It's your time. If it keeps me out of class, that's fine with me.
COUNSELOR: Good. So, what do you think of your new school?
TINA: It's okay.
COUNSELOR: What can you tell me that you like about the school?
TINA: What? Don't you have any idea yourself?
COUNSELOR: Well, I would like to hear from you about what you think of school here. I've been here for so long I'm not sure I can even answer that question myself. I thought maybe you could give me a new perspective on things.
TINA: Some of the kids here are nice.
COUNSELOR: Well, that's great to hear. Is there anything else?
TINA: I guess some of the teachers are nice.
COUNSELOR: Wonderful, that's very refreshing to hear. Usually all I hear are the bad things.
TINA: Well, some of them can be kinda mean.
COUNSELOR: In what way?

TINA: They always want something from you. Always demanding that you get your work done.

COUNSELOR: I see. Can you give me some examples?

TINA: I guess when it comes to doing work in class and getting my homework done.

COUNSELOR: Homework? It sounds like some of these demands are also occurring at home?

TINA: Yep. That can be worse.

COUNSELOR: So, how do you usually respond to these demands?

TINA: Usually, I don't like them, and I let people know that I don't like them.

COUNSELOR: And how do you communicate to adults that you don't like these demands? Could you give me an example?

TINA: I usually yell at them and tell them to leave me alone.

COUNSELOR: I see. I guess that lets them know something. Tina, I have a questionnaire that could help us talk about stuff like this. It's called the Social Skills Rating System. It describes situations with school, teachers, and other kids and asks what you do in situations like those described. If you could fill out the questionnaire, it would give me a better sense of what happens for you at school. Could you take a couple minutes to answer the questions? And then after you answer all the questions we can talk about some of your answers.

TINA: Great—more demands.

COUNSELOR: No, no. [with laughter] It consists of only 34 questions that ask you to rate "how often" you might respond to a certain situation. There aren't any right or wrong answers—just what you think. Do you think you could do that?

TINA: Yep.

After Tina took approximately 15 to 20 minutes to complete the Social Skills Rating System instrument, she and the counselor discussed her responses. Specifically, Tina and the counselor focused on her strengths in addressing and interacting with adults by discussing her responses to questions on the Social Skills Rating System.

COUNSELOR: Thanks for being so diligent in completing the questionnaire. Let's take a look at some of your answers. I notice that you circled *sometimes* as it relates to disagreeing with adults without fighting or arguing.

TINA: Yes.

COUNSELOR: That's great. It sounds different from what you described earlier. Can you tell me what's different those times that you "sometimes" disagree with adults without fighting or arguing compared to those times that you might disagree by fighting or arguing?

TINA: Well, I have only hit my mom one time, and I have never hit a teacher, but sometimes if one of my teachers makes me mad, I will argue with her.

COUNSELOR: But I notice you said *sometimes*, so there must have been times when one of your teachers made you mad or demanded something from you, but you didn't argue with her. Could you give me an example when something like that has occurred?

TINA: Sure, just the other day my biology teacher asked us to read chapter 8 in class and to answer the questions at the end of the chapter. I did it without arguing with her about the assignment.

COUNSELOR: Can you tell me what was different about this particular day or assignment?

TINA: I don't know. I guess it was the way she asked me.

COUNSELOR: I'm not sure I follow you. How did she ask you?

TINA: She was nice, and she smiled a lot.

COUNSELOR: What about for you?

TINA: What do you mean?

COUNSELOR: Well, there must have been something occurring with you. I'm sure other adults, who were not as pleasant or friendly, have asked you to complete things and you still completed the task.

TINA: I guess so.

COUNSELOR: So, what kind of things do you think about or do that allows you to sometimes agree with adults without arguing or fighting?

TINA: Well, I try to think about what might happen if I yell at one of my teachers or my mom.

COUNSELOR: What might happen? Can you give me some examples?

TINA: If I yell at my teachers, I might have to stay after school. If I yell at my mom, I might get smacked.

COUNSELOR: So it sounds like you try to think about the possible negatives or consequences associated with yelling or arguing with teachers or your mom. Good. You think things through.

TINA: Yep.

COUNSELOR: What might be some of the positives that occur when you don't yell or argue with your teachers or your mom?

TINA: They get off my back.

COUNSELOR: Anything else?

TINA: I also try to think about the rewards I might get if I go ahead and do what they ask.

COUNSELOR: Oh, so you think about good things that happen when you cooperate. Can you give me some examples of requests you might honor?

TINA: Like doing my class assignments or helping my mom with my younger brother.

COUNSELOR: And what might be the positives that result from those?

TINA: I guess the teachers and I would get along better and my mom would give me some money for helping her with my baby brother.

COUNSELOR: Excellent, this sounds like something you have done before.

TINA: Yes.

COUNSELOR: It sounds like you have recognized an important strength you possess in sometimes getting along with teachers and adults without arguing or fighting.

In using the Social Skills Rating System as an assessment and intervention tool that would tap into Tina's strengths, the counselor identified specific items that assessed her behavioral strengths with teachers and adults. Before proceeding with the session, the counselor identified two additional social skill items that Tina indicated she "sometimes" displays pertaining to her behavior with adults.

COUNSELOR: Tina, I also noticed that you circled *sometimes* in responding to the item "I listen to adults when they are talking to me."

TINA: Yes.

COUNSELOR: Tell me, what are some of the things you do "sometimes" to listen to adults when they are talking to you?

TINA: In my classes I try to stop talking to some of my friends when the teacher wants our attention.

COUNSELOR: That sounds like a good idea. What about at home? What do you do if your mom is trying to talk to you about something?

TINA: I try to give her my attention, but sometimes things are so noisy with the TV and my older sister and younger brother, that it's hard.

COUNSELOR: I see. Talk to me a little more about that. Tell me what it means to give someone your attention.

TINA: I guess it means respecting them and listening to what they have to say, like what we're doing right now.

COUNSELOR: Sounds like you already have an idea as to what you can do to listen when adults are talking to you.

TINA: Yes, I like it when people are looking at me when I'm talking to them.

COUNSELOR: Most people do.

TINA: Mmmm.

COUNSELOR: Tina, before you head back to class, there is one more response you circled on the questionnaire that I would like to talk about.

TINA: Which one?

COUNSELOR: The one where you stated that you "sometimes" end fights with your parents calmly.

TINA: What about it?

COUNSELOR: Can you tell me what's different about those times when you end the fights you have with your parents calmly compared to those times when you don't?

TINA: Well, I have a stepfather and usually if he's involved in the argument, we just yell and yell at each other.

COUNSELOR: I noticed you said "usually." Tell me about times when an argument with him ends calmly. What's different about those times?

TINA: I guess I do the same thing I do with my teachers. I just listen to what they have to say without yelling back at them.

COUNSELOR: Interesting. And what kind of effect does that have on your teachers or your stepfather?

TINA: They don't yell at me so much.

COUNSELOR: Really! So by not engaging in the yelling with them, it helps to end the argument or fight more calmly?

TINA: Seems like it.

The counselor used the Social Skills Rating System instrument as an assessment as well as an intervention tool to amplify Tina's strengths, talents, capacities, and resources pertaining to behavior and situational demands presented by teachers and other adults. The counselor sidestepped some of Tina's provocative statements by taking a curiosity stance, identifying items to which Tina responded "sometimes." This allowed the counselor to develop a strengths-based dialogue during the counseling session. Tina was able to explore those times when she exhibited the necessary strengths and resources concerning the demands presented by teachers and her parents. Sessions that followed with Tina were spent discussing her recent successes and revisiting her initial responses on the Social Skills Rating System. In addition, time was spent discussing some of the skills that were uncovered when she took the Social Skills Rating System and how these skills might fit in her life as a junior high school student.

The Strengths and Difficulties Questionnaire

The Strengths and Difficulties Questionnaire (SDQ; Goodman, 1997) is a brief instrument concerning attributes of behavior of youth ages 3–16 years old. The SDQ has 25 items, some of which are positive and some negative, rated on a three-point scale of "not true," "somewhat true," and "certainly true." This instrument is not designed from a strengths perspective, but it does purport to measure strengths. Scoring the measure generates a prosocial behavior scale and four problem scales. The prosocial behavior scale includes the following items: considerate of other people's feelings; shares readily with other children; helpful if someone is hurt, upset, or feeling ill; kind to younger children; often volunteers to help others. The problem scales (conduct problems, inattention-hyperactivity, emotional symptoms, and peer problems) may be summed to yield a total difficulties score. Some of the items for the problem scales are phrased in a strengths-based way: generally obedient, usually does what adults request; thinks things out before acting; sees tasks through to the end, good attention span; has at least one good friend; generally liked by other children. Parallel versions of the questionnaire exist to obtain responses from parents, teachers, and youths (ages 11–16) themselves. The various versions of the instrument are available free on the Internet (www.sdqinfo.com).

The SDQ can be used in screening, assessment, or as an outcome measure. In practice from a strengths perspective, the practitioner should pay most attention to the prosocial behavior scale and the other positively worded items to avoid a problem focus.

Conclusions and Implications for Practice

This chapter is an attempt to collect measurement instruments that could be used with families in practice from a strengths perspective. This review is limited to self-report instruments, because an important aspect of practice from a strengths perspective is obtaining clients' views of their situations (strengths, functioning, resources). Of the 13 instruments identified and described here, 5 are from an explicit strengths perspective (Family Support Scale; Family Resource Scale; Family Functioning Style Scale, from Dunst, Trivette, & Deal, 1994; Family Empowerment Scale, from Koren et al., 1992; and Behavioral and Emotional Rating Scale, Epstein & Sharma, 1998). These instruments are clearly consistent with practice from a strengths perspective. Although the remaining instruments may contribute information about strengths, the social worker practicing from the strengths perspective would want to pay close attention to their use and interpretation to avoid introducing a problem focus.

The measures illustrated in this chapter can assist the practitioner in focusing on the desired end state or goal, through obtaining family members' perceptions of how they want their family to function or to communicate and the behaviors they would like to see from themselves and other family members. These measures can also be used to identify elements of the system (family and environment) to modify, as well as to monitor progress to see that the desired end state is reached. Using measures such as these can help human service workers meet client needs and accountability demands. More important, if used sensitively, these instruments should not introduce a pathology focus into the interaction between worker and family but should instead identify strengths on which to build.

A General Procedure for Using Measures in Direct Practice

- *Select a measure:* Selection of particular measures to use may be determined by one or more of the following: use the same few measures with all clients who are similar in a particular program (e.g., a parent education program); use a measure that matches the client's presenting situation (e.g., child has emotional problems).
- *Explain how to fill it out:* The worker should be thoroughly familiar with the instrument so that the explanation is smooth. It would be a good idea to get a colleague, family member, or friend to assist in a mock session to practice introducing the measure, scoring it, and verbally reporting results before using it with a client. In the explanation, assure clients that there are no right or wrong answers. One justification to provide to clients for using a measure is that it is a quick way to get information that will help the clinician understand more about how to help.
- *Time, space, and materials:* Allow ample time. Most of the measures presented here can be completed in at most 25 minutes. Many of them take less time than that. There should be a hard writing surface, such as a desk or a clipboard. Appropriate writing utensils (pencil if the measure will be computer scored) should also be provided.
- *Answer questions, clarify:* It is important to assess clients' literacy levels, whether children or adults. If necessary, read each question and response to the client. If a client is unsure of an answer, he or she should be encouraged to provide what he or she thinks is the "best" answer. Workers should avoid interpreting the items or questions.
- *Score the measure:* Most of the measures described are easy to score. Ideally, this should be done when the client is still present so that he or she may receive immediate feedback from the clinician. If the scoring protocol is more difficult, the worker may instead choose particular items that seem to pertain closely to the particular intervention being provided, exceptions to "the problem" or clear strengths the client possesses.
- *Share the scores:* This is the most artful part of the process. The worker not only tells the client what some or all of the scores are but also comments on them. Some are interpreted as exceptions, some as strengths; others may provoke a question as to whether the item(s) represent an area the client wishes to work on.
- *File the measure:* The completed measure should be filed. Agencies may need to develop particular procedures for places assessment

measures are kept. Of course, they should be treated as confidential information. It is important to have completed measures available for later follow-up and assessment of outcomes.

• *Repeat the measure at a later date:* Using the same measure one or more times later provides both the client and the worker with an assessment of change. This is an important step in motivating clients, solidifying gains they have made through the therapeutic process, and documenting outcomes for accountability purposes. Use similar procedures each time the measure is repeated.

References

Berry, M., Cash, S. J., & Mathieson, S. G. (in press). Validation of the strengths and stressors tracking device with a child welfare population. *Child Welfare*.

Bowen, G., & Richman, J. (1997). *School success profile*. Chapel Hill, NC: Jordan Institute for Families, School of Social Work, University of North Carolina at Chapel Hill.

Combs-Orme, T., & Thomas, K. H. (1997). Assessment of troubled families. *Social Work Research, 21,* 261–269.

Corcoran, K., & Fischer, J. (2000). *Measures for clinical practice* (3rd ed.). New York: Free Press.

Cournoyer, B. R., & Powers, G. T. (2002). Evidence-based social work: The quiet revolution continues. In A. R. Roberts & G. J. Greene (Eds.), *Social worker's desk reference* (pp. 798–807). New York: Oxford University Press.

Cowger, C. D., & Snively, C. A. (2002). Assessing client strengths. In D. Saleebey (Ed.), *The strengths perspective in social work practice* (3rd ed.). Boston: Allyn & Bacon.

Deal, A. G., Trivette, C. M., & Dunst, C. J. (1988). Family functioning style scale. In C. J. Dunst, C. M. Trivette, & A. G. Deal (Eds.), *Enabling and empowering families: Principles and guidelines for practice* (pp. 175–184). Cambridge, MA: Brookline.

DeJong, P., & Miller, S. D. (1995). How to interview for client strengths. *Social Work, 40,* 729–736.

Dunst, C. J., Jenkins, V., & Trivette, C. (1984). Family support scale: Reliability and validity. *Journal of Individual, Family, and Community Wellness, 1,* 45–52.

Dunst, C. J., & Leet, H. E. (1987). Measuring the adequacy of resources in households with young children. *Child: Care, Health and Development, 13,* 111–125.

Dunst, C. J., Trivette, C. M., & Deal, A. G. (Eds.). (1994). *Supporting & strengthening families. Vol. 1: Methods, strategies and practices.* Cambridge, MA: Brookline.

Dunst, C. J., Trivette, C. M., & Mott, D. W. (1994). Strengths-based family-centered intervention practices. In C. J. Dunst, C. M. Trivette, & A. G. Deal (Eds.), *Supporting & strengthening families. Vol. 1: Methods, strategies and practices* (pp. 115–131). Cambridge, MA: Brookline.

Early, T. J. (2001). Measures for practice with families from a strengths perspective. *Families in Society, 82,* 225–232.

Early, T. J., & GlenMaye, L. F. (2000). Valuing families: Social work practice with families from a strengths perspective. *Social Work, 45,* 118–130.

Epstein, M. H., & Sharma, J. (1998). *Behavioral and emotional rating scale: A strengths-based approach to assessment.* Austin, TX: PRO-ED.

Epstein, N. B., Baldwin, L. M., & Bishop, D. (1983). The McMaster family assessment device. *The Journal of Marital and Family Therapy, 9,* 171–180.

Fraser, M. W. (Ed.). (1997). *Risk and resilience in childhood: An ecological perspective.* Washington, DC: NASW Press.

Gilgun, J. F. (1999). CASPARS: New tools for assessing client risks and strengths. *Families in Society, 80,* 450–459.

Goodman, R. (1997). The Strengths and Difficulties Questionnaire: A research note. *Journal of Child Psychology and Psychiatry, 38,* 581–586.

Goodman, R. (2001). Psychometric properties of the Strengths and Difficulties Questionnaire. *Journal of the American Academy of Child and Adolescent Psychiatry, 40,* 1337–1345.

Gresham, F., & Elliott, S. (1990). *Social skills rating system.* Circle Pines, MN: American Guidance Service.

Hazzard, A., & Christensen, A. (n.d.). *Parent perception inventory.* Available from Andrew Christensen, Department of Psychology, University of California, Los Angeles.

Hazzard, A., Christensen, A., & Margolin, G. (1983). Children's perceptions of parental behaviors. *Journal of Abnormal Child Psychology, 11,* 49–59.

Kirk, R. S., & Reed Ashcraft, K. (1998). *User's guide for the North Carolina Family Assessment Scale, version 2.0.* Chapel Hill, NC: Jordan Institute for Families, University of North Carolina School of Social Work.

Koren, P. E., DeChillo, N., & Friesen, B. J. (1992). Measuring empowerment in families whose children have emotional disabilities: A brief questionnaire. *Rehabilitation Psychology, 37,* 305–321.

McCubbin, H. I., & Thompson, A. I. (Eds.). (1991). *Family assessment inventories for research and practice.* Madison: University of Wisconsin.

Olson, D. H., McCubbin, H. I., Barnes, H., Larsen, A., Muxen, M., & Wilson, M. (1992). *Family inventories.* Manual available from Life Innovations, Minneapolis.

Rapp, C. A. (1997). *The strengths model: Case management with people suffering from severe and persistent mental illness.* London: Oxford University Press.

Richman, J., & Bowen, G. (1997). School failure: An ecological-interactional-developmental perspective. In M. W. Fraser (Ed.), *Risk and resilience in childhood: An ecological perspective* (pp. 95–116). Washington, DC: NASW Press.

Ronnau, J., & Poertner, J. (1993). Identification and use of strengths: A family system approach. *Children Today, 22,* 20–23.

Skinner, H. A., Steinhauer, P. D., & Santa-Barbara, J. (1995) *Family assessment measure III manual.* Toronto, Canada: Multi Health Systems.

Strom, R., & Cooledge, N. (1987). *Parental strengths and needs inventory research manual*. Tempe: Arizona State University.

Strom, R., & McCalla, K. (1988). Perspectives on childrearing competence. *Exceptional Child, 35,* 155–164.

Trivette, C. M., Dunst, C. J., Deal, A. G., Hamby, D. W., & Sexton, D. (1994). Assessing family strengths and capabilities. In C. J. Dunst, C. M. Trivette, & A. G. Deal (Eds.), *Supporting & strengthening families. Vol. 1: Methods, strategies and practices* (pp. 132–138). Cambridge, MA: Brookline.

Tutty, L. M. (1995). Theoretical and practical issues in selecting a measure of family functioning. *Research on Social Work Practice, 5,* 80–106.

Walton, E., Sandau-Beckler, P., & Mannes, M. (2001). *Balancing family-centered services and child well-being*. New York: Columbia University Press.

Weick, A., Rapp, C., Sullivan, W., & Kisthardt, W. (1989). A strengths perspective for social work practice. *Social Work, 34,* 350–354.

Weick, A., & Saleebey, D. (1995). Supporting family strengths: Orienting policy and practice toward the 21st century. *Families in Society, 76,* 141–149.

behavior theory (*continued*)

    parent management training, 134

    system level of change, 66

    See also cognitive-behavioral therapy

Behavioral and Emotional Rating Scale, 365, 369, 378–79

behavioral management, 318, 319

behavioral marital therapies, 208–23

belief systems, 179–81, 257–61

brainstorming, 33, 51, 98, 157, 178

caregiving, 77–78

causal attribution, 44

CD. *See* conduct disorder

change

    and behavior theory, 37–40

    and cognitive-behavioral therapy, 43–45, 62, 63, 65

    and engagement, 72

    future-oriented questions, 88, 90

    and goal setting, 91

    and motivational interviewing, 24–34, 62, 63, 65, 137–43

    plan for, 32–34

    and self-motivational statements, 79

    and solution-focused therapy, 5, 6, 8, 63, 64, 65

    and strengths-and-skills-building model, 68

    and substance abuse, 195–96

    system level of, 66

    and woman battering, 234–44

    See also stages of change model

child welfare, 268–88, 293–324

    case studies, 275–88, 293–324

    cognitive-behavioral therapy, 271, 273–74, 306–7, 318

    decisional balance, 300–2

    engagement techniques, 294–99

    exception finding, 309–11

    goal setting and case plans, 311–18

    motivational interviewing, 269, 270, 271, 272–73

    problem exploration, 299–302

    solution exploration, 305

    solution-focused therapy, 269, 270–72

    strengths-and-skills-building model, 268, 270–71, 275, 293–324

    and substance abuse, 272, 273–74, 275–88

    taking action for, 318–24

    tracking problem sequences, 304–5

circular questions, 11

Circumplex Model of Family Functioning, 363, 375

clarifying free choice, 31

classical conditioning, 38–39, 40, 66

cognitive-behavioral therapy, 43–54

    for adolescents, 133–34

    and child welfare, 271, 273–74, 306–7, 318

    compared with other models, 59–60, 69

    compliance with, 65

    coping questions, 77

    for depression, 164

    empirical evidence for, 54, 66

    goal setting, 88

    intervention principles, 45–53

    nature of problems and change, 43–45

    normalizing, 75

    reframing, 73

    for sexual abuse, 329

    stance toward behavioral change, 63

    strengths versus deficits, 61–62

    for substance abuse, 190, 191–92, 205

    system level of change, 66

    type of client, 64–65, 67

    and validity of thoughts, 47, 49

cognitive deficit, 44

cognitive distortion, 44, 45, 179, 258

cognitive restructuring, 45–46, 219–20, 349

cognitive therapy, 47

collaboration

    and child welfare, 294, 318

    and sexual abuse, 345–47

    in strengths-and-skills-building model, 97–101, 109

    and woman battering, 254–57

commitment, 93, 361

communication skills, 50–53, 321–23, 352–53, 375
communication training, 220–21
complainant relationship, 8–9, 64, 72, 74, 92, 234, 235–38
compliance, 65
complimenting, 11–12, 52, 220, 320
compulsive behaviors, 39
conditioning, 38–39, 40
conduct disorder (CD), 131, 143
confidence, 32–33
consciousness raising, 254
constructivism, 5, 7, 65–66
    social constructivism, 5
contemplation, 21–23, 25, 32, 231
coping
    cognitive, 46, 48, 50–53, 349–51
    definition of, 77
    mechanisms, 170
    skills, 91, 218, 343–45
    questions
        and adolescent behaviors, 135
        and child engagement, 297–98
        and depression, 168–71
        in strengths-and-skills-building model, 76–78, 115, 121
        and woman battering, 237–38
covert modeling, 39–40
cross-cultural competence, 103
cultural diversity, 103–4, 255
customer relationship, 8–9, 64, 72, 74

decisional balance, 31–32, 82
    and adolescent behavior problems, 142
    and child welfare, 300–2
    and depression, 180
    and sexual abuse, 336–38
    and substance abuse, 196–97
    and woman battering, 245–47, 260–61
deductive questioning, 320, 347
deductive reasoning, 258
definitive phrasing, 7
denial, 28, 30
depression, 163–86
    cognitive-behavioral therapy, 164
    engagement techniques, 166–68

externalizing, 174–76
feeling identification and management, 177–79
goal setting through scaling interventions, 181–83
medication use, 185
problem exploration, 177–81
solution exploration, 168–77
solution-focused therapy, 164–65
strengths-and-skills-building model, 166–86
symptoms of major, 167
taking action against, 183–85
termination questions, 185–86
didactic teaching, 46
disruptive behavior disorders
    adolescents with, 131–59
    application of strengths-and-skills-building model, 132–59
    case example, 132
    engagement techniques, 134–36
    goal setting, 151–53
    problem exploration, 137–44
    solution exploration, 144–51
    taking action against, 153–58
domestic violence. See woman battering
double-sided reflection, 28, 30, 112
double standard technique, 46
downward comparisons, 237–38
dream question, 88, 90, 247–48

effort-based consequences, 319
emotions, 146–47, 177–79
empathy, 26, 72, 76, 109, 126
engagement techniques
    for adolescent conduct disorders, 134–36
    aligning with client's position/perspective, 78
    and child welfare, 294–99
    coping questions, 76–78, 115, 121, 135, 168–71, 237–38, 297–98
    for depression, 166–68
    joining strategies, 8–12, 71–72
    normalizing, 75–76, 167–68, 235, 298–99

engagement techniques (*continued*)
    reframing, 30–31, 33, 73, 74, 75, 236–37, 296
    for sexual abuse, 330
    with solution-focused and behavioral marital therapies, 213–14
    in strengths-and-skills-building model, 71–78
    for substance abuse, 193–93
    for woman battering, 233–34
Erickson, Milton, 6
exception finding
    with adolescent behavior disorders, 144–47
    and child welfare, 309–11
    with depression, 173–74
    guidelines for, 12
    and solution exploration, 82–86
    with substance abuse, 201–3
    and woman battering, 248–50
externalizing, 13–14, 147–49, 200–1, 218–19
extinction, 319

families
    case example, 371–74
    See also children; child welfare; parents
family violence. *See* child welfare; domestic violence; sexual abuse; woman battering
feelings. *See* emotions
functional analysis, 80–82
    applied to adolescents, 143–44
    definition of, 40–42
    pitfalls and solutions, 84
    sample assessment questions, 41
    with substance abuse, 198–99

goal setting
    in behavior theory, 41–43
    and child welfare, 311–18
    for depression through scaling interventions, 181–83
    miracle questions, 151–52
    scaling questions, 93–97, 152–53
    and sexual abuse, 339–45

with solution-focused and behavioral marital therapies, 216–17
    in strengths-and-skills-building model, 88–97, 151–53
    with substance abuse, 203–5
    and woman battering, 250–51
grief, 75–76

hypothetical change questions, 88, 90

idiosyncratic language, 10–11, 166–67
ignoring, 28, 30. *See also* extinction
indirect complimenting, 11–12
internalization of success, 149–50
interruption, 28, 30
irrational beliefs. *See* cognitive distortions

journaling, 177

language
    attention to, 72
    idiosyncratic, 10–11, 166–67
    nonblaming, 124
    presuppositional, 250
    and solution-focused therapy, 5, 7, 8, 10–11, 63, 66
    tentative, 97–98
learned helplessness, 229
letter writing, 158–59, 175–76, 186, 204
listening, 26, 50–51, 52, 166, 321
love, 261–62

marital therapies, 208–23
McMaster Model of Family Functioning, 376, 377
measurement, 359–91
    miscellaneous measures for families, 363–64, 374–77
    procedure in direct practice, 390–91
    strengths-based measures for children, 365–66, 377–89
    strengths-based measures for families, 361–62, 367–74
measures
    Behavioral and Emotional Rating Scale, 365, 369, 378–79

Family Empowerment Scale, 362,
369, 370
Family Resource Scale, 361, 367–68,
369, 373
Parent Perception Inventory, 363,
370, 376
School Success Profile, 365–66, 370,
378, 379–83
Social Skills Rating System, 366, 370,
378, 383–88
Strengths and Difficulties
Questionnaire, 366, 370, 378, 388–
89
strengths-based measures for, 365–66,
377–89
medication, 149–50, 165, 185
Mental Research Institute brief therapy
model, 6
miracle questions
with adolescents, 151–52
in case studies, 119–20, 124–25, 307–8
and child welfare, 305, 307–8, 309
definition of, 14
and goal setting, 88, 90
pitfalls and solutions, 89, 91
and woman battering, 247–48
modeling, 39–40, 66, 320
motivation assessment, 299
motivational enhancement therapy. *See*
motivational interviewing
motivational interviewing, 19, 24–34
for adolescents, 133, 137–43
and child welfare, 269, 270, 271, 272–
73
compared with other models, 59–62,
68–69
compliance and resistance, 65
empirical support, 25–26
exception finding, 146
guidelines for, 27
hypothetical change questions from,
88, 90
reframing, 73
stance toward behavioral change, 63
strengths versus deficits, 62–63
for substance abuse, 25, 190, 191–92,
196–97

system level of change, 66
techniques, 26–34
type of client, 64, 67
and woman battering, 238–39

negative reinforcement, 39
negativity, 76, 164
normalizing, 75–76, 167–68, 235, 298–99

ODD. *See* oppositional defiant disorder
operant conditioning, 39, 40, 66
oppositional defiant disorder (ODD),
131, 143

paradox, 6, 31
paradoxical stance. *See* pessimistic
stance
Parent-Adolescent Communication
Scale, 363, 370, 374, 375–76
Parent Perception Inventory, 363, 370,
376
Parental Strengths and Needs
Inventory, 363, 370, 375
parent training, 39
parent management training, 134, 155–
56
parents of sexual abuse victims, 327–54.
See also children; child welfare
pattern interruption, 221–22
pessimistic stance, 15, 150–51
pleasurable activities, 222–23
point-counterpoint technique, 46
positive behaviors, 93
positive reinforcement, 39, 169
possibility phrasing, 7, 102
precontemplation, 20–22, 32, 72–73, 231
pressures to change model, 20
problem exploration
with adolescent conduct disorders,
137–44
and child welfare, 299–302
with depression, 177–81
for sexual abuse, 331–39
with solution-focused and behavioral
marital therapies, 214
in strengths-and-skills-building
model, 79–82

task setting, 183, 217–18, 251
teens. *See* adolescence
time-out, 319
time-sequenced incident drawing, 198–99

unilateral therapy. *See* reinforcement training

validation, 166
values, 146–47
video talk, 210
violent relationships, 227–64
visitor relationship, 8–9, 64, 72, 74, 134, 235, 238–43

White, Michael, 13, 147
woman battering, 115–17, 227–64
  case study, 115–17
  cycle of violence, 254–55
  engagement techniques, 233–34
  feminist perspectives on, 228–31
  goal setting, 250–51
  loosening attachment for batterer, 261–64
  problem exploration, 243–47
  and relationship to change process, 234–43
  solution exploration, 247–50
  strengths-and-skills-building model applied to, 230–64
  taking action against, 251–64